Mildred B. Wohlford

Philosophical Foundations
for Physical, Health,
and Recreation Education

PRENTICE-HALL INTERNATIONAL, INC., *London*
PRENTICE-HALL OF AUSTRALIA, PTY., LTD., *Sydney*
PRENTICE-HALL OF CANADA, LTD., *Toronto*
PRENTICE-HALL FRANCE, S.A.R.L., *Paris*
PRENTICE-HALL OF INDIA (PRIVATE) LTD., *New Delhi*
PRENTICE-HALL OF JAPAN, INC., *Tokyo*
PRENTICE-HALL DE MEXICO, S.A., *Mexico City*

Philosophical Foundations for Physical, Health, and Recreation Education

EARLE F. ZEIGLER

Professor of Physical Education
University of Illinois

Prentice-Hall, Inc.
Englewood Cliffs, N. J.

© 1964 by
PRENTICE-HALL, INC.
ENGLEWOOD CLIFFS, N. J.

Library of Congress
Catalog Card No.:
64-15598

PRINTED IN THE UNITED STATES OF AMERICA
66225-C

To

John S. Brubacher
a fine scholar, a great teacher, and a good friend

Preface

This text is designed to help the reader understand the philosophical foundations underlying physical, health, and recreation education in the Western world. It is hoped that through such an understanding he will be stimulated to examine himself and to build his own personal philosophy. There is no doubt in my mind that there is a great need for this book. All about us we find programs that are the results of inconsistent and illogical thinking. This criticism is not leveled at physical, health, and recreation education only; it is evident as we look at the entire educational system. Whichever way the wind blows, we are apt to find the shaky educational reed inclining. Witness the panic in evidence when Russia showed certain superiority in missile construction, or the desire to jump on the bandwagon when a member of the medical profession claimed that American children were not physically fit.

In contrast to many of our current "principles" texts, no effort will be made to indoctrinate the reader to any particular philosophy. I am well aware that I am, of necessity, standing on the shoulders of my predecessors, however firm or shaky that perch may be. For the help of the many leaders of the past and present I am grateful; it probably would be inappropriate to cite particular names, but it would be unfair not to express appreciation to my colleagues, teachers, and students in the YMCA of Connecticut, Arnold College (now a division of the University of Bridgeport), Yale University, Columbia Teachers College, The University of Western Ontario, The Society of Directors of Municipal Recreation of Ontario, and The University of Michigan. The friendship, guidance, and inspiration I received from John Seiler Brubacher, of Yale University and now of The University of Michigan, has been immeasurable. Richard B. Morland of Stetson University has been a good friend and a highly valued consultant.

This volume has seven parts or divisions. Part One serves to introduce the reader to aims and objectives of the book and to orient him to philosophy of history and philosophy in general. Parts Two through Five follow an identical pattern—each of the *three main philosophies of the Western world,* as well as naïve naturalism of the past, is discussed through the medium of the recurring problems that they present. In each part the implications of the specific philosophy for education are then presented. Finally, there is a chapter in each of these parts in which I have postulated what each philosophy of education means to the special field of physical, health, and recreation education.

It was not advisable or possible to go into too much detail with each of the philosophies of education, since these areas are not primarily the function of professors of physical, health, and recreation education—and space is limited. Because of this, I have tried to explain them as succinctly as possible. Every effort has been made to organize and write this material in such a way that it may be used by upperclassmen as well as by graduate students.

The best approach, some would say, would be to develop our undergraduate professional curricula so that each student would follow a progression from a course in general philosophy to a course in the philosophy of education and finally to a course in the philosophy of physical, health, and recreation education. But even this presumed ideal approach appears to have its weaknesses. Many undergraduate majors in our field cannot seem to get interested in general philosophy in their sophomore year. Subsequent philosophy of education courses do not seem to strike a spark either, for a variety of reasons. Lastly, a course in the principles of physical, health, and recreation education is usually required of majors so early in their four-year programs that they often do not see or care about the connections with, and the implications from, the other subject matters and related fields. Thus, a student may emerge from his undergraduate career with so many different presentations of aims and objectives (usually discussed briefly at the beginning of each of his undergraduate professional courses) that he eventually becomes bored with the whole matter. But he is actually in a most bewildered state of confusion as to his own goals for his chosen field. It is because of all these difficulties that I have followed the comprehensive plan outlined above.

In Part Six, some of the persistent problems which our field has met in the past, is meeting at present, and will meet in the future are presented. I have selected and delineated these problems over a period of years with the help of members of my classes. A structural philosophical analysis is presented for the consideration of the student. How he and his colleagues decide that these problems should be met will be determined largely by the particular philosophical position they eventually accept.

Part Seven is called *Consensus and Summary.* Because there appears to be a great need for consensus in theory as well as in practice, the possibility and significance of such agreement is considered. Finally, some concluding recommendations are made in the form of five stages of development through which the professional educator may pass.

Students may wish to refer to the glossary which was included to help them with many terms that may be new. The bibliography was arranged to coincide with the successive chapters in the text.

A word about the appendixes seems in order. I have become convinced that debating, used as a classroom technique for clarification of one's own beliefs and the development of communicative skill, offers great value to the professional student. Some twenty-five controversial topics are listed which may be used for class debates as a type of laboratory experience. There is a presentation of the rules of debating and a discussion of methods of organizing debating materials and of evaluating the debates themselves.

Appendix B includes a few suggestions about pretests, examinations, and term papers which have been used successfully.

It is my sincere hope that students who use this text will make sound progress toward the achievement of a life purpose couched in a philosophical structure that will guide them throughout the years in their chosen profession. Many centuries ago, Socrates took a stand and, in the vernacular of the late Robert Frost, " . . . bet his sweet life" on the rights of free thought. He said, "the unexamined life is not worth living." Leaders in physical, health, and recreation education must make this wager themselves about the worth of their field and should have "examined lives" and wise purposes. They should ever be ready to help others who are seeking the truth of the good life for themselves.

E. F. Z.

Contents

Introduction   *xv*

PART ONE

ORIENTATION

1. *Philosophy of History*   **3**

    Perspective. Ten Peaceful Revolutions. Questions and Answers. The
    Possibility of Historical Research. Toynbee's Philosophy of History.

2. *Orientation to Philosophy*   **10**

    Brief Historical Outline. The Various Aims of Philosophy. Methods
    Involved in the Practice of Philosophy. Philosophy Contrasted with
    Science. Philosophy Contrasted with Art. Philosophy Contrasted with
    Religion. Philosophy Contrasted with Education. The Branches of
    Philosophy. Some Definitions of Terms Used.

3. *A Brief History of the Ideas and Problems of Philosophy*   **23**

    One Persistent Problem Viewed Historically. Historical Highlights
    of the Philosophy of Naturalism. Historical Comparison of Idealism,
    Realism, and Pragmatism. Early Modern Philosophy. The Twentieth
    Century. The Present Situation in the Western World—A Brief
    Summary.

PART TWO

NAÏVE NATURALISM AS A PERVASIVE INFLUENCE

4. *Naïve Naturalism in Philosophy and Education*   **45**

    The Philosophy of Naturalism. Questions about Reality (Metaphysics). Theory of Knowledge Acquisition (Epistemology). Exact Relating of Ideas (Logic). System of Values (Axiology). Society, School, and the Individual. Educational Aims and Objectives. The Process of Education. Summary.

5. *Naïve Naturalism in Physical, Health, and Recreation Education*   *54*

Aims, Objectives, and Methods. Summary. Strengths and Weaknesses.

PART THREE

EXPERIMENTALISM

6. *Experimentalism in Philosophy and Education*   *69*

Metaphysics. Epistemology. Logic. Axiology. Society, School, and the Individual. Educational Aims and Objectives. The Process of Education. Summary.

7. *Experimentalism in Physical, Health, and Recreation Education*   *87*

Aims and Objectives. Methodology. Summary. Strengths and Weaknesses.

PART FOUR

REALISM

8. *Realism in Philosophy and Education*   *113*

Metaphysics. Epistemology. Logic. Axiology. Society, School, and the Individual. Educational Aims and Objectives. The Process of Education. Summary.

9. *Realism in Physical, Health, and Recreation Education*   *136*

Aims and Objectives. Methodology. Summary. Strengths and Weaknesses.

PART FIVE

IDEALISM

10. *Idealism in Philosophy and Education* **169**

Metaphysics. Epistemology. Logic. Axiology. Society, School, and the Individual. Educational Aims and Objectives. The Process of Education. Summary.

11. *Idealism in Physical, Health, and Recreation Education* **201**

Aims and Objectives. Methodology. Summary. Strengths and Weaknesses.

PART SIX

SYSTEMATIC PHILOSOPHIES AND SOME PERSISTENT PROBLEMS IN PHYSICAL, HEALTH, AND RECREATION EDUCATION

12. *Systematic Philosophies and Some Persistent Problems in Physical, Health, and Recreation Education* **247**

Introduction. Progress in Physical, Health, and Recreation Education Through the School. Values in Physical, Health and Recreation Education. Politics and Nationalism. Economics. Methods of Instruction. The Role of Administration. Professional Preparation. The Healthy Body. Physical Education and Recreation for Women. Dance in Physical Education and Recreation. The Use of Leisure. Amateur, Semi-professional, and Professional Sport. Conclusion.

PART SEVEN

CONSENSUS AND SUMMARY

13. *The Possibility of Consensus* **283**

The Importance of a Continuing Search for More Agreement. Some Common Denominators in Education. Some Common Denominators in Physical, Health, and Recreation Education. Issues That Stand in the Way of Greater Consensus. Concluding Statement.

14. Building Your Own Personal Philosophy   *291*

Five Possible Stages of Development. Conclusion.

Appendix A   *295*

Appendix B   *301*

Glossary   *317*

Bibliography   *324*

Index   *347*

Introduction

A great many people have philosophical beliefs, but they are vague about them. Unfortunately the man in the street still thinks of philosophy as something that is beyond him—a most difficult intellectual activity. Consequently, he makes decisions based on common sense. This isn't necessarily bad, but it could be a lot better! The development of a philosophy would help him fashion a better world for the future based on the past and the scientific discoveries of the present. Without philosophy we can never know if we have the correct goals in life.

Some may ask immediately whether science might achieve this for us by its everlasting probing into the unknown. But we should understand the relationship between philosophy and science. Both are most interested in knowledge; they ask questions and want answers. Scientific investigators turn in facts; the philosopher must be cognizant of these advances. Actually, philosophy starts where science leaves off by attempting to synthesize. What do these facts mean? When you become concerned about the ultimate meaning of these facts, then you are philosophizing in the best sense.

A person striving to function intelligently in society needs a philosophy of life and/or religion. In addition, a physical educator, or health educator, or recreator should have a philosophy of education that is in harmony with his philosophy of life. To top this off, he should develop still further a philosophy of physical, health, and recreation education that, once again, does not clash with the rest of his beliefs about life and education. The achievement of this total philosophy may well become a lifelong task. The reflective thinking required to accomplish this task, however, is a mighty cheap price to pay for a well-ordered life.

We have only to look at present programs with their shifting emphases to realize that we are, to quite a degree, vacillating practitioners. This is true both within the school and in public recreation.

Why is this happening? Probably because even many experienced leaders have not worked out personal philosophies that are consistent and logical in their various phases! So where does that leave the rest of us?

When a person assumes the role of leadership in the educational profession in the area of school health, physical education, and recreation, or in the recreation profession, he is implying that he has a life purpose. But, strangely enough, many leaders become hazy when they are asked to express a philosophy. To be sure, they have a lot of opinions, isolated and often quite contradictory. It's a little like saying, "I'm for good and against sin!" The difficulty comes when we are asked to define what's good and what's bad.

Where does physical, health, and recreation education fit into life's picture today? What is it? Why is it needed? What does it do to a boy or girl, or to a man or woman? How can we prove that it does what we say it does? What is its future? What could its future be? What should its future be?

The Need for Determination of a Philosophy of Physical, Health, and Recreation Education

The time has come for the true professional in physical, health, and recreation education to adopt a basic philosophy. Science and philosophy have complementary roles to play in aiding the field to find its place in the educational system and in society. For too long we have ignored the wisdom of both of these branches of learning in carrying out our program. Lately there has been a greatly increased interest in science with a corresponding loss of interest in philosophy.

Philosophy can help us to attack the basic problems of physical, health, and recreation education in a systematic fashion. In the first place, philosophy will enable the physical- and health-education teacher (and the director of recreation) to view their professions as a whole. They will not see themselves merely as athletic coaches, health-education teachers, playground leaders, physical conditioners, sports-skill teachers, community-center directors, or corrective specialists. In this sense, philosophy would be a criticism of experience.

Philosophy will help the physical educator, for example, to fashion for himself a mental image of what physical education ought to be in the light of his own personal philosophy of education. It will be prospective in the sense that it will form a vanguard leading practice in the field. It is true that there will be conflicting philosophies, but at least people will be logical and consistent in their approaches no matter which educational philosophy they accept.

A philosophy of physical, health, and recreation education would eventually have to be practical, or it would be worthless in the eyes of many. An instrumental philosophy would necessarily imitate science in part, but it would serve only as a plan for action. Science can describe physical education as it exists; philosophy can help to picture it as it should be. The same can be said for the field of recreation, of course. Philosophy, in addition, will fill in for science temporarily, since its methods are faster.

Methods in physical education and/or recreation must wait for philosophy to outline a plan of action. Following this, the philosophical differences can be tested in the practical execution of the program. Actually philosophical analysis and methodology do not oppose each other; they are dependent on each aspect being carried out effectively.

A philosophy of physical, health, and recreation education, actually a part of the entire division of educational philosophy, has a relationship to the general field of philosophy. On this point there are varied and conflicting views. Most obvious is that which holds a philosophy of life basic and primary to a philosophy of education. To the former is assigned the establishment of fundamental principles (except for pragmatism); to the latter is given their application in the educational process. If this viewpoint is acceptable, it is obviously of utmost importance that one's general philosophy be sound.

The determination of at least progressive and essential philosophies of physical, health, and recreation education can help our field in innumerable ways. At least, physical educators will be able to determine for themselves under which banner they stand. At present many professionals are dilettantes and hence present no solid educational arguments for many of the beliefs they may hold. We should at least know which side of the fence we are on; then, we can decide if we want to stay there when dark clouds threaten.

Today there are many serious problems and conflicts dangerously splitting the field of physical education itself, and also dividing physical education from school-health education and from community recreation. Some say there is no such thing as *physical* education. Others say that physical fitness is our primary task and that we should be about our business and forget concomitant learnings. Do we have a responsibility for adapted physical-education programs? Is military training an adequate substitute for physical education? Are we stressing competition and winning too much? Can organized sport be true recreation?

These, of course, are only a few of the problems which are preventing the field from presenting a united, determined, and powerful front at a time when the worth of our programs in the educational picture is being challenged continuously. The answers to these questions, and many others not mentioned, cannot be given by the uninformed or the misinformed. The highest type of reflective thinking is needed. A personal stand can come only through the development of a consistent philosophy of physical, health, and recreation education.

PART ONE

Orientation

CHAPTER ONE

Philosophy of History

A professional in physical, health, and recreation education must start from the beginning to comprehend the role of his own specialized field in society. For this reason we are taking a brief excursion into the area of philosophy of history. A philosophy of history would be a systematic body of general conceptions about history.

Perspective

Living our lives from day to day we sometimes forget that the planet Earth originated some 4 billion years ago. Early man, we are told, had his beginnings some 1 million years ago and has used crude tools for something less than half that time. Three-hundred thousand years have elapsed since the mutation of subman into man. The beginnings of the first civilizations were actually less than 10,000 years ago, which means that there was a gap of some 290,000 years more or less. The great religions are the products of the past 2,500 years. Democracy, the youngest of infants, had its origins during the past several centuries. Is it any wonder that perfection appears to be a long way off?

Ten Peaceful Revolutions

During the second half of the twentieth century we are told that at least ten *peaceful revolutions* are having a significant effect on our nation and on the world. Political candidates with an eye to the future are discussing such problems and the resultant implications in their plans and campaign speeches. The peaceful revolutions are as follows: (1) the "exploding" cities; (2) the mechanization of the farm; (3) the vastly increasing birth rate; (4) the extended life expectancy; (5) the technological improvements in production; (6) the use of electrical and atomic energy; (7) the development of a higher standard of living; (8) the development of weapons [hardly a "peaceful" revolution item]; (9) the rapid growth of population in underdeveloped nations least able to support it; and (10) a developing nationalism evident throughout the world.

Questions and Answers

As our thinking about this subject progresses, we begin to realize that there are a number of unanswered questions. We must come up with answers to these questions that satisfy us. We might ask the question, "What is history?" Is everything historic? Are we referring to the actual order of events or to the order of events as seen by an interpreter (the historian)? A student of history might ask whether the philosophy of history challenges the democratic way of life. This would imply that there is just one way of looking at history or that there is simply one philosophy. If there are a number of philosophies of history, can we say that one is paramount?

Approaching this issue from another angle, we might question the validity and reliability of historical research. Is it possible to construct a valid philosophy of history that is fact and not fiction? Is it possible for historians to record facts scientifically? It has been said that good history has depth as well as surface. Mommsen, however, has asserted that "history is neither made nor written without love or hate."

For example, Woody deprecates the fact that those who have written about education and its history have slighted "physical culture" perhaps through bias.

Despite the fact that lip-service has been paid increasingly to the dictum "a sound mind in a sound body," ever since western Europe began to revive the educational concepts of the Graeco-Roman world, there is still a lack of balance between physical and mental culture, both in school programs and among those who write of education. This is evident in many quarters, even where a certain universality of outlook ought to reign. Turn where one will, it is impossible to find physical culture adequately presented in books dealing with the general history of education. Written in keeping with a dominant rationalism, these books have been concerned chiefly with intellectual movements and institutions for mental improvement.[1]

[1] Thomas Woody, *Life and Education in Early Societies* (New York: The Macmillan Company, 1949), p. vii.

History appears to have begun with the ancient Greeks. It was written also, but perhaps not quite as well, by the Romans. We have to decide, of course, whether a disinterested observer can write history as effectively as someone who has lived through the passing events.

This introduces a disturbing problem which is difficult to answer. What constitutes acceptable history? Is a simple chronological listing of events satisfactory? Some would argue that history must show the connection between a series of events. Furthermore, it should cover a broader field and should extend over a fairly long period of time.

And then we find some histories of the world with religious overtones that would have us believe unequivocally that God's purpose is gradually coming to pass. We must ask ourselves if there has been moral evolution. Despite the fact that history is destructive as well as cumulative, many feel that the history of man shows strong trends toward emergence. Are we evolving a formula that will help all the people of the world live together in relative peace and harmony?

The Possibility of Historical Research

There is no argument but that historical writers need to uncover as many primary sources as possible to write the best history. If only one mind passes between the historian and the material about which he is writing, there is a much greater chance of an accurate report. The possibility of a forged document, for example, or of a firsthand observer's inaccurate report only increases the difficulty of writing fine history.

Because it may be so difficult also to locate an objective observer, some historians have felt it necessary to retrace the steps of the incidents which the historian hopes to describe later. Witness the historian of the twentieth century who felt it advisable to hire an elephant to prove that it had been possible for Hannibal to cross the Alps by this means of transportation. One further step may be required: the historian may find it essential to employ the highest type of reflective thinking before completing his work.

Experimental researchers, and even those who undertake survey research, may repeat and check on their earlier observations. Unfortunately (for the historian at least) history does not repeat itself. Because the historian cannot himself "see" what has happened, his attitude will undoubtedly influence his work. He must make some assumptions as to the rationality of the universe. Presumably this would have to be true if a rational human hoped to make sense out of the world in which he lives.

Thus we might agree that complete objectivity of history is an impossibility. Perhaps our best hope is that someone with penetrating insight will have flashes of intuitive genius while writing and interpreting the history of man. Such a person would undoubtedly be employing a type of speculative philosophy as part of his approach to the problem of historical interpretation. In this manner one or more philosophies of history evolve.

Having employed empirical methods involving experiment and experience, scientists in many of the more exact sciences have been able to predict future developments. In this respect historians are fighting against a handicap, but they have made definite progress. By attempting to meet the exacting requirements of the more empirical sciences, it has been possible to develop a type of philosophy of history. As a result many kinds of history may be examined using present criteria for adequacy and accuracy. History makes a stout effort to define the future. Any such definitions reflect the mood of the times and the predispositions of the historian. Man must continue to strive, and it appears he must continue to act on faith.

Toynbee's Philosophy of History

One such historical analysis or philosophy of history, which has been popularized, is that of Arnold J. Toynbee, an eminent British historian.[2] He explains that the story of man may be told through his life in twenty-one major "civilizations." [3] We learn that five of these civilizations are still alive but that only Western civilization is still relatively healthy.[4] The other four—Far Eastern, Hindu, Islamic, and Orthodox Christian (largely Russian)—are weakening and are being incorporated into a "Great Society" with a Western cast.

CIVILIZATION'S PATTERN OF GROWTH. Most civilizations seem to have gone through a fairly identical pattern of birth, growth, breakdown, and disintegration. A society is but a group of individual humans with an infinite number of interrelationships. It could go on indefinitely, although none has to the present day. Toynbee parts company with Spengler who believed that a civilization is an organism whose life path is predetermined. Toynbee denies also the theory that a superior race is necessary to found a civilization,[5] or that a civilization is created only by a most favorable environment.[6]

THEMES OF ACTION. Toynbee endows history with the possession of

---

[2] Arnold J. Toynbee, *A Study of History,* abridgement by D. C. Somervell (New York and London: Oxford University Press, 1947), Vols. I-VI. There are, of course, many other conceptions of the development of civilizations.

[3] Ibid., p. 34.

[4] *Ibid.,* p. 8.

[5] *Ibid.,* p. 55.

[6] *Ibid.,* p. 57.

certain "themes of action." They all seem to have a one-two rhythm such as "challenge-and-response" as the society develops, and then "withdrawal-and-return" or "rout-and-rally" as it begins to disintegrate.[7] Man answers the right challenge presented by his environment. He is thereby started forward on the path to civilization. This does not mean that man has the help of a favorable or easy environment. Conversely, he is confronted with many difficulties that stimulate him.[8] He develops as he responds to the various stimuli. Subsequently, the developing society faces a number of other stern challenges such as war, unfavorable environmental conditions, and other conceivable moral or physical pressures.

BREAKDOWN OF CIVILIZATION. If a civilization meets its challenges, it survives. Its life is measured by the number of challenges that are met successfully. Trouble comes when an incorrect response is made to a specific challenge or stimulus. Then the society is faced with what Toynbee calls a *Time of Troubles*. This period in the civilization's development is not necessarily a catastrophic fall to oblivion; it may go on for hundreds of years. It does, however, usually result in a *Universal State*.[9] This occurs when the conflicting countries have order imposed on them by some stronger force. An example of this might have been Rome's Augustan dictatorship. Such a Universal State may extend over what seems to us a very long period such as the 2,400 years of Egypt's two empires.

CHARACTERISTICS OF THE UNIVERSAL STATE. Actually, the beginning of the Universal State appears to some as the foundation of a stable society. In reality, however, it is a symptom of the disintegration of the society, since the people no longer follow the rulers of their own accord. This period of decline is accompanied by a "wanderings of peoples," as occurred in Europe when the Roman Empire was on the wane.

One of the characteristics of such a period may be the adoption of a new religion by the proletariat. For example, consider the growth of the Christian Church, which developed into a Universal Church.[10] Subsequently, it served as a basis of a second or "affiliated" civilization. Thus we are told that Western civilization grew out of the Greek-Roman society via the Universal Church of Christianity. In like manner, it may be reasoned that the Far Eastern civilization of China-Japan-Korea developed from the earlier Sinic civilization via Buddhism. Toynbee states in essence that these are the broad outlines of the

---

[7] *Ibid.*, p. 67.
[8] *Ibid.*, p. 87.
[9] *Ibid.*, p. 12.
[10] *Ibid.*, p. 24.

twenty-one civilizations that the world has seen. *This theory of the development of civilizations is, of course, not agreed upon by all historians. Some feel that it does not fit all civilizations exactly, while others assert that it is derived too exclusively from an analysis of the Greek-Roman civilization.*

SUBMAN BECOMES MAN. Although we are concerned primarily with an analysis of so-called civilization, it should not be forgotten that the mutation of subman into man took place in a social environment over 300,000 years ago. We should consider the idea that this transformation is perhaps a more significant amount of growth than has taken place yet under the banner of civilization.

PROGRESS OF CIVILIZATIONS. Toynbee suggests the interesting metaphor of civilizations having arrived at various ledges on the way up a rocky mountainside.[11] Each civilization is depicted by a man in the dress of that particular society. Most of these "men" are lying dead on a ledge situated at a fairly low level. These include the Egyptiac, Sumeric, Hittite, Babylonic, Indic, Minoan, Hellenic, Syriac, Sinic, Andean, Mayan, Yucatec, and Mexic civilizations. Five other civilizations appeared to have been halted on nearby ledges. Of these five, the Spartan and Ottoman civilizations are dead. The remaining three—Polynesian, Nomadic, and Eskimo—are represented by individuals in a sitting position; they are the arrested civilizations.[12]

THE STATUS OF WESTERN CIVILIZATION. As mentioned above, five civilizations are still climbing, but only the Western civilization is relatively healthy. The other four—Far Eastern, Hindu, Islamic, and Orthodox Christian—appear to be "weakening" because of Western influences. To continue with the suggested metaphor, we may ask the question, "How much farther will Western man climb?" Could it be that our *Time of Troubles* started during the time of the religious wars of the sixteenth century?[13] Proceeding from this premise, both Napoleon and Hitler failed to create a Universal State. It could be that another great power will be the conqueror that will begin the time of the Universal State.[14]

We must ask ourselves further if certain symptoms of world decay are evident to a critical observer.[15] When civilizations disintegrate, there is a "schism of the body social" into three parts known as the *dominant minority,* the *internal proletariat,* and the *external proletariat.* Toynbee explains this as follows:

---

[11] *Ibid.,* p. 49.
[12] *Ibid.,* p. 16.
[13] *Ibid.,* p. 245.
[14] *Ibid.,* p. 239.
[15] *Ibid.,* Part IV.

We have seen, in fact, that when, in the history of any society, a creative minority degenerates into a dominant minority which attempts to retain by force a position that it has ceased to merit, this change in the character of the ruling element provokes, on the other side, the secession of a proletariat which no longer admires and imitates its rulers and revolts against its servitude. We have also seen that this proletariat, when it asserts itself, is divided from the outset into two distinct parts. There is an internal proletariat, prostrate and recalcitrant, and an external proletariat beyond the frontiers who now violently resist incorporation.

On this showing, that nature of the breakdowns of civilizations can be summed up in three points: a failure of creative power in the minority, an answering withdrawal of mimesis on the part of the majority, and a consequent loss of social unity in the society as a whole.[16]

Certainly in our society we do not find the internal proletariat ready to secede because of a dominant, creative minority. Nor is asceticism present. Thus it would appear that our civilization is not very far advanced on its way to disintegration.

SPECULATION ABOUT THE FUTURE. If earthmen learn to live with each other in relative peace, the world may not see devastating hydrogen-bomb warfare with its seemingly inevitable results. It could be that the West and the East will no longer be reacting on each other by A.D. 5000. Perhaps the world may be united into a single civilization through the agency of religion. Toynbee suggests this in his belief that religions may be the "intelligible field" of historical study rather than the investigation of civilizations. As mentioned above, it may be that religions serve as the connecting link between one civilization and its successor.[17] Could it be that the purpose of civilizations is to spread opportunities among men for a fuller knowledge of God? If this is true, what will future religion be like? Will it help us achieve the ultimate goal of all human endeavors? What is this aim? Is it the transformation of Man into Superman?

No matter what we may believe about these conjectures, there is every likelihood that the goal is still a long distance away. After all, the earth is only about 4 billion years old. According to Sir James Jeans's calculation for the habitability of this planet, man, having survived at the rate of twenty-one civilizations in 6000 years, still has 1743 million civilizations ahead of him.

---

[16] *Ibid.*, p. 26.
[17] *Ibid.*, p. 24.

CHAPTER TWO

Orientation to Philosophy

The man in the street does have philosophical beliefs of one type or another, but he is generally quite vague about them. Strangely enough, he uses a variety of philosophical terms; yet, if he were asked to be more explicit, the resultant attempt might embarrass him.

THE AVERAGE MAN'S PHILOSOPHY. If one of our friends has a lot of queer ideas, or perhaps doesn't reason correctly, we might say that he has a warped philosophy of life. We usually do have other friends who believe in taking a long-range approach when they think about problems, and we ordinarily call such individuals *philosophical*. Most people do have some sort of philosophy by which they conduct their daily affairs, and this philosophy they conceive as an interpretation of what is important and basic in life. We do find, however, that their beliefs and their principles are often contradictory and illogical.

ROLE OF THE PHILOSOPHER. And so we find that, although the term is used frequently in everyday conversation, the average person still thinks of the subject-matter philosophy as a very difficult intellectual activity. The professional philosopher is a mental giant who lives only to ponder about abstractions that really aren't of any immediate, practical value. More highly educated people, on the other hand, would have a somewhat better image of philosophers as scholars dedicated to and ultimately responsible for the outlook and values of certain societies and cultures. Actually, it may be safely said that the philosopher tries to evaluate what we know and believe about the universe and our own sphere of human affairs. Subsequently he evolves a systematic and coherent plan that may give the ordinary person an understanding of life. It may help to give him a focus so that he can determine that which is important and significant. Thus it can help him decide what he should do in the years ahead.

Brief Historical Outline

Philosophy had its beginning in Greece over twenty-five hundred years ago where the word meant *knowledge* or *love of wisdom*. The main method used by philosophers was speculation. Practical knowledge gained through experience and observation was differentiated from speculative knowledge. These men were seeking some logical view of the universe. Heraclitus, a Greek philosopher of Ephesus, believed in the universality of change. To him everything seemed to be in the process of becoming. Pythagoras felt that the first principle was number or harmony. The Pythagoreans asserted that these numbers were fundamental in the universe and had a real objective existence.

THE SEPARATION OF PHILOSOPHY FROM SCIENCE. Much later everything was interpreted in the terms of evolution by Darwin and Spencer. As a result of this theory the road was paved for William James to advance the pragmatic outlook. Before this, of course, when the precise Arabic numerical system had been introduced, and the invention of instruments of measurement and investigation took place, it wasn't long until sciences such as physics, astronomy, and chemistry were developed. Philosophical thought thus became distinguished from these practical sciences. Philosophy had speculated about everything and all matters. At this stage it was crowded out of the material world with the result that ethical and moral principles appeared to be its entire remaining province. The thought was that the true nature of things could now be analytically determined through accurate scientific measurement; thus, philosophy had only values left with which to concern itself. One's philosophy became a scheme of life accomplished by means of the guidance provided by certain values and ideas. Strangely enough, modern civilization seems to find itself in an analogous position to that of the ancient Greeks. Science has advanced so rapidly that the greatest scientists seem to be writing philosophy as they try to explain what their discoveries and inventions mean.

The Various Aims of Philosophy

Thus far, we might say that philosophy is that branch of learning (or that science) which investigates, evaluates, and integrates knowledge of reality as best as possible into one or more systems embodying all available wisdom about the universe. Science is therefore the essential material foundation of philosophy which is summarized and synthesized. The knowledge of life is interpreted by an attempt to explain the universe and to ponder over the achievements of civilization. Furthermore, it asks if men's actions are expedient and right.

Philosophy's problems are as many as the questions philosophers ask. They want to know the nature of the world, the problem of good and evil, the possibility of free will, whether God exists, if some values are more important than others, whether knowledge is possible to man, and the possibility of beauty—just to name a few of life's many enigmas.

Methods Involved in the Practice of Philosophy

How do philosophers arrive at any conclusions about the problems they face? In all probability the first method used to obtain knowledge was speculation, pure and simple. Quite probably imagination and intuition played a large part in this method also. Furthermore, it was generally accepted at that time that truth could be achieved through direct revelation. A later method employed was the acceptance of a priori principles. These principles were postulated dogmatically and thereafter followed blindly. Subsequently, and concurrently to a degree, problems were resolved by the application of principles which were taken as truths without any further thought given to the matter. *Deductive logic* is the term usually applied to this type of thinking, and much reasoning of this nature still goes on in the world. Oddly enough, many people still accept feeling as the criterion by which they determine their method of philosophy. In the best modern tradition the method usually applied is reflective thought involving accurate analysis and synthesis of gathered data. Conclusions are arrived at only after all known facts are taken into consideration.

CONFLICTING VIEWS ABOUT PHILOSOPHY.   Today there are many conflicting views on philosophy and philosophic thought. Some seem to feel that philosophy has no subject-matter or method and is merely common sense. Another school of thought finds truth in the idea that philosophy has to do with the rational, much in the same way as Plato conceived it. This idea of the rational has been interpreted in many different fashions. One group is looking for the absolute, while another faction resolutely damns the absolute. A third school wishes to make philosophy the science of sciences by maintaining that its function is to unify the true concepts underlying all the special sciences. A fourth group may have the best answer to the question, since it wants philosophy to determine ends and values, to evaluate the findings and conclusions of science on the basis of these goals, and to formulate standards for the guidance of action and conduct.

Imagine that the task of philosophy is to afford a logical view of the world. The only difficulty seems to be that the view of one man differs so completely from the view of another. One seems always to be looking back at the wonderful accomplishments of the past and the superior wisdom of his forerunners. Naturally, he is anxious to preserve the *status quo*. The opposite extremist refers constantly to the view that traditions and mores are stifling any hope for the future; everything is so outmoded, and it is so difficult to shake off this deadening influence. In between these two points of view we find a great many who wish to strike a happy medium of one type or another. This type of reasoning has had its effect on the school as well. The composition of the core curriculum has been a perennial battleground, the effects of which influence all phases of education.

Philosophy Contrasted with Science

Philosophy included all knowledge in early recorded history. Men had no ways or means other than their own thinking processes for determining accurately and precisely information about the stars, the earth, or man himself. The remarkable thing is that often their deductions concerning many fields turned out to be very close to accepted, modern scientific fact. As scientific method gradually and progressively came to include many of the aspects of the earth which were originally under the domain of philosophy, and the need for philosophic speculation lessened a great deal. One of the strange results of this development was that many continued to employ speculative thought without apparently any reference to the known facts. One of the reasons for this was probably that these men doubted that the "facts" were facts. Often they felt that their well-tried values were superior to so-called facts.

THE DECLINE OF PHILOSOPHY. Thus it was eventually that philosophy was forced off the battlefield for all practical purposes. As Durant reports:

Philosophy is in flight today before the sciences, one after another of which have run away from her into the productive world, until she is left chill and alone, like a forsaken mother with the vitals gone from her and almost all her cupboards empty. Philosophy has withdrawn herself timidly from her real concerns—men and their life in the world—into a crumbling corner called epistemology, and is in danger every moment of being ousted by the laws that prohibit habitation in flimsy and rickety structures. . . . Philosophy, like everything else, must secularize itself; it must stay on the earth and earn its keep by illuminating life.[1]

---

[1] Will Durant, *The Story of Philosophy*, rev. ed. (New York: Garden City Books, 1938).

A POSSIBLE RECIPROCAL RELATIONSHIP.   Several tentative conclusions may be drawn up to this point. In this relationship between philosophical analysis and scientific method it must be understood that the philosophers must give heed to all the available material determined by scientific investigation. Scientists should not be averse to considering the many questions raised by the better philosophers, since this would negate one of the basic principles of the scientific method itself. Very important as well is the interpretation of all knowledge in terms of philosophical values. The scientist might say that he questions the ability of the philosopher to interpret the various scientific data critically and correctly. This might be partially true; yet, it is the rare scientist who has the ability (or wishes to take the time) to interpret his scientifically determined truths for the benefit of all mankind. Both are interested in knowledge; they ask questions and want answers. But science wants factual knowledge, whereas philosophy (except pragmatism) wants ultimate knowledge. The one has a limited scope, while the other seeks to develop a comprehensive outlook.

THE REALM OF PHILOSOPHY.   Many feel that philosophy will eventually become unnecessary, because science will in time answer all the questions that men will ask. Actually, the scientific facts mark the dividing line between the two disciplines. Science does set up facts, to be sure; but, as far as the earth and its inhabitants are concerned, decisions are made to a great extent by what men think and do about these facts. Philosophy starts with the facts and then synthesizes. One enters philosophy's realm when he becomes concerned with the ultimate meaning of these facts. If we grant the possibility of philosophical research, philosophizing demands the same rigid and careful approach that is found in a more exact science.

If they are honest, philosophers must be careful to consider the possibility of the need for changing their ends and values as new scientific truth is presented. To neglect such an adjustment would bring about loss of all respect in a short time.

The fact that philosophers often seem to (and do) disagree should not cause undue alarm. Scientists have always disagreed until one man came up with the "final" proof concerning a problem. Then, fifty years later, another learned individual reopened the case and proved that the earlier final proof was not final at all. So it should be with philosophy. Eternal disagreement seems to serve as a constant stimulus to new and better thought.

THE PROSPECTIVE NATURE OF PHILOSOPHIC THOUGHT.   Philosophic conclusions serve another most important function in that they are often prospective—"ahead" of scientific fact. In this way tentative conclusions may be formulated, which may later be revised. It is possible that philosophical thinking of the highest type can in many instances point the way for future scientific investigation.

Philosophy Contrasted with Art

A second branch of learning or discipline which may be contrasted with philosophy is the field of art. The scope of the artist is necessarily much more limited than that of the philosopher. Certainly both branches are equally anxious to understand and interpret both knowledges and experiences. The artist conveys his feelings through the medium of form, color, or sound, while the philosopher offers a more inclusive but obviously theoretical approach. The artist finds certain aesthetic qualities in an experience and allows himself to be caught up in the emotion necessary to express his feelings adequately and accurately. The philosopher is concerned with the promotion of a plan that will bring to man a rich, full life. He is conscious of his intent at all times.

Philosophy Contrasted with Religion

At first glance it might seem that philosophy and religion tend to be synonymous, or that one might be attempting to supplant the other. Both branches seek the truth, although it might be stated that science and philosophy are more intellectual in their quest. Actually, philosophy is not religion, and it probably will never take its place except in the case of relatively few individuals.

Butler makes an interesting comparison between the two that helps to clarify the approaches.[2] He states that religion (in our Western world) has at least three essentials: (1) experience of worship of God; (2) a community of believers; and (3) a constructive program of service such as missionary work or social reform. If we were to apply these criteria to philosophy, it is explained, the following three statements would be evident: (1) a philosopher has an intellectual love of God (unless he is an atheist or an agnostic); (2) the philosopher works with his colleagues in a sincere search for truth; and (3) a philosopher is generally concerned with improving man's everyday life.

Philosophy Contrasted with Education

"The history of education," according to Woody, "ranging from

---

[2] J. Donald Butler, *Four Philosophies,* rev. ed. (New York: Harper & Row, Publishers, Inc., 1957), pp. 8-9.

the blindly groping to the most highly purposive process, is the record of man's reconstruction of his ideals and institutions, and his efforts to mold each generation to them with such skill and insight as he could command." [3]

Philosophy, we have said earlier, is that branch of learning which evaluates and integrates knowledge as best possible into a system embodying all available wisdom about the universe and its many facets. Thus we can see that philosophy is theoretical and that education is practical. There is, of course, such a special, or specialized, philosophy as philosophy of education. This specialized philosophy may be listed under that division of philosophy known as *axiology* that has to do with a system of values.

The relationship between the two comes into focus most sharply when we realize that philosophy offers us a world view (or, more correctly, world views) which dictates or guides the path which education must or may follow. This is not a one-way street, however, since education of each generation results in experiences which philosophy must consider in future planning.

The Branches of Philosophy

There does seem to be some general agreement concerning the branches of philosophy, although there will probably never be anything like complete unanimity. Windelband explains the historical development of "the conception, the task, and the subject-matter of philosophy" briefly in the following way:

The oldest philosophy knew no division at all. In later antiquity a division of philosophy into logic, physics, and ethics was current. In the Middle Ages, and still more in modern times, the first two of these subjects were often comprised under the title, theoretical philosophy, and set over against practical philosophy. Since Kant a new threefold division into logical, ethical, and aesthetical philosophy is beginning to make its way. [4]

Butler offers a division of the field of philosophy into four branches upon which we will find considerable agreement. [5] He accepts the categories of metaphysics, epistemology, logic, and axiology. For our purposes these four divisions may be explained as follows:

1. Metaphysics—questions about reality.
2. Epistemology—acquisition of knowledge.

---

[3] Thomas Woody, *Life and Education in Early Societies* (New York: The Macmillan Company, 1949), p. 3.

[4] Wilhelm Windelband, *A History of Philosophy*, rev. ed. (New York: Harper & Row, Publishers, Inc., 1901), Vol. I, 18-19.

[5] Butler, *Four Philosophies*, pp. 48-54.

3. Logic—exact relating of ideas.
4. Axiology—system of values.[6]

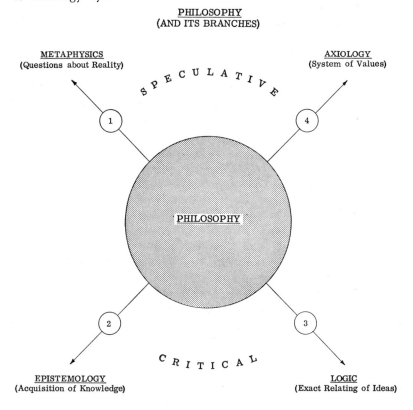

PHILOSOPHY
(AND ITS BRANCHES)

METAPHYSICS
(Questions about Reality)

AXIOLOGY
(System of Values)

S P E C U L A T I V E

1

4

PHILOSOPHY

2

3

C R I T I C A L

EPISTEMOLOGY
(Acquisition of Knowledge)

LOGIC
(Exact Relating of Ideas)

A FORMULA FOR ACTION

$$\frac{\text{PRESENT}}{\text{VALUES}} + \frac{\text{SCIENTIFIC}}{\text{ADVANCES}} + \frac{\text{CONDITIONING}}{\text{OF EMOTIONS}} = \frac{\text{WHAT WE}}{\text{DO}}$$

Metphysics and axiology are generally considered to form what may be called *speculative philosophy,* because they treat the postulation of first principles and the subsequent recognition of values. Epistemology and logic comprise what is often designated as *critical philosophy;* they attempt to explain how man acquires knowledge and how thought becomes verified.

NO PRESCRIBED PROGRESSION FOR THE NOVICE. There does not appear to be definitely prescribed progression by which the beginning student of philosophy may approach the subject; yet, it is sometimes suggested that epistemology be approached prior to metaphysics.[7] We could study

---

[6] See accompanying diagram.
[7] Butler, *Four Philosophies,* pp. 315 and 445.

various histories of philosophy, which usually consist of a chronological treatment of the development of certain theories regarding the branches of the field. Often such books are built around the biographies of outstanding philosophers. Another approach might be to read progressively and probably chronologically from the translated works of the world's greatest thinkers. A third means of entry might be to investigate the major recurring questions of philosophy chronologically, *but one at a time.* In this way each chapter of a book could start and finish with present-day interests. It is possible that beginning students would not get discouraged wading through a long book before they arrived at the twentieth century. Brubacher has followed this method in writing about the departmental or special philosophy of education.[8] It is a most interesting approach and one which the writer uses with physical, health, and recreation education later in this book.[9]

A SUGGESTED PROGRESSION FOR YOU.   Another way to begin the study of philosophy might be to consider established principles and then trace these beliefs back to the philosophies from which they emanated. Up to the present time in the specialized field of physical, health, and recreation education, for example, outstanding individuals have written texts about the principles of physical education, or the principles of health education, or the principles of recreation. While these efforts have been significant and noteworthy aids in the development of our field in the present century, they have not given the prospective teacher, or the mature professional for that matter, the opportunity to fully comprehend the source and derivation of these "principles." For this reason, and because it seems much more logical and challenging, it is now recommended that you should start at the beginning (insofar as the field of philosophy is concerned) and work your own way through to those beliefs that you feel you can accept in the light of your own educational background and life experience. Actually, you will find that in the main a more comparative approach has been used among the various philosophies, although every effort has been made to treat recurring problems and living issues whenever possible.

Some Definitions of Terms Used

As you now delve into the various branches of the general field of philosophy, some of the terms used will be new and seemingly quite complex (as indeed they often are), but there is every reason to believe that you will find the quest a most rewarding and enlightening experience.

Metaphysics treats questions about the nature of reality. One sub-

---

[8] J. S. Brubacher, *Modern Philosophies of Education,* 2nd ed. (New York: McGraw-Hill Book Company., Inc., 1950).
[9] See Chapter 12.

division of this branch of philosophy is *cosmology,* which inquires into the orderliness and harmony of the universe. One view *(evolutionism)* is that the universe developed by itself, while a second view *(creationism)* accepts the role of God as the Planner of an orderly system.

Secondly, cosmology treats the nature of man; here an *idealist,* for example, believes that man is a spiritual being. The *physical realist* conversely accepts the position that the self and the body are one and the same thing. Still further, the *experimentalist* has come to the conclusion that man is a social-vocal phenomenon. A further subdivision of the nature of man might inquire into the nature of the relationship between body and mind. (The technical terms that are used here appear in the glossary in the appendix.)

Thirdly, cosmology includes the problem of man's freedom. If man is not free *(determinism),* then all of his actions are determined by some power infinitely greater than he is. If, however, man is free *(free will),* this means that he has the power to choose all his courses of action throughout his life. A third position, peculiar to the experimentalist, takes an intermediate position between determinism and free will.

Fourthly, cosmology inquires about man's conceptions of God. If man believes there is no power or reality behind the cosmos *(atheism),* this sets him apart from *deism, pantheism, polytheism,* and *theism,* etc. The deist believe that God exists but that He is apart from and disinterested in the universe as we know it. The pantheist takes a directly opposite approach, because to him God is identical with the universe. The polytheist believes that there is more than one God, while the theist sees God as personal and immanent in the universe (as opposed to deism). A fifth conception accepts the belief that God is evolving along with the physical universe.

Teleology (whether there is purpose in the universe) makes up a fifth heading under the subdivision of cosmology. If a philosophy includes the belief that there is (and has been) purpose in the cosmos, that philosophy is called *teleological. Nonteleological* systems of philosophy assume that the universe is mechanistic and was created by chance. The experimentalist believes that man is the one who puts purpose in the world.

The belief that reality is fixed is called *absolutism,* while *relativism* means just the opposite—reality is constantly changing.

A seventh heading under cosmology considers the matter of quantity in ultimate reality. *Monism* stands for a unified reality; *dualism* sees two (sometimes antithetical) realities such as good and evil; and *pluralism* envisions a world made up of many realities considered equally real such as mind, energy, etc.

Lastly, *ontology* inquires as to the sense of life as such. What does existence mean from the standpoint of time and space? Are we all part of God or dependent upon Him (e.g., idealism)? The experimentalist, conversely, sees everything as part of change, which denies the validity of existence in any ultimate sense.

Epistemology is the second large subdivision of the field of philosophy to be discussed briefly. This branch is concerned with various theories about the nature and kinds of knowledge possible.

One of the first questions to be considered under this second subdivision is whether any knowledge of the ultimate reality is possible. The *agnostic* does not believe it is possible for man to have any real knowledge of what is behind the cosmos even if there were a God. The *skeptic* is not quite so definite about this question; he is merely somewhat dubious about the possibility of ultimate knowledge. Another position is, of course, the position that man can acquire some of the true facts about the nature of reality. Once again, the experimentalist takes a different stand; he believes that functional knowledge is possible, but that it comes to man fractionally, never totally.

Secondly, epistemology consists of a heading which treats the kinds of knowledge possible. A priori knowledge is reasoning that deduces consequences from principles assumed to be true. A posteriori knowledge is just the opposite; it is the inference of causes from effects, or that type of reasoning which arrives at generalizations after the facts are in, so to speak. The experimentalistic outlook is again somewhat different from a posteriori knowledge, which may be described as induction. He puts knowledge into play in order to promote still greater and more meaningful experience.

Lastly, epistemology investigates the instrument of knowledge. Knowledge gained *empirically* comes to man through the senses, while *rationalism* is the position that he acquires knowledge through his own reason. *Intuitionism* describes the belief that man gains knowledge of reality through immediate apprehension. *Revelation* means that God has disclosed his intentions to man, and *authoritarianism,* which is closely related, asserts that such an indisputable authority as the Church has guaranteed the validity of particular, important knowledge.

Logic, the third subdivision of philosophy, treats the exact relating of ideas as a science.[10] It is concerned with distinguishing correct thinking from incorrect thinking. When we reason from certain particulars to a general conclusion, or from the individual to the universal, that is called *induction. Deduction* is a directly opposite type of reasoning; the process moves from general premises to their necessary conclusion, or from the universal to the individual. The *syllogism,* a form once used much more extensively for deductive reasoning, is an analysis of a formal argument in which the conclusion necessarily results from the given premises. Modern scientific investigation now uses what may be

---

[10] See Chapter 9 for a detailed discussion of formal logic.

called *experimental reasoning* or *problem solving*. This thought process is largely inductive (but may revert to deduction as well). We start with a problem about which we may have a hypothesis. Then after considering all related information we decide upon the method of research which is most applicable to the type of problem involved. Certain research techniques are employed at this point to gather data relating to the problem. Finally, after analysis and interpretation of results have been completed, we arrive at some conclusions which may bear out or negate the original hypotheses. If it isn't possible to conduct detailed research as described above, then reflective thinking of the highest type is used that employs a similar type of reasoning.

Axiology, the fourth and last subdivision of philosophy, is most important and the end result of philosophizing. This involves the development of a system of values that is consistent with your beliefs in the other three subdivisions just considered. The nature and theory of value is considered, as are the various kinds of value.

Some believe that values exist only because of the interest of the valuer *(the interest theory)*. *The existence theory,* on the other hand, asserts that values exist independently, although they are important in a vacuum, so to speak. They are essence added to existence. The experimentalist *(the experimentalist theory)* views value a bit differently. Values which yield practical results that have "cash value" bring about the possibility of greater happiness through more effective values in the future. One further theory, *the part-whole theory,* is explained by the idea that effective relating of parts to the whole brings about the highest values.

Lastly, the various domains of value must be examined under the subdivision of axiology. First and foremost, we must consider *ethics,* which considers morality, conduct, good and evil, and ultimate objectives in life. There are several approaches to the problem of whether life, as we know it, is worthwhile. A person who goes around all the time with a smile on his face looking hopefully toward the future is, of course, an optimist *(optimism)*. On the other side of the fence is the individual who gets discouraged easily and soon wonders if life is worth the struggle *(pessimism)*. In between these two extremes we find the golden mean *(meliorism)* which would have us facing life and striving constantly to improve our situation. This position assumes that we can't make any final decisions about whether good or evil will prevail in the world.

A second most important question to be considered under ethics is what is most important in life for the individual. This might be described as the ultimate end of our existence. Under this heading we encounter the belief that pleasure is the highest good *(hedonism)*. A philosophy which has more or less distinct leanings in this direction is called hedonistic. One approach under hedonism that has developed in modern history is known as *utilitarianism*. Society becomes the focus, since the basic idea is to promote the greatest happiness for the greatest number in the community. Thus, although there are types of pleasure which range from intense, momentary, emotional pleasure to a pleasure that is reflected in a placid life of contentment, a hedonist believes that the seeking of his type of pleasure will result in the fulfillment of his own moral duty. Another important way of looking at the *summum bonum* (or highest good) in life is called *perfectionism*. Here the individual is aiming for complete self-realization, and he envisions a society of the highest type as well.

A logical progression following from an individual's decision about the greatest good in life is the standard of conduct that he sets for himself. The naturalist, for example, would not have you do anything through which you might destroy yourself; for him self-preservation is an important principle of life. Kant, who spent his days in Königsberg in the late eighteenth century, felt that a man should base his actions upon what he would wish might become a universal law. Of course, orthodox religion tells us that we must obey God's wishes, because He has a purpose for us all. The experimentalist, however, suggests a trial run in our imaginations to discover the possible consequences of any of our actions.

Certain interests are apt to guide our conduct in life. If we are too self-centered, people say we are egotistical *(egoism)*. Some people go the other way completely; they feel that an individual fulfills himself best and most when he plays down the realization of his own interests in order to serve society or some social group therein *(altruism)*. Once again, Aristotle's concept of the "golden mean" comes to the fore as perhaps a desirable aim for a man to fulfill within the span of his life.

There are, of course, other areas of value under the Axiology subdivision over and above ethics which treat moral conduct. One of these areas has to do with the "feeling" aspects of man's conscious life *(aesthetics)*. Aesthetics may be defined as the theory or philosophy of taste, and man has inquired whether there are principles which govern the search for the beautiful in life. Because there has been a need to define still further values in the life of man, we now have specialized philosophies of education and religion. We often refer further to a man's social philosophy. What is meant here is that men make decisions about the kind, nature, and worth of values which are intrinsic to, say, the educational process.[11]

---

[11] The author must express his debt at this point for the sequential alignment of certain of the philosophical branches and subdivisions to Professor J. Donald Butler, *Four Philosophies*, pp. 48-54.

CHAPTER THREE

A Brief History
of the Ideas and Problems
# of Philosophy

There are at least six possible approaches when one considers tracing historically the ideas and problems of philosophy.[1] For example, the development of philosophical thought could be told as a *chronological narrative* that is blended with *historical facts*. A second approach might be to present each of a number of recurring problems separately and chronologically (i.e., a so-called *longitudinal approach*). One such recurring problem could be the development of man's thought about the nature of God.

A third approach could be called *comparative*, since its objective would be to trace each of three main philosophies of the Western world chronologically. Thus, the reader could be shown (perhaps with the aid of a comparative chart) the highlights of such philosophies as naïve naturalism, realism, idealism, and pragmatism.

A fourth idea or means of approach is sometimes called the *great-man approach*. Here the story of philosophy could be built around the leading philosophical figures of the ages and their philosophical positions could be clarified by a listing of their main ideas. If these main ideas (or *Kerngedanken*) are traced progressively, it could be that this *course of development approach* would represent a fifth approach to the subject.

A sixth approach will be mentioned at this point, and its use makes an assumption about the history of philosophy. The stress here would

---

[1] Cf., p. 5 ff.

be to show (if this were the belief of the author) that the *tendency of the time* influenced the philosophical thought of that particular era. It would seem logical that the opposite of the above assumption might also be true, but to a much lesser extent.

To conclude this brief discussion about how we might approach the history of philosophy, a few opinions offered by Boas seem to make a great deal of sense.[2] He believes that it is not possible to write a history of a single subject matter called *philosophy,* because the methods and interests of philosophers have varied such a great deal. Secondly, he stressed that practically no philosopher has had a complete system of philosophy. Usually he has had a number of leading ideas determined both deductively and inductively, and influenced greatly by the then current historical trend. Finally, Boas explains that it would be dangerous and misleading to extract a philosophical idea and to examine it without considering also the remainder of the intellectual thought of that particular historical period. Having made this third point, he concludes by stating that "histories of various philosophical ideas, taken singly, would be more fruitful than a history which would attempt to synthesize all of them into a general history of philosophy." [3]

One Persistent Problem Viewed Historically

Let us now trace one philosophical idea historically—a persistent problem which has been plaguing man for many centuries. What is the universe in which man lives? If philosophy's goal is to suggest answers or solutions to man's recurring problems, this question is perhaps his most universal problem.

What is the universe, or the world? Plato (427–347 B.C.) interpreted man's world as an imperfect copy of the actual or "ideal world." Aristotle (384–322 B.C.), his pupil and contemporary, did not agree with his teacher on this point. He believed that the world of sense is the real world. In this world, form is present inherently in matter and is always struggling to realize itself.

Much later, Francis Bacon (1561–1626), who gave the world the beginning of a new method of scientific inquiry, realized the consistency of phenomena which occurred in the universe. He recommended simple experimentation as a means of determining the physical laws which give order to the world.

Descartes (1596–1650) has been called the *father of modern philosophy.* His aim was to apply the laws of mathematics to the study of philosophy.

---

[2] Yervant Krikorian, ed., *Naturalism and the Human Spirit* (New York: Columbia University Press, 1944), pp. 152-153.

[3] *Ibid.,* p. 153.

He realized that these laws applied to the universe and the matter of which it is composed. He believed that matter filled all space, and the whole was divided into small particles continually changing positions according to law. Thus, the real properties of a physical object are quantitative and measurable. To carry this line of thought further, the qualities of objects are subjective configurations of the human mind. This is the theory of Cartesian dualism, which split our world into two worlds (the scientific, quantitative world and the human, qualitative world).

Spinoza (1632–1677) wasn't satisfied with Descartes's approach to the makeup of the universe. He carried the concept of mind and matter further by suggesting that there are two ways of looking at the same substance. What is this basic substance? It is God—the basic "material" of the universe!

Locke (1632–1704) raised a question in his *Essay Concerning Human Understanding* that had not been considered in such detail before his time. He believed that man could learn about the universe only through his senses. Because he deplored loose thinking, he wanted men's ideas to be put to the test of experience. He couldn't be certain that the evidence of his own senses was true.

Kant (1724–1804) considered this basic question about the nature of the universe. The conclusion he came to had tremendous implications for the future development of philosophy. He stated unequivocally that it is not possible for man to know that which lies outside of the realm of his own thought. This is the "unknowable" world—the "thing-in-itself." He postulated that our reason constructs a universe of idea, and that it is this universe that we are capable of knowing. Thus, we have two worlds: (1) a scientific, phenomenal world of experience; and (2) a practical, noumenal world of reason. Kant's metaphysics indicate that we really can't be positive about anything in the world outside experience.

William James (1842–1910) accepted this distinction between two "types" of worlds. He believed that we should turn only to the "practical" world of human experience. He urged that man forget about the world that he can't know about. Why should man be concerned about it?

James was a meliorist, who worked for a better world by attempting to eliminate the evil in it. The universe was for him a plural world consisting of separate, imperfect, and contradictory elements. Man's task was to adjust himself to a practical, pragmatic world. Men, working together, can overcome those forces which hold back the progress of mankind.

Lastly, let us consider the views on this question of the idealist Bergson

(1859–1941). His contention was that the world as explained by scientists was deficient, because too much was left out. He refers to the process of "creative evolution," because he believes that man can work right along with God to determine man's own destiny and that of the entire universe. For him the world is developing according to a design; it is growing and creative and will undoubtedly develop into something vital and unforeseeable.

Historical Highlights of the Philosophy of Naturalism

Now that we have traced one philosophical idea (what is the universe?) historically, albeit rather sketchily, let us now examine the historical development of what has often been called naïve or unrefined naturalism. Such an examination will lead us subsequently to even more of a comparative approach. At this later time we will consider also idealism, realism, and pragmatism.

Naturalism appears to be the oldest philosophy in the Western world. It has often been called an *elusive philosophy,* perhaps because it crops up in other philosophies (often conflicting) just as humanism appears frequently in theistic religions. To the naturalist, nature exhibits order, and a dependable order at that. His intuition and his reason tell him that nature must take its course.

This philosophy may be traced back to Thales, who lived in Asia Minor in the sixth century B.C. He, along with several others, founded what has been called the *Milesian* school. His bold approach, which stamped him as a naturalist, emphasized that water was an essential element of all matter and that it was to be found throughout and within nature. Anaximander, one of his contemporaries who was also a philosopher and astronomer, theorized that all animals were descendants from fish through some sort of successive transformation.

Naturalism got its start also, and perhaps even a bit more strongly, from Leucippus and Democritus (early fifth century B.C.) who theorized that nature could be reduced to empty space and atoms. Atoms were the smallest possible indivisible units which moved around in various combinations in the void of empty space. Still further, nature evolved from these basic structures and not by chance. These men believed that it was important to live in harmony with nature in a practical and simple way. There should be a balance between work and the quiet pleasures of life. These beliefs were echoed to a large extent by Epicurus (342–270 B.C.) and Lucretius (95–54 B.C.). It has been said that Epicurus was less deterministic than Democritus, because he foresaw the possibility of chance operating when atoms mixed in space. He believed further that there were a number of superior creatures known as gods, but that they did not create the world nor interfere with its processes. Lucretius is not thought to have added to the doctrines of Democritus and Epicurus, although he did proclaim them enthusiastically and beautifully.

It is quite a jump from 54 B.C. to the sixteenth century that we make at this point. Certainly there would be some traces of naturalism present in at least several of the philosophers who wrote during this long period of history. Hook, in referring to Murray's *Four Stages of Greek Religion,* points out that Murray felt that for a period of 400 years there appeared a lack of character that might be designated as "failure of nerve." [4] At such times there is much greater emphasis on asceticism, mysticism, and, for that matter, pessimism. A corresponding loss of self-confidence, conversion of the soul to God more readily, and loss of faith in man's efforts were evident to a considerable extent.

After the invasion of the barbarians, and the subsequent downfall of the Roman Empire, philosophy retreated into the monasteries. For this reason we see very few traces of naturalism, because searches for truth were not welcomed during the Middle Ages. In the eighth century, however, the Arabs penetrated into Spain and established many universities. The name of Averroës (who lived in the twelfth century and was known as an Aristotelian) should be mentioned as one who believed in the eternity of nature, and who indicated that the universe was evolving of its own initiative. In the thirteenth century, Roger Bacon (*c.* 1214–1294?), who is not to be confused with Francis Bacon born almost 200 years later, displayed certain naturalistic tendencies in his philosophy and has been celebrated chiefly for his interest in natural science and experimentation through direct observation.

Thomas Hobbes (1588–1679) took up the thread of naturalism where some of the ancients had left off. He developed a natural philosophy which was concerned with the physical properties of "bodies" that are moving in space. He stressed that these bodies exist independently of man. Occupying space, they move from one position to another, and time elapses. Hobbes believed further that man acquires knowledge through his senses. In regard to man's freedom of will, he believed that man could follow his inclination within limits but could not escape nature's framework of cause and effect. Finally, we must confess that Hobbes was not a pure naturalist; he removed religion from the realm of philosophy arbitrarily—a religion which was theistic in its essence.

Although Rousseau (1717–1778) proclaimed himself to be a deist, much of the evidence indicates that we can safely call him a naturalist. In the first place, he believed strongly that man should live a simple existence and should not deviate from a life which followed closely the ways of nature. In his classic of educational literature, he desired

[4] *Ibid.,* p. 40.

an education for *Émile* in which nature could bestow her many good ways on the child raised simply without "benefit" of society's many "opportunities." And so we find that Émile developed eventually a natural religion wholly free from creed. This leads us to another main idea of Rousseau which pointed up the evil and corruption of society in France of that time. The basic thought was that society was artificial and evil, while nature was completely reliable and free.

Moving forward into the nineteenth century, we encounter Herbert Spencer (1820–1903) who has been designated as the most important naturalist (albeit naïve) of this period in Europe. Whereas Rousseau has been extremely emotional about his naturalistic beliefs, Spencer appears to have gone about his writing over a thirty-three year period in a completely matter-of-fact manner despite being plagued by poor health. Whereas previous philosophers wrote in times when organized religion held a stranglehold on man's thoughts, Spencer was undoubtedly influenced by the many scientific discoveries of his day. He believed that reality was unknowable, although he did not deny an Ultimate Being. But he felt that God was utterly incomprehensible for mere man. Spencer gave himself the fantastically difficult task of describing all scientific knowledge in one gigantic scheme. He believed in man's evolution and dissolution into the dust of the earth. Feeling that he was incapable of understanding the makeup of God, he defined this Power as force or energy.

To conclude this discussion of the development of naturalistic thought, we may now consider naturalism in America very briefly. Larrabee tells us that "the career of naturalism in America is the history of the slow growth of an attitude rather than of a specific philosophical doctrine." [5] He explains further that actually the leading philosophy, which has been expressed both in institutions of higher learning and through various publications, has been idealistic with a very strong theological base. But despite this speculation of a metaphysical nature, American thought and American living generally have strayed from the beam of this light largely because of the rapid advancement of science and invention throughout this nation, and the rest of the world for that matter. This trend, of course, has been disconcerting and most disturbing to many theologians and some philosophers, who have often decried the trend of the American people toward so-called materialism. Furthermore, it has done untold damage to the former position of the technical philosopher who may have assumed that he was exerting a certain amount of influence on American life. According to Larrabee, therefore, we find a situation where the division between idealistic, organized religion and realistic business practice and applied science has steadily widened.[6]

---

[5] *Ibid.*, p. 319. (See Part Two of this book for a detailed discussion.)

Such developments as industrialization and war have fostered this attitude. With the fantastic scientific development of the twentieth century gathering momentum daily, there is every reason to believe that a naturalistic attitude will continue to grow. We must keep in mind, however, that unrefined naturalism of the past has been confined to a very large extent to the branch of metaphysics. *In this century both realism and pragmatism have borrowed heavily from naturalistic thought.* On the other hand, despite the effect of global war, interest in philosophy of religion seems to be growing. What this naturalistic development will mean is impossible to predict. We can't even understand the significance of the situation at present because of the lack of historical perspective. It is safe to say that a naturalistic outlook on man and his world will continue to influence American philosophy to a very great extent.

Historical Comparison of Idealism, Realism, and Pragmatism

Now that we have traced one recurring metaphysical problem (what is the universe?) through the thinking of leading historical philosophical figures, and also through one philosophical school of thought *(naturalism)*, it is time to make some sort of a historical comparison of the three leading Western philosophies of the latter half of the nineteenth century—*idealism, realism,* and *pragmatism.* The influence of these schools of thought has certainly not lessened in the twentieth century despite the influence of two "new" philosophies—*philosophical analysis* and *existentialism.*

To treat each of these philosophies in exactly the same way that unrefined naturalism was covered would make this chapter far too long, and also would not serve the purpose of a fairly direct comparison among them. For these reasons, a separate analysis of the ideas of some of the leading philosophers representing each school of thought will be developed concurrently on the following pages. The author realizes the inadequacy of so brief a treatment insofar as the achievement of a complete understanding of the developing movements is concerned; nevertheless, it should serve at least *two* purposes: (1) it will give the reader some orientation as to the time and historical setting of each of the philosophers and philosophies included; and (2) it will help to form a most necessary base upon which a philosophy of education (and a philosophy of physical, health, and recreation education) can be built. Furthermore, it will be obvious to the serious-minded individual that he is just beginning a most exciting adventure in the world of ideas.

---

[6] *Ibid.,* p. 324.

HISTORICAL DEVELOPMENT

IDEALISM (Idea - ism)

A man is a real, existent being with a soul.

In each man is a spirit or mind which is basically real; the essence of the entire universe is in some way mind or spirit, also.

A man is a son of God, who was the Creator of the universe; he is not merely a high-grade monkey.

Plato (427?–347 B.C.)

Ideas have direct relationship with ultimate reality. They endure, and are imperfectly embodied in physical objects. Man's focus should be on a life of reason, as all else stems from this. Absolute knows truth, beauty, and goodness; there are ideas not represented in physical form. Impossibility of knowing anything save psychical reality. The developing organism becomes what it inherently is (a process of recollection).

REALISM

Man lives in a world which is undoubtedly real; things actually happen exactly the way man experiences them.

Man's experience does not change any knowledge that may enter into his consciousness; things are just the same as they were before such experience occurred.

The reality "out there" is independent of man's mind.

Aristotle (384–322 B.C.)

He made an attempt to describe all phases of the natural order analytically. God is defined as the first cause and thereby is responsible for all existence. Things seem to change, but actually their essential character remains the same. Man is unique because of his ability to reason. Nature is primary and self-evident and is a starting point for philosophy. Truth corresponds with reality.

PRAGMATISM

The world is constantly undergoing change.

An idea is not true until it is tested through experience.

When an idea is put into practice, we can learn by the experience what it really means.

We can't really find out what the nature of the universe is.

Heraclitus (540?–470? B.C.)

The world is characterized by change and movement.

The Sophists (Fifth century B.C.)

It is actually impossible for man to discover what ultimate reality is. Through the experience of sense perception man makes his closest approach to knowledge or truth. This means that values are not fixed and may change according to the mores of the time.

HISTORICAL DEVELOPMENT (Cont.)

IDEALISM

Hebrew–Christian Tradition
in Religion

This tradition appears to have definite relationship with the idealistic conception of reality being basically spiritual. God, according to the Bible, created the world and the creatures in it. Man received a special place, because he is said to be unique in that he is likened to his God. This great God and Creator has a most rational character and represents reason as seen in Platonic thought.

René Descartes (1596–1650)

Exerted a tremendous influence on modern philosophic thought. Several of his basic ideas definitely develop the thread of idealism: (1) the self is for each person immediate and most real; (2) each of us can conceive of a Perfect Being and that is God. Is remembered for his famous "I think, therefore I am." Thus to know anything we must begin with the self before analyzing experience.

REALISM

St. Thomas Aquinas (1225?–1274)

He shared the realist spirit as did Aristotle and achieved still greater stature than St. Augustine. Some modern realists still agree with his position. He did believe in matter's reality but decided after consideration that God had actually created it. He was the first cause and has no limits being eternal and infinite. He defined matter as follows: "It is being in potentiality." Today many realists define matter as physical energy and thus agree.

René Descartes (1596–1650)

The seeming contradiction evident in the thought of Descartes should not unduly disturb us. Asking if the outside world was real, he agreed that it was because God is perfect and would not deceive us. The world is also a physical, material, and mechanistic entity; thus, his philosophy served as a basis for mathematical physics. Matter is quantitative, but qualities of things are subjective in the mind.

PRAGMATISM

Francis Bacon (1561–1626)

His *Novum Organum* challenged man's thought processes in the past. Science really did not have an effective method of investigation. He outlined common errors used to determine "knowledge" and asked for an inductive logic based on careful observation. In his *New Atlantis* he anticipated modern pragmatism; he felt true science should guide society's development. He wanted scientists to pool their research in an effort to help society solve all of its problems.

John Locke (1632–1704)

Added to realistic thread, also, but asked the question, "How do we determine truth?" He stated, "Let us put the ideas of our mind, just as we put the things of the laboratory, to the test of experience."

HISTORICAL DEVELOPMENT (Cont.)

IDEALISM

Baruch Spinoza (1632–1677)

Gave evidence of idealistic thinking as well as realistic. Believed in an enduring substance behind the cosmos which is more basic and unchanging than matter. This substance is God who is "absolutely infinite." This idea unites the basic metaphysical belief of Aristotle and St. Thomas (and Descartes's Perfect Being) with the natural world. God's two attributes are extension and thought.

Gottfried W. Leibniz (1646–1716)

Believed that the universe is a "vital living being." Offered a theory of "monadism" to describe the makeup of the world. There are three categories of monads: (1) simple—innumerable and more "mental" than physical organisms; (2) complex—comparable to man's "soul"; (3) still more complex—comparable to man's "spirit," which involves reason that distinguishes man from animals. God belongs to last type, but He is infinite without limitations.

REALISM

John Amos Comenius (1592–1670)

Took an elementary, simple realistic position. Did not add to realistic thinking but definitely helped to clarify it. Compared the mind of man to a "spherical mirror suspended in a room." Also, it "reflects images of all things that are around it." This postulates man's mind as a "passive recipient" of the world's images and means that he will have no lasting influence that might promote change in the surrounding world.

Baruch Spinoza (1632–1677)

Is included under idealism also. His theory about substance is basically realistic also, because of enduring reality. Extension is a basic attribute of existence; extension in time and place is necessary for the second attribute—thought. God is the "only existing substance," but the basic frame of reference is substance and not mind. Another realistic element in Spinoza's thought is the theory that will is not free in God or man.

PRAGMATISM

As mentioned previously, both *Francis Bacon* and *John Locke* made contributions to the development of philosophical pragmatism in the sixteenth and seventeenth centuries. Most important as well was the growth of the scientific spirit started by *Copernicus* (1473–1543), and followed by *Kepler* (1571–1630), *Galileo* (1564–1642), *Newton* (1642–1727). Other important early scientists were *Vesalius* (1514–1564), *Fabricius* (1537–1619), *Harvey* (1578–1667), *Boyle* (1627–1691), and *Huygens* (1629–1695).

HISTORICAL DEVELOPMENT (Cont.)

IDEALISM

George Berkeley (1685–1753)

Revolted against commonly accepted belief that universe is matter moving in space; we must comprehend the true character of knowledge to understand reality. A mind is necessary to perceive that matter and meanings are real. Thus if a mind gets ideas from the world, the true reality must be mind or spirit. The only world we know is that which we perceive; thus, behind the objective world must be a Spirit that gives us the ideas and meanings. God creates and perceives.

Immanuel Kant (1724–1804)

He analyzed the acquisition of knowledge very carefully and expressed metaphysical beliefs of an idealistic nature. Says it is our conscious experience which gives world a unity. Sensations are "representations" within man. From reason, man receives twelve categories or conceptions, which are grouped according to quantity, quality, relation, or modality. Out there behind it all is the "thing-in-itself"—God—that is unknown to man. There is moral law and immortality.

REALISM

John Locke (1632–1704)

Propounded famous *tabula rasa* theory that mind is a blank sheet upon which the world makes its impressions. As there are no innate ideas at birth, any knowledge must come from man's experience—by sensation and reason. He suggests that "primary qualities" as we experience them coincide with the external objects "out there." But "secondary qualities" are different and man's mind participates in "translation."

Immanuel Kant (1724–1804)

Some of his ideas must be classified under realism also. They belong to his epistemological theory, however, not his metaphysics. The "representative" theory of knowledge is accepted by the critical realists as well, but not by the neorealists. The doctrine that the "thing-in-itself" may not be "known" is definitely realistic, because this refutes the idealistic claim that God must be rational—a Universal Mind.

PRAGMATISM

No contemporary to those above may be listed until *Comte*. Undoubtedly there were a number of early scientists such as *Simon* (astronomy), *Hutton* (geology), *von Haller* (physiology), and *Lamarck* (biology), who did much to promote the rise of experimental method.

Auguste Comte (1798–1857)

Man's progress includes three stages: (1) theological—belief in supernatural powers; (2) metaphysical—some force underlying existence; and (3) the positive (highest stage in the evolution)—exact scientific laws explain the fundamental structure of the universe. His positivistic metaphysics and social interest relate his thought to pragmatism. Comte did believe, however, that universe displayed order and that there had been progress through evolution.

Historical Development (Cont.)

IDEALISM

Georg Hegel (1770–1831)

Proposed a complex, idealistic philosophy in which the parts must always be seen in connection with the whole. Man has a similar relationship to the universe. Went a step beyond Kant in that the "unknowable thing-in-itself" became an Infinite Being possessing knowable attributes. Mind is greater than nature (the latter being a finite aspect). His *Dialectic* concluded that progress came through thesis, antithesis, and synthesis.

Nineteenth Century European Idealism

After idealism reached such heights through the work of *Kant* and *Hegel,* this influence spread throughout the other countries of Europe. Such names as *Bergson* (France), *Croce* (Italy), and *Gentile* (Italy) became well known and exercised significant influence. The materialism of *Marx* and others arose in opposition. In England and Scotland, *Coleridge, Carlyle, Jowett,* and the *Cairds* promoted idealism.

REALISM

Johann F. Herbart (1776–1841)

Is known more in education than in philosophy. Attempted to establish psychology as a science. Defined mind as a "group" of self-preserving concepts which are developed through "representation" not "presentation." These tend to cluster together and there is a struggle to "rise above the threshold of consciousness." Mind, therefore, is not striving to bring about change; it is a composite of all impressions made on the soul.

William James (1842–1910)

Is identified primarily with pragmatism, but his epistemological belief ties him in also with American realism. To him, consciousness has been defined as a bodily function; furthermore, objects are "presented" in consciousness, not "represented." He believed also in a multiverse, not a universe. To him, man was (and is) present and observes experience "taking place" in time.

PRAGMATISM

Charles S. Peirce (1839–1914)

Appears to have been basically a realist, but is responsible for the coining of the term *pragmatism*. Tried to make up for what he felt was a lack in Kant's idea regarding the possibility of analysis of reality. He said, "To determine the meaning of any idea, put it into practice in the objective world of actualities and whatever its consequences prove to be, these constitute the meaning of the idea." Try the idea out in the objective world!

William James (1842–1910)

Believed strongly in the freedom of will, because it meant so much to him. We want to be free so that we can make the world better if possible. Pragmatism is prospective; we are challenged to improve our lot and that of the world. His pragmatism was not atheistic, since he believed in a spiritual pluralism as opposed to *Dewey's* later naturalism. Man helps positively to determine certain aspects of unfinished realities.

HISTORICAL DEVELOPMENT (Cont.)

IDEALISM

Late Nineteenth and Early Twentieth Century American Idealism

German idealism ultimately had a strong influence on America. In the first place, the writings of *Carlyle* and *Coleridge* were widely read in the United States, where subsequently Ralph Waldo *Emerson* (1803–1882) expressed what was known as New England Transcendentalism. He had studied in Germany in his youth but was regarded as more of a literary figure than as a philosopher. His writing did much, however, to prepare the way for the growth of philosophical idealism in America. Secondly, many German scholars emigrated to America for a variety of reasons and were significant factors in the development of idealism. Two of these men were Carl *Follen* (1796–1840) and Francis *Lieber* (1800–1872) [coincidentally, both were strong proponents of German gymnastics]. Two other important figures were Frederick A. *Rauch* (1806–1841) and Louis *Agassiz* (1807–1873). A third influence promoting idealism was that of a number of eminent Americans who studied abroad.

Some of these leaders were Henry Wadsworth *Longfellow*, Henry *Barnard*, Horace *Mann*, and G. Stanley *Hall*. The St. Louis Philosophical Society was established in 1866. It was formed to provide a vehicle for the promotion of idealism in America. In 1867 the first issue of the *Journal of Speculative Philosophy* appeared and continued for twenty-six years to spread Hegelian idealism. William T. *Harris* edited this first American philosophical journal and spearheaded idealism in America. Other important names in American idealism were George H. *Howison* (1834–1916), later professor of philosophy in the University of California; Borden Parker *Bowne* (1847–1910), a Boston University professor; Josiah *Royce* (1855–1916), a great figure in American idealism who taught at Harvard for many years; and many others following such as *Brightman, Hocking, Calkins,* and *Horne.*

REALISM

The Critical Realists (c. 1916–1920)

A reactionary group within the ranks of realists took a stand in opposition to the neorealists. They included George *Santayana* of Harvard and Roy Wood *Sellars* of Michigan among others. This group published some essays in 1920 in which they agreed as to epistemology but disagreed on their metaphysical beliefs. They wished to correct the neorealistic epistemology, since they believed that objects were represented (not presented) in consciousness.

The Neorealists (c. 1910)

In 1910, a group known as neorealists decided to make their position known as being opposed to the prevailing idealism. This group, which included Ralph Barton *Perry* and others, published a group of essays in 1912. They wished to contradict the position of idealism which stated simply that knowledge effected a change in the object known. Secondly, they believed that the knowing experience was not as complicated as had been suggested. An object was presented directly to man's consciousness.

HISTORICAL DEVELOPMENT (Cont.)

PRAGMATISM

John Dewey (1859–1952)

Although much of his earlier background pointed him in the direction of idealism, Dewey eventually became the twentieth century's strongest exponent of experimentalism. In the 1890's Dewey gave up the metaphysics of idealism and believed that the individual could be explained as completely behavioristic. He thought of man as a social phenomenon interacting in society with the cultural environment exerting tremendous influence on his thoughts and ideas. While discarding the idea that the universe is undergirded by the Absolute Mind, he turned to man instead and emphasized the need for intelligence to have a social function in order to provide for a better world in the future. He saw that the world has many problems and that answers to these problems only created more problems. Thus man must turn to science if he wishes to solve all the problems that he faces, whether they be in the realm of science or social values. Dewey taught at Michigan, Chicago, and Columbia Universities. He has exerted a tremendous influence on American education in the twentieth century, and this influence has been felt in many other countries. *Democracy and Education* (1916) is considered by many to be his greatest book; it is said to represent his mature pragmatic philosophy. In it philosophy is deemed to be comparable to a general theory of education. Dewey is revered by many, reviled by many, and misunderstood by a great many people. None can dispute his great influence on American education; the question seems to revolve around whether this influence has been beneficial and in the ultimate best interests of America's future. Obviously, for the pragmatist and experimentalist there is no question. The task is to put his theory to practice; the consequences will tell us about the worth of the idea.

Early Modern Philosophy

As we have seen in the chronological sequences of idealism, realism, and pragmatism immediately preceding, Descartes exerted a tremendous influence on the development of philosophic thought. Some say he started the modern epoch in philosophy (and perhaps "modern" times also) when he offered a philosophy that was designed to serve as a foundation for mathematical physics. His philosophy has become known as Cartesian dualism, because he proposed a split between the human world and the scientific world. The basic properties of a physical object are considered to be the quantitative ones, and this matter, which is extension, can be measured objectively. Qualities (as opposed to quantity) were thought to be subjective and belonged to the human mind. This dualism is still with us to a degree, as man is way ahead in his ability to make use of matter. But when it comes to meeting and conquering the problems of man in relationship to his fellow man, he has made only a meager beginning.

This type of reasoning caused rational man to ponder long over his situation. Kant came to the rescue in 1781 to a certain extent when he postulated that many of the ideals of Christian civilization (i.e., man's freedom, the human soul and possible immortality, and God himself) cannot be known through the medium of human reason. These things were simply beyond man's grasp as they referred to ultimate things. Scientific method could be most exact, but it could be employed only with temporal objects. Despite this earth-shaking postulation, Kant, undoubtedly influenced by the tenor of the time, stated subsequently that man should not deny the existence of God and the human soul.

Although Kant's metaphysical beliefs were essentially idealistic, many of the idealistic philosophers after him felt that it was necessary to strengthen their position by re-establishing man's spiritual entity. Hegel (1770–1831) went so far as to state that ultimate realities which affected man must be within the realm of man's reason to comprehend them. He asserted that reason could fathom all aspects of human experience. Philosophy, therefore, had but to determine all the laws by which reason functions within man. That there would be many who would rebel against this philosophical position is not difficult to comprehend. Arthur Schopenhauer (1788–1860) was one such philosopher whose *The World as Will and Idea* was published in 1818. Europe at this point, of course, was in terrible condition because of ruinous war; a generation of hope seemed to have been swallowed up in despair and frustration. Schopenhauer's pessimistic contribution fell on the eyes and ears of people who were too exhausted to care or to hope. It wasn't until much later in his life that people appreciated the work of a philosopher who made a fairly intelligible survey of real-life phenomena, albeit a most pessimistic effort. Despite the emphasis placed on an individual will that was dynamic, life had dealt so many blows to Schopenhauer that he became a recluse.

Herbert Spencer was another strong anti-Hegelian influence whom we discussed earlier in this chapter.[7] His *Synthetic Philosophy* gave expression to the bio-social implications of Darwin's *Origin of the Species.* In Spencer's publication, to which he devoted much of his life, he surveyed man's and nature's evolutionary development and dedicated himself to an agnostic realism which asserted that man cannot know the Absolute, only that which is finite. His influence on social and moral thought was considerable.

Because we have not mentioned the name of Friedrich Nietzsche (1844–1900) before under the banner of any particular philosophical thread, it seems appropriate to introduce this bold German philosopher at this point. Here was a man who saw that Spencer's ethical philosophy coincided with Darwin's theory of evolution. He believed further that the world belonged to the strong who were able to survive. This type

---

[7] Cf., p. 29.

of thought rejected altruistic Christianity and demanded in its place strong, intelligent men who could win in the battle of life. In a sense this man became a spokesman for a Germany led by a powerful figure—Bismarck. Influenced by Richard Wagner, the great musician, and stirred by the German victory of 1871, he dreamed of a society in which superior men ruled, and the worship of mediocrity (as in democracy) was thrust aside. Whether we can agree with Nietzsche's theories or not, it remains that he served as a refreshing critic of certain established institutions and that he forced society to consider many of the ethical implications of Darwinism.

The Twentieth Century

It is most difficult to gain historical perspective on the philosophical trends and developments of the past 100 years. It is apparent, however, that there have been strong attacks on many of the traditional approaches that have been enumerated in this chapter. Certain of the developments will now be highlighted briefly followed by a summary of the present situation as it appears in the twentieth century. As we have seen naturalism and materialism were moving ahead despite the fact that those philosophies expressed (in America, for example) continually refuted this outlook on life. Prior to World War I the idealism that had emanated from Kant, perhaps as a reaction to the Englishmen Locke and Berkeley, had lost some of the prestige that it enjoyed in the late 1800's. The defense of scientific investigation by Spencer and Darwin was a tremendously powerful influence. As usual, there were those who sought a middle position which stressed man's will and the desire for positive action as a recommended compromise between the two extremes.

Pragmatism continued to be influential, especially in the United States. It gathered much strength from naturalism and from the rise of the spirit of scientific inquiry. Great emphasis was placed on the desirability of testing hypotheses through experience in order to gain "true" knowledge. In fact, it was stated that we couldn't even know the meaning of an idea before it was put into practice. Furthermore, science should be so directed as to solve man's social problems. From this approach comes a new type of ethical theory which states than man will find workable solutions to his problems as truth is wrought in action. After World War I, the term *instrumentalism* was coined and is largely synonymous with pragmatism of which it is an extension. Still later it became known as *experimentalism,* an educational philosophy which accepts only scientific, experimental method as a valid and reliable means of determining truth and resultant practice.

Philosophical analysis has been another interesting development that has gathered momentum in the past forty years. Despite the fact that various citizens of the Western world have been engaged in philosophical thought for more than two thousand years, there is still an argument over what the exact nature of philosophy is. As we have seen, early Greek philosophers thought that philosophy should serve a function not unlike that which we attribute to contemporary science. Today, of course, we employ scientific method which involves reflective thought and hypothesis, long-term observation, and experimentation prior to subsequent generalization. Thus, many of today's philosophers ask themselves, "What kind of activity am I engaging in?" They wonder whether philosophical activity does result in knowledge after all. Some are fearful that the scientific method has clearly demonstrated that true knowledge can only come from this type of experimentation. If this is true, what is the justification for philosophy?

In the twentieth century there have been three developments within philosophy that have sought to answer this question: (1) logical atomism; (2) logical positivism; and (3) ordinary language philosophy. The main idea behind these approaches is that philosophy's function is analysis. The difficulty is that they look at analysis differently, but there is agreement that philosophy must be approached through the medium of language analysis to a greater or lesser extent.

Logical atomism involved a new approach to logic as devised by Bertrand Russell (1872–   ) and Alfred North Whitehead (1861–1947) called *mathematical logic*. It had been thought that Aristotle had said the last word on this subject, but these two great philosophers developed a logic that was much broader in scope. This logic dealt more with propositions rather than with only classes. Thus, in addition to saying something like, "All cats are vertebrates, all vertebrates are animals," and therefore "all cats are animals," Russell showed the implication between two statements by saying, "If an apple falls from the tree, it will land on the ground." This doesn't sound very startling, but it did open a much broader logical system for investigation. Furthermore, Russell demonstrated that mathematics had a relationship to logic. His next step was to show that a language like English had essentially the same basic structure as mathematics. Because our language was not exact enough, however, it was thought that mathematical logic would help man explain the components of language such as sentences which give us "world facts." Carried through to its logical conclusion, the philosopher would then be in a position to find out everything about the structure of the world by using philosophical analysis to rearrange our ambiguous language so that the new logically arranged sentences would become crystal clear. This approach, which flourished for twenty or more years in some quarters, was thought to offer us a new metaphysical system, but it was superseded by logical positivism which carried mathematical logic a step further.

In the 1920's a group subsequently known as the *Vienna Circle* came to believe that it was not possible for logical atomism to provide the world with a system of metaphysics. Their answer was logical positivism which presented philosophy as an activity—not as theories about the universe. They felt that philosophy's task was to analyze and explain what statements meant. Some statements would be able to "withstand being subjected" to the *verifiability principle*. This means that a sentence might be factually significant to a given person, if he understands those observations which would enable him to accept or reject the proposition therein contained. Thus, some sentences may be significant factually, others are not directly applicable to this world, although they appear to be analytically true, and a third group are actually nonsensical or nonsignificant. Now it can readily be seen how devastating such an approach to philosophical activity would be to traditional philosophical approaches. The usual philosophical statement is definitely not empirically verifiable, which means that the various traditional approaches were mere conjecture and not important to man. This new approach, however, gave philosophy a distinctly new role—analysis of ordinary language statements into logical, consistent form. In this way it could be told whether a problematical question could be answered either through mathematical reasoning or scientific investigation. The philosopher does not, therefore, give the answers; he analyzes the questions to see what they mean.

Ordinary language philosophy is the third approach to philosophy which involves language analysis, but in a slightly different way. It was started in the 1930's by Ludwig Wittgenstein (? –1952) who had earlier been one of the originators and developers of logical atomism. In the period between the 1930's and 1952 (when Wittgenstein died) he decided that it would not be possible to devise a language so perfect that the world would be accurately reflected. Accordingly, he came to believe that much of the confusion and disagreement over philosophy emanated from misuse of language in various ways. With this approach the task of the philosopher was not to transpose the problems of philosophy into certain language terms; rather, it was to decide what the basic philosophical terms were and then to use them correctly and clearly so that all might understand. Thus, it would seem to become something akin to semantics, the science of meanings. Wittgenstein was more anxious to learn how the term was used than he was to discover how people defined it. With this approach it may be possible for philosophy to solve some problems through clarification of the meaning of certain terms which have been used synonymously (albeit often incorrectly). In this way man might achieve certain knowledge, at least about the world, through the medium of ordinary language philosophy—a very new type of philosophical analysis.

During the past 100 years still another philosophy has emerged as a significant force—*existentialism*. Sören Kierkegaard, prior to 1850, had become concerned about so many influences within society that were taking man's individuality away from him. Since that time many others have felt a similar concern. Originally, existentialism started as a revolt against Hegel's idealism, which was a philosophy stating that ethical and spiritual realities were accessible to man through reason. Kierkegaard decided that religion would be next to useless if man could reason his way back to God. Then along came Nietzsche who wished to discard Christianity since science had shown that the transcendent ideals of the Church were nonsense. Man's task, therefore, was to create his own ideals and values. After all, he was only responsible to himself. Twentieth-century existentialists are striving to further this tradition, and their efforts are meeting with a fair amount of acceptance.

Some of the beliefs which characterize modern existentialism involve a continuation of Cartesian dualism that split the world in two. We live in a human world; the world of science extends into mathematical space. Man is part and parcel of this human world and may be distinguished from any and all other animals. Still further, it is not possible to understand man completely through the efforts of natural scientists. There appear to be several different types of truth, including that possible through scientific investigation. This belief places existentialism in opposition to the belief that science will eventually answer all of man's questions and problems. It becomes a philosophy through which man makes a valiant attempt to look at himself objectively in a world in which God may be dead. Under such a circumstance it is up to man to blend the past, present, and future together so that the world (the human world) assumes meaning and direction. Man must ask himself what it all means! So he *is* a unique historical animal; now what does he do? Can he so direct and guide his own existence that responsible social action will result? Some say he should begin a more intensive search for God; others are turning toward the development of a humanism which gives him a much greater power of self-determination than he has ever had before.

The Present Situation in the Western World—A Brief Summary

What is the answer to the many philosophical questions posed in this chapter? It is safe to say that no one person or group has the answer organized in such form that anywhere nearly universal acceptance would result. As matters stand, pragmatism (including instrumentalism and experimentalism) shows no decline in interest especially insofar as philosophy of science and social philosophy are concerned. Traditionally, philosophy has been a search for truth, goodness and beauty. In the past forty years, however, this approach has been challenged vigorously by the various types of philosophical analysis such as logical atomism, logical positivism, and ordinary language philosophy. For these people, philosophy's role is to clarify meanings in one way or another. Although they have been influenced by these movements, idealism and realism are by no means in a state of general collapse. In fact, they seem to be striving for greater intercommunication while concerning themselves with statements regarding specific problems instead of evolving large, speculative systems. Of course, no society can go through such an experience as World War II without much soul-searching. What is going to happen to the world as we think we know it? Should we all turn to an existentialistic belief which negates the idea of a personal God? Must man rely on himself completely for the future? Catholic neoscholastic philosophy continues to have a broad appeal to a great many of the world's people, because it offers assurance and comfort. Upon what basis of consensus can we proceed?

PART TWO

Naïve Naturalism as
a Pervasive Influence

CHAPTER FOUR

Naïve Naturalism
in Philosophy and Education

As we move forward to a consideration of the three leading philosophical tendencies of the twentieth century and their implications for education, and still more specifically for physical, health, and recreation education, the plan is to treat each philosophy in a fairly identical fashion. This plan will be followed by a discussion of naïve naturalism as well because of its importance as a pervasive influence. First, we will present the metaphysics (questions about reality), epistemology (acquisition of knowledge), logic (exact relating of ideas), and axiology (system of values) in education. Then, we will turn to the implications of the particular philosophical tendency for the recurring problems of education which we have designated as: (1) society, school, and the individual (the relationship among); (2) educational aims and objectives; and (3) the process of education. In the chapter immediately following, the implications for aims, objectives, and methods of physical, health, and recreation education will be indicated. A brief statement as to possible strengths and weaknesses will be given also.

The Philosophy of Naturalism

Naturalism has been called the oldest philosophy in the Western world. It has been said further that it is the most elusive. We should be fully aware also of the fact that naïve naturalism can be described quite accurately, *but it tends to become either more pragmatic or realistic* as it moves from questions about reality (metaphysics) into theory about the acquisition of knowledge (epistemology). *For this reason many feel that its place has been usurped in the modern world of the twentieth century by realism and pragmatism.* And yet it represents an attitude that we cannot escape just as the philosophy of idealism is ever present to influence our thoughts and actions. *For this reason it is still included as a separate section in this text but should be considered mainly as a pervasive influence.*

Questions about Reality (Metaphysics)

Butler tells us that a major philosophy seems to be built on an attitude that most people are willing to accept.[1] Such is the case with naturalism. Here we find the belief that nature is reliable and dependable—"Let Nature take her course," we are told. It is easy to understand why people are often willing to let this happen and do not wish to tamper with that which appears to be developing "naturally." Early naturalists felt that perhaps one "substance" was characteristic of all nature; later Spencer discarded what has been called a *materialistic approach,* because he felt that energy was the basic "substance" out of which the universe was constructed.[2] But concurrently Auguste Comte, known as a *positivist,* took the more critical position that science was the only true way to knowledge. In the twentieth century Schneider took a still more advanced position (quite similar to pragmatism) which viewed nature as a process exhibiting a continuity despite changing of laws and substances.[3] Thus we can see why Butler believes that "refined" naturalism has been supplanted in many ways by realism and pragmatism.

Theory of Knowledge Acquisition (Epistemology)

Here again we find a distinction between naïve naturalism and critical naturalism. Early naturalists believed that objects presented images of themselves in the viewer's mind. In the seventeenth century Thomas Hobbes gave a somewhat better explanation of sensory knowledge. About the same time Francis Bacon recommended substitution of induction for deduction through the observation of the specifics in

---

[1] J. Donald Butler, *Four Philosophies,* rev. ed. (New York: Harper & Row, Publishers, Inc., 1957), pp. 81–82.

[2] Ralph B. Perry, *Present Philosophical Tendencies,* 3rd print. (New York: George Braziller, Inc., 1955), pp. 70–71.

[3] Yervant H. Krikorian, ed., *Naturalism and the Human Spirit* (New York: Columbia University Press, 1944), pp. 121–124.

nature to gain reliable knowledge of the world. Auguste Comte in the 1800's argued for scientific investigation as the best and highest means of acquiring true knowledge. Still later, Herbert Spencer strengthened this approach and belief that we can only learn about our world through scientific investigation.

Exact Relating of Ideas (Logic)

The logic of naturalism is the same logic as we find in science. This means, of course, that naturalism relies on induction much more than deduction, because the emphasis is placed on discovering nature's laws and relationships as they seem to exist at the time of examination. Regarding what appear to be nature's uniformities, however, Nagel states that "no demonstrable ground has yet been found which can guarantee that such regularities will continue indefinitely or that the propositions asserting them are necessary." [4]

It must be explained though that a variety of methods of logic are used by different naturalists. Induction only is (or has been) recommended by naïve naturalists. As we move forward into modern naturalism, we find that those espousing realism give deduction a somewhat greater role to play. Moving over to pragmatism, we find that the opposite is the case; induction is extended to a still more pliable means of problem solving where hypotheses are formulated and tested as progress is made. This obviously lessens the need for an attentuated period of induction. These approaches will naturally be discussed more fully when we treat realism and pragmatism in subsequent chapters.

Thus it boils down to "careful observation of Nature, accurate description of what is observed, and caution in formulating generalizations." [5] The belief is that careful, painstaking amassing of facts will make eventual formulation of generalizations about nature self-evident.

System of Values (Axiology)

The study of a philosophy's value structure is, of course, extremely important and is for many its most meaningful and rewarding aspect. Naturalists have ever been concerned with the many values that life has to offer; in fact, they believe that these many values are inherent in nature itself, which is just that sort of order. The apparent means whereby the individual may achieve peace and happiness in his life is through the gearing of his life to the "natural order" of events.

Ethically, naturalism is hedonistic in that it stands for the achievement

---

[4] *Ibid.,* p. 210.
[5] Butler, *Four Philosophies,* p. 92.

of pleasure. But there is much discussion as to what constitutes pleasure for man. Many naturalists assert that pleasure achieved must be "refined and abiding" in order to be of highest value for them. Conversely, man encounters much that may be termed *evil* in nature. Physical evil is certainly a fact of nature which plagues man in some corner of the earth every day. There isn't much that can be done in this regard save to ameliorate some of the effects when possible. But man does seem to be involved in various types of moral evil which he often inflicts upon his neighbor. This does appear to be more of a social problem than an individual one. His best plan, however, is to make choices throughout his life so that he will achieve, insofar as possible, the highest type of abiding pleasure for himself, his family, and his neighbors.

Aesthetically, the naturalist searches for experiences that are purely natural. Vivas describes the aesthetic feelings of a sentient organism when he says, "The aesthetic experience is an experience of intransitive, rapt attention on any object which may elicit interest." [6] Of course the naturalist sees no supernatural factors at work in the object of his attention. It is merely a matter of experiencing life in its natural forms by an organism with a highly complex nervous system. Man in the course of time has achieved the ability to retain and interrelate meanings that yield him the highest type of aesthetic experience.

Religiously, the naturalist is concerned with those values which arise from the nature of the world in which we live. For him it is life now, not at some indefinite future date, that is significant. If there are values that we are not fully achieving at present, the naturalist wants to bring them into realization at the first possible moment. This is his "religious imperative," which means that for the naturalist religious value is exactly the same as over-all value realization.

Socially, we find that the naturalist devotes much more attention to the individual and his development in relation to the physical universe than to human society. Social goals appear therefore to be secondary values for the naturalist, even though he realizes that men have been forced to band together for common good. But he can't escape from the feeling that society may be inherently evil and exerts a most disturbing influence on the individual. It appears almost to be a choice of accepting the lesser evil of organized society as opposed to the difficulties which chaotic anarchy seems to bring.

Society, School, and the Individual

Although it would be very difficult to locate someone who would call himself a teacher that subscribes completely to a naturalistic philos-

---

[6] Krikorian, *Naturalism and the Human Spirit,* p. 100.

ophy of education, there is no doubt that the philosophy of naturalism exerts a considerable influence on the educational process as we know it in the Western world. Such naturalism is often embodied in the epistemology of the pragmatist or the realist. Furthermore, Brubacher speaks of a number of progressives who subscribe to what might be called *romantic naturalism.*[7] These people seem to take their lead from such educational theorists as Rousseau and Froebel. The task of the educator in their eyes is to learn just what the laws of human nature are. Believing that the instincts of the child will reflect accurately what his needs are, the romantic naturalist is ready and anxious to build the school program around these indicators. It must be confessed also that such theorists tend to be somewhat disturbed about strong governmental influence on education, since they would believe that people would display a natural self-interest in the education of children and youth.

Most naturalists, on the other hand, feel that the school has an important place and a sound basis for existence in society. Almost from the time of conception, certain types of learning are taking place within the individual. No one can deny that learning is a natural process, and it is natural also that adults need to teach children as they gradually mature. Man's exceptionally long period of growth, as contrasted with other animals, makes such careful instruction necessary. Other animals, of course, are guided very strongly by set instinctive patterns. With man, therefore, adults have the opportunity to mold many of his traits and may possibly mold him to great achievements in society. On the basis of this premise, the naturalist believes strongly that education is an absolute necessity.

Educational Aims and Objectives

In order to avoid getting involved in semantics while discussing educational aims and objectives, we will state that "aims" are long range and quite probably not completely attainable. "Objectives," on the other hand, will be considered to be realizable educational goals. One of the finest statements of the naturalistic position in existence was made by Herbert Spencer in one of his four famous essays on education, *What Knowledge Is of Most Worth?* Written at a time when he was arguing for inclusion of science as the most important aspect of the educational curriculum, Spencer used the phrase *complete living* as the general aim of education. This state, he felt, might be achieved by joining moral responsibility with practical self-direction. He recommended the follow-

---

[7] J. S. Brubacher, *Modern Philosophies of Education,* 2nd ed. (New York: McGraw-Hill Book Company, Inc., 1950), pp. 305–307.

ing classification of leading activities, which he felt constituted human life:

(1) Those activities which directly minister to self-preservation; (2) those activities which, by securing the necessaries of life, indirectly minister to self-preservation; (3) those activities which have for their end the rearing and discipline of offspring; (4) those activities which are involved in the maintenance of proper social and political relations; (5) those miscellaneous activities which fill up the leisure part of life, devoted to the gratification of the tastes and feelings.[8]

It is important to note further that Spencer listed these activities in "their true order of subordination"—that is, in their order of importance.

Thus we find a position which views the child as a little animal that has an instinct for self-preservation. It is obvious that he must be a healthy, rugged organism capable of standing up under life's many strains and stresses. As Spencer points out, "knowledge immediately conducive to self-preservation is of primary importance."

Secondly, Spencer argues, man must learn how to earn the means of his livelihood. This, of course, requires a set of knowledges and competencies; society should provide him with the opportunity to acquire them through some system of education over and above that which he secures by his own spontaneous activity and through the educative influence of his parents.

Thirdly, the naturalist is concerned with the welfare of the family and the propagation of the race. Since, according to chronological order, the family preceded the state, youth must learn the duties of parents as an important part of their education. If we educate the young person in the art and science of enlightened parenthood, the state will eventually be greatly improved. Spencer felt very strongly on this point, because he believed that England in the nineteenth century placed far too great an emphasis on what he considered to be secondary, classical training and preparation for girls to conduct themselves adequately in polite society. Because of this belief, he recommended giving educational methodology a fundamental role in any hierarchy of school subjects.

Fourth in the order of importance he stressed the need to understand the pattern of the social structure. Throughout a person's entire life he will be faced with a variety of social and political actions which will mark him as a responsible citizen or as an incompetent. Education must equip the adult for intelligent self-direction in society.

Lastly, Spencer recognizes that the individual has a responsibility to use his leisure wisely. This is important to round out his concept of "complete living." He mentions "the enjoyments of music, poetry, paint-

---

[8] H. Spencer, *Education: Intellectual, Moral, and Physical* (London: C. A. Watts & Co., Ltd., 1949), pp. 10–15. Originally published in 1861.

ing, etc.," which will come to the adult who has studied literature and the fine arts. Professional recreators of the twentieth century will undoubtedly find themselves in complete agreement at this point.

The Process of Education

Such a set of educational aims proposed in the order of their importance needs to be presented to the young citizen in a way that will be most effective. Spencer is not suggesting that we should leave the child alone so that he may follow his own desires and whims without any interference from parents and other teachers. Quite the contrary, the recommendation is that education is a natural function of the elders in a society who are anxious to promote the present and future welfare of their community, state, and nation. It is imperative that parents and teachers be directly involved because of man's prolonged maturation period of almost two decades.

ROLE OF THE TEACHER. Immediately we must understand that each child undergoes a natural period of growth and development. It is the duty of the educator, therefore, to discover just how this development takes place. Failure of the teacher to comprehend this basic tenet cannot help but result in an education that is artificial and deficient.

NEED FOR EDUCATIONAL RESEARCH. Spencer, as we have pointed out, was most anxious to encourage educational research which would result in the best possible educational practice designed to implement most effectively his aims of education. He recommends a number of *principles* of educational methodology, which he feels are "all in logical order."

In the first place, he believes that education must exhibit a progression from the simple to the complex.[9] He encourages the introduction of a few subjects at first with the gradual addition of others until all those deemed necessary are being studied by the student. Thus we find progression from the simple to the more complex battery of subjects, as well as a similar progression with the individual subject itself.

Secondly, we must keep in mind that the intellect is only able to "discriminate rudely" at first. This means that we will encounter difficulties when the teacher attempts to "put precise ideas into the undeveloped mind." The mere learning and memorization of verbal forms does not result necessarily in any clear perception of underlying meanings.

Thirdly, it is important to proceed from the concrete to the abstract in true learning. Don't start out with first principles which imply understandings that the mind has not yet at that point the ability to grasp. Introduce many practical examples as you proceed from the particular to the general in the learning process.

---

[9] *Ibid.,* p. 87.

Fourthly, the history of civilization should serve as a valuable guide as we plan our educational methodology. Spencer believed that the "genesis of knowledge in the individual must follow the same course as the genesis of knowledge in the race." If man as a species obtained his knowledge of the world in a certain way, it stands to reason that a similar order in the acquisition of knowledge may be advisable with each individual within the group.

Fifthly, we need to employ a "purely experimental introduction" with a course of study. Spencer believes that science will eventually develop from a like art "proceeding from the empirical to the rational." An example of this would be to offer language practice prior to the introduction of rules of grammar.

Sixthly, Spencer is most anxious to promote self-instruction on the part of the learner. He implies that we should "tell" the student as little as possible, while encouraging him to investigate for himself and to draw his own conclusions from what he studies firsthand whenever possible. There is far too great a tendency in education to introduce the facts as we see them in a particular order to the student, whether he shows any interest or not.

Lastly, Spencer encourages us to make use of the "spontaneous activity to which children are thus prone." He believes with Fellenberg that idleness is completely foreign to the nature of boys and girls.[10] When we see laziness, he asserts, it is the result of either poor methods of instruction or poor health.

Summary

Initially, from the standpoint of the metaphysics of naturalistic philosophy, naturalists feel that nature is reliable and dependable. From an early belief that nature was composed of one substance, naturalists later accepted the concept that energy was the "substance" out of which the universe was constructed. Now nature is viewed as a process exhibiting continuity. The epistemology of naturalism, starting with the idea that objects presented images of themselves in the mind, advanced to an improved understanding of sensory knowledge. The observation of specifics in nature (induction) was suggested as complementary to the earlier idea of deduction. Still later, scientific investigation was recognized as the only true means of gaining knowledge about the world. The logic of naturalism relies heavily on induction—the "method of science." Generalizations about nature become self-evident when facts are amassed carefully and painstakingly. The axiology of naturalism is based on the many values inherent in Nature itself. Ethically, naturalism is hedonistic

---

[10] *Ibid.*, p. 95.

—the achievement of the highest type of abiding pleasure for all is basic. Experiences that are purely natural bring the naturalist aesthetic pleasure. Religious value is identical with over-all value realization; life now is what is significant. Social goals are secondary values; the relationship of the individual to the physical universe is paramount. A social system is accepted since it is better than anarchy.

The naturalist believes that each child has a natural growth and development. Education must be synchronized with the natural rhythm of this pattern. Thus, education may well serve as a delaying action while maturation (the natural rhythms of development) takes place. The teacher will be aided greatly by the inborn self-activity which is present in each child. The naturalist relies on scientific method and makes every effort to acquire all kinds of information and factual knowledge. Inductive methods of instruction are basic, and the experience should be interesting and pleasurable. Punishment and reward are part of this process, but they should come about naturally as consequences of the action. We should not be unduly harsh when the child makes a mistake. Lastly, it is very important that there be a balance between education for the mind and education for the body.

CHAPTER FIVE

Naïve Naturalism
in Physical, Health,
and Recreation Education

In this chapter we will point out what appear to be the implications for physical, health, and recreation education from the philosophical *tendency* known as naïve naturalism. Some of the aims, objectives, and methods listed will undoubtedly come up again in a somewhat different order of importance when we treat the leading philosophical positions of pragmatism, realism, and idealism. Although we will be stressing the differences in philosophic approach to problems in physical, health, and recreation education, it is important to keep in mind that there is much agreement as well. We should not forget either, in our eagerness to promote that approach to education which we feel will bear the greatest fruits, that it is vitally important that we search unceasingly for increasingly more agreement. We should understand that the aim of educational science is to prove that we should follow common goals and methods. Of course, such agreement has tremendous significance in the achievement of the "one-world concept."

Aims, Objectives, and Methods

In the preceding chapter the general aim of education was given as "complete living." Subsidiary objectives were listed as self-preservation, learning how to earn a livelihood, caring for one's family, understanding the pattern of the social structure, and learning how to use leisure wisely.

These objectives were given presumably in their order of importance. That they hold important implications for physical, health, and recreation education is self-evident.

NEED FOR A MORE RUGGED ANIMAL. The naturalist is primarily concerned that man (and woman) be a rugged animal fit to withstand the excessive wear and tear that life's informal and formal activities may demand. The impact of this objective strikes to the heart of the problem as many of our professionals see the situation today. For many reasons children and young people on the North American continent have "enjoyed" a way of life which has not been conducive to the achievement of the objective—a rugged animal. We were told a few years ago that a great many boys and girls cannot do one pull-up; that only 10 per cent of our elementary-school children receive regular, organized physical-education classes; that only 50 per cent of our high-school youth get such instruction; that draft statistics in World Wars I and II showed high rejection rates; that the average adult female is sixteen pounds overweight and that the average male is twenty pounds overweight; and that many people twenty-seven years of age are old physically. What is the answer?

Strangely enough, as long ago as 1861 Spencer called the public's attention to this serious matter. He believed that a "nation of good animals" was a "first condition" before national prosperity could be achieved and maintained. Even in the "contests of commerce" he saw the need for workers with bodily endurance. As we listen to the following words, who would not agree that his statements make great sense in today's world:

The competition of modern life is so keen, that few can bear the required application without injury. Already thousands break down under the high pressure they are subject to. If this pressure continues to increase, as it seems likely to do, it will try severely even the soundest constitutions. Hence it is becoming of especial importance that the training of children should be so carried on, as not only to fit them mentally for the struggle before them, but also to make them physically fit to bear its excessive wear and tear.[1]

Spencer goes on to state again his major thesis that the findings of science should be applied to education. Rather critically he stated pointedly that our children should be participating in the benefits that "sheep and oxen are deriving from the investigations of the laboratory."

From the standpoint of the naturalist it is only a short step forward to the conclusion that nature wants men and women to have good physiques since the welfare of posterity is of the greatest importance. He (Spencer) points out that a "cultivated intelligence" in a "bad physique" may die

---

[1] H. Spencer, *Education: Intellectual, Moral, and Physical* (London: C. A. Watts & Co., Ltd., 1949), p. 177. Originally published in 1861.

out in a few generations. Conversely, he feels that a good physique is worth saving, because we may be able to improve the mental endowments of his descendants.

DEVELOPMENT OF HEALTH HABITS. The unrefined naturalist is quite properly concerned about man's health habits and the necessary instruction that should be offered to the child to protect him from ailments and diseases caused by infractions of nature's physiologic law. Spencer wrote his treatise on naturalistic education shortly after the time that the first medical course was offered by an American university. He, of course, was concerned about the health habits in his native England and quoted from the *Cyclopaedia of Practical Medicine,* which was the authoritative reference of the period. Speaking about overeating and undereating, he felt that city dwellers had reacted perhaps too violently to some of the past extremes in indulgence. Formerly, a child had been exhorted to eat as much as possible, but then Spencer found that this emphasis had changed, except perhaps in rural districts. He was disturbed about it since he believed that undereating was much worse than overeating. He wondered why we should discourage something so natural as an individual's appetite. In the twentieth century, of course, we encourage children to eat a balanced diet, and we like to see them have a healthy appetite generally speaking. On the other hand, overweight adults are encouraged to abstain while keeping balance in their diets. Innumerable vitamin tablets are consumed in the United States every day.

Spencer points out that "generally, we think, the history of the world shows that the well-fed races have been the energetic and dominant races." [2] He explains further that animals can work harder when they are fed more nutritiously. The point he wishes to make is that a sound diet is necessary for both energy and growth.

IMPORTANCE OF SENSATIONS. Consistent with his naturalistic approach, Spencer disagrees with a then prevalent notion that sensations were to be disregarded. He postulates that this would indeed be a peculiar world if such were the case. It is not eating, drinking, breathing, or even exercising when we feel like it that is bad; it is doing these things when nature indicates there is no need or urge to do so that causes all the difficulties. He answers those who say that the sensations do not seem to have provided adequately for people who have persistently led unhealthy lives in the following way:

People who have for years been almost constantly indoors, who have exercised their brains very much and their bodies scarcely at all, who in eating have obeyed their clocks without consulting their stomachs, may very likely be misled by their vitiated feelings. But their abnormal state is itself the result of trans-

---

[2] *Ibid.,* p. 191.

gressing their feelings. Had they from childhood never disobeyed what we may term the physical conscience, it would not have been seared, but would have remained a faithful monitor.[3]

Clothing, or the lack of it, is another subject that is discussed by Spencer at some length in regard to its relationship to health. He does not believe in an excess of clothing, but he is concerned about scantiness in apparel which results in the wearer being continually cold. Here again it is a question of following the dictates of nature. He points out that people can adjust to extreme cold, but they do it at the expense of their body. Clothing which preserves the body's warmth serves as an equivalent for a particular amount of food.

GIRLS SHOULD BE RUGGED. The naturalist applies the standard of a good animal to girls as well as to boys. He asks the question whether girls' constitutions are so different from those of boys that they don't need vigorous exercise. This question might well be asked today of women physical educators in North America who help to set a pattern of mild exercise for girls and young women. What happens to these young animals when they mature is a sight to behold, and this is the American ideal! Of course, on the other side of the coin the adult male on this continent would not exactly create a sense of awe within the onlooker either.

There can be no doubt, however, that women are most concerned with their appearance. At the present time physical-education courses which cater to posture, figure, and carriage seem to have crowded sections at the college and university level. Television programs and magazine articles appear daily which encourage women to exercise regularly through the medium of a series of calisthenics. As fine as these efforts may be, they represent an artificial approach to a problem that can be met in a much more natural way through games and sports embodying the fundamental skills. Nor do they give adequate emphasis to the need for circulo-respiratory efficiency in every vital animal, human or otherwise. Spencer saw the existence of this problem in London a century ago when he took the citizenry to task for the encouragement of an excessive amount of study as follows:

Hence, the much smaller proportion of them who grow up well-made and healthy. In the pale, angular, flat-chested young ladies [witness the female models in our newspaper and magazine advertisements today], so abundant in London drawing-rooms, we see the effect of merciless application, unrelieved by youthful sports; and this physical degeneracy hinders their welfare far more than their many accomplishments aid it. Mammas anxious to make their daughters attractive, could scarcely choose a course more fatal than this, which sacrifices the body to the mind. Either they disregard the tastes of the opposite sex, or else their conception of those tastes is erroneous. Men care little for erudition

---

[3] *Ibid.,* p. 197.

in women; but very much for physical beauty, good nature, and common sense.
. . . The truth is, that out of the many elements uniting in various proportions
to produce in a man's breast the complex emotion we call love, the strongest
are those produced by physical attractions; the next in order of strength are
those produced by moral attractions; the weakest are those produced by intellectual attractions; and even these are dependent less on acquired knowledge
than on natural faculty—quickness, wit, insight.[4]

Sadly enough, in the past few years, we find a disproportionate emphasis
being placed on intellectual development and so little for the body. In
this manner would the naturalist speak!

ELIMINATE ARTIFICIALITY.   As far as the physical-education program
itself is concerned, the naturalist makes a strong plea for the elimination
of all types of artificial exercises insofar as possible. He wants to see
exercise patterns that develop naturally and spontaneously from play and
sport activities. Spencer points out that it is very difficult to prescribe a
sufficient number of exercises that would be as varied as those the individual would perform naturally while taking part in an active game.
There is a danger also that artificial exercises might tend to produce
bodily development that is disproportionate.

PLAY ELEMENT IS BASIC.   The factor of amusement and a state of
happiness that should accompany the correct kind of exercise looms
large for the naturalist. The belief here is that a natural activity involving varied play a highly invigorating influence. The naturalist feels
that the "riotous glee" accompanying games and sports is as important
as the strenuous exercise involved. He won't go so far as to say that
"gymnastics" don't do any good, but he does feel that they can never
serve in place of the exercises prompted by Nature. It seems reasonable
to assume here that the introduction of a play element and freedom of
choice to all sorts of formalized gymnastics and calisthenics would go
far toward making them more palatable to the naturalist.

BODY IS NEGLECTED.   The naïve naturalist can't help being disturbed
by the imbalance that he sees in operation in our "civilized" society.
He is vitally concerned with the child's growth and development pattern,
and he believes that the years from six to sixteen are being burdened
by an excess of mental application. The pattern in many schools today
seems to be as little as possible for the body and as much as possible
for the mind. We are told that the Western world is engaged in a fierce
struggle for its very existence and that life is a serious business. Our
answer appears to be the encouragement of intensive application to the
"important" subjects in the curriculum. Children are being asked to do
hours of homework after sitting in classrooms for the large part of the
daylight hours. The child who is gifted in motor capacity seems to be

---

[4] *Ibid.*, pp. 226–227.

getting his share of attention, but the average youngster gets either no regular physical-education periods or else one or two inadequate periods a week. The result is a child that is weak physically with poor body mechanics and deficient play skills. Everyone appears to give lip service to the Roman ideal of a "sound mind in a sound body," but very few follow through and do anything about achieving this desirable state. The final result is an adult who is "impoverished physically" and who doesn't appear to have the inclination or energy to do anything about it. We are warned that "Nature is a strict accountant; and if you demand of her in one direction more than she is prepared to lay out, she balances the account by making a deduction elsewhere." [5]

METHODOLOGY IS IMPORTANT. The methodology to be employed by the teacher of physical education or the director of recreation with naturalistic tendencies must be considered briefly, because it is so necessary to the achievement of naturalistic aims and objectives. In the first place, naturalism does not imply a roll-out-the-ball approach. The teacher must be directly involved with the child's education because of the human's long period of maturation. It seems logical also that the teacher or recreation leader should be fully cognizant of the growth-and-development approach that has been stressed so admirably in certain quarters in recent years. Activities should be introduced naturally when the boy or girl is ready for them. This confronts us directly with the need for a decision on the variety of program features that have been spelled out for us in different quarters in the past few decades. How shall health instruction be integrated into the curriculum and at what level? How much stress should be placed on children's rhythms? Are we educating *through* the physical, or should we be more concerned with education *of* the physical? What about movement education at the elementary level? Others are most anxious to get the youngster, both male and female, started on organized sports just as soon as possible. The naturalistic answer to many of these questions should be apparent at this point.

NATURALISTIC ORDER OF INSTRUCTION. A logical order of instruction seems to relate most closely to the naturalistic position. As teachers and leaders, we should move from the simple to the complex in our instructional patterns. We should make every effort to avoid the introduction of artificial movements and activities into the health, physical-education, and recreation curriculum. The counterpart of this is obvious—we should encourage spontaneous activity at every opportunity. This would seem to indicate further that a child's natural curiosity for investigation and experimentation should be exploited for all that it is worth.

The naturalist would tend to give credence also to the recapitulation theory in education. This has clear implications for our profession. If we

---

[5] *Ibid.*, p. 217.

want to help the child to adapt himself to life in the present, then we must allow him as an individual to pass through all the stages of culture that man has experienced along the way. The child starts out as a savage and ends up as a civilized man in modern culture.

WILLIAMS AND THE NATURAL MOVEMENT. Two outstanding physical educators of the twentieth century discussed at some length some of the implications from naturalism for health, physical education, and recreation. Jesse Feiring Williams, formerly of Columbia Teachers College, was strongly identified with what has been called the *natural movement* in physical education. He believed that we could answer many of our problems if we would but turn to the evidence presented by nature. It was for this reason that he helped to lead us away from the various foreign systems of gymnastics that were so popular around the turn of the century. He urged the adoption of a program "based upon natural motor movements which represent the racial motor activities of man." [6] According to Williams:

The fact that man presents in the racial patterns of his nervous system certain underlying predispositions to function in well-defined motor activities characterized in type and quality by his motor experiences over thousands of years, that he is urged on by his very nature to exploit these established organizations, and that, under proper guidance, such expressions may be made to serve high causes and noble ends is of outstanding import. [7]

Williams makes it clear, however, that the dictates of nature are not always necessarily right. Many natural tendencies are such that we would want to control them, and physical education can serve in such a way as to negate them. The important thing is not to include activities or teaching methods which work against natural laws. We should keep in mind further that the profession has been able to improve on nature in certain ways. Witness the improvements that have been made in such activities as swimming, throwing, and pole vaulting, to name just a few. Environment has served to modify many of the outdoor activities we engage in as well. The difficulty comes when children's education is neglected in such a way as to prevent them from following their natural proclivities resulting in a narrow adulthood devoid of the exercise and pleasure which can offer so many benefits to both sexes.

MC CLOY'S INTERPRETATION OF NATURALISM. The late C. H. McCloy of the State University of Iowa was most concerned with naturalism in physical education with perhaps certain differences in emphasis from those of Dr. Williams. To McCloy's way of thinking, it was fundamental that natural activities should be stressed as much as possible. He did

---

[6] J. F. Williams, *The Principles of Physical Education,* 7th ed. (Philadelphia: W. B. Saunders Company, 1959), p. 134.

[7] *Ibid.*

believe though that much of the thinking about naturalism in physical education pointing toward the inclusion of games and sports in the program and the exclusion of gymnastics ought to be reconsidered. As Dr. McCloy said:

It seems to me that the monkey in us would point toward apparatus work as being as natural as basketball, merely needing to be reorganized, purged of its 'exercises,' and properly taught. I am convinced that the dropping of this type of activity is not at all complimentary to our professional intelligence.[8]

Dr. McCloy suggested further that we should examine method even more than content if we wished to promote naturalism. He explained that the Greeks used dumbbells (halteres), but that they employed them for bodily development more than for drill. He felt that it was equally as natural to exercise for the development of a fine body as it was to follow the artificial pursuit of hitting a golf ball, perhaps more so. Thus, he believed that the desire to have a fine body was equally as important for a man as the urge to play and compete in sports.

McCloy held these opinions until the end of his life (at age seventy-three in September, 1959). In one of his last addresses, he related how he had taught in a new government university in Nanking, China in the year 1913–1914.[9] Not knowing which foreign system he should use, he had been encouraged by the president to teach the "best" system. With this encouragement he employed a considerable amount of experimentation with disturbing results. A questionnaire survey given to the students at the end of the first year disclosed that about 90 per cent of them hated it because it "had no meaning." Therefore, he "did a good deal of experimenting by mixing natural types of activity, which were pointed towards the development of skills, and the artificial types, which were pointed directly to exercise and physical development." At this point in his address Dr. McCloy reiterated what he had said twenty years before—that we tend to use the word *natural* very loosely. He asked what was natural about the western roll in high jump or about the complicated routines on the trampoline. Furthermore, he stated that "anything that you do in golf that is natural is wrong."

As far back as 1927, Dr. McCloy encouraged the use of natural teaching materials and methods in order to make possible the greatest use of the individual's nature. He made seven strong points which merit consideration, discussion, and further investigation in our laboratories as follows:

[8] C. H. McCloy, *Philosophical Bases for Physical Education* (New York: Appleton-Century-Crofts, Inc., 1940), p. 97.

[9] C. H. McCloy, "A Half Century of Physical Education," *The Physical Educator,* XVII, No. 3 (October 1960), 83-91.

1. Opportunities should be provided to exercise the desirable instinct mechanisms through which the development of socially useful traits may be motivated and further developed.
2. The "racial activities" should be used where possible to the relative exclusion of the artificial activities. Neuromuscular skills that have innate elements should be stressed in preference to those entirely lacking these elements.
3. The various parts of the body should be used according to their natural functions, so far as possible.
4. The posture of the body should be dynamic, not static. That is, the posture should be the posture of action, not of "attention"; of efficiency, not of rigidity.
5. There should be every attempt to conserve the reciprocal innervation of the antagonistic muscles, and to avoid resistance of antagonists and general rigidity.
6. There should be as small an energy-activity ratio as possible; that is, the skills should be learned so thoroughly that the results attained are as great as possible in relation to the amount of energy expended.
7. There should be much emphasis upon the development of skills at the various speeds for which there will be a demand.[10]

But with these emphases there are also some warnings against certain naturalists of the time as McCloy saw them. For example, he believed that certain natural urges could in all probability be served by activities that are unnatural. He stressed also that dancing and stunts are as natural as games and sports if performed informally.

NATURALISM IN PLAY AND RECREATION. Most of the attention in this chapter has been given to health and physical education with brief reference to the concept of play of a more or less physical nature. But what about the developing profession of recreation and the implications of naturalism for man's recreational pursuits of all types? Here the picture is rather confusing, much depending on whether recreation education is seen as basic or ancillary to the core curriculum. Naturalism would, of course, seem to point the way in the current movement toward outdoor education (or nature study) as a regular part of the curriculum through the medium of such programs as school camping. Such attention at this stage of the educational process would no doubt foster appreciation of nature as a source of healthful recreation throughout maturity.

The naïve naturalist builds his theory of play and recreation from a biological base. Spencer was largely responsible for a detailed surplus-energy theory in regard to play. Man as a higher animal earned a certain amount of leisure depending on his ability to cope with his environment. Consequently he had time and energy unused and certain basic desires and urgings had to be satisfied. Groos explained Spencer's approach most concisely.[11] He carried theory on this subject much further as well.[12]

---

[10] McCloy, *Philosophical Bases for Physical Education*, pp. 35-37.
[11] Karl Groos, *The Play of Animals* (New York: Appleton-Century-Crofts, Inc., 1898), p. 6.
[12] Karl Groos, *The Play of Man* (New York: Appleton-Century-Crofts, Inc., 1901).

Explaining that the use of surplus energy would result only in aimless play, he pointed out that there must be a second phase to such a physiological theory—*re-creation of exhausted powers.* There appeared to be no reason why these two phases couldn't take place simultaneously. Furthermore, Spencer saw this type of play as being imitative of serious activity. This is certainly partially true in a particular time and place, but it cannot be said to be universal. In fairness to Spencer, it must be stated further that he had a relationship in addition with what has been called the *instinct theory.* He believed that self-assertion and imitation could be classified as instincts and that these helped to evoke play in certain forms.

Groos, of course, made a very important addition to the theory of play which has meaning for us at this point, although it does overlap somewhat with other philosophical positions. He is known generally with what has been called the *preparation for life* theory of play. His entire theory, however, was based on a belief that play is primarily the result of instinct and that surplus energy comes into the picture allowing practice of these instincts not yet fully developed. In addition, he stressed that play is pleasurable.

A third contribution to the biological and physiological theories of play, prior to the entrance of the so-called psychological theories, was made by G. Stanley Hall known for his *inheritance* or *recapitulation* theory. For him every play movement can be traced to some hereditary tendency; this meant that the child was reliving in his own experience each cultural epoch of his predecessors.

What then has naïve or unrefined naturalism to offer to the field of recreation today? If play at present is considered to be a phase of the more-inclusive term *recreation,* then we must recognize that the theories expressed above go a considerable way toward explaining man's urge to play. They do *not,* however, present a complete picture; that will come when psychological and sociological aspects are added to the discussion.

To return to the implications of naturalism for recreation in the twentieth century, we find that opportunities abound for all members of the family to return to nature. Brightbill points the way admirably in his chapter *What Comes Naturally* by describing the many facets of this phase of recreation.[13] He explains how the fisherman, hunter, gardener, and camper, etc., realize the many advantages it offers. We like to view the beauty of nature, and many people even in crowded cities make an effort to keep a bit of the earth close at hand in an urn or pot. Brightbill describes further that nature provides an escape for many of civilization's unnatural pressures and tensions. It gives us the chance to

---

[13] Charles K. Brightbill, *Man and Leisure* (Englewood Cliffs, N.J.: Prentice-Hall, Inc., 1961), pp. 135-154.

use all of our senses in a pleasurable way. In our poetry, song, and other forms of art, we praise nature in its many forms—its sights and sounds of all descriptions. When we desire real challenge and adventure, it may be discovered in any one of a number of directions. He concludes by expressing the belief that the earth offers us great security, because it is basically a source and a builder of life. Who will say that families cannot grow and develop best in every way in a *natural* setting?

Summary

AIMS AND OBJECTIVES.   The naïve or unrefined naturalist believes that man, to be a good animal, must be fit to withstand the excessive wear and tear of life. According to this position, nature wants men and women to have good physiques, since the welfare of posterity is of the greatest importance. Necessary instruction should be offered to the child to protect him from ailments and diseases caused by infractions of nature's physiologic law. The standard of a good animal applies to girls as well as to boys. This may be achieved through exercise patterns which are developed naturally. We should eliminate all types of artificial exercises and encourage those natural types of exercise which cause amusement and a state of happiness and glee. Play through games and sports will stimulate interest, and in this way proportionate bodily development will be promoted. Lastly, it is very important to maintain a balance between physical and intellectual education.

METHODS.   The teacher must be *directly* involved with the child's education because of the human's long period of maturation. As this education proceeds, the teacher or recreation leader should be fully cognizant of the growth-and-development approach. Following a logical order of instruction, teachers should move from the simple to the complex in their instructional patterns. Spontaneous activity should be encouraged at every opportunity while avoiding artificiality as much as possible. This may be achieved, according to Williams, by encouraging the child's natural curiosity for investigation and experimentation, basing the program upon natural motor movements which represent the racial motor activities of man, and avoiding activities or teaching methods which work against natural laws. As a profession, physical, health, and recreation education should work to improve on nature whenever possible.

McCloy believed that we should examine method even more than content if we wish to promote naturalism, and that "opportunities should be provided to exercise the desirable instinct mechanisms through which the development of socially useful traits may be motivated and further developed." [14] He stressed further that we should encourage active, dynamic bodily posture, not posture that is rigid and static. In this way the various parts of the body will be used according to their natural functions. In keeping with these ideas, he believed that "there should be every attempt to conserve the reciprocal innervation of the antagonistic muscles, and to avoid resistance of antagonists and general rigidity." [15] If we learn skills thoroughly, the results obtained will be as great as possible and the amount of energy consumed will be minimum. Stress should be placed upon performance of the skills "at the various speeds for which there will be a demand." [16]

Strengths and Weaknesses

When we consider naturalism as an underlying philosophical current or tendency, and from the standpoint of its implications for education, its strength as well as its weakness appears to lie in its simplicity. [17] Our lives are very complex, and this complexity is increasing all the time. Upon first consideration, naturalism strikes us like a fresh breeze that will help us to unravel some of the interwoven strands of modern life. Life is largely external, and the complexities of introverted experience are definitely secondary. Furthermore, society has presented us with many artificialities and disturbances that a return to nature can help us avoid in the future.

Unfortunately, naturalism's opponents argue that its simplicity represents a shallowness of approach that will simply not suffice. Its metaphysics is such that it does not meet the test today in the face of scientific analysis. Secondly, it is pointed out that nature is not all sweetness and light as its earlier proponents seemed to believe. There is much that is frightening and dangerous to man's existence in the universe that must be somehow harnessed for man's benefit.

When considering its application to education, some of naturalism's basic inferences appear to make very good sense, but it does not go far enough. Consider, for example, the statement of Williams relating to "improvement on nature" in connection with swimming, throwing, high jumping, and polevaulting. [18] McCloy, also, was quite worried about the profession's interpretation of the implications of naturalism (e.g., the belief that only games and sports were true natural activities).

Writing about the future of physical, health, and recreation education,

---

[14] McCloy, *Philosophical Bases for Physical Education*, p. 36.

[15] *Ibid.*, p. 37

[16] *Ibid.*

[17] J. Donald Butler, *Four Philosophies*, rev. ed. (New York: Harper & Row, Publishers, Inc., 1957), pp. 121-127.

[18] Cf., p. 60.

McCloy warned that we must think "in terms of the environment of today" despite all the good that can come from focusing on "man's original nature and his instinctive likes and dislikes." [19] He referred us to Charles A. Eastman's book *Indian Childhood,* in which was described a truly natural form of physical education. The only difficulty is that it requires about twelve hours a day, and we don't have that much time to devote to the program. If we are lucky, we find children being allotted two 40-minute periods a week often with very inadequate facilities. McCloy wondered whether we have an obligation to "adapt our natural programs more and more to our unnatural environment, and even to motivate some unnatural activities—as the Scandinavians have so well done—in order that a larger number of people may benefit when the best types of activities are not available or convenient." [20] This is a recurrent theme with McCloy, whose naturalism appeared to veer into realism rather than pragmatism. He often urged re-examination of the naturalistic position, either because it has been interpreted incorrectly, or because it is impractical for one of several reasons.

[19] McCloy, *Philosophical Bases for Physical Education,* pp. 297-298.
[20] *Ibid.*

PART THREE

Experimentalism

CHAPTER SIX

Experimentalism in
Philosophy and Education

This chapter covers the second of the three leading philosophical tendencies of the twentieth century and its implications for education. We have chosen the name *experimentalism* rather than pragmatism or pragmatic naturalism, because it seems to be more useful philosophically in the light of present conditions. Geiger offers some substantiation for this decision, as he prefers the use of this terminology over and above the name *instrumentalism* (which enjoyed brief popularity) as well.[1] The term *progressivism* is not used, as there are progressivists who are not experimentalists.

Generally speaking, experimentalism proceeds on the assumption that it is only possible to find out if something is worthwhile through experience. This approach is not new in the history of mankind, but twentieth-century experimentalism has organized this type of thinking into a philosophical tendency that has been accepted in many quarters, especially in educational and scientific circles.

There are some who believe that epistemology (theory about the acquisition of knowledge) looms so large in the consideration of experimentalism that this aspect of the philosophy must be discussed first. This may be true from one standpoint, but we decided to remain

---

[1] George R. Geiger, "An Experimentalistic Approach to Education," *Modern Philosophies and Education, Fifty-fourth Yearbook* of the N.S.S.E. (Chicago: University of Chicago Press, 1955), Part I.

with the pattern decided upon initially throughout the discussion of the three leading philosophical positions.

The metaphysics, epistemology, logic, and axiology of each philosophical tendency will be presented first in the order mentioned. In the latter part of the chapter, the recurring educational problems will be presented in the "light" that they would be seen from the "reflection" of experimentalism.

Metaphysics

THE LIMITING OF THE FRAME OF REALITY TO THE SYSTEM OF NATURE. It has often been said that this philosophy has no interest in a general world view and that method is its only concern. This statement may be partially true; yet, the assertion that the experimentalist has no interest in a general world view cannot be accepted. It is doubtful whether any rational being ever goes through life without many times asking questions as to the basic "whys and wherefores" of the universe in which he lives.

The experimentalist has arrived at the stage where he realizes that it is beyond man's power to do anything about the course of the physical universe. He believes further that man is only deluding himself when he attempts to speculate about the infinite. His problem, therefore, is to interpret what he finds. He looks at nature and, quite naturally, he asks questions about it. How is it to be interpreted? Is nature an inexorable process which is advancing according to a universal plan? Is the onward surge of nature a kind of emergent evolution? To the question of interpretation of nature, the experimentalist says that he will take what he finds and function from there. To the question as to whether nature is an inexorable process working out according to a universal plan, he maintains that he doesn't actually know. At times he probably hopes so, because this would certainly afford a sense of security; but, for the greater part of the time he hopes not—individual freedom is much too important a matter for him. The experimentalist believes that scientific fact has proved that nature is an emergent evolution; yet, this raises a further question in his mind immediately—emerging toward what?

This philosophy limits man's frame of reality to nature as it functions. If he does make any assumptions about the nature of reality, they are only hypotheses to be held tentatively. The future is always to be considered, because situations are continually changing. The belief is that the ongoing process cannot be dealt with finally at any one time. Activity must be related to past experience as well.

WORLD IS CHARACTERIZED BY ACTIVITY AND CHANGE. Even these preceding statements cannot be considered entirely free from inferences regarding the nature of reality. It is argued that the world is characterized by activity and change. All that is known concerning the human response to nature can be known without first definitely making a final statement about the universe as a whole. Thus, experience or interaction with the environment is all that the experimentalist has by which to live his life. If his environment doesn't give him an accurate account of reality, then it would seem that humans are the victims of a fantastic hoax.

WORLD IS YET INCOMPLETE. The experimentalist believes further in organic evolution and that rational man has developed in this process. The logical conclusion to draw from this assumption is that the world is yet incomplete. This doesn't mean, of course, that everything is in a state of change. Some elements and structures appear to be relatively stable. But this quality of stability is very often deceiving; the experimentalist, consequently, looks upon the world as a mixture of things relatively stable and yet incomplete. This makes all life a great experiment. It is the task of education to make this experiment an intelligent one.

THE THEORY OF EMERGENT NOVELTY. The experimentalist believes that reality is constantly undergoing change. For example, he denies that fundamentals in education remain the same. He will not accept the idea that there is an end to progress. Progressive education is a process of continuous growth. Brubacher offers an example of novelty which strikes a strong blow against the theorists who maintain that any emergence is merely the uncovering of some antecedent reality.

This is true about the individuality of any particular boy or girl. It is inescapably unique since any given offspring of bisexual reproduction is the only one of its kind. Such a child commences and lives his life at a juncture of space and time which simply cannot be duplicated for anyone else.[2]

He theorizes further that if this is novelty, then the future must, of necessity, be uncertain in outcome. Thus, the physical and social environment of the experimentalist is characterized by the constant possibility of novelty, precariousness, and unpredictability, since life and education are the interaction of man and his environment.

THE IDEA OF FREEDOM OF WILL. Many of the philosophies allow for freedom of will, and this is definitely one of the strong points of the experimentalistic outlook. Man's future must allow for freedom of will. He does not conceive of free will as a motiveless choice, and his belief certainly does not coincide with the essentialist who allows for enough freedom so that the world can unfold properly. The experimentalist's

---

[2] John S. Brubacher, *Modern Philosophies of Education* (New York: McGraw-Hill Book Company, Inc., 1939), p. 35. There are 1950 and 1962 revised editions of this work.

contention is that all beings are in process of interaction with other "existences." He inquires about the quality of this interaction and how great a role the individual can play in this process. He would urge man to determine the character of this process from within. As the experimentalist understands life, the individual truly learns only through experience. Thus he is most anxious to control the educative process for each individual so that this inclination to learn from activity and experience will be gradually and as fully developed as possible. Freedom developed in this manner is achieved through continuous and developmental learning from experience.

Childs summarizes the problem of freedom and education in one of his early works as follows:

> In a changing world the only person who can become free and who can maintain his freedom is the one who has 'learned to learn.' A democratic society can hope to succeed only if it is composed of individuals who have developed the responsibility for intelligent self-direction in cooperation with others. From these two basic considerations the experimentalist draws the conclusion that the most fundamental objective of education is to arrange its procedures so that all of them contribute to the realization of these purposes. He believes that it is a sound psychological principle which states that we learn what we practice. He urges, therefore, that schools be placed on the experience basis in order that children may practice learning from experience, and in so doing acquire those habits and attitudes, together with the mastery of those techniques, which lead to increasing ability to control their own experience—which is freedom.[3]

Epistemology

THE RELATIONSHIP BETWEEN TRUTH AND KNOWLEDGE. An adequate definition of knowledge has tried the insight and ingenuity of learned men for many centuries right down to the present day. If knowledge is fact, and fact is truth, then truth is knowledge. Knowledge has been described as *a knowing-about-something, an awareness, a comprehension, or an understanding.* Here it becomes a subjective matter, and it has to do with the inner workings of the mind. Still others believe in a type of knowledge called *objective*—knowledge existing in a world outside the individual. Such knowledge is there to be known by the intellect. Up to this point knowledge may be defined as something which is known or which can be known. The problems of knowledge have troubled many. What does it consist of? How does the individual truly know what he believes he knows? Can human knowledge comprehend all? Is it possible for men to have knowledge about the infinite? These queries could be legion.

SOME HISTORICAL BACKGROUND. After men had speculated for hundreds

---

[3] J. L. Childs, *Education and the Philosophy of Experimentalism* (New York: Appleton-Century-Crofts, Inc., 1931), p. 168.

of years, there gradually arose a body of evidence that has since been called the science of psychology. This is a separate branch of study which examines the processes of the mind, and the varied states of knowing in the individual mind. Locke said that all knowledge must come through experience—that is, it must be obtained by means of the senses. Kant maintained that there was also knowledge which has not been experienced; in fact, his theory of *der Ding an sich* asserted that there is a realm of reality which cannot be known by man. Still later, Hegel set this aside for himself and argued that the real is in the mind—a manifestation of intelligence.

A NEW THEORY OF KNOWLEDGE. Modern scientific development, after Darwin's evolutionary theory, opened the way for a new theory of knowledge—the pragmatic or experimentalistic idea of knowledge and truth. It seemed to make sense in a world where scientific method was influencing almost all thought and was marching on with great rapidity. William James took the lead in expounding this theory in which knowledge is the result of a process of thought with a useful purpose. Truth is not only to be tested by its correspondence with reality, but also by its practical results. This pragmatic treatment of knowledge lies between the extremes of reason and sense perception with some ideas that are not included in either rationalism or empiricism. Truth, therefore, not only is true, but it becomes true. Knowledge is not present because it has been acquired through the years; it is there because it has been earned through experience. It must work! It is an instrument of verification. This type of knowledge, which is literally *wrought in action,* should help in the battle for survival.

THE FUNCTION OF MIND. Brubacher explains how the pragmatist naturalizes mind as follows:

The pragmatist is inclined to make mind a part of the order of nature, to naturalize it. He views intelligence as a relatively late-comer on the world scene. He adopts the evolutionary viewpoint that mind has evolved in the natural order as a more flexible means of adapting the organism to a changing environment. It is definitely an instrument of survival. This fits very neatly with the theory that reality is a mixture of the stable and the precarious. The educational procedure it mandates is necessarily experimental.[4]

For the experimentalist, therefore, the function of mind is to give man a more flexible means of adapting himself to his world. If the mind were not functioning, man would lose his control of the earth. This mind helps to form knowledge or truth by undergoing experience. It must be adaptable because of the possibility of novelty and the consequent precariousness of man's relationship with the world.

THE RELATION OF BODY AND MIND TO THE LEARNING PROCESS. The ex-

---

[4] Brubacher, *Modern Philosophies of Education,* p. 60.

perimentalistic position, in connection with this problem, is more or less of an intermediate one. It does not coincide with the behaviorist, who believes that the mind and the central nervous system are identical and that the mind is therefore only another bodily organ. Conversely, he (the experimentalist) rejects the postulate that the mind is immaterial and entirely extraneous from the body. The experience of the mind must be taken into consideration in order to satisfy him. That the mind and body interact, he does not deny. It is precisely this interaction that concerns him. Mind, through evolution, has become that part of the whole of man which enables him to cope with the surrounding world. Through experience, man's many problems have been, are, and will be solved. An intelligent mind makes this possible.

DEWEY'S EXPERIMENTAL METHOD. This theory of knowledge leads to Dewey's experimental method for the solving of problems, which is characterized by the following steps:

1. Life is characterized by movement, the smoothness of whose flow may be interrupted by an obstacle.

2. This obstacle creates a problem; the resultant tension must be resolved to allow further movement to take place.

3. Man marshals all available and pertinent facts to help with the solution of the problem.

4. The data gathered falls into one or more patterns; subsequent analysis offers a working hypothesis.

5. This hypothesis must be tested to see if the problem may be solved through the application of the particular hypothesis. When the problem is solved, movement may begin again. A hypothesis which turns out to be true offers a frame of reference for organizing facts; subsequently, this results in a central meaning that may be called *knowledge*. The experimentalistic theory of knowledge acquisition (epistemology) merges with its value theory at this point, inasmuch as such knowledge frees man to initiate subsequent action furthering the process of movement and change.

Logic

There seems to be rather general agreement that logic is primarily concerned with the methods of reasoning that man employs in his search to find answers for the problems that confront him. From this rather general definition one could make a good case for the argument that logic is the most fundamental branch of philosophy. Thinking and reasoning are necessary for study of all aspects of the subject. Consequently the importance of correct thinking is self-evident.

A RADICAL DEPARTURE FROM TRADITIONAL LOGIC. As the reader might suspect, experimentalism (pragmatism) is a philosophy that represents a radical departure from traditional logic. Dewey, as the recognized leader of this philosophical approach, decried the inadequacy of Aristotelian logic since he felt it to be completely out of place in the twentieth century.[5] He reasoned that a system of logic which regarded nature as a fixed system simply could not meet the challenge of a universe which seemed to be boundless and perhaps expanding. What Dewey desired was a revised system of logic—"a unified theory of inquiry through which the authentic pattern of experimental and operational inquiry in science shall become available for regulation of the habitual methods by which inquiries in the field of common sense are carried on." [6]

THE PATTERN OF LOGIC. The pattern of logic bears a strong relationship to the learning theory described under the epistemology of experimentalism. Dewey speaks first of *the indeterminate situation* which raises doubt in an individual's mind. The second stage is called *institution of a problem* and takes place when a person realizes the indeterminacy of the situation and the need for clarification of the issue or problem. Next in order is *the determination of a problem-solution,* which is pretty much the same as the establishment of a hypothesis in a scientific experiment. At this point we find the introduction of ideas which may be instrumental in determining the solution to the problem-situation. The fourth stage as outlined by Dewey is called *reasoning.* Possible solutions may come to mind as answers, but they never seem to fit the problem-situation in exactly the same way as they may have done previously. Hence an adaptation with possible subsequent modification takes place that must be reasoned through with extreme care. It is important to understand that Dewey treats facts as functional inasmuch as they contribute to the movement toward solution of the problem. This is referred to as *the operational character of facts-meanings.* It is more difficult for us to comprehend how meanings can be considered operational as well. But he explains that meanings are closely related to operation because they are in a sense inseparable from it as they give direction to any further observation as the problem-solution movement takes place.

This pattern of logic is so fascinating, because it appears to bridge the gap between traditional logic and twentieth-century scientific inquiry. Butler, for example, emphasizes how now the pattern of logic available to science can be employed by the average man in his daily, common-sense problem-situations.[7] It creates a two-way street, because scientific inquiry now has a common-sense base.

Butler points up further four *characterizations of the pattern* which

---

[5] J. Dewey, *Logic, The Theory of Inquiry* (New York: Holt, Rinehart and Winston, Inc., 1938).

[6] *Ibid.,* p. 98.

[7] J. D. Butler, *Four Philosophies,* rev. ed. (New York: Harper & Row, Publishers, Inc., 1957), p. 464.

make it such an innovation. First, patterns of thought peculiar to induction and deduction cannot be applied to a problem-situation arbitrarily, since each situation is unique. Secondly, there is a very close relationship between this pattern of logic and life on earth as we know it—in other words, "man and Nature are continuous." Thirdly, such a pattern of logic seems to fit man's sociological development as well as his biological progress. Lastly, it is very interesting to note that such an approach to logic has application for individual as well as group and societal problems.[8]

Axiology

The system of values of the philosophy of experimentalism is, of course, consistent with the other aspects of this philosophical tendency. *A value is that fact which, when applied to life, becomes useful.* An experience is adjudged as valuable by the human organism which is attempting to adapt itself to the environment in the best and most profitable manner. The comparison of values in order to determine the best ones is a problem of deciding which value or values will help achieve life's purposes in the best way. But it is important to understand that these goals may be only temporary ones.

What are the main values? For the experimentalist, that depends on when, where, and how the individual is living. Innumerable attempts have been made to set up various standards and value systems for people living in modern, complex society. The experimentalist believes that "values must be closely related to the world in which man finds himself." [9] Man must choose which means and ends he will accept and which he will reject. His progress depends upon critical examination of values prior to intelligent selection.

Ethically, the experimentalist finds himself facing continually new situations in which he must exercise wise judgment in keeping with the apparent elements of the indeterminate situation. It is argued that experimentalism offers the possibility of avoiding what has been most troublesome in ethical behavior up to this time—how to resolve a situation where one's motives are good, but his action violates currently acceptable standards. When the experimentalistic steps of logic are employed, progressing from the indeterminate situation through the institution of a problem, the determination of a problem-solution, to reasoning, and to the operational character of facts-meaning for further observation of the proposed course of action, it is possible to blend inner motives

---

[8] *Ibid.,* pp. 264-266.
[9] Geiger, *Fifty-fourth Yearbook,* Part I, p. 142.

and outer behavior in planned, purposeful action to meet each new situation in a fresh, unbiased manner.

Aesthetically, we are concerned with experiences which convey beauty and meaning of an enduring nature to man. For the experimentalist, aesthetic appreciation is closely related to the nature of the experience. In life we fluctuate between tension and pleasure depending on whether indeterminate situations are resolved to our satisfaction. When we find the answers to our problems, tensions are eased and enjoyment results. It is noted, however, that there is no permanent state of aesthetic pleasure for man, since life's rhythm of experience does not function in such a way as to make this possible. Thus, aesthetic satisfaction comes when close identification is maintained with the ebb and flow of life's indeterminate situations. We are all anxious to preserve a state of enjoyment and release, but if it is held too long and disturbs life's rhythm, troublesome difficulties arise. The psychological problems arising from life in a dream world are only too well known. Fortunately, various types of artists help us freeze many of these aesthetic values for subsequent enjoyment. The man who would achieve the greatest amount of aesthetic enjoyment for himself must possess and develop continually those habits which promote keen insight. In conclusion, it must be mentioned that Dewey assigns a lesser role to values which are the opposite of beauty. For example, tragedy and horror may be preserved as art forms. As we look back at these past experiences of our own, or of others, we can feel this experience in some perspective and accept it as a form of beauty with calm mien.

Religiously, the experimentalist assumes a completely naturalistic approach. For him religion would have to be defined in a considerably less orthodox fashion.[10] Any worship of the supernatural is obviously not present. The religious experimentalist would be a person who is most anxious to reach pragmatic values whenever and wherever possible by living purposefully. Man's task is to thrust himself into life's many experiences; only there will he find the opportunity to give his life true meaning.

Socially, we find that the experimentalist places great emphasis on this aspect of life. Social values are fundamental, since life (or society) is "an organic process upon which individuals depend and by which they live."[11] Any individual who would withdraw from relationships with his fellow man in order to devote himself to the realization of other values in his life would appear to be making a rather drastic error. Recluses injure society by withdrawing from their responsibility to it, and it is quite possible that they do themselves still greater harm. Such

---

[10] Cf., p. 48.
[11] Butler, *Four Philosophies,* p. 475.

social values as loyalty, cooperation, kindness, and generosity can hardly be achieved in a vacuum. The experimentalist sees the highest possible relationship between the individual and the society existing in a democracy. Pragmatic values are most in evidence when the individual has the opportunity to develop to the highest of his potentialities, so long as the development does not interfere with the good of the whole. It is impossible to develop many social values in other types of society, but it seems logical to state that the experimentalist finds a much better balance in a democracy.

Society, School, and the Individual

There is no doubt but that experimentalism has exercised a significant influence on education in the United States as well as in certain other countries. A careful examination would indicate, however, that it has not had as much influence as many of its opponents would have us think it has. As the experimentalist sees it, *education is very definitely a social institution;* as a social phenomenon it is one of the basic means by which society progresses and regenerates itself. Furthermore, under this philosophy it is a moral affair—a value enterprise. To carry out best its true role there is no escaping the fact that the school of necessity must maintain a close connection with society.

THE INDIVIDUAL IN THE DEMOCRATIC SOCIETY. It is essential to consider the relative importance, educationally speaking, of the individual and the society. We must resolve the question of whether the student and his development are *the* end of education. Or shall the interests of the individual be subordinated to those of the state? Experimentalism and democracy as we know it do seem to go hand in hand. As far back as 1934 Burton offered the fundamentals of this democratic philosophy as follows:

Thus we see that democracy is not equalitarianism, nor majority rule, nor blind conformity, nor ruthless individualism, nor paternalistic guarantee of individual happiness. What, then, is it? It means not only government of, for, and by the people, but also industry, art, science, opportunities for enjoyment, all the activities of the common life to be of, for, and by the common people. Democracy is participatory group life, enjoyed by free individuals possessing maximum opportunities for participation. Its chief characteristic in regard to individuals is, in current happy phrase, 'respect for personality.' In regard to the group its chief characteristic is the flexible and evolutionary nature of group institutions. Free participation in cooperative group life under evolutionary institutions and with respect between individuals are the earmarks of democracy. Democracy is a system of attitudes, social insights, values, and personal disciplines by means of which all men seek and enjoy the good life.[12]

---

[12] W. H. Burton, *Introduction to Education* (New York: Appleton-Century-Crofts, Inc., 1934), pp. 179-180.

Thus, in a democracy there is ample room for individual freedom and development. On the other hand, sharing is the other great principle of the democratic philosophy of life. As long as one of these values does not interfere materially with the development of the other, this way of life is possible. It is somewhat difficult to "reconcile these two ideas to each other." On occasion, however, one of them simply *must* not outdistance the other. The experimentalist believes that, despite certain failings, experience has shown that this type of society offers the best solution yet discovered for this earth.

In any society the influence of the economic and political systems on education is very great indeed. If the people of a society have to work from sunup to sundown to maintain a meager existence, naturally they will not have much of any formal education. Likewise, if a society is run by a group of people who have come into power by force or deception, it is quite possible that the underlings will have little or no opporunity for formalized education. The experimentalist is therefore vitally concerned about a societal medium where the democratic philosophy of life prevails.

THE DUAL ROLE OF FORMALIZED EDUCATION.   For the experimentalist, formalized education serves a dual role. The social heritage must be preserved and handed down from generation to generation. Its second role is equally as important as the first; it must siphon out the more important qualities of this "intellectual sea" while directing and guiding the student in the formation of new ideas regarding his world. This creative function must in time cause major changes in the structure of the society itself. Each faction, the conservative and the progressive, tend to have a restraining influence on the other. This influence is beneficial in the long run, as it seems to hold radical, possibly harmful, influences in check. If they are allowed to present all sides of an issue at hand and to help the students form independent personal conclusions, teachers have the opportunity to become some of the most important leaders in a society.

WHICH AGENCY SHALL EDUCATE?   Discussion often arises as to which agency shall educate the individual—the home, the church, the state, or some private agency. In resolving this question the most important problem is to determine whether any agency is capable of performing the whole task alone. In a democracy each agency has a specific function to perform in completing the entire task. In Nazi Germany the state attempted to handle the majority of the responsibility and failed. In the United States the Catholic Church combines with the home to perform this all-important function and has succeeded to a great degree. The experimentalist would certainly not agree with much of Catholic methodology and curriculum content. He would tend to place the major responsibility on the home and the school, whether this school was sponsored by the local community and the state or by some private institution. Many under the progressive banner may well believe that the church has a definite task to fulfill in educating the spiritual nature of man, but the experimentalist can visualize that this function be successfully performed by the ideal school. In the United States today, however, parents must decide for their own children about the possibility of the inculcation of religious values.

Educational Aims and Objectives

It has been stated often by various experimentalists that the general aim of education is more education. Geiger tells us that "education in the broadest sense can be nothing less than the changes made in human beings by their experience." [13] With such a fluid approach we find that ends become means in a continuing process as students receive experience in coping with an ever-changing environment.

To make the educative process meaningful *the necessity of an aim* is self-evident. The aims that are chosen, at first undoubtedly by a minority, will give the individual some standards by which to set his course. When realized, there should be no painful transition, since life experiences are part and parcel of the ideal experimentalistic curriculum. Future aims will arise out of experience and therefore take their place naturally in man's future outlook.

THE ROLE OF STUDENTS.   The relationship of students to the formation of aims and objectives is so important to this approach that it must be mentioned at this point as well as under educational process. Dewey made it clear that such participation was absolutely essential in order to generate all-important desired interest.[14]

THE AIM OF SOCIAL EFFICIENCY.   It must be mentioned that the social aim of education is extremely important for the experimentalist; in fact, for Dewey social efficiency was the general aim of education. Brubacher points out that for the experimentalist "membership in society is recognized as the surest access to the social treasures necessary for the development of the pupil's personality." [15]

INSTRUMENTAL VALUES.   The experimentalist's ethical values cannot actually be separated from his educational aims. Generally, therefore, we can say that for the experimentalist values are instrumental—"subject to individual purpose and circumstance." Thus, there are *no fixed*

---

[13] Geiger, *Modern Philosophies and Education*, p. 144.

[14] J. Dewey, *Experience and Education* (New York: The Macmillan Company, 1938), p. 90

[15] Brubacher, *Modern Philosophies of Education*, p. 298.

values; they arise from experience. Pupil growth, as interpreted by the experimentalist, is all important.

Specifically, under the above-mentioned conditions, the experimentalist could subscribe to the seven cardinal principles of education as published in 1918 by the U. S. Bureau of Education: (1) health; (2) command of the fundamental process; (3) worthy home membership; (4) vocational efficiency; (5) civic participation; (6) worthy use of leisure; and (7) ethical character.[16] Brubacher suggests that religious education might have been added to this list in order to make eight principles.[17] The specific objectives necessary to achieve each of the above-mentioned aims would be almost endless in number. It should be understood further that the experimentalist would emphasize that such aims and objectives would have to arise from the practical experiences of the students, parents, and teachers.[18] Such cardinal principles viewed in this light might serve as guidelines that help perhaps to keep a balance among what appear to be the more important ethical values of the experimentalist.

Process of Education

In the educational process recommended by the experimentalist, we find that *the individual,* not the subject matter, is placed at the center of the educational experience. This represents a radical revolt against all educational formalism. Here the idea of *growth* is a central one with experience playing a primary role. With this approach the teacher acts more like a guide and a counselor. Its methodology includes the use of creative projects with study units modeled after cycles of human experience. In this way thinking becomes actual problem solving in a life experience.

The *unity of the human organism* is accepted today by modern psychologists. No longer are the mind and body viewed as separate entities; the mind is now often considered a function of the organism. In the effort to escape the mind-body dichotomy, however, care should be taken not to go to the opposite extreme.

The experimentalist tries to discover any basic facts of the learning process. He wants to know its physiological basis and the laws of its operation, insofar as this is possible. No completely adequate theory is tenable at present from the realm of natural science. Experimentalism will accept no truth that is not "earned" through experience.

---

[16] U.S. Bureau of Education Bulletin 35 (Washington, D.C.: Government Printing Office, 1918).

[17] Brubacher, *Modern Philosophies of Education,* pp. 110-111.

[18] *Ibid.*

HOW LEARNING TAKES PLACE. The experimentalist asserts that learning takes place when interest and effort unite to produce the desired result. When the element of interest is present, learning follows. Effort alone will produce learning of a sort, but the process seems much slower. Interest is purposeful and does not abate until the immediate learning situation has passed by. Interest and effort combine in the initial learning; interest of a more remote kind, such as the interests of life aims, will usually bring effort into play when the primary tension of the first interest is slackened. Often this sort of interest tension occurs and reoccurs when a certain amount of initial learning causes both immediate and future aims to develop continually as experience progresses.

THE DIFFICULTY OF OBJECTIVE EVALUATION. One of the most difficult problems facing modern education is determining if learning has taken place. An elaborate system of tests and measurements has been devised in an effort to solve this problem; yet, the objectivity of these tests is always open to question. As we can understand, the experimentalist has unusual difficulty in evaluating, because his aims and objectives are likely to change as experience seems to indicate new answers. This fact leads the conservative to insist that the experimentalist has only a house built upon sand. The latter counterattacks with the statement that life takes place in exactly this manner; for him, education is life, and the individual learns only what he experiences. Thus, it would seem that objective evaluation is only within the realm of possibility if the judge is able to determine a person's adjustment to his environment accurately.

LOGICAL ORDER AND PSYCHOLOGICAL ORDER. The temporal order of the experimentalistic curriculum may follow both a logical arrangement (from the simple fact to the complex conclusion) and a psychological order (problem solving as explained through scientific method). The problem-solving method fits in much better with progressive education, however, since it attempts to answer the first question arising out of the reciprocal meeting of the organism and the environment.

The structural order demands the problem-solving method as well, since the individual is taught how to think and how to adjust himself to life. Reflective thinking arises from the interaction of man with his environment; the resultant knowledge of what works and what fails aids him to act successfully. There is always a social context to learning, and the curriculum must be adapted to the particular society for which it is intended.

ACTIVITY IS NECESSARY FOR LEARNING. The experimentalist believes that true learning takes place only when activity is involved. The emphasis should be upon directing the seemingly boundless energy of the child. Improvement is sought by building the curriculum around this basic assumption of biological activity. Effective adaptations are made daily to the many environmental problems. The experimentalist tries to discover the method and conditions which favor these adaptations. The learning process is very complex. Human beings tend to try to fulfill certain basic wants in order to achieve satisfactions. The learner often chooses experiences which tend to result in these satisfactions; however, learning may not always accrue from this satisfied condition. If a learner has a certain amount of success with a particular method or technique, he may not be willing to try anything new.

MIND IS A FUNCTION. Since mind is viewed by the experimentalist as a function rather than as a structure, teaching becomes a conditioning process partially; yet, there is more to the total process. The student of experimentalism must necessarily agree at this point that the mind reaches out to make its own knowledge from experience. The actual learning process is enigmatic. The ability of mind to react to a complicated stimulus and to make it part of the learner's own knowledge is amazing. It seems certain that this involves more than just mere imitation, or more than just a conditioned reflex. Concept formation seems to take place through some unique power of the mind when a synthesis of the new and old takes place. Each school of thought in psychology arrives at this idea of concept formation in a different manner. Mind, a relative newcomer to the world scene, helps the experimentalist adapt himself to his world.

ANSWERS COME ONLY AFTER PARTICIPATION. Experimentalism realizes that the doctrine of the conditioned response has assumed an important place in the field of education, but the experimentalist isn't too happy about it. Most educators seem to feel that it is their role to give the answers concerning life's problems to their students. They may do this not so much to force their own particular beliefs on the student, but to save the developing person from the hard knocks and the pitfalls which almost inevitably he must face. The experimentalist would be quick to point out that such teachers are forgetting that understanding and true learning result from actual participation in the process of problem solving.

LEARNING IS MORE THAN A CONDITIONED RESPONSE. The experimentalist is wary about accepting the stimulus-response description of human behavior and learning, because he realizes that possible acceptance of this might make it seem that man has no creative capacity. In his earlier statement of the educational implications of experimentalism, Childs analyzed this possible danger as follows:

In sum, educational conceptions associated with "connectionism" have given intellectual support to an educational practice which has tended to make much of drill and the development of motor skills, but which has not been so well calculated to arouse interest in the creative possibilities of the individual, nor to focus attention upon the importance of the development of procedures which would call out these creative capacities.[19]

LEARNING BY DOING.   The activity theory of learning is an important contribution of experimentalism. This theory emphasizes that true learning is an active and not a passive matter. This is where the slogan *learning by doing* started. We find in this approach recognition of man's biological nature. The child learns when he gets firsthand, active experience in that which he wishes to accomplish. By experimenting with various hypotheses, we can learn through verification of the correct approach to a problem. As a result of such activity, there may be an actual change in the particular environment under consideration. Furthermore, there is an answer to those who state that some subjects such as history are not learned through activity. To this the experimentalist would agree that some types of learning are not immediately practical, but such scientific knowledge was probably gleaned from earlier experience that was essentially most practical in nature.[20]

There are, of course, a number of different theories as to how learning takes place. One group known as *The Eclectic School* takes what are considered to be acceptable beliefs from the various schools of thought and employs them in an effort to make a seemingly proportionate body of thought. With this approach there is recognition that many factors influence learning, no matter how the process is conceived. Factors such as whole-and-parts method, transfer of training, the learning curve, the conditioned reflex, inhibition, behavior and past experience, overlearning of motor skills, distribution of practice periods, motivated learning, and confidence are all deemed worthy of careful consideration.

IMPORTANCE OF ENVIRONMENTAL ADAPTATION.   The experimentalist emphasizes that organic behavior is characterized by responses which help the individual adapt to his environment. He believes that reflective thinking is a sequential and ordered process which progresses toward problem solution. As blocks hinder this progress, the individual, conscious of the process taking place, makes adjustments to create more efficient means of realizing evolving goals—goals which are always tentative in the light of future experience. Many modern psychologists have emphasized the need for purposeful participation on the part of the learner in his own experience. Thus, the gradual shift is coming about—the placing of the individual at the center of the educative process.

---

[19] Childs, *Education and the Philosophy of Experimentalism*, p. 192.
[20] Brubacher, *Modern Philosophies of Education*, pp. 86-87.

Summary

The experimentalist limits the individual's frame of reality to the system of nature as we know it. It is only from experience that anything can be known about the world. The world is constantly changing and presents a complicated and uncertain existence to modern man. Freedom is achieved through continuous learning from experience.

Knowledge is that which is known through experience or which can, in the future through improved experience, be known in this manner. The human mind has developed through many thousands of years and has acquired knowledge by means of a process of thought with environmental adaptation as its purpose. The term truth can be used synonomously with knowledge and should be tested mainly by practical results. Truth should correspond with reality; it is literally wrought in action. Mind and body are not separate entities; they interact within the individual as an aid in adaptation to a changing world.

Value is a fact which has become useful through application to life. As there are many values, it is necessary to select those which help achieve evolved aims in the best way. Ethically, the experimentalist finds himself facing continually new situations in which he must exercise wise judgment in keeping with the apparent elements of the indeterminate situation. Aesthetically, satisfaction comes when close identification is maintained with the ebb and flow of life's indeterminate situations. Religious values are pragmatic as well and are achieved by living purposefully. Social values are fundamental to experimentalism, since life is a process of an organic nature upon which individuals are absolutely dependent.

For the experimentalist, a belief in democracy as a way of life seems to be the most practical solution, because in this type of society there is opportunity for the free growth of the individual as well as for the sharing of the cultural and social heritage. Furthermore, a democracy tends to have an economic system whereby the majority of children and young people can take time away from helping to earn the family living in order to enjoy better educational opportunities.

The school has a creative function—to guide the student as he develops an understanding of and an ability to cope with the new and changing factors of his environment. Thus, the school not only preserves the social heritage to a great extent, but it helps to create a new heritage for the future. The experimentalist believes that the home and the public school should play the leading roles in the education of most children. The place of the private school in a democracy is a doubtful one, as is that of the church in connection with religious education. Some religious faiths play an important part in the child's development, but in most Protestant faiths religious education leaves much to be desired and should probably be handled by the school. This is such a controversial issue that the likelihood of this taking place in the near future is remote.

Aims and objectives are necessary to make the educative process meaningful. Experimentalism suggests that "education in the broadest sense can be nothing less than the changes made in human beings by the experience." [21] If these goals are realized, the child should be prepared for present-day life; future aims can and should grow out of continuing experience. The curriculum should be mainly dependent on the aims and objectives which have been set by the ever-increasing few. These goals may vary slightly as the curriculum is presented and experienced.

The social aim is especially important for the experimentalist. Values, which cannot actually be separated from educational aims, are instrumental and tend to arise from experience. Pupil growth is extremely important.

The individual is at the center of the educative process. Creative projects related to the student's daily experience are essential to the educational methodology employed. Thinking becomes actual problem solving in a life experience.

It can be determined partially when learning has taken place through the use of educational measurement and testing. In the final analysis, the individual's adjustment to his environment is the best method of ascertaining whether learning has been effected.

---

[21] Cf., p. 80.

CHAPTER SEVEN

Experimentalism in Physical, Health, and Recreation Education

The implications of the philosophical position of experimentalism for physical, health, and recreation education follow logically and consistently from those presented in relation to education generally. Despite the fact that many of our fine contemporary principles texts display distinct experimental leanings in their approach, students are unfortunately asked to accept these beliefs without a clear understanding of the philosophical bases underlying the position. As a result, the debate between proponents of education through the physical against those who favor education of the physical has raged on unabated. Unfortunately it is not an easy matter for the professional student to decipher; in fact, the mature professional teacher needs to clarify his thinking on this matter as well. Clarification of the problem would be quite simple if the experimentalist could say that he, as a progressive, is firmly committed to education through the physical, and that the essentialist therefore accepts the position that education of the physical is the correct approach. This statement is probably true to a considerable degree, but we cannot leave it at that. Much more careful analysis is necessary, because the individual professional must find his place on a spectrum rather than merely accepting one side or the other of an either-or dichotomy.

In 1943, Cobb stated that four basic beliefs were evident from a study of physical-education literature and the views expressed by many educators. They are:

1. There is no place for physical education in education.
2. Physical education is for the maintenance of health in order that students may carry on their intellectual work with the least strain.
3. Physical education should develop students physically, mentally, and morally (mind-body dichotomy implied).
4. Physical education should contribute to the growth of the individual as an integrated personality by discovering the health, recreation, and personality needs of each student, and helping him to meet those needs through the activity program.[1]

The last definition listed states the case fairly clearly for the experimentalistic position, but it is not complete. The other three beliefs could be traced to their underlying philosophical tendencies as well. Let us now examine the aims, objectives, and methods of the experimental approach.

Aims and Objectives

In the foundational chapter we listed Geiger's definition that "education in the broadest sense can be nothing less than the changes made in human beings by their experience.[2] This is a far cry from a definition of education as the liquidation of ignorance.

The experimentalist would immediately challenge the name *physical* education! He feels it is an unfortunate designation carried over from another era, and a rapid change should be effected. He bases his case on the acceptance of the unity of the human organism by modern psychologists, which no longer views mind and body as separate entities.

CONCERN WITH TOTAL FITNESS.   According to this approach, "the focus of the individual should be in society and not in his muscles."[3] This means that the experimentalist is much more interested in promoting the concept of *total fitness* rather than what he would consider to be a much narrower physical-fitness approach.[4] As Williams expresses it:

This concept of a physically educated person differs sharply with views that would make physical education a body-building, disciplinary, obedience-developing function in the schools. It maintains that we do not exercise muscles to strengthen them, but we educate individuals through motor activities which incidentally strengthen muscles.[5]

This educational position is amplified further by Williams and Hughes

---

[1] L. S. Cobb, *Physical Education* (New York: Columbia University, Teachers College Contributions to Education, 1943), p. 6.
[2] Cf., p. 80.
[3] J. F. Williams, *The Principles of Physical Education*, 7th ed. (Philadelphia and London: W. B. Saunders Company, 1959), p. 265.
[4] R. Cassidy, *New Directions in Physical Education for the Adolescent Girl in High School and College* (New York: A. S. Barnes and Company, 1938), p. 71.
[5] Williams, *The Principles of Physical Education.*

as they describe the purpose of education and explain the purpose of health, physical education, and recreation as a phase of this process as follows:

The purpose of education is to be stated in terms of living. After all, the disciplines of vocational import are only a phase of life and the purpose of a college is to educate for fine living and not for a narrow vocational interest. Since fine living involves more than vocational activities, innumerable experiences in school and college will contribute. The best preparation for broad interests, wholesome recreations, and socialized living after school days is experiencing broad interests, wholesome recreations, and socialized living during school days. Student organizations, athletic contests, and recreative enterprises offer numerous opportunities for the setting up of fine ideals and worthy standards of conduct.[6]

AN INTEGRAL SUBJECT IN THE CURRICULUM. As the experimentalist sees it, therefore, physical education can become an integral subject in the curriculum if it shows itself to be useful. The implication is that we are only beginning to realize the potential in physical, health, and recreation education for the realization of educational values (as defined by the experimentalist).

VALUE HAS NOT BEEN REALIZED. Larkin pointed out this opportunity in 1937 when he stated that "the fact that as youths and as adults we have played games, taken time for recreational exercise, indulged in competitive sports and throughout life exhibited a zeal for the outdoors, was never taken for its true significance."[7] In 1959 Williams pointed out that such was still the case when he indicated that, "it has rarely occurred to schoolmen to use physical education for worthwhile goals."[8] If such is the case—recent statistics seem to bear out the fact that only 50 per cent of our high-school youth get some type of regular physical education and that only 10 per cent of elementary schools have this benefit—then the answer would appear to be that these educational administrators have implied philosophies of education which do not see these values to which Williams refers.

WIDE SELECTION OF PRACTICAL ACTIVITIES. There should be a wide selection of activities according to the experimentalistic approach, and such activities should be practical and useful. The activities which the individual takes part in would depend a great deal on the needs of the person relative to his pattern of growth and development as well as to his interests. Morland emphasizes this when he indicates that the experimentalist would "start with the experiences that the pupils already

---

[6] J. F. Williams and W. L. Hughes, *Athletics in Education* (Philadelphia and London: W. B. Saunders Company, 1937), p. 55.

[7] R. A. Larkin, "The Influence of John Dewey on Physical Education" (Master's thesis, Ohio State University, 1936), p. 67.

[8] Williams, *The Principles of Physical Education*, p. 225.

have and broaden out into other areas as subsequent experiences are related to the activity at hand." [9] This means there would be no inflexible syllabus imposed by the authority of the teacher.

THE GOAL OF SOCIAL INTELLIGENCE. Most important for the experimentalist, of course, is that a great many socializing activities be included in the curriculum. Here it is not intended to imply that we should only offer social activities as typically conceived. What is meant is that the curriculum should provide experiences which would develop "social intelligence—the power of observing and comprehending social situations—and social power—trained capacities of control—at work in the service of social interests and aims." [10]

IMPORTANCE OF NATURAL ACTIVITIES. Great emphasis is placed also on activities which bring natural impulses into play. [11] Since naturalism undergirds both pragmatism and realism, this approach is to be expected. Williams speaks to this point at some length when he explains that the foundations of human nature biologically and psychologically demand this:

Physical education in the selection of activities should recognize that man is prepared by nature to engage in certain kinds of activity. Many of the persistent problems in physical education today are clarified by reference to the facts of nature. For example, a program of physical education based upon natural motor movements which represent the racial motor activities of man, and a program based upon the artificial creations of "systems" of gymnastics are readily evaluated by reference to the facts of nature. Thus, the fact that man presents in the racial pattern of his nervous system certain underlying predispositions to function in well-defined motor activities characterized in type and quality by his motor experience over thousands of years, that he is urged on by his very nature to exploit these established organizations, and that, under proper guidance, such expressions may be made to serve high causes and noble ends is of outstanding import. [12]

EVALUATION OF EXPERIENCE. In keeping with experimentalistic education the word *evaluation* should be substituted for the phrase *tests and measurements* that has been so popular. Not that the experimentalist is against the whole idea of measurement; nothing could be farther from the truth, since the very name *experimentalism* implies use of scientific method wherever it may be applied. The point is that the experimentalist is strongly opposed to the idea of national norms and/or

[9] R. B. Morland, "A Philosophical Interpretation of the Educational Views Held by Leaders in American Physical Education" (Ph.D. thesis, New York University, 1958), p. 54.

[10] J. Dewey, *Democracy and Education* (New York: The Macmillan Company, 1916), pp. 42-43.

[11] E. C. Davis, *The Philosophic Process in Physical Education* (Philadelphia: Lea & Febiger, 1961), pp. 76-77.

[12] Williams, *The Principles of Physical Education,* pp. 133-134.

standards that tests and measurements imply. His concern is with the individual and his progress in relationship to his adjustment to his environment. Although he is most concerned with evaluation through measurement, such evaluation is unusually difficult, because aims and objectives may change if experience indicates such change is desirable. Thus, we can see why the word *grades* disturbs the experimentalist; he is more concerned with pupil growth and evaluation of this progress. Academic credit as a concept would be eliminated or altered in nature, because it bespeaks the traditional course approach and semester hours of credit which will eventually be added up to make the requisite number of hours for graduation. It makes a great deal more sense to the experimentalist to place most emphasis on the experience that the student has and what knowledges and competencies have resulted from this experience.

THE MAJORITY SHOULD BE SERVED. Physical-education classes and intramural sports are more important to the experimentalist than interscholastic and intercollegiate competition in sports activities. The reasoning behind this statement is quite logical. In a democracy we are dedicated to the idea that the individual should be developed to the maximum of his potential, *but* that individual's development should never be allowed to interfere with the development of the majority of the children and youth. Unfortunately, we in physical education (not in health education and community recreation) have been putting the cart before the horse for years. The experimentalist would view women physical educators favorably, inasmuch as they give more attention to the development of the average girl than their male counterparts do with the boys. Women believe typically that men physical educators place altogether too much emphasis on interscholastic sports for the few. If they were to follow a similar approach, the average girl would simply not get the attention she deserves.

COMPETITIVE SPORT CAN BE EDUCATIONAL. Despite the stand concerning the experience of the majority of youngsters, the experimentalist can give full support to team experiences in competitive sports, because they can be vital educational experiences. Commercialization would be eliminated, however, because educational values are usually negated under such circumstances. The experimentalist, in addition, is most concerned about the attitude of cooperation which can be fostered in such situations; the competitive elements of the contest would be secondary, although obviously necessary for a lifelike experience.

A FINE AESTHETIC EXPERIENCE. The experimentalist believes further that physical-educational activity or athletic and physical-recreational activity at a reasonable level of skill can be an aesthetic experience of a fine type. This is implied by the joy of effort in which one pictures a well-conditioned boy or girl taking part in a sports activity with form and vigor. In speaking of Dewey's position on this question, Larkin says:

He implies that an activity that exhibits honesty, is deliberately organized and produced, stimulates work that serves some good and leads to an enjoyable perception of other things, also exhibits fineness of art.[13]

SYNONYMITY OF MORALS AND SOCIAL INTELLIGENCE. Another important aspect of experimentalistic educational theory is the stress placed on the continuous development of standards to guide conduct. Dewey's stand in this matter is quite clear:

Moral character in schools is practically hopeless when we set up the development of character as a supreme end, and at the same time, treat the acquiring of knowledge and the development of understanding, which of necessity occupy the chief part of school time, as having nothing to do with character.[14]

Once again, we can appreciate Dewey's belief that "ultimate moral motives and forces are nothing more or less than social intelligence—the power of observing and comprehending social situations—and social power—trained capacities of control—at work in the service of social interests and aims." [15]

MORAL VALUES IN PHYSICAL EDUCATION. Both Hetherington and Mc-Cloy seem to echo this belief. In speaking about moral values in physical education, Hetherington points out that "this judgment of the moral quality of the act, in the midst of the experience, is the keynote of the laboratory method in moral training." [16] McCloy, designated as an *essentialist*,[17] seems to be speaking of the same thing when he talks about educational situations in connection with basketball coaching, but he does not use the word *moral*. Writing in 1928, he stated:

Thus the promotion of coaching of basketball should not be considered as a means of just securing good basketball teams, but as a tool for securing educational situations which can and will be so presented as to cause such responses in the individual under such psychological conditions as will make for the change in attitudes and concepts, that will bring the desired educational results.[18]

A concern for the planned occurrence of educational situations within sports competition is important to the experimentalist. Larkin expressed his concern with practices in interscholastic and intercollegiate sports a quarter of a century ago—practices which are still all too evident today:

---

[13] Larkin, "The Influence of John Dewey on Physical Education," p. 66.

[14] Dewey, *Democracy and Education,* p. 411.

[15] Cf., p. 80.

[16] C. Hetherington, *School Program in Physical Education* (Yonkers, N.Y.: World Book Company, 1922), p. 87.

[17] Morland, "A Philosophical Interpretation . . ."

[18] C. H. McCloy, "Physical Education as Part of General Education," *Journal of Health and Physical Education,* XXXI (November 1928), 45.

When the playing of football, basketball, and other interscholastic sports originate in the minds of outsiders, and when aims are obscure or remote, these activities run the same risk of being misunderstood and therefore dropped or indulged in for vicarious reasons. The group that plays football under these conditions becomes the agent of others, and therefore the sport becomes branded as professional and outside the list of recreations that carry responsibility of observing, anticipating, and arranging. The desire to reduce team play to matters of mechanics represents the authoritative control so necessary when aims lay outside those who do the playing.[19]

A UNIFIED FIELD. We must mention again at this point that the experimentalist would do away with the term *physical* education as soon as possible. When phrases such as *development of the total individual for self-satisfaction, preparation of the individual for community living by effective solution of present day problems,* and *development of understandings through physical experiences that enable the individual to formulate social judgments of value in a democratic society* are used to describe the experimentalistic position, it is difficult to envision the field as being composed of areas of extreme specialization. The experimentalist would be more concerned with integration and unity and might be inclined to discourage separate undergraduate majors in health education, physical education, or recreation. He would at least be most anxious to see the field united in every way possible to achieve experimental educational aims and objectives.

AIMS OF HEALTH EDUCATION. Keeping the above statements in mind, let us now move to a consideration of some of the aims and objectives of health education as seen through the eyes of the experimentalist. In the first place, here again we find a naturalistic undergirding. The experimentalist would concur in the beliefs that man must be a rugged animal, and this standard should apply to girls as well as to boys. Secondly, he would agree that the child needs health instruction and that natural types of exercise promote sound mental health.

COOPERATION NECESSARY FOR SUCCESS. Health is therefore a primary objective of education for the experimentalist. The success of the school health-education program depends on the degree of cooperation among home, school, and community agencies. Today an educated person must understand the difference between health and disease, and he must know how to protect and improve his own health, that of his dependents, and that of the community both large and small.

UNIFIED PROGRAM ADMINISTRATION RECOMMENDED. The experimentalist takes the position that health, physical education, and recreation should be administered as a unified program within a school system. He feels that these efforts may be coordinated, because they are related in many ways. Through unity, these structures which are basically

---

[19] Larkin, "The Influence of John Dewey on Physical Education," pp. 25-26.

related could probably serve the needs of school children and youth much more effectively than is the case so often at the present. This approach would see no reason for the creation of a separate agency or department every time a need becomes apparent.

A MORE POSITIVE DEFINITION OF HEALTH. To be truly effective, health education must be concerned with helping the individual to lead a rich, full life. This means more than providing a health service so that students can maintain minimum health needed to pursue intellectual work with the least amount of strain. As Williams has indicated, health should be defined positively—as that quality which enables us to live most and serve best. The experimentalist, therefore, would concur with the approach that perceives school health education as being composed of three distinct, yet most closely related, divisions as follows: *healthful school living*—"development of an environment that facilitates their students' optimal growth and development"; *health instruction*—"programs definitely organized to promote specific learnings in the area of health"; and *health services*—"provision for (a) the care of emergency sickness or injury, (b) specific procedures for the prevention or control of communicable diseases, (c) health appraisal, and (d) health counseling." [20]

STRONG PRAGMATIC INFLUENCE IN PROFESSIONAL PREPARATION. Downey's study completed in 1956 found that the chief influence being exerted in the professional preparation of health educators is pragmatic (experimentalistic). His research identified the philosophical beliefs of certain teacher educators in the field of health education. He attempted to discover whether the basic beliefs of these educators were idealistic, pragmatic, or realistic. He devised the *Teacher Education Beliefs Indicator for Health Education* which covered thirty-one areas of teacher preparation. Forty per cent of the areas covered were determined to be definitely pragmatic in direction in regard to both aims and objectives and methodology:

The purpose of education is to prepare the students to take their places in our democratic society. Health is defined as appropriately acting and reacting to problems. Learning is the result of new techniques gained from biosocial experiences which may be used to solve old and new problems. A liberal education develops a desire and willingness on the part of the student to find out things about living and biosocial interactions. Guidance of students should be personal but non-directive. The social sciences should form the major content of the professional curriculum, and this curriculum should have as its aim the preparation of the student in the solving of his professional problems. Placement is primarily a student problem and is a learning experience for him.

---

[20] American Association for Health, Physical Education, and Recreation, H. C. Kozman, editor and chairman, *Democratic Human Relations* (Washington, D.C.: A.A.H.P.E.R., First Yearbook, 1951), pp. 77-80.

The follow-up program is for the improvement of the preparing institution's curriculum in light of its graduates' experiences and the problems on the job. In-service training should be a teacher-centered and -conducted program.[21]

RECREATION EDUCATION. Shifting our emphasis now to the area that has been designated as recreation, and our concern is primarily with its role in the educational system, it should be mentioned again that the experimentalist is much more concerned with a unified approach whereby the three specialized areas would provide a variety of experiences involving knowledges and understandings that will enable the individual to live a richer, fuller life through superior adjustment to his environment. It is certainly true that physical, health, and recreation education reflects the value system of the culture where it takes place.

NINE CHARACTERISTICS OF RECREATION. There are innumerable definitions of play and recreation, and it is very easy to get lost in a maze of biological, psychological, and social considerations which may possibly be recognized in a particular definition. Meyer and Brightbill have outlined nine fundamental characteristics of recreation that merit careful consideration. As they see it, recreation has the following qualities or characteristics: (1) involves activity; (2) has no single form; (3) is determined by motivation; (4) occurs in unobligated time; (5) is entirely voluntary; (6) has therapeutic value; (7) is universally practiced and sought; (8) is serious and purposeful; and (9) is flexible.[22]

THE EXPERIMENTALISTIC POSITION. Our task in this chapter, however, is to discover how the experimentalist views play and recreation. Initially, three points may be made which are perhaps self-evident. Education for leisure is basic to the curriculum of the school—a curriculum in which pupil growth, as defined by the experimentalist, is all important. Secondly, play shall be conducted to foster desirable moral growth. Thirdly, overorganized sport competition is not true recreation, since the welfare of the individual is often submerged in the extreme emphasis which is so frequently placed on winning.

DEWEY ON PLAY. In his monumental work *Democracy and Education,* Dewey devotes considerable attention to the subject of *Play and Work in the Curriculum.*[23] He pointed out how "going to school is a joy, management is less of a burden, and learning is easier," when "children have a chance at physical activities which bring their natural impulses into play." [24] But this is not the point that Dewey wants to make; these

---

[21] Robert J. Downey, "An Identification of the Philosophical Beliefs of Educators in the Field of Health Education" (Ph.D. thesis, University of Southern California, 1956), pp. 25-26. Abstract.

[22] H. D. Meyer and Charles K. Brightbill, *Community Recreation: A Guide to Its Organization* (Englewood Cliffs, N.J.: Prentice-Hall, Inc., 1956), pp. 32-37.

[23] Dewey, *Democracy and Education,* chap. 15.

[24] *Ibid.,* p. 228.

are the reasons why essentialists of the more conservative type encourage play activities on the school premises, but only during recess when a change from the basic curriculum seems desirable.

EDUCATION IS LIFE NOW. Dewey was most anxious that educators should learn "the place of active occupations in education." Just because children and youth usually take part in play and work outside of school proper is no reason why educators should think that something completely different should take place when school is in session. His reasoning on this question was as follows:

When exercises which are prompted by these instincts are a part of the regular school program, the whole pupil is engaged, the artificial gap between life in school and out is reduced, motives are afforded for attention to a large variety of materials and processes distinctly educative in effect, and cooperative associations which give information a social setting are provided.[25]

RECREATION CAN BE EDUCATION. There is also a strong recommendation for the inclusion of all sorts of arts-and-crafts occupations in the curriculum. Furthermore, Dewey suggested that such "active pursuits with social aims" as "outdoor excursions, gardening, cooking, sewing, printing, book-binding, weaving, painting, drawing, singing, dramatization, story-telling, reading and writing" be included as well.[26] It is evident that Dewey would concur with those who would like to see the name *recreation* be changed to *recreation education*. These activities, involving "modes of experience which are intrinsically valuable," are "truly liberalizing in quality." [27]

THE IMPORTANCE OF PLAY. Of course, it should be made clear that Dewey doesn't regard work and play as being so far apart in meaning as one would think they are. He explains that we shouldn't "confuse the psychological distinction between play and work with the economic distinction." [28] Play, for Dewey, may not be defined characteristically as "amusement or aimlessness." It is more a matter of emphasis—"when fairly remote results of a definite character are foreseen and enlist persistent effort for their accomplishment, play passes into work." [29] He explains that our work often becomes drudgery, but the need for play exists in our makeup. Then we need something which is stimulating and exciting, or at least something which will make the time pass. Our very nature makes an urgent demand for recreation, and we can't escape it. This is why Dewey recommends the importance of education which offers the opportunity to enjoy wholesome recreation and to learn how

[25] *Ibid.*, pp. 228-229.
[26] *Ibid.*, p. 230.
[27] *Ibid.*, p. 235.
[28] *Ibid.*, p. 241.
[29] *Ibid.*, p. 239.

to find it when the occasion demands. He explains the urgent need for recreation education in the curriculum in the following way:

Education has no more serious responsibility than making adequate provision for enjoyment of recreative leisure; not only for the sake of immediate health, but still more if possible for the sake of its lasting effect upon habits of mind.[30]

NEED FOR THE CULTIVATION OF LEISURE. Dewey, of course, is not alone in the ideas that he expressed about the importance of education for leisure. Geiger feels strongly about the need for "cultivation of leisure" in America today. The experimentalist, as we have mentioned earlier, sees education and growth as synonymous. As Geiger sees it:

Not by leisure but by the cultivation of leisure can men grow. Therefore, education for the citizen must aim to enrich the free time that the march of technology seems to promise (assuming, of course, the gradual solution of basic economic and political questions). This is not to be interpreted as regimentation or discipline or some devious first step to cultural totalitarianism. What is intended here is that men must be granted at least the chance to employ their free time creatively and fruitfully and not be delivered by default to the tender mercies of comic strip and pulp fiction, soap operas, gigantic orgies of professionalized sports and entertainment, all presided over by the advertising impressaria. Instead, encouragement of artistic talents, appreciation of great music and literature, introduction to the fascination of science and philosophy, cultivation of hobbies, training in the handicrafts—these are but a sample of the paths possible.[31]

PLAY AND WORK SOMETIMES OVERLAP. Brubacher concurs in the idea that the activity curriculum must offer greater promise for educational growth. He is somewhat concerned also about traditional conceptions of work and play being antithetical. In a modern industrial community he feels that it may be justifiable to include play in the school program.[32] He explains how difficult it is to tell where play leaves off and work begins. If our goals are long range, he suggests that an activity may be more akin to work than if we are engaging in a game, for example, for immediate pleasure and fun. He uses the analogy of the boy heading for the playground to play baseball after school; this is play. If, however, this boy gets in a league at an early age, and follows up this interest by becoming a varsity ballplayer in high school and college (perhaps on an athletic scholarship), and has professional baseball in mind as a possible career, then it begins to seem like work as his purpose gets increasingly serious. Of course, it will probably retain certain play aspects as well.[33]

---

[30] *Ibid.*, p. 241.

[31] George R. Geiger, "An Experimentalist Approach to Education," *Modern Philosophies and Education, Fifty-fourth Yearbook* of the National Society for the Study of Education, chairman J. S. Brubacher (Chicago: NSSE, 1955), pp. 150-151.

[32] J. S. Brubacher, *Modern Philosophies of Education* (New York: McGraw-Hill Book Company, 1950), p. 227.

[33] *Ibid.*, pp. 238-239.

WILLIAMS'S POSITION. Others classified as experimentalists or reconstructionists have called for an increased emphasis on recreational interests. Williams, for example, feels that "education for leisure marks a proper emphasis in physical education today." [34] Interestingly enough, he points out that watching *human* art in football and baseball contests is called *spectatoritis,* while a similar type of observation in connection with art or music is considered highly desirable.

RECONSTRUCTIONISM. Brameld feels that there is an urgent need for a reconstructed philosophy of education, especially since it appears to many that the organized progressive-education movement is on the wane. He recommends, therefore, reconstructionism as a logical outgrowth of progressivism and believes that it is the approach needed in the second half of the twentieth century. For Brameld, the use of the figure of a wheel to describe the core curriculum of this approach is appropos. Although he lists certain areas of experience as *extracurricular activities,* Brameld is quick to make the following statement:

Quite as integral as spoke and hub studies are extracurricular activities—so much so, in fact, that the prefix 'extra' is misleading. Frequently the last period of the day may extend beyond 4 P.M. because students are interested in building stage equipment, rehearsing a musical program, or practicing a debate. In the area of physical education little time, if any, is devoted to competitive interscholastic sports; rather there is emphasis on intramural games, on the dance as recreation and as an art form, and other shared activities.[35]

He goes on to point out that the plan is to meet the needs of all students through "fusion of the curricular and the extracurricular." If such "fusion" doesn't seem to be taking place as completely as desired, then he recommends the substitution of what appears to be needed in place of scheduled assemblies or discussion periods. Brameld indicates also that the school should be open for use during a much longer period than what has been accepted as the usual school day:

. . . its recreational and adult program extends into the late afternoon and evenings and into Saturdays and Sundays. Obviously, a staff large enough to accommodate this extensive schedule is essential.[36]

The position of the reconstructionist may seem to be opposed to interscholastic athletic competition, and we suppose this is true because of the ideal of social self-realization which it holds and the excesses of athletic contests in the past and present. Experimentalism seems to favor this stand also, but it would seem that the experimentalistic progressive is tremendously concerned about the individual and his

[34] Williams, *The Principles of Physical Education,* p. 226.

[35] Theodore Brameld, *Toward a Reconstructed Philosophy of Education* (New York: The Dryden Press, Inc., 1956), p. 217.

[36] *Ibid.,* p. 214.

development as well. Hence it would appear that a carefully planned program of interscholastic sports built upon a sound physical-education and intramural, athletic base should not be viewed unfavorably. If a choice had to be made, however, between intramural sports and voluntary recreational activities and a varsity athletic program, the experimentalist, as well as the reconstructionist, would base their choice on the greatest good for the greatest number without question.

Methodology

What teaching methods shall the experimentalist employ? Now that we have looked fairly carefully at the question of aims and objectives, it is time that we shift our emphasis to methodology. It is often possible to get a certain amount of consensus about long-range objectives between conflicting educational positions. Consider, for example, the seven cardinal aims of education published widely since 1918, which included health, command of the fundamental processes, worthy use of leisure, etc. Almost everyone would agree on these aims; the difficulty comes when we try to get consensus on a hierarchy of educational values and how we should teach to bring about the achievement of any objectives agreed upon.

AIM AND METHOD MUST SHOW RELATIONSHIP. Larkin felt that it was important for aims and method to go hand in hand. "Trading the drill master of calisthenics for the domineering coach of football does not appear to be enough." [37] He summarized further the salient qualities of the experimentalist teacher of physical, health, and recreation education as follows:

In restating the desirable methods in a physical education program the pattern appeared to be this: a broad social outlook, great consideration for the learner, well prepared teachers, and a minimum of inherited technique as such. [38]

PROBLEM SOLVING AND ATTITUDE DEVELOPMENT. The experimentalistic teacher should aid the student in the development of skill for problem solving. This skill is more than a conditional reflex; the learner needs to develop insight into the nature of the anticipated outcome. As the experimentalist sees it, knowledges are essential, but attitude development is vital! What health educator doesn't realize the importance of this statement!

A NEW CONCEPTION OF THE CURRICULUM. "As teachers we must make ourselves progressively unnecessary," says Kilpatrick, because "we face thus a new conception of the curriculum as consisting properly of such

---

[37] Larkin, "The Influence of John Dewey on Physical Education," p. 67.
[38] *Ibid.,* pp. 37-38.

a succession of school experiences as will best bring and constitute the continuous reconstruction of experience." [39] It is important to start at the student's level and to give him "as much freedom as he can use wisely. And again the test is the learning that results." [40]

INTEREST AND INVOLVEMENT ARE BASIC.   The experimentalistic teacher has a definite responsibility to find material which is interesting and significant to the student. After all, this is the only guarantee of attention. Dewey expresses it as follows:

The problem of instruction is thus that of finding material which will engage a person in specific activities having an aim or purpose of moment or interest to him, and dealing with things not as gymnastic appliances but as conditions for the attainment of ends. [41]

He points out further that we as teachers will find a greatly different attitude if we involve the student as "an agent or participant" rather than as a spectator. He states that the latter is usually quite indifferent about any enterprise in which he is not actively involved. The participant, however, "is bound up with what is going on; its outcome makes a difference to him." [42]

INTERACTION WITH ENVIRONMENT IS VITAL.   There is simply no question as to the importance of methodology in the eyes of Dewey. The teacher as the agent of the school should create an environment in which "play and work shall be conducted with reference to facilitating desirable mental and moral growth." The mere introduction of handwork, games, plays, and manual exercises will not suffice. "Everything depends on the way in which they are employed." [43] We must present an environment offering great opportunity for interaction between an individual and his surroundings, both natural and social. This "interaction" is vital for Dewey, because it "will effect acquisition of those meanings which are so important that they become, in turn, instruments of further learnings." [44]

A FLEXIBLE CURRICULUM.   Standardization of the curriculum from year to year is something that the experimentalist is most anxious to avoid. There should be opportunities for changes in plan and program often involving student choice. Morland, for example, explained that an experimentalistic curriculum should be flexible and not systematically arranged. He stressed further that in such a curriculum the teacher

---

[39] W. H. Kilpatrick, *Education for a Changing Civilization* (New York: The Macmillan Company, 1926), p. 123.
[40] *Ibid.*, p. 129.
[41] Dewey, *Democracy and Education*, p. 155.
[42] *Ibid.*, p. 146.
[43] *Ibid.*, p. 230.
[44] *Ibid.*, p. 320.

would never impose a syllabus upon a class.[45] This avoidance of prescription is fundamental to this approach. The student must have the chance to use and develop his own judgment in such matters.

DISCIPLINE COMES FROM THE GROUP. The attitude of the experimentalist toward discipline is interesting as well. The belief is that disciplinary measures should, insofar as possible, arise from the actions of the class itself. This does not mean that the experimentalist wishes to replace teacher domination with pupil domination—far from it! It does mean that he wants to see the group control the actions of its own members, that this approach will bring about increased social efficiency, and that management will be much less of a burden when children are active in a flexible curriculum marked by completely apparent purpose.

BEST POSSIBLE LEARNING SITUATION. The idea is, therefore, that the best possible learning occurs when the student aids in the origination and planning of his own educational experience, when he has a part in the execution of the enterprise, and when he has the opportunity to evaluate the success or failure of the whole venture.

EVALUTION OF GROWTH. The matter of grades, term marks, testing, and all other varieties of measurement must be considered also. The experimentalist rejects measurement of an absolute nature. He would substitute the term *evaluation,* because he is most interested in individual pupil growth rather than whether a particular student comes up to a national norm in pull-ups. The experimentalist realizes, as Clarke has indicated, that there may be as much as a four-year difference in the physiological maturity of two students the same age.[46] Furthermore, Ulrich reports that some students do not perform up to their capabilities in "testing situations, where the psychosocial factors encourage stress." She feels that there is "ample evidence that the 'good performer' is that individual whose performance pattern improves under stress elicited by the physical educator stressor." Because "there does not appear to be any way in which stress immunity is acquired," [47] the testing of all students indiscriminately to measure physical fitness may actually be a measurement of certain factors other than physical performance for many. The experimentalist would be unwilling to build a program of evaluation on such an approach. He would much rather consider the individual's body type, his continuing health record, and his past performances before testing him to determine whether individual pupil growth had taken place.

---

[45] Morland, "A Philosophical Interpretation . . ."

[46] Statement by Dr. H. H. Clarke at a summer conference in Eugene, Oregon, the University of Oregon, on June 28, 1961.

[47] Celeste Ulrich, "Implications of Stress and Stressors for Physical Education," a paper presented at a summer conference held at the University of Michigan, July 24-25, 1961.

EXPERIMENTALISTIC TEACHING METHOD. Authoritative use of texts and preplanned lectures do not fit into the experimentalist's teaching pattern as a daily procedure. There is an element of uncertainty with a considerable measure of contingency when an experimental problem-solving approach is employed in the teaching of a class. It would seem that it would be much easier for the teacher (but perhaps not so beneficial for the student) to employ an authoritarian technique. Dewey, of course, wanted the student to be presented with a life experience. Presented with a problem the student, guided by the teacher, searches for ways and means to solve it. If the teacher steps in with *his* answer or *an* answer too soon, it is obvious that the student will probably relax his own effort to consider all possible solutions. A desirable third stage, then, is when the student comes up with a proposed solution which he proceeds to test by putting it into practice (a fourth stage). If the plan of action works, or it appears that it might work through a reasonable amount of practice, then learning is a result of the experience. This particular learning experience should enter upon a fifth stage when it is correlated with previous experiences to give broader meaning and perspective to the entire educational process.[48]

THE ROLE OF THE TEACHER. It seems perfectly reasonable to the experimentalist that this approach can be used in the curriculum of health, physical education, and recreation. Of course, it all depends on objectives, and presumably the best method is the one that brings about the objective (or objectives) desired. As Williams explains:

With the goal of the highest individual development in relation to social welfare uppermost, it ought to be clear that the teacher must stand ready to meet situations rather than give allegiance only to a theory of action. There are times when play breaks down due to disturbing individuals. There are individuals who have never learned any self-direction at all. To give such persons unlimited freedom without opportunity to learn what liberty means, and how it is attained, is a serious mistake in method. The teacher must be ready to help out in the management of an activity. The teacher, as a member of the group, is therefore a responsible leader as well as a thoughtful follower upon occasion.[49]

If we as teachers are convinced that students learn best when their interest in the experience is maintained, this should be an important indicator of the type of methodology necessary.

A PRACTICAL EXAMPLE. If a teacher is instructing a boy in the sport of wrestling, he may first explain to him and his classmates the general idea of the sport and then ask two upperclassmen to wrestle a short demonstration match. At this point he might pair off the class members

---

[48] Brubacher, *Modern Philosophies of Education*, pp. 255-256.
[49] Williams, *The Principles of Physical Education*, p. 273.

and allow them to wrestle very briefly, being very careful not to over-match any one individual too greatly. Upon the completion of a short tussle, the instructor might conceivably ask the students to sit in a circle in order to discuss the various categories of skills (or groups of skills) comprising the sport. The problem, of course, is to put the opponent's shoulders (scapulae) to the mat for two seconds in order to score a fall. If both men start originally on their feet, it won't be long before the boys will figure out that takedowns, rides, pinning combinations, and escapes are the basic groups of skills to be mastered for proficiency in the sport. The first lesson might feasibly include one skill from each of the above-mentioned four groups of skills. A teacher in the experi-mentalistic pattern will guide the boys in such a way that they will use their reasoning ability in the selection of one skill from each category.

THREE ASPECTS OF LEARNING. Although the teacher may have a very specific objective in mind at this point—helping the boy to figure out one method of taking his opponent off his feet—he must not forget that there may be a variety of learnings in a class experience. There is the *technical* learning of how to bring a man to the mat, but there is also the *associated* learning that you will have to follow—a rigorous training routine in order to be fit for the activity. In addition, there are a num-ber of important *concomitant* learnings that accompany the sport of wrestling. For example, an amateur wrestler in an American high school or college can never be permitted to lose because he may be injured by his opponent. It is up to the referee to see to it that no punishing hold is permitted. Wrestling encourages a boy to give the best that is in him; this is a most important concomitant learning in our society.[50]

FIVE UNIVERSITY PROGRAMS. Moving from experimentalistic teaching methodology of a technical learning in a particular sport, it might be advantageous to consider the question somewhat more broadly—the organization and methodology employed in several different university programs of physical, health, and recreation education. Three of five programs to be discussed are required for the freshman year in university (the very word *requirement* negates an important quality of an experi-mentalistic program—interest). The fourth program to be considered may be required anywhere from six weeks to thirty weeks depending on the results of a proficiency testing and evaluation program. The fifth pro-gram is completely elective. The organizational patterns of the five institutions are:

University A—Freshmen must take physical education between Thanksgiving and Easter. Proficiency testing is conducted in swimming, physical fitness, body mechanics, combatives, and leisure skills. If a student does not meet prede-termined norms and standards in each of these program areas, he must attend

---

[50] *Ibid.*, pp. 271-272.

classes in swimming, physical fitness, etc., in that order until the standard is met. If Easter arrives before the standards are met in each of the areas, the student is released. He must, however, swim 100 yards before graduation. Students are encouraged to take part in intramural and intercollegiate sports. Intercollegiates may be substituted.

University B—Freshmen must take physical education for the entire first year at the university. No proficiency testing is given typically. A student elects one activity each semester according to his own wishes; some difficulty occurs when students cannot get into certain sections, because they are already full and must therefore take a second or third choice. Intercollegiate athletics, marching band, or ROTC may be substituted.

University C—Freshmen must take physical education for the entire first year at university (a two-year requirement was just lowered to one for budgetary reasons). All students must enroll in an orientation program during which there is an introduction prior to three periods of testing to obtain a self-image. Subsequently, students are told how to effect physical changes and then engage in an intensive two-week training program. Then through lectures, the how-and-why of personal physical maintenance is explained. At this point students are exposed by film and participation to the various sports taught in the program. Finally, the "student completes the guidance section of his workbook in which he is forced to consider carefully the role of sports in his life. The student, however, guides himself into the instructional courses he will take to complete his physical education requirement. Body type, future place of residence, intended occupation, emotional release and carry-over values are classed as the activity needs. These are matched against the student's activity interests and skill level to determine the priority listing of courses to be taken. Proficiency examinations will be offered to permit reduction of the requirement in cases where a high need is well satisfied by interests and skills. Finally, a personal prescription for effective living in the present and future is completed." [51]

University D—Freshmen may be required to take up to one year of physical education depending on the results of proficiency testing. A physically educated student can conceivably bypass the requirement and move immediately into either intramural sports and voluntary recreational activities or intercollegiate sports. A number of introductory orientation lectures are offered to all at the outset. Proficiency testing is offered in swimming, body mechanics, motor fitness, combatives, and indoor and outdoor leisure skills. Physical-education courses and intercollegiate sports may be elected for credit throughout the four years at university and count toward the graduation hour requirement.

University E—There is no requirement whatsoever at this university. Students may elect physical-education courses for credit throughout their university undergraduate years.

PHILOSOPHICAL ANALYSIS.　When we consider the aims and objectives discussed earlier in this chapter, it becomes immediately apparent that some of the above-mentioned physical-education programs are much more experimentalistic than others. *University A* seems to have a program that is decidedly essentialistic; everything appears to be decided

---

[51] W. D. Van Huss, "Orientation to Instructional Physical Education at Michigan State University," *Proceedings* (College Physical Education Association, December 28-30, 1959), pp. 95-98.

in advance for the student—how long he takes physical education, in what order he must take its various phases, what standards must be met, and the place of leisure skills with carry-over value in the scheme of things. Quite the opposite—except for the omnipresent one-year requirement—appears to be the case with *University B*. Here the student may elect any course in which he can find room. At least the interest factor is given serious consideration, and this point makes the experimentalist fairly happy inasmuch as learning may follow when interest is present. Negatively, however, we find that marching band and ROTC (as well as intercollegiate athletics) may be substituted for the requirement. Furthermore, the experimentalist cannot see any evidence in the approach that the school is serving a creative function. There appears to be no evaluation of total fitness, no guidance insofar as election of activity is concerned in keeping with needs as well as with interests. A student may well elect an activity of doubtful carry-over value, and no growth may be the result.

University C seems to be coming much closer to the experimentalistic ideal than *University B*. The initial orientation program for all is a desirable type of introduction and evaluation. The idea of obtaining a self-image contributes to the establishment of motivation for future growth. Then through visual aids and activity the student is guided to the realization of his own potential. There is opportunity for student choice of activity, for the development of skill for problem solving, for measurement of status and progress, and for adjustment of his own organism to nature (self) and society. Students may also, through proficiency, earn exemption in certain aspects of the requirement. Emphasis is placed on a personal prescription for effective living in the present and future as worked out by the student and his counselor.

University D's program has strong experimentalistic leanings also. There seems to be somewhat less emphasis on orientation and guidance, although orientation lectures are offered. The possibility of passing proficiency examinations to reduce the requirement and the opportunity to elect physical-education classes or intercollegiate sports for credit toward a degree because of their educational value would be pleasing to the experimentalist.

The lack of any requirement whatsoever at *University E* may be considered experimentalistic, as long as socializing activities (not social), catholic selection of activities, and evaluation and guidance are available. This analysis would be correct, also, if the concept of total fitness is promoted and if physical education is considered an integral subject in the curriculum.

EXPERIMENTALISTIC APPROACH TO ADMINISTRATION. The experimentalistic approach to administration within the educational system is in keeping with the aims and objectives of this philosophical position expressed earlier. The administrator makes every effort to conduct the affairs of the department as a "democratic enterprise in which all concerned share in its operation." He makes it clear that he is interested in democratic living and "his actions are in keeping with his words." [52] Students and staff are not afraid to come to him with their problems. When he does criticize any staff member or student, it is done in such a way that a minimum of antagonism occurs. The individual concerned is encouraged to present his side of the story as well. The end result should be that the person concerned leaves with a desire to improve his performance in order to live up to the confidence that the administrator has placed in him.

Such an administrator encourages both staff and students to offer constructive criticisms in a variety of ways. All departmental policy is decided through democratic procedure. The administrator sees himself as a chairman at meetings. He may well speak of the various issues and problems at hand, and perhaps without the formality of leaving the chair. His democracy-in-action approach is quite apparent throughout the program and is reflected in the attitudes of the staff and the students toward the enterprise. A staff member given responsibility finds that the authority to carry it out is present as well. Such an administrator treats his staff members as co-workers. He encourages staff study projects and wants all staff members to improve themselves professionally. When staff members do something that merits praise, this man sees to it that their work is recognized both within and without the department.

The experimentalistic administrator works to create an atmosphere in which all can make a full contribution to the progress of the department. The best possible human relations are encouraged. If such an administrator takes another position, it would not be unusually difficult for a qualified staff member to assume the chairman's position. A successor does not have to learn the tricks of the trade through bitter experience.

Such an administrator realizes that there are many relations and determinants that influence a person's behavior in any given situation. He views administration as a developing social science. He knows that he can't expect cooperation on the part of all concerned to develop by chance. If all are involved in policy formation, and the lines of communication are kept open insofar as possible, emotional acceptance to necessary decisions will probably follow. In this way there is a much greater possibility that the goals of democratic, experimental education will be realized.[53]

---

[52] Morland, "A Philosophical Interpretation . . . ," p. 295.

[53] Earle F. Zeigler, *Administration of Physical Education and Athletics* (Englewood Cliffs, N.J.: Prentice-Hall, Inc., 1959), pp. 5-6 and 225-227.

Summary

AIMS AND OBJECTIVES. The experimentalist is much more interested in promoting the concept of total fitness rather than physical fitness alone. He believes that physical education should be an integral subject in the curriculum. Students should have the opportunity to select a wide variety of useful activities, many of which should help to develop social intelligence. The activities offered should bring natural impulses into play. To him, physical-education classes and intramural sports are more important to the large majority of students than interscholastic or intercollegiate sports and deserve priority if conflict arises over budgetary allotment, staff available for guidance and instruction, and use of facilities. He can, however, give *full support* to team (as well as to individual and dual) experiences in competitive sports, because they can be vital educational experiences if properly conducted.

The experimentalist believes that man should be a rugged animal, and this standard should apply to girls as well as to boys. Health, as he sees it, is a primary objective of education, and the child needs health instruction. The success of the school health-education program depends on the degree of cooperation among home, school, and community agencies. An educated person should understand the difference between health and disease, and he should know how to protect and improve his own health, that of his dependents, and that of the community. As he sees it, the program of school health, physical, and recreation education may be administered as a unified program within a school system. He believes that natural types of exercise promote sound mental health. All these aspects of the total program may be coordinated because they are related in many ways. Through unity these subdivisions, which are basically related, could probably serve the needs of school children and youth much more effectively more often than it does now. To be truly effective, school health education must be concerned with helping the individual to lead a rich, full life. This means more than providing a health service so that students can maintain minimum health needed to "pursue intellectual work with the least amount of strain." Health should be defined positively as *that quality which enables us to live most and serve best.*

The experimentalist is inclined to favor the adoption of the name *recreation education* rather than recreation in the educational system. He sees advantages in a *unified* approach whereby the three specialized areas of health, physical education, and recreation (in schools) would provide a variety of experiences that will enable the individual to live a richer, fuller life through superior adjustment to his environment.

To him, education for the worthy use of leisure is basic to the curriculum of the school—a curriculum in which pupil growth, as defined broadly, is all important. Play shall be conducted in such a way that desirable moral growth will be fostered. Overly organized sport competition is not true recreation education, since the welfare of the individual is often submerged in the extreme emphasis which is so frequently placed on winning. The experimentalist believes that it is a mistake to confuse the psychological distinction between work and play with the traditional economic distinction that is generally recognized. All citizens should have ample opportunity to use their free time in a creative and fruitful manner. The experimentalist does not condemn a person who watches others perform with a high level of skill in any of our cultural recreational activities, including sport, as long as the individual keeps such viewing in a balanced role in his entire life.

Methodology

For the experimentalist, objectives and methodology must go hand in hand. Experimentalism in physical, health, and recreation education is characterized by "a broad social outlook, great consideration for the learner, well prepared teachers, and a minimum of inherited technique as such." [54] The instructor should begin his teaching at the student's level and give him "as much freedom as he can use wisely." A physical-education program which is interesting and significant to the student is the sole guarantee of attention.

Dewey believed that the learning experience is greatly improved if we involve the student in activity just as soon as possible. Of course, there should be opportunities for changes in plan and program often involving student choice. The experimentalist urges that disciplinary measures should, insofar as possible, arise from the actions of the class itself.

The students should have the opportunity to evaluate the success or failure of the whole educational venture. The experimentalist rejects measurement of an absolute nature concerning student progress if it is to be used for open comparison with others; he is vitally concerned with the evaluation of individual pupil growth.

Authoritative use of texts and preplanned lectures do not fit into the experimentalist's teaching pattern as a daily procedure. He believes in an element of uncertainty with a considerable measure of contingency when an experimental problem-solving approach is employed in the teaching of a class. He guides his students in such a way that they will use their reasoning abilities in the realization of the technical, associated, and concomitant learnings available in the learning of sport skills.

---

[54] Cf., p. 99.

Strengths and Weaknesses

STRENGTHS. Generally speaking, experimentalism seems to be strong because it encourages us to meet each daily experience fully—one step at a time. In an age when scientific discoveries are legion, it would seem that emphasis on experimental method can accomplish much good more rapidly in the world. If we believe that ours is indeed a changing world, then experimentalism would appear to be a very practical approach to life.

In education, experimentalism (often called *pragmatic naturalism*) breaks down the distinction between life in the school and life out in the world by keeping teacher and student close to experience and by making every effort to destroy much academic artificiality. The aim is to place the student at the center of the educational process, not the teacher *or* the subject matter. Pupil freedom (at least as much as can be used wisely) is certainly appealing to those concerned most directly; yet, there is great concern for society and the social implications of the educational process. If we wish to develop initiative and self-reliance, such freedom might well bring about these qualities more quickly and much more fully. This approach should have great appeal to a people devoted to the concept of an evolving political democracy. Stress on interest as the basis for motivation of instruction should bring greater involvement on the part of the student and should, therefore, be a strength. Furthermore, experimentalism promotes easy interchange of diverse cultural viewpoints; this is a vital point as we seek to promote better understanding among various races and creeds at home and throughout the world.

The experimentalistic position offers a great deal of strength to our specialized field. Physical education can become an integral subject in the curriculum, if it realizes its educational potentialities. Secondly, experimentalism encourages the various subdivisions of our total field to unite in order to meet the needs and interests of students; such unity, which is possible, would offer us greatly increased strength to fulfill our role as envisioned by the experimentalist. Thirdly, a teaching method based on pupil interest affords much strength for the task.

WEAKNESSES. From a general standpoint first, experimentalism seems to be weak, because it does not provide the stability that many people seem to need; critics say that its house is built on sand. The thought of no fixed aims or values in advance can be very disturbing to men who are fearful for the future of the world as we know it. Furthermore, opponents point out that life appears to include much that may never be solved by experimental method.

In education, many teachers and administrators ridicule the experimentalistic philosophy. They say that physical fitness is the unique contribution of physical education and that we should be about our business, because America is getting soft. In keeping with this belief, health education is important because it can contribute to total fitness, which is something else again. In this context, health education is an allied field. Recreation is an allied field also, it is said. It serves as a form of relaxation against life's many stresses—a catharsis which is necessary, but not an integral part of the curriculum. Critics point out further that experimentalism is not yet an entirely complete philosophy of education; some of the other philosophies of education seem to be more consistently inclusive. Many grant that the whole concept of progressivism did have much to offer at the beginning of the twentieth century, but it has now served its purpose and should be cut back from some of the excesses promoted by misguided professional educators. Opponents do admit that an exceptionally good teacher can use the experimental approach with certain types of youngsters, but, they say, it should be apparent that we don't have even a minority of teachers of this caliber available in the field.

In health, physical education, and recreation, the experimental approach, its opponents say, spreads us too thin. The idea is that it is difficult enough to achieve physical fitness, so why should we concern ourselves directly with such things as socializing activities, total fitness, the development of personality traits, and the evaluation of individuals according to the growth and development pattern of each unique individual. In our schools we have a prevailing essentialistic system of grades and academic credit; so, why fight it? Besides, classes are so large anyhow in the typical school situation; how can we hope to give the individual attention so necessary for the best type of experimentalistic education?

In the area of methodology, critics of experimentalism hit the hardest. They say that much educational material should be indoctrinated and that interest will come later. Children and youth need a strong hand today; there would be much less juvenile delinquency if this were the case. Why ask the child to evaluate his own educational experience? This is apt to bring nothing but pooled ignorance. This same type of reasoning applies to theory of administration at all levels; someone has to call the shot. Committees take too much time and never really accomplish anything. Experimental teaching by progressivists of the twentieth century has brought about a general weakening of the moral fiber of American youth. As a result, children are weaker, less able to read, write, and speak adequately and accurately, and juvenile delinquency rates have never been higher. Critics say that these are the weaknesses of experimentalism in action.

PART FOUR

Realism

CHAPTER EIGHT

Realism in Philosophy and Education

The second of the three leading philosophical tendencies of the twentieth century is called *realism*. In this chapter we will consider realism first as a philosophy and subsequently in regard to its implications for education. There may be some question in the reader's mind as to the advisability of introducing realism prior to idealism, since it does represent a viewpoint distinctly in opposition to the metaphysical beliefs of the idealist—not to mention the still greater difference between the two from the standpoint of epistemology (theory of knowledge). Furthermore, idealism as a distinctive philosophy definitely precedes realism historically, which has gathered great strength as a school of thought in the twentieth century. The justification for this order of arrangement, therefore, is that realism has a number of similarities to experimentalism in regard to the basic categories under consideration, and especially as to the involvement of the scientific method as the major means whereby the problems of education may be solved.

It was pointed out earlier that naïve naturalism undergirds much of the twentieth-century positions of realism and experimentalism.[1] Naturalistic belief holds that nature is reliable and dependable. Experimentalism stresses the importance of experience as the only means of discovering whether something is worthwhile. Realism, generally speaking, is the philosophical approach which accepts the world at face value.

---

[1] See Chapter 4, p. 46.

From the viewpoint of man, the world *is* exactly as he experiences it. It is as it seems to be, and our experiencing it changes it not one whit.

In this chapter the metaphysics, epistemology, logic, and axiology of realism will be presented in order, following the previously established pattern. Then, in the second half of the chapter, the three recurring educational problems chosen for consideration will be viewed in the light of the philosophy of realism.

Metaphysics

As we have indicated, the world is just what it seems to be to the realist. As Wild expresses it, "the world exists in itself, apart from our desires and knowledges." [2] In his essay *Whitehead's Philosophy of Organism,* Feibleman states that Whitehead has seen "that realism in philosophy is demanded by the development of modern physics, particularly by the theory of relativity." [3] "Whitehead argues that there is only one reality; what appears, whatever is given in perception, is real." [4] Here we find Whitehead placing great emphasis on ontology (explanation of ultimate nature of being or existence) rather than continuing the stress on epistemology (theory of knowledge acquisition) which had actually taken philosophy far out on a limb in the late nineteenth and early twentieth centuries.

A PATTERN MAY BE DISCERNED.   Actually, it is extremely difficult to explain the metaphysical beliefs of realists, because there is such extreme variance. Wild gives some help at this point, which is described as follows:

The Metaphysical Thesis. The universe is made up of real, substantial entities, existing in themselves and ordered to one another by extramental relations. These entities and relations really exist whether they are known or not. To be is not the same as to be known. We ourselves and the other entities around us actually exist, independent of our opinions and desires. This may be called the thesis of independence. [5]

Butler explains that it may be possible to discern some pattern in the metaphysical beliefs of the varieties of realists despite the fact that they vary all the way from atheism to a distinctly theistic position. To do this, he views their beliefs in relation to pluralism, determinism, mind, the world, and God. [6]

---

[2] John Wild, "Education and Human Society: A Realistic View," in *Modern Philosophies and Education,* ed. N. B. Henry (Chicago: University of Chicago Press, 1955), p. 17.

[3] James Feibleman, *The Revival of Realism* (Chapel Hill, N.C.: The University of North Carolina Press, 1946), p. 46.

[4] *Ibid.,* p. 48.

[5] Wild, *Modern Philosophies and Education,* p. 17.

[6] J. Donald Butler, *Four Philosophies,* rev. ed. (New York: Harper & Row, Publishers, Inc., 1957), pp. 320-331.

ALL DO NOT AGREE ON BASIC UNITY. If we were to ask realists what their position is in regard to the unity of the universe, we would find that many of them cannot agree that there is a *basic* unity present. They hold dual or pluralistic positions—that is, a nonunified cosmos with two or more substances or processes at work. A particular dualist might argue that good and evil represent a basic conflict in the world.

A WORLD OF CAUSE AND EFFECT. Generally speaking, realists would adhere to a form of determinism rather than any postulation about an open-ended world in which anything could happen. They have a healthy respect for science and the exactness which it appears to bespeak. The implication is, of course, that things don't just happen; they happen because many interrelated forces make them occur in a particular way. Man lives within this world of cause and effect, and he simply cannot make things happen independent of it.

MIND HAS BODILY EXISTENCE. The realist's attitude toward mind is that an individual's mental life has bodily existence as its basis. This implies that there is an extremely close relationship between mind and body. Other realists would carry this concept still further and explain that mind is a basic function of the organism which serves as the means of relating the individual to his environment. Others would say that man's mind consists of those cerebral processes that take place in a highly developed animal that has increased its ability to cope with its environment greatly in the past 300,000 or 400,000 years. A less widely held belief sees mind as something new and unique in man's evolutionary development—something that conscious man uses to relate meaningfully to his environment, but which somehow appears to be above and beyond the physical organism.

AN ORDERLY WORLD, BUT . . . In keeping with the metaphysics of this approach, man lives in a world which is regular and orderly—one that is governed by the laws of physics. This, as you will recall, is quite similar to the belief of most naturalists. The one difficulty at this point is that many physicists now seem to view their field of endeavor as a descriptive science—in other words, they describe what they find in outer space; however, there may not be only *one* set of physical laws throughout the universe, whatever the term *universe* may mean. This concept may well imply the presence of a multiverse.

VARIETY OF BELIEFS ABOUT GOD. Perhaps the most difficult aspect of the metaphysics of realism to comprehend is the great variety of beliefs present in relation to the problem of God. There is a variance from the one extreme (atheism) to the other (spiritual pantheism). Atheists see the world as being completely naturalistic or mechanistic. Pantheists believe that everything in the universe is part of the essential nature of God. Polytheistic believers see more than one force or power at work in the world and postulate the possibility of a limited God, while a few others can conceive that that God is developing or emerging just as the world appears to be emerging. Spiritual pantheism is that belief which ascribes purpose to a world which is part of God's essential nature.

Epistemology

TWO MAJOR EPISTEMOLOGICAL THEORIES. Undoubtedly the most distinctive phase of realism is its theories about how knowledge is acquired by man. As Broudy expresses it: ". . . the aim of knowledge is to bring into awareness the object as it *really* is." [7] Similarly, Wild states that the thesis of direct realism is "to know something is to become *relationally* identified with an existent entity as it is." [8] These men are both stating one of the two major epistemological theories of realism—the theory called *epistemological monism* by Butler. [9] These men, Broudy and Wild, believe that objects of the world outside man are "presented" directly into man's consciousness. When man perceives an object, he is seeing exactly what is out there. In an attempt to make this theory understandable to his readers, Butler uses an analogy from the area of physical education—a tennis racket. He describes the various qualities of a racket that might be your own and explains how certain of your senses are involved in making an analysis of it and its possible effectiveness in helping you to hit a ball back over a net to an opponent. The crux of his argument is that you are able to assess a racket made of physical materials correctly through your "awareness" or "consciousness." [10]

Now to look at the other side of the coin, we must consider *epistemological dualism,* which states that man's consciousness and the *actual* tennis racket perceived never intersect; thus, when we look at an object there are really two objects. According to this belief, the object is represented in consciousness, not presented. It seems, therefore, that the neorealists believe that the mind is more than part of the brain and the nervous system and reaches out to establish a relationship with the world that it is interpreting to the human organism, while to the epistemological dualists just described the direct connection is completely inseparable.

Logic

Generally speaking, logic is the systematic study of certain general principles upon which correct thinking is based. It treats propositions

[7] Harry S. Broudy, *Building a Philosophy of Education,* 2nd ed. (Englewood Cliffs, N.J.: Prentice-Hall, Inc., 1961), p. 106.
[8] Wild, *Modern Philosophies and Education,* p. 18.
[9] Butler, *Four Philosophies,* pp. 316-318.
[10] *Ibid.*

and the subsequent interrelations which may be inferred from these statements. Aristotle derived the form known as the syllogism, which is a formalized scheme of deductive reasoning. It may be described as a means of demonstrating an argument that is based on a major premise and a minor one. If the statements are true, the conclusion which follows these statements would also be necessarily true. The most famous example of a syllogism is: "All men are mortal; Socrates is a man; therefore, Socrates is mortal." [11]

FORMAL LOGIC MUST BE EXTENDED. Realists would concur that formal logic must be extended to be adequate in today's scientific world. Feibleman points out that logic is not threatened by science and experimentation; they actually go hand in hand.[12] He explains that experiment and logic are both vital parts of scientific method; scientific investigation could never ignore the laws of logic if it is hoped that results will have any true meaning. Conversely, various theories postulated must stand the rigid test of scientific investigation. The important thing is that science through this endless experimentation into the nature of the world gives us the factual bases for major premises. We must use these premises in the various syllogistic patterns through which man's ideas can be related accurately to one another.

STEPS IN SCIENTIFIC METHOD. Typically, scientific method gives valid results through a series of steps as follows:

1. Problem definition
2. Observation of all factors bearing on problem at hand
3. Determination of hypothesis
4. Evaluation of hypothesis by controlled experiment

Feibleman reduces scientific method to the following two main steps: (1) examination of conditions existing in order to form inductively an underlying hypothesis, and subsequent testing of hypothesis to see if it may be allowed or rejected; and (2) reconciliation of this hypothesis with knowledge "already in" to determine if the hypothesis is consistent with the established body of knowledge in the particular branch of science.[13] Science, of course, is searching continually for laws which are wider and more inclusive. We can see that Feibleman's "reduction" is actually an extension of the four steps listed under scientific method above. His explanation shows how induction, experimentation, and deduction are all part of true scientific method.

IMPROVED LOGIC HAS GREAT POTENTIAL. Realists, therefore, would concur in the belief that formal logic is basic to philosophy. This formal

---

[11] Carter V. Good, *Dictionary of Education* (New York: McGraw-Hill Book Company, Inc., 1945), p. 404.

[12] Feibleman, *The Revival of Realism*, pp. 253-254. See chap. 11 on Idealism for a detailed explanation of formal logic.

[13] *Ibid.*, pp. 252-253.

logic has been expanded tremendously in the past century through the efforts of a number of philosophers, many of whom are classified as realists. They realized that the improved logic contained great potential as a scientific instrument.[14] Such a logic involves a diligent search to discover standards or principles of reasoning that will apply to as many of life's activities as possible.[15]

Axiology

There appear to be two general theories in the ethical system of realists as follows: (1) when man experiences something that is valuable, he knows it although he can't necessarily define it; and (2) rational, experiencing humans develop attitudes on which value is dependent.[16] Perry, a foremost American realist of the twentieth century, subscribes to the latter of these two theories. Writing on the subject of value, a favorite subject with him, Perry states his belief that:

A philosophy of life must always contain two principal components, a theory concerning the nature of goodness or value, and a theory concerning the conditions and prospect of its realization. The former is the central topic of ethics, and the second is the central topic of a philosophy of religion.[17]

Despite this emphasis on a belief that value, generally speaking, stems from a relation to interest and is not independent of the consciousness of man, Perry concurs that values are "absolute in the sense that they are independent of opinion." [18]

MORAL LAW OR NATURAL LAW.   Realists believe generally in what is called *moral law* or *natural law*. This law, upon careful inspection, may be discovered in the very nature of the world. Obedience to it is required for the completion of human nature, as we know it. St. Thomas Aquinas described *eternal law,* which becomes *natural law* to rational man.[19] Wild states that it is "a universal pattern of action applicable to all men everywhere." [20]

Ethically, the realist would be inclined to concur with John Stuart Mill and his belief that the greatest happiness to the greatest number

---

[14] Morris R. Cohen, *Logic* (New York: Holt, Rinehart and Winston, Inc., 1944), pp. ix-xi.

[15] Max Black, *Critical Thinking*, 2nd ed. (Englewood Cliffs, N.J.: Prentice-Hall, Inc., 1952), pp. 3-10.

[16] Butler, *Four Philosophies*, pp. 334-335.

[17] Ralph B. Perry, *Present Philosophical Tendencies* (New York: George Braziller, Inc., 1955), p. 331.

[18] *Ibid.,* p. 335.

[19] Anton C. Pegis, ed., *Basic Writings of Saint Thomas Aquinas* (New York: Random House, Inc., 1945), Vol. I, 750.

[20] John Wild, *Plato's Modern Enemies and the Theory of Natural Law* (Chicago: University of Chicago Press, 1953), p. 65.

is a most desirable ethic in a world such as ours. Wild refers to *The Ethical Thesis* of realism which follows directly from the knowledge that it is possible to acquire of man's human nature.[21] Man possesses higher tendencies or traits than subhuman animals whose life is guided by many inflexible instincts. Because of the flexibility of his tendencies and the knowledge which he has gained through the power of cognition that he has developed, it is possible for man to set up a pattern of living for himself. As mentioned previously, this "pattern of action" is both individual and social. Down through the centuries it has become a moral law or natural law which he must use as a helpful and reliable guide. Common sense, a realistic aid, must be extended and improved upon through the means of philosophy as a civilization develops.[22] The end result is a "moral imperative" that can work for man in approximately the same way as the idealistic "categorical imperative" of Kant.

Aesthetically, the realist is faced with the problem of whether his own individual preferences are definite and final. If he rejects modern art by saying, "I don't like that 'stuff' and that's that," it is quite possible that he simply doesn't comprehend it. According to Roy Wood Sellars, for example, there is much beauty in the world that is good. If man would improve and refine his power to discern keenly, he would appreciate the worthwhileness of these qualities in a thing which can afford pleasure to his senses.[23] It is quite possible, of course, that the most desirable state to achieve is a mingling of apprehension and physical sensation. Man's creative and aesthetic interests range through all aspects of his culture. He has communicative recreational interests, social recreational interests, learning recreational interests, and physical recreational interests, as well as aesthetic and creative recreational interests. Whether he is watching or actively taking part, there is the possibility of objectification of a large variety of emotions in these ventures.

Religiously, we find diverse possibilities within realism for value achievement in life depending on whether or not the individual realist believes in a Divine Being. For believers, faith and hope would be religious values; for the agnostic or atheist, they would obviously hold no value. Wild says that man may violate the moral law if he so desires; there is no determinism in that sense. Man must understand, however, that he really doesn't have complete freedom of choice if he wants to lead a good life. This is true, because laws beyond our control determine

---

[21] Wild, *Modern Philosophies and Education*, pp. 18-20.

[22] John Wild, ed., *The Return to Reason* (Chicago: Henry Regnery Company, 1953), pp. 357-363.

[23] Roy W. Sellars, *The Philosophy of Physical Realism* (New York: The Macmillan Company, 1932), pp. 451-452.

thoughts and action.[24] Broudy says, ". . . to be morally right, therefore, an act must be intended to fill not any claim, but a claim to some good in life." [25] Religious phenomena are strange things (a great philosopher like Santayana found beauty in the ceremony of the Roman Catholic Church, but he did not believe that the dogma was true and would deny the possibility of such phenomena[26]) and appear to occur universally "in the consciousness which individuals have of an intercourse between themselves and higher powers with which they feel themselves related." [27] It would seem to be fair to say that realism generally takes a middle position (if we may exclude the realism of the Roman Catholic Church for the moment). Perry sums up as follows:

There is nothing dispiriting in realism. It involves the acceptance of the given situation as it is, with no attempt to think or imagine it already good. But it involves no less the conception of the reality and power of life. It is opposed equally to an idealistic anticipation of the victory of spirit, and to a naturalistic confession of the impotence of spirit. In this sense all bold and forward living is realistic. It involves a sense for things as they are, an ideal of things as they should be, and a determination that, through enlightened action, things shall in time come to be what they should be.[28]

Socially, the realist believes that the physical universe is more basic to life and thought than is society. In this regard there is considerable agreement with the position of the naturalist, for whom the physical world holds great importance also. Realists are more concerned with the individual and his relationship to the universe than they are with society as a primary unit. To clarify this further, society and the social process depend on the aforementioned two primary units (the individual and the universe). Butler offers the following realistic formula of social value as being fairly standard:

Social value will result when it is determined what the desired social values are, when real incentives are recognized which will make people act in the direction of these values, and when mechanics of social organization are used which are real—real because they are based on real incentives.[29]

The entire position might be summarized by saying that the world is composed of actual, "substantial entities" related to each other by certain physical laws. Through a process of cognition, it is possible for man to know some of these entities and their relationships directly.

---

[24] Wild, *Modern Philosophies and Education,* p. 23.

[25] Broudy, *Building a Philosophy of Education,* p. 236.

[26] Will Durant, *The Story of Philosophy,* new rev. ed. (New York: Garden City Books, 1938), pp. 543-544.

[27] William James, *Varieties of Religious Experience* (New York: Longmans, Green & Co., Inc., 1929), p. 465.

[28] Perry, *Present Philosophical Tendencies,* p. 347.

[29] Butler, *Four Philosophies,* p. 342.

Knowledge thus gained provides man with natural or moral law that includes set principles to guide all individual and social action. Man's common sense is a great help in the determination of conduct.

Society, School, and the Individual

There is no question that the philosophy of realism and its subsequent implications for education are receiving increased consideration in the second half of the twentieth century. This has been called an *era of new conservatism.* The world situation has forced many people to turn from idealistic and pragmatic considerations and to take a hard look at many of the cold realities facing us. We are told that it is foolish and un-realistic to look at the world any other way. The titanic "cold war" struggle between democracy and communism has jarred the Western world, and the resultant renewal of certain emphases in education has been the work of both conscious and unconscious essentialism. The essentialist is one who believes that there is an urgent need to prescribe a large part of the curriculum for all children in our schools. These people are most concerned with transmission of the cultural heritage— certain essentials that the educated individual must master before he can take his rightful place in society. Such words as *discipline, moral stamina, authority* and *past experience* loom large in the educational system in which essentialism prevails.

COMENIUS ON EDUCATION. Writing in the seventeenth century, John Amos Comenius explained that man needs the manifold influences of society and culture to achieve all his innate potentialities.[30] Thus, the school is the place where a great deal of man's formation takes place.

Wild reinforces this position through a comparison of human society and animal communities. He explains that there are two fundamental differences: (1) man as an infant does not possess the same fixed instinct patterns of animals, and this flexibility during childhood must be directed into certain patterns by his parents and society; and (2) man has been favored with a "cognitive capacity" of great power that must be "properly exercised" to insure his development and the perpetuation of society.[31]

REALISM HAS A PLACE IN A DEMOCRACY. There are some who say that an essentialistic pattern of education is inconsistent with the basic tenets of a democratic country. Breed takes exception to such a position which implies that experimentalism is the only approach possible in our democracy. He points out that the doctrine of liberty with its re-

---

[30] John Amos Comenius, *The Great Didactic,* ed. and trans. M. W. Keatinge (London: A. & C. Black, Ltd., 1907), Part II, p. 228.

[31] Wild, *Modern Philosophies and Education,* pp. 24-25.

spect for individuality is not inconsistent with realism. He insists, however, that the school should not be "child-circumscribed." "If growth receives its direction from social as well as from individual demands," Breed finds the "individual-growth objective" quite acceptable to the modern realist.[32]

EDUCATION'S PRIMARY RESPONSIBILITY. All realists are not as compromising as Breed appears to be, as may be seen from a statement by Kandel when he says that the primary responsibility of education is to "reproduce the type, to transmit the social heritage, and to adjust the individual to the society." [33]

GOVERNMENT MUST CONTROL FORMAL EDUCATION. Writing fifteen years later, Broudy subscribes to a similar theory when he points out that all types of government have varying amounts of control over education. Whatever type of government we may have, it must control formal education, since education is a social institution that affects all other institutions in the society.[34]

THE CATHOLIC CHURCH'S PRIMARY ROLE. The position of the Catholic realists must be clarified in this connection also. They believe that the Catholic Church has a primary role in the education of children and young people. Redden and Ryan make it absolutely clear that the state is not the only agency which must be considered. Their position asserts that human control *cannot* be the only jurisdictional power in such a basic responsibility.[35] Obviously, this stand is entirely consistent with the underlying philosophical position of Roman Catholics.

If these various statements of position seem confusing and occasionally inconsistent with each other, we must remember that there was extreme variance in the metaphysical and epistemological divisions of the realistic philosophy.[36] Brubacher sheds light also by explaining what he considers to be the four primary philosophical positions in educational philosophy under essentialism: (1) idealism; (2) naturalistic realism; (3) rational humanism; and (4) Catholic supernaturalism.[37] *He points out that the transition from progressivism to essentialism is not necessarily an abrupt one.* The entire group is deemed essentialistic, however, because it is "fully aware of the relentless pressure with which society enforces the customs which are basic or essential for maintaining its unique char-

[32] Frederick S. Breed, "Education and the Realistic Outlook," in *Philosophies of Education, Forty-First Yearbook* of the National Society for the Study of Education (Chicago: University of Chicago Press, 1942) , Part I, p. 131.
[33] Isaac L. Kandel, *Conflicting Theories of Education* (New York: The Macmillan Company, 1939), p. 32.
[34] Broudy, *Building a Philosophy of Education,* pp. 97-98.
[35] Butler, *Four Philosophies,* pp. 346-347.
[36] Cf., pp. 114-116.
[37] John S. Brubacher, *Modern Philosophies of Education,* 2nd ed. (New York: McGraw-Hill Book Company, Inc., 1950), pp. 307-324.

acter." [38] Idealism is the only one of the four positions that will not be included in the discussion at this time.

Educational Aims and Objectives

The question of educational aims and objectives is fairly straightforward for the realist, although we do find certain variations depending on which type of educational realism is being considered. One definition of educational realism offered by Good is "a philosophy holding that the aim of education is the acquisition of verified knowledge of the environment and adjustment to the environment; recognizes the value of content as well as of the activities involved in learning, and takes into account the external determinants of human behavior; advocates freedom of the individual limited by consideration of the rights and welfare of others." [39] Such a definition doesn't hold much meaning until we examine some of the underlying premises.

THE ROLE OF THE SCHOOL. Broudy, who seems to begin from the philosophical position of the rational humanist while concluding in a fairly strong naturalistic tone, deplores the fact that many educational debates are meaningless, since the protagonists almost always argue from a different position as to what constitutes the good life. In addition, the problem of semantics makes it difficult for people to communicate effectively with each other. [40] He criticizes experimentalism by stating that *real* needs are probably much more important than *felt* needs. The fundamental problem is how to make life good for man. This means that the role of the school is to "transcribe the good life, the good individual, and the good society into learnings that presumably will contribute to their production." [41]

EDUCATION SHOULD BE USEFUL. Whitehead, a foremost philosopher of realism, delivered a series of essays on the subject of education between 1912 and 1928. These essays were subsequently published in one volume. [42] He concerned himself generally with education on its intellectual side. The central theme of his realistic position is expressed by Whitehead as follows: "The students are alive, and the purpose of education is to stimulate and guide their self-development. It follows as a corollary from this premise, that the teachers also should be alive with living thoughts. The whole book is a protest against dead knowledge, that is to say, against inert ideas." [43] Whitehead's stand for an education that

---

[38] *Ibid.,* p. 309.

[39] Good, *Dictionary of Education,* p. 332.

[40] Broudy, *Building a Philosophy of Education,* pp. 21-26.

[41] *Ibid.*

[42] Alfred N. Whitehead, *The Aims of Education,* 10th print. (New York: The Macmillan Company, 1929).

[43] *Ibid.,* Preface.

is useful is definite and unequivocal. He wants a reasonable number of subjects taught, and he feels they should be taught thoroughly. "Education is the acquisition of the art of the utilization of knowledge," he says, and "this is an art very difficult to impart." [44] Furthermore, Whitehead recommends elimination of "the fatal disconnection of subjects which kills the vitality of our modern curriculum. There is only one subject-matter for education, and that is Life in all its manifestations." [45]

BREED'S REALISTIC STAND. Writing in the early 1940's, Frederick S. Breed, a proponent of realism in educational philosophy, described the revival of this approach in the twentieth century. He told how, in his opinion, pragmatism "had made a successful attack on the stronghold of absolute idealism and, following a period of destructive criticism, had undertaken to become constructive in its own right." [46] This was the point where the pragmatists ran into difficulty, because many philosophers could not accept the metaphysical implications of this position. Breed praised Whitehead for "adopting much that is precious in pragmatism while avoiding its anti-intellectualism and, withal, remaining fundamentally realistic." [47]

THE TRANSMISSION OF KNOWLEDGE. Certainly one of the finest statements of the aims and objectives of the philosophy of realism for education has been made by Wild writing for the National Society for the Study of Education.[48] He explains that since the time of Plato, realists have understood that education is fundamental to life and that it is necessary to analyze human society critically for direction. It is so difficult to achieve knowledge, and many errors are made along the way. When man does achieve some knowledge, it is anything but a simple matter to hand it down to the next generation. The shortness of life for any one individual increases this difficulty. So, as Wild sees it, the primary task of education is to transmit knowledge, without which civilization cannot continue to flourish.

FORMAL EDUCATION HAS PERSISTENT DEFECTS. Because of man's social nature, education has always been accomplished through informal methods. As societies have developed, formal education has assumed a greater role in the system. Unfortunately, this process seems to be marked by certain persistent defects. In the first place, the process of imitation, although eminently practical, tends to become blind routine unless we strive constantly for theoretical justification for any such action pattern. This leads to an ever-present defect of inflexibility in our customs as

---

[44] *Ibid.,* p. 16.
[45] *Ibid.,* p. 18.
[46] Breed, *Forty-first Yearbook,* Part I, pp. 91-92.
[47] *Ibid.*
[48] Wild, *Modern Philosophies and Education.*

well as in our educational process. There is a tendency further for a type of disunity to set in. Wild explains that "another defect is the incoherence and disorder of many blind routines devised to meet isolated needs and interests. An *ad hoc* unity may be achieved by mythical construction. But this is in constant danger of being overthrown by new and unwelcome fact. Genuine, stable integration of the whole culture can be attained only by universal principles grounded on observation." [49]

NATURALISTIC REALISM. Brubacher, in his excellent chapter called *Systematic Philosophies of Education,* summarizes the position of the naturalistic realist in essentialism.[50] He explains how this group takes an uncompromising position in regard to education—that is, man must use his mind ("a naturalized product of nature") to survive in a universe governed by inexorable law. The experimentalist theory of education, which believes that reconstruction of the surrounding universe is possible, is replaced by a theory which states that the aim of education is to conform to the world as it exists. Whatever man has discovered to be true because it conforms to reality must be handed down to future generations as the social or cultural tradition.

BROUDY'S PROBLEM—CENTERED CURRICULUM. Now that we have considered the aim of education for the naturalistic realist generally, let us turn to a discussion of the curriculum more specifically. Once again, Broudy comes to our assistance with his view of the curriculum as habits and skills and content. He summarily rejects the subject-centered curriculum of the more traditional school.[51] He discredits it because it cannot solve the problem of motivation, it cannot guarantee that information will be retained, and it most certainly cannot develop a desirable type of thinking. He states:

Our own view is that the objectives of the curriculum are habits or tendencies to acquire, use, and enjoy truth. In this we agree with the objectives of the problem-centered curriculum. But it is suggested that the way to form these habits is by mastery of organized subject matter. Once we realize what it means to master such subject matter, we shall be disabused of the notion that it is merely the memorization of facts.[52]

Habits, therefore, go hand in hand with content.

"Organized subject matter, group problems, and personal problems provide the content." [53] Subject matter includes the humanities, the social sciences, and the natural sciences. The humanities are "whatever concerns man as distinct from physical nature, especially as expressed

---

[49] *Ibid.,* pp. 24-27.
[50] Brubacher, *Modern Philosophies of Education,* chap. xiv, pp. 296-325.
[51] Broudy, *Building a Philosophy of Education,* chap. xii, pp. 283-310.
[52] Broudy, *Building a Philosophy of Education,* 1st ed., p. 181.
[53] *Ibid.*

most adequately in the great or classic achievements of humanity in literature and art." [54] Social science is "the branch of knowledge that deals with human society or its characteristic elements, as family, state, or race, and with the relations and institutions involved in man's existence and well-being as a member of an organized community." [55] Natural science is typically subdivided into physical science and biological science. Physical science is "the science that deals with matter and its properties except as these are concerned with life processes; represented by physics, chemistry, astronomy, geology, meteorology, and other specialized branches closely related to these." [56] Biological science is "the science of life processes and of living things and their relation to factors in their physical environment; represented by botany, physiology, bacteriology, zoology, and ecology." [57]

As the amount of material available in these disciplines increases, it obviously becomes a physical impossibility to teach it all to students. Broudy suggests that "each subject be reduced to its basic concepts, facts, principles, and modes of investigation. These minimum essentials should then be taught for as thorough mastery as the maturity and competence of the pupil will permit." [58] He stresses further the necessity for problems courses involving analysis of the culture as well as for a continuing guidance program.

Moving now slightly to the right of the essentialistic position of naturalistic realism, the educational philosophy of rational humanism will be considered briefly. This group takes its strength from Aristotle's *philosophia perennis* that was subsequently altered somewhat by St. Thomas Aquinas because of the implications of Christianity for education. This latter position will be described briefly also under the heading of Catholic supernaturalism.

RATIONAL HUMANISM. The rational humanist believes that man has a unique faculty of reason which is part of the very fiber of human nature. From this position we learn that the main aim of education should be identical for all men anywhere anytime. Educators must help man to develop his intellect to its highest potentiality; they have no choice in this regard whatsoever. If a particular subject matter demands a great amount of reasoning before mastery is achieved, it would, of course, rank high in the scale of educational value. Because the curriculum, of necessity, must include all the truth that has been uncovered by man, the student has relatively less chance for election in his choice of subject

---

[54] Good, *Dictionary of Education,* p. 207.

[55] *Ibid.,* p. 361.

[56] *Ibid.*

[57] *Ibid.,* p. 360.

[58] Broudy, *Building a Philosophy of Education,* 1st ed., p. 208.

matter along the way. As Adler, one of the principal exponents of this position, states:

Education is the process by which those powers (abilities, capacities) of men that are susceptible to habituation, are perfected by *good* habits, through means artistically contrived, and employed by any man to help another or himself achieve the end in view (i.e., good habits). In so far as this definition that education should be the same for all men (i.e., should aim at the same end), its truth is proved by the establishment of the proposition that the ends of education are absolute and universal.[59]

Through a series of syllogisms, he explains a number of the propositions which become self-evident to educators who subscribe to this educational philosophy, but he does not list the specific objectives that result from the belief that the first principles of education are absolute and universal. Brubacher clarifies this position by stating that "the subjects with the greatest rational content, of course, are the liberal arts, and among the liberal arts, the humanities. These are best exemplified in the 'Great Books' of our culture." [60] Education for freedom is achieved by conformity to truth—the essential nature of the universe which man must uncover through his reasoning power.

EDUCATIONAL OBJECTIVES IN RUSSIA. In passing, mention should perhaps be made of the materialistic realism which dominates Soviet educational thought. This is a metaphysical position in which only matter in the universe is real. It is considered by many to be an atheistic approach, because the universe is conceived as purposeless. Collective life is very important in the U.S.S.R., and there appears to be considerably less emphasis on the worth of the individual. Butler tells us that three extremely important educational objectives of the Russians are the development of devotion to the Party, great respect for labor, and dedication to strong personal discipline.[61]

CATHOLIC REALISM (SUPERNATURALISM). Ignoring the momentary digression to consider Russia's materialistic realism, which is probably closer to the naturalistic realist position, the next movement to the right on the educational spectrum takes us to the position of the Catholic realist (supernaturalist). Here we should keep in mind Brubacher's comment that "the Catholic supernaturalists agree with the rational humanists as far as they go but declare that they do not go far enough." [62]

ELEMENTARY AND SECONDARY SCHOOLS. For Catholic realists the illumination of revelation and theology are vital considerations when the

---

[59] Mortimer J. Adler, "In Defense of the Philosophy of Education," in *Philosophies of Education, Forty-first Yearbook* of the National Society for the Study of Education (Chicago: University of Chicago Press, 1942), Part I, p. 246.

[60] Brubacher, *Modern Philosophies of Education,* p. 319.

[61] Butler, *Four Philosophies,* pp. 364-366.

[62] Brubacher, *Modern Philosophies of Education,* p. 319.

school curriculum is considered. The explicit theological implications are based on the belief that the good life emanates from cooperation with God's grace. Christ's example and teaching offer us a pattern to use as a guide. In speaking of the function of the elementary school, McGucken explains that:

> The elementary school aims to impart those knowledges and skills, habits and appreciative attitudes that will fit the child to be an intelligent practical Catholic, a good citizen, a good member of society, including the various groups to which he belongs, family, working group, neighborhood, and the like.[63]

The secondary school as well "must find its objectives within the frame of reference that is common to all Catholic institutions—the supernatural." [64] Furthermore, "for the Catholic secondary school, development of the Christian virtues is obviously of greater worth than learning or anything else." [65] Christian citizenship, Christian character, and supernatural virtues are, of course, the concern of the home as well. "The purpose then of the Catholic high school, as I understand it, is to develop Catholic boys and girls along intellectual lines, to turn out intelligent Catholic citizens with an appreciative knowledge of their heritage as American citizens and an appreciative knowledge of their Catholic heritage." [66]

From this statement of Father McGucken, it seems reasonable to draw certain conclusions. In the first place, if there are unchanging educational objectives, man must concern himself on earth with the means necessary to achieve ultimate union with God. This view of education as preparation means that the child must be prepared for an eventual life of reason, and, obviously, the three R's are basic along with science, literature, geography, history, and perhaps a foreign language. As has been mentioned above, character training is tremendously important at this stage. At the secondary level, every young person should have a greater or lesser amount of general education and preparation for life through the learning of a trade if he is not going on to university. Foreign languages, including Greek and Latin, and such subjects as mathematics, grammar, rhetoric, and logic are stressed because they help man to reason. Of course, the "Great Books" cannot be overlooked. It must be pointed out, however, that there are varieties of opinion among those who subscribe to the essentialistic position of Catholic supernaturalism in education.

---

[63] William McGucken, "The Philosophy of Catholic Education," in *Philosophy of Education, Forty-first Yearbook* of the National Society for the Study of Education (Chicago: University of Chicago Press, 1942), Part I, p. 267.

[64] *Ibid.*

[65] William J. McGucken, "Intelligence and Character," *The National Catholic Educational Association Bulletin,* XXXVI (May 1940), 10-12.

[66] *Ibid.*

The Process of Education

Now that we have given consideration to the aims and objectives of the various branches of realism, we are faced with the questions relating to the actual educational process. What kind of activities do students engage in according to these beliefs (and in what way) in order that the end result will be satisfactory to those concerned?

BROUDY'S REJECTION OF OTHER APPROACHES. Immediately we discover that Broudy does not recommend a continuation of the traditional subject-matter approach, and, of course, we could not expect him to accept wholeheartedly the type of activity curriculum that developed as a result of John Dewey's efforts. In the first place, he criticizes the lack of motivation, the poor retention, the failure to develop reasoning power, and the compartmentalization of subject matter apparent in the traditional approach to learning.[67] On the other hand, problem solving in the school community based on the interests of the pupils, which results in a *doing* continuously as the student *grows,* does not seem to meet with his unqualified approval either. In this latter instance, despite the guidance of the teacher, he cannot agree that immature pupils have anything but immature interests. He explains further that all problems that they face do not necessarily require the application of scientific method—just plain thought about a difficulty can take place which does not even require the presence of a school. So, while the subject-matter curriculum can and does founder in search of the realization of its objectives, the activity curriculum based on problem solving has not come up with a scheme that will guarantee mastery of the necessary material often called the *cultural heritage.* He does agree that it often is capable of bringing about the realization of certain desirable attitudes on the part of the students toward community life.

A THIRD ALTERNATIVE. In the place of these two tried and unproven educational processes, he suggests a third alternative. The curriculum, Broudy believes, should provide for the development of certain habits and skills: (1) those involved with acquiring knowledge; (2) those involved with using knowledge from the standpoint of practical analysis for problem solution as well as for comprehension of life's broader issues; and (3) those involved with the realization of enjoyment in life through the many values that life has to offer to those individuals who have the capacity and ability to take advantage of these opportunities.[68] For this type of educational development, Broudy recommends four kinds of educational activity as follows:

---

[67] Broudy, *Building a Philosophy of Education,* 2nd ed., pp. 285-287.
[68] Broudy, *Building a Philosophy of Education,* 1st ed., p. 157.

1. Systematic study of organized subject matter with emphasis on the skills of learning.

2. Problems courses attached to each major area of knowledge with emphasis on *understanding* actual problematic situations.

3. Guidance programs in which the individual confronts himself with his own problematic situations and tries to solve them in the light of the best knowledge available.

4. Aesthetic creativity as a means of developing and testing one's ability to enjoy such values. The other value areas are explored in the problems courses and in the guidance program.[69]

This third alternative suggested by Broudy seems to be almost identical to that suggested earlier by Breed, in which he recommends the need for the problem approach in educational method and states that it seems to be "psychologically and philosophically inescapable." Furthermore, Breed states:

Man proposes, but nature disposes. The child projects, but the teacher directs. This is the essence of the definition that teaching is the *guidance* of learning. The test of truth is conformity with something not of one's own creation, and the content objectives of a good curriculum are but selections of values thus attested.[70]

Social or cultural tradition, therefore, stands for external reality as best known to date. This, in essence then, is the educational process of the naturalistic realist. Here is an educational philosophy which has limited the system of nature as it has been uncovered by scientific research. It would seem to rely heavily on stimulus-response learning and encourages greatly the scientific measurement approach to education.

METHODOLOGY OF THE RATIONAL HUMANIST. The rational humanistic approach, based on Aristotle and his *philosophia perennis,* appears to be more traditionalistic or essentialistic than that described above. Here the concern is with the development of the intellect—the greater the amount of reasoning required to learn a subject, the more important is that subject in the curriculum. Since the principal aim of education must be the same for all men at all times in all places, it is obvious that students should have only a slight amount of election in their program of studies. The rational humanist does, however, allow room for two orders of learning: (1) the logical (essential) order; and (2) an order where you start with the student's interest and then move back to the essential subject matter at the first opportunity. If education for freedom is achieved through conformity to truth, such freedom does not come early in the child's educational pattern. As Hansen states:

If the individual has his reason fully developed, through exhortation or logical processes, then he can be allowed a great deal of freedom. But since, according

---

[69] *Ibid.,* p. 158.
[70] Breed, *Forty-first Yearbook,* Part I, p. 126.

to this view, reason does not develop very well very early, the child of elementary or high school age probably should be kept under pretty tight rein.[71]

CATHOLIC REALISM. The educational process of Catholic realism or supernaturalism will seem quite similar to that of rational humanism, because it is built on the same foundation. Revelation and theology have, of course, added certain additional implications. For example, education is the process by which man seeks to link himself ultimately with his Creator. McGucken tells us that the Catholic as a Catholic is not concerned with curriculum and method.[72] Whatever may happen in school, his (the Catholic's) primary concern is that religious instruction be placed first (a seeming contradiction!). McGucken indicates that the Catholic supernaturalist may use drill, the project method, the problem method, the child's interest, and a variety of other teaching methods so long as:

Every acceptable method of learning must be based on the theory that all education is self-education. Consequently method, as distinct from techniques or mere tricks of the education profession, must have as its aim the teaching of the child to think for himself, to express adequately his own thoughts, and to appreciate in a humane way the true, the beautiful, and the good.[73]

PERSEVERANCE, INDOCTRINATION, AND AUTHORITY. Despite the above statement by McGucken, which certainly appears to have a progressive ring in spots, Brubacher has pointed out quite clearly that the Catholic supernaturalist believes fully that the curriculum ("essentials of the culture") takes precedence over interest. The student must persevere when interest lags, because he has a responsibility to learn. Interest will undoubtedly come later in many cases when the learner comes to realize the value of what is being taught. Thus, because the educational objectives are stable, it is quite legitimate for the teacher to indoctrinate a curriculum that is made up in advance of the learning activity itself.[74] Redden and Ryan concur fully at this point when they define the teacher as "one who has authority over others for the purpose of instructing them in knowledge, skills, attitudes, and ideals consonant with their true nature, ultimate end, and highest good." [75] In fact, as Butler points out, this authority which the teacher possesses comes from God Himself.[76]

THE DIRECT METHOD IS BEST. Further argument for the direct method

---

[71] Kenneth H. Hansen, *Philosophy for American Education* (Englewood Cliffs, N.J.: Prentice-Hall, Inc., 1960), p. 162.

[72] McGucken, *Forty-first Yearbook,* Part I, p. 286.

[73] *Ibid.*

[74] Brubacher, *Modern Philosophies of Education,* pp. 319-324.

[75] John D. Redden and Francis A. Ryan, *A Catholic Philosophy of Education* (Milwaukee: The Bruce Publishing Company, 1942), p. 339.

[76] Cf., Romans 13:1, *Four Philosophies,* p. 373. As quoted by Butler.

as opposed to the indirect or incidental method is given by Redden and Ryan when they point out that "the incidental technique or informal method favors the creation of a moral atmosphere or environment, designed to permeate imperceptibly, as it were, the teaching of all subjects." But as Catholic supernaturalists, they are far from satisfied with such teaching method when they point out, "in regard to the indirect method, the reader should note carefully the lack therein of a positive moral sanction and an authoritative procedure which serve to discipline the child and cause him to discipline himself." [77] Sister Raby asks an interesting question in this connection when she says, "Is there not a greater value to the child in sitting down and attacking the geography lesson which he does not want to study than in working on the airplane? This view proceeds from the principle that it is better to do what we do not want to do than what we do want to do." [78] She continues by pointing out that this is "truly Catholic" and it is "in some manner bound up with Christian asceticism."

Summary

From the standpoint of metaphysics, the realist believes that the world is real and is just what it seems to be. The substantial entities, of which the universe is composed, exist *whether they are known or not* by any creature within its boundaries. There does appear to be disagreement on whether a basic unity is present; some realists take a dualistic or pluralistic position concerning the nature of the universe.

Realists, generally speaking, accept a deterministic world in which things happen because many interrelated forces make them occur in a particular way; it is, therefore, a world of cause and effect. To some realists the mind is a basic function of the organism which serves as the means of relating the individual to his environment. Realists believe that man lives in a world which is orderly and regular.

When the problem of God is considered, there is a great deal of variance in the positions taken by realists—all the way from a belief in an atheistic, mechanistic world to one that is spiritually pantheistic or part of God's essential nature.

Epistemologically, neorealists believe that objects of the world outside man are presented directly into man's consciousness—a theory known as *epistemological monism*. When man perceives an object, they say, he is seeing exactly what is out there. Epistemological dualists, however, state that man's consciousness and the *actual* object perceived never intersect.

---

[77] Redden and Ryan, *A Catholic Philosophy of Education,* pp. 280-281.
[78] Sister Joseph Mary Raby, *A Critical Study of the New Education* (Washington, D.C.: The Catholic University of America Press, 1932), p. 89.

In this case the object is represented and not presented to the mind of man. In the former instance, the mind is more than part of the brain and nervous system, because it reaches out to establish a relationship with the outside world.

The logic of realism attempts to explain certain general principles upon which correct reasoning is based. Progressing from Aristotle's formalized scheme of deductive reasoning in which the syllogism is employed, realists now concur that formal logic must be extended to be adequate in today's scientific world. The claim is that logic goes hand in hand with experimental science. Science offers factual bases upon which major premises are built. Scientific method consists of: (1) problem definition; (2) observation of all factors bearing on the problem at hand; (3) determination of hypothesis; and (4) evaluation of hypothesis by controlled experiment. Realists, therefore, concur in the belief that formal logic is basic to philosophy.

Two general theories in the ethical system (axiology) of realists are: (1) when man experiences something that is valuable, he knows it although he can't necessarily define it; and (2) rational, experiencing humans develop attitudes on which value is dependent. Realists believe generally in what is called *moral law* or *natural law,* which is present in the very nature of the universe. By virtue of this, man has a mandate to follow certain action patterns at all times in all places. A desirable ethic in our world for the realist could well be that it is important to provide the greatest happiness to the greatest number of our citizens.

Aesthetically, under the axiology of realism, it is up to the individual to develop his powers of discernment so that he can recognize that which is beautiful and good. Religiously, the many possibilities within realism for value achievement depend on presence of, or lack of, belief in a Divine Being. A moral act, according to Broudy, is one that fulfills a claim to certain good in life; man, therefore, does not have complete freedom of choice as to his actions.

Socially, the realist believes that the physical universe is more basic to life and thought than is society. He is more concerned with man and his relationship to the universe than he is with society as a primary unit. Social values must be determined and real incentives provided to make people work for their achievement. A mechanics of social organization based on these real incentives must be developed.

The implications of the philosophy of realism for education are receiving increased attention in the western world today. The cold war struggle between democracy and communism has brought about a renewal of the demand to prescribe a large part of the school curriculum. The essentialist is vitally concerned with the "transmission of the cultural heritage" so that the individual can take his rightful place in society.

Breed feels that realism and democracy are compatible and that the "essentialistic pattern" of education can subscribe to an "individual-growth objective." Kandel appears somewhat less compromising when he states that the primary responsibility of education is to "reproduce the type, to transmit the social heritage, and to adjust the individual to society." Catholic realists believe that the Church has a primary role in the education of youth, since human control *cannot* be the only jurisdictional power in such a basic responsibility.

Brubacher postulates four primary philosophical positions under essentialism: (1) idealism; (2) naturalistic realism; (3) rational humanism; and (4) Catholic realism (supernaturalism). Explaining that the transition from progressivism to essentialism is not necessarily abrupt, he classifies these four positions as essentialistic because they are "fully aware of the relentless pressure with which society enforces the customs which are basic or essential for maintaining its unique character."

Turning from the relationship among society, school, and the individual to a more specific consideration of aims and objectives, Broudy, a classical realist, feels that the fundamental problem of education is to make life good for man; the role of the school is to "transcribe the good life, the good individual, and the good society into learnings that presumably will contribute to their production." Whitehead believes that "education is the acquisition of the art of the utilization of knowledge." Wild stresses that accrued knowledge must be transmitted so that civilization can continue to flourish.

As Wild sees it, the primary task of education is to transmit knowledge. He explains that "genuine, stable integration of the whole culture can be attained only by universal principles grounded on observation." Whatever man has discovered to be true because it conforms to reality must be handed down to future generations as the social or cultural tradition. This is basically the position of the naturalistic realist in essentialism.

In rejecting the subject-centered curriculum of the more traditional school, Broudy sees habits being developed hand in hand with content; group problems and personal problems should be stressed in courses which involve analysis of the culture. This recommendation would seem to be a compromise between extreme traditionalism and extreme progressivism.

The rational humanist believes that education must help man to develop his intellect to its highest potentiality; his is a unique faculty of reason, and it must be expanded through mastery of subject matter —all the truth that has been uncovered by man to date. As Brubacher explains it, "the subjects with the greatest rational content, of course, are the liberal arts, and among the liberal arts, the humanities."

The Catholic realist (supernaturalist) believes that there are unchanging educational objectives also. He has added revelation and theology to the educational position of the rational humanist. Man must concern himself on earth with the means necessary to achieve ultimate union with God. Character education is tremendously important along with the basic curriculum subjects. At the secondary level, general education as well as the learning of a trade is essential for those not going on to university.

The educational process recommended by the various proponents of realism follows quite directly from the aims and objectives expressed. Broudy is anxious about the possible continuation of certain trends that have proved ineffectual in both traditionalism and progressivism. He recommends that students develop habits and skills involved with acquiring knowledge, with using knowledge practically to meet life's problems, and with realizing the enjoyment that life offers.

The rational humanist believes that the child develops his intellect by employing reasoning to learn a subject. The subject which involves a greater amount of reasoning for mastery is more important in this approach. There is room for two orders of learning in this approach that states the principal educational aim must be the same for all men at all times in all places. But the psychological order of learning moves back to the essential subject matter at the first opportunity.

For the Catholic realist, as explained previously, education is the process by which man seeks to link himself ultimately with his Creator. Therefore his primary concern is that religious instruction be placed first. Herein and thereafter the curriculum takes precedence over interest. Because educational objectives are stable, it is quite legitimate for the teacher to indoctrinate a curriculum that is made up in advance of the learning activity itself.

CHAPTER NINE

Realism in Physical, Health, and Recreation Education

There is no question that education is receiving a more realistic appraisal in the second half of the twentieth century. The cold war struggle between democracy and communism has assumed frightening proportions and has thereby brought about a vigorous renewal of the demand to prescribe a large part of the school curriculum. The "transmission of the cultural heritage"—a heritage that is increasing at a fantastic rate—places an almost superhuman task upon the agencies of both formal and informal education.

When we consider the implications of the realistic outlook for physical, health, and recreation education, the educational philosophies of naturalistic realism, rational humanism, and Catholic realism (supernaturalism) become our primary targets for analysis.[1] The idealistic outlook, placed by Brubacher under the essentialistic position also, will be treated separately in a subsequent chapter. In a very real sense this exclusion does make it possible to state that the realistic position typically accepts education of the physical as the primary emphasis in this specialized area. It is, of course, not such a simple matter, or else this particular analysis could stop at this point. Much more careful analysis is demanded because of the variety of differentiated positions within the realistic outlook. An important additional consideration is the belief that the

---

[1] John S. Brubacher, *Modern Philosophies of Education,* 2nd ed. (New York: McGraw-Hill Book Company, Inc., 1950), pp. 314-325.

individual professional should find his place on a spectrum through careful self-examination rather than blithely accepting one philosophical tendency or the other because of momentary appeal.

Aims and Objectives

In the foundational chapter immediately preceding this one, Broudy's definition of education was offered for consideration. He believes that the role of the school is to "transcribe the good life, the good individual, and the good society into learnings that presumably will contribute to their production." [2] Contrast this with Geiger's definition stating that "education in the broadest sense can be nothing less than the changes made in human beings by their experience." [3] Or move farther to the left on the educational spectrum to read a statement of Brameld, a reconstructionist. He believes that "the one task of education before all others is to help reconstruct the cultures of the world to the end that people shall attain maximum satisfaction of their material and spiritual wants, including the satisfaction of building and ruling their own civilization everywhere on earth—theirs to design, to possess, and to enjoy." [4]

PHYSICAL DEVELOPMENT IS IMPORTANT.   Whereas the experimentalist is dissatisfied with the name *physical education,* the realist would have no particular objection to the use of this term to describe the function of the field. In fact, the realist, especially the naturalistic realist, would be quite apt to say that progressive influences have led physical educators astray in the past thirty years or so. Witness a statement by McCloy in 1941 in which he asks for "a return to fundamentals" as follows: "Many leaders of the 'educational school' have led us to believe that it is something to be ashamed of to seek health and physical development directly." [5] Clark, in what is probably the first study in physical education involving an analytical and comparative approach to philosophical research, states that: "The development of physical stamina and well-being claims prior value over recreation, according to Realism." [6] Simi-

---

[2] Harry S. Broudy, *Building a Philosophy of Education,* 2nd ed. (Englewood Cliffs, N.J.: Prentice-Hall, Inc., 1961), p. 25.

[3] George R. Geiger, "An Experimentalistic Approach to Education," in *Modern Philosophies and Education, Fifty-fourth Yearbook* of the National Society for the Study of Education (Chicago: University of Chicago Press, 1955), p. 144.

[4] Theodore Brameld, *Toward a Reconstructed Philosophy of Education* (New York: The Dryden Press, Inc., 1956), p. 18.

[5] Charles H. McCloy, "A Return to Fundamentals," *Proceedings* (College Physical Education Association, 1941), p. 76.

[6] Margaret C. Clark, "A Philosophical Interpretation of a Program of Physical Education in a State Teachers College" (Ph.D. dissertation, School of Education, New York University, 1943), p. 270.

larly, she asserts that realism is concerned with "the development of the maximum of physical vigor." [7]

Support for the importance of the "physical" in physical education comes from a variety of sources. Alfred North Whitehead, one of the great exponents of the philosophy of realism, deprecated the neglect of the body in the "post-renaissance Platonic curriculum" as follows:

I lay it down as an educational axiom that in teaching you will come to grief as soon as you forget that your pupils have bodies. This is exactly the mistake of the post-renaissance Platonic curriculum. But nature can be kept at bay by no pitchfork; so in English education, being expelled from the classroom, she returned with a cap and bells in the form of all-conquering athleticism. [8]

Wegener has developed what he has called the *Organic Philosophy of Education.* In so doing he states that "the philosophical orientation is 'organic' in the tradition from Plato and Aristotle to the contemporary thought of Alfred North Whitehead." [9] Although this is presented as a new philosophy of education, much of its undergirding is naturalistic and realistic. In writing about man's physical function, Wegener concurs with "the ancient Greek ideal which emphasized the education of the physical and mental aspects of man's nature." [10] Statements like "no organic philosopher minimizes the importance of the body in all of its varied functions and what it contributes to the beauty and utility of life," [11] and "there are the instrumental values of strong and healthful physical functions as they provide the physical and psychological energies, drives, emotions, feelings, and desires to carry on the intellectual, moral, social, domestic, and other functions of man." [12]

Conant, former President of Harvard University, conducted a four-year study of the American high school and junior high school under the auspices of the Carnegie Corporation. He speaks of "vicious overemphasis" on competitive athletics in our schools and colleges, but he does not downgrade the importance of a realistic position in regard to the physical training of our youth. He states that we must win the real struggle of a long "cold war." The following are some of his other statements portraying what might be a realistic emphasis:

That we need to have concern with the physical development of our youth goes without saying. . . . I have come to believe that all public-school pupils should devote a period every school day to developing their muscles and body

---

[7] *Ibid.,* p. 317.

[8] Alfred N. Whitehead, *The Aims of Education* (New York: The Macmillan Company, 1929), p. 60.

[9] Frank C. Wegener, *The Organic Philosophy of Education* (Dubuque, Iowa: William C. Brown Co., 1957), xi.

[10] *Ibid.,* p. 395.

[11] *Ibid.*

[12] *Ibid.,* p. 425.

co-ordination. . . . But there is little real concern for what is of prime importance, namely, the physical fitness of all youth, both boys and girls.[13]

Shortly before his election in 1960, the late President Kennedy was so concerned about the physical condition of young Americans that he wrote an article entitled *The Soft American.* Speaking realistically, he made these remarks in his urgent plea for greater emphasis on physical fitness:

But the harsh fact of the matter is that there is also an increasingly large number of young Americans who are neglecting their bodies—whose physical fitness is not what it should be—who are getting soft. And such softness on the part of individual citizens can help to strip and destroy the vitality of a nation. For the physical vigor of our citizens is one of America's most precious resources. If we waste and neglect this resource, if we allow it to dwindle and grow soft then we will destroy much of our ability to meet the great and vital challenges which confront our people. We will be unable to realize our full potential as a nation.[14]

A HIERARCHY OF VALUE. Despite what would appear to be the urgency of the situation, Brubacher reminds us that essentialistic philosophy of education includes a hierarchy of value in which "intrinsic values stand higher . . . than do instrumental ones." [15] He continues by saying that "consequently physical education, valuable as it is, must yield precedence to intellectual education." [16] This realistic position is echoed by the 1961 statement of the Educational Policies Commission.

The school must be guided, in pursuing its central purpose or any other purposes, by certain conditions which are known to be basic to significant mental development. The school has responsibility to establish and maintain these conditions. . . . *An adequate physical basis for intellectual life must be assured.*[17]

MC CLOY AS A REALIST. Except for periods of emergency in the twentieth century, there have been relatively few realistic voices within the field of physical, health, and recreation education. The late C. H. McCloy was one of these people. Although he saw certain values in the progressivistic position, down through the years he spoke out consistently in favor of education of the physical. In his very interesting book *Philosophical Bases for Physical Education,* published in 1940, McCloy included sixteen essays explaining his position on a number of subjects

---

[13] James B. Conant, "Athletics: The Poison Ivy in Our Schools," *Look Magazine* (January 17, 1961), p. 57.

[14] John F. Kennedy, "The Soft American," *Sports Illustrated* (December 26, 1960), p. 16.

[15] Brubacher, *Modern Philosophies of Education,* p. 99.

[16] *Ibid.,* p. 100.

[17] Educational Policies Commission, *The Central Purpose of American Education* (Washington, D.C.: National Education Association, 1961), p. 15.

within the field. He sets the stage for what is to follow (in the foreword to his work) when he offers a few beliefs which undergird the subsequent essays:

1. that our science, our philosophy, and our technology are becoming much more complex;
2. that new ideas are coming to light from time to time, and need to be carefully considered; but
3. that the discovery and validation of a *new* idea does not thereby invalidate an unrelated *old* idea; and
4. that the rather current tendency to run after first one fad, then another, is an indication of relative intellectual incompetence, even though it *is* difficult to keep so many aspects of our sciences in mind at once.[18]

McCloy stresses further that other professions like law and medicine do "keep many aspects in mind," and he asks why we have been unable to develop such a competency. He then explains how this particular volume is an attempt to present "many sides of a philosophy of physical education." The reader should note that he says "a" and not "the," "our," or "an American" philosophy. McCloy admits that there are some new ideas, but he wishes to retain many of the old ideas that he believes are still sound. He concludes by saying that "after all, there *should* be *some* fundamentals in our science that do not change with the advent of each new system of psychology! We *are* still animals—even if we have 'stresses' and—sometimes—insight!" [19]

From this point on—the very beginning—McCloy, with the exception of a few places such as in 1937 when he pointed out that it did not seem to him that "there is any essential conflict between *education through the physical* and *education of the physical*," [20] makes a great many references to his basic realistic position. Even the title of his 1937 article is *Forgotten Objectives of Physical Education*. In his chapter entitled *How About Some Muscle?* he asserts that we have "abandoned overnight . . . twenty-five centuries of good experience." He explains further how "the basis of all physical education—developmental, educational, corrective, or any other—is *the adequate training and development of the body itself*." [21]

Continuing along through this volume we find that he believed that the YMCA got so educational that "it departed from the practice of emphasizing the physical in man," and thereby "was troubled with turn-over and lack of interest." He argued further that the "education through the physical" proponents "held back the stream of progress . . .

---

[18] Charles H. McCloy, *Philosophical Bases for Physical Education* (New York: Appleton-Century-Crofts, Inc., 1940), viii.
[19] *Ibid.*
[20] *Ibid.*, pp. 57-74.
[21] *Ibid.*, p. 81.

as much as they have helped it." [22] McCloy then proceeds to make his point in the strongest possible way as follows:

Why *not* education of the physical? Our ancestors for millions of years stressed the education of the physical, and it put us, evolutionarily speaking, where we are today. We praise the Athenians of ancient Greece for their civilization— and about half of their education was education of the physical.[23]

In a subsequent essay, he makes his position still clearer (if that is possible!) when he makes a careful analysis of progressive education. Discussing "progressive reverence for the personality" he points out:

In American democracy, if we are realistic, we find that we quite generally have to fight our way. Only the idealist respects our personalities very much. Integration of this personality is not just contentment in an educational Utopia. Life has many foci, and the child who will be the best-integrated is the one who, in the long run, can adjust himself to those who don't reverence his personality as well as to those who do.[24]

In 1960, C. O. Jackson, editor of *The Physical Educator* of Phi Epsilon Kappa, paid special tribute to McCloy by publishing in its entirety in September, 1959, one of his final talks given shortly before his death at the age of 73. This final statement, of a man who was undoubtedly one of America's great physical educators, emphasizes many of the definitely realistic beliefs that he fought for so valiantly down through the years of the twentieth century. In his final paragraphs he concludes magnificently in a "typically McCloy" penetrating analysis of the current position of the field; in his final summation he inserts traces of naturalism, experimentalism, and idealism as he searches for Aristotle's golden mean. This statement is printed in its entirety.

A CHALLENGE

I hope that the next fifty years will show physical educators to be much more literate; to be able to read the physical education literature of the world; to seek for facts, proved objectively; to supplant principles based on average opinions of the people who don't know, but who are all anxious to contribute their averaged ignorance to form a consensus of uninformed dogma. I would hope that the time would come when men and women will work out their philosophy of physical education together rather than—as it is now in far too many cases fighting blindly and far too often unintelligently: and let me hasten to say that the unintelligent contributions are about equally distributed as to the sex of origin. Often there is heat enough to run a locomotive, but not enough light to light a small room.

While so long as I live I never expect to come to the word "finally," as my last point, *I hope the time will come in the United States when all physical education will be planned not only to help unfold the personalities and the*

---

[22] *Ibid.*, p. 96.

[23] *Ibid.*, pp. 96-97.

[24] *Ibid.*, pp. 239-240.

*characters of school children and to develop their health and abilities to func-
tion to the fullest, but will become part of a way of life that will aid in the
evolution of the person not only during the school years, but from birth to
senescence. I hope further that physical education will become a part of the
habits of our lives to the end that we may become not only healthier and
physically more efficient, but that we may develop much richer lives in many
respects—which lives, according to the present best estimate, will be prolonged
to a much greater average age than is the case today.*[25]

Up to this point we have devoted considerable attention to what the
realist might designate as his primary objective—a sound body. There
are other objectives as well. For example, Clark emphasizes that the
learning of sportsmanship and desirable social conduct is important.[26]
Broudy tends to agree with this as an objective when he states that,
"in our own country, team sports are supposed to result in a strong
sense of fair play, courage, loyalty, and perseverance. No doubt this is
true, although in the nature of the case it would be difficult to prove
or disprove such a claim." [27] He postulates further that the commer-
cialism of high school and college sports may leave this subject open to
question.

QUALIFIED APPROVAL TO INTERSCHOLASTIC SPORT. Actually, there are
many realists who believe that competitive sport can make a positive
contribution to the development of young people. After considerable
investigation, Morland came to the conclusion that essentialism gives
"qualified approval" to interscholastic athletics.[28] McCloy, in keeping
with his most persistent theme, gave varsity athletics some "back-handed
praise" when he ventured the opinion that "though many in our profession have protested against certain administrative abuses of high-school
and college varsity athletics, at least these activities have not sinned by
providing no exercise for their participants." [29]

EXTRACURRICULAR ACTIVITIES. Broudy, speaking of *recreational values*
in connection with sport (he does not even mention the term *physical
education* anywhere in his entire text), takes a most interesting position
in this regard, but he is not really speaking about competitive athletics
in the usual sense. He asserts that every child should be required to
learn one team game and two individual sports that can be played as
an adult before graduation. But, he quickly explains, this should not be

[25] Charles H. McCloy, "A Half Century of Physical Education," *The Physical Educator*, XVII, No. 3 (October 1960), 91.

[26] Margaret C. Clark, "A Philosophical Interpretation of a Program of Physical
Education in a State Teachers College," *Research Quarterly*, XV, No. 4 (December,
1944), 327.

[27] Broudy, *Building a Philosophy of Education*, 2nd ed., p. 169.

[28] Richard B. Morland, "A Philosophical Interpretation of the Educational Views
Held by Leaders in American Physical Education" (Ph.D. dissertation, New York
University, 1958), p. 295.

[29] McCloy, *Philosophical Bases of Physical Education*, p. 72.

considered as part of the regular curriculum; it is extracurricular and should come after the official school day is over.[30] Broudy, in reply to those who would include sports education as part of the regular daily curriculum, points out that there are many other recreational skills equally as important and that there is no guarantee that students will continue with these activities as adults. Hopefully, the adult milieu into which they are thrust will not exert such a strong influence that they would discard those activities that they have learned well. For those who would abolish varsity sports for intramural athletics, Broudy has a typically realistic answer:

Some hardy souls draw a further conclusion: that interscholastic sports should be replaced by intramural sports. This is good logic but poor educational politics because the people will not cheerfully be deprived of their spectacles.[31]

DOES SPORT HAVE EDUCATIONAL VALUE? It is unfortunate, however, that varsity sports in many educational institutions and at all levels of the educational system have gone to such extremes that they have drawn such sharp criticism from many educators. Conant places the blame for the "exploitation" of children on the community itself. When he says that "the burden of proof is upon the proponents to show the educational values of *any* junior-high interscholastic athletics," [32] and that he knows of none, certainly this places a crucial challenge which measurement people in the physical-education field should meet squarely. We should prove what athletics do for youth under certain conditions —good or bad. If the answers are favorable, varsity sports deserve continued support. If, however, the results of experimentation shows more negative than positive results, there is only one answer and that is to correct the situation insofar as this might be possible. Sport has been receiving support from high places, however, as can be seen from these words of the late President Kennedy:

Throughout our history we have been challenged to armed conflict by nations which sought to destroy our independence or threatened our freedom. The young men of America have risen to those occasions, giving themselves freely to the rigors and hardships of warfare. But the stamina and strength which the defense of liberty requires are not the product of a few weeks' basic training or a month's conditioning. These come only from bodies which have been conditioned by a lifetime of participation in sports and interest in physical activity. Our struggles against aggressors throughout our history have been won on the playgrounds and corner lots and fields of America.[33]

POPE PIUS XII ON SPORT.   Even the late Pope Pius XII spoke a number

---

[30] Broudy, *Building a Philosophy of Education*, 2nd ed., p. 167.
[31] *Ibid.*
[32] Conant, *Look*, p. 57.
[33] Kennedy, *Sports Illustrated*, p. 16.

of times about the importance of sport and physical culture in society. First, in 1945, he spoke to the athletes of Rome upon the invitation of the Central Office of Athletics. His discourse, based on a Pauline text, stressed the role of athletics in the formation of a Christian character. To those who criticized the Church for lack of interest in the body, the Supreme Pontiff replied:

As if the body, just as much a creature of God as the soul, should not have its share in rendering homage to the Creator! . . . After all, what is sports if not a form of education of the body? This education has strong ties with morality. How then could the Church not be interested? . . . Now, what is primarily the duty and scope of sports, wholesomely and Christianly understood, if not to cultivate the dignity and harmony of the human body, to develop health, strength, agility and grace? . . . Sports is a school for loyalty, courage, endurance, determination, universal brotherhood; all natural virtues, but which serve as a solid foundation for the supernatural virtues and prepare one to withstand without weakness the weight of more serious obligations. . . . Sports—really worthy of the name—render a man courageous in the face of danger, but does not authorize him to enter a serious risk without a corresponding reason. . . . For the Christian sportsman, and also for you beloved sons, sports must not become the supreme ideal, the ultimate goal, but they must serve to tend toward that ideal, toward obtaining that goal. If sports serve you as a recreation and stimulus to accomplish your work and study with freshness and enthusiasm, then they can be said to be significant and worthwhile and accomplish what they should. And if, besides this, sports become not only a symbol, but in some way also an execution of your highest duty, if, that is, you set yourselves through sports to render the body more docile and obedient to the soul and to your moral obligations; if besides, with your example you contribute to modern sports a form more corresponding to human dignity and the divine precepts, then your physical culture takes on a supernatural value.[34]

Again, in 1952, Pius delivered a major address to delegates attending the Italian Congress on the Pedagogic and Hygienic Problems of Sports and Gymnastics about the Christian attitude towards sports. He emphasized how important the body is in its subservience to the soul: "Sport which does not serve the soul is nothing more than a vain movement of the body's members, an ostentation of passing attractiveness, an ephemeral joy." [35] Finally, upon the opening of the Olympic Stadium in Rome on May 16, 1953, he blessed the new structure and lay down some fundamental principles of Christian conduct for the spectator in athletic events as follows:

The very tone of the voice, which rises strongly from the stadium of a Christian city should resound in a manner different from that of the strident

---

[34] Pope Pius XII, "Physical Culture and Youth," *Catholic Newsletter,* No. 288 (May 26, 1945). Translated by Rev. J. La Manna.
[35] Pope Pius XII, "Sports and Gymnastics," *Catholic Mind,* No. 51 (September 1953), pp. 569-576.

yells of a pagan stadium. In dignity and restraint of language, it should be such as not to differ too much from the solemn tone of the choruses and cheering that is heard, rising to heaven, from the same people in those same stadia on the occasion of civic and patriotic celebrations and of religious rites.[36]

ANOTHER STATEMENT OF POSITION. Before leaving the subject of the importance of physical-education classes and athletics viewed according to the educational philosophy of realism, a few more statements of position should be considered briefly. Finney, an essentialist writing just over thirty years ago, showed what might be considered a fairly consistent and typical pattern in regard to extracurricular activities. He points out that:

It is true that children learn fair play by learning to play fair, and all that; but it is going altogether far when one implies that these participatory social experiences are the most important part of the school's program. They are minor, secondary, and quite incidental matters. . . . Incidental practice in teamwork and sociability are important, therefore, in the modern school; not because that is what the school is for, but because that is what much schooling must not be allowed to prevent. However, it is a shallow sociology that ascribes to extracurricular activities a major function in the school program, and a faddish pedagogy that overworks them in practice. The main thing is the curriculum![37]

But having said this, and it does seem very clear and explicit, Finney, just a few pages later, does seem to contradict himself to a considerable degree. He begins by mentioning that "civilized societies have evolved techniques of play and recreation only less elaborate than their techniques of industry; and it may be that the former have by right a larger claim upon the curriculum maker than we are in the habit of assuming." [38] He then stresses the importance of play in a civilization which has removed man from "a state of nature." We are told how certain historic schools "used games and sports as a means of developing personality and moral character," but Finney would not agree for a minute that such an objective has been achieved with any degree of success in public high schools in the United States. In concluding his remarks on this subject, however, Finney does take what might be considered a realistic position without actually saying directly that such activities should ever be required (as Broudy did somewhat later!):

Such a philosophy would doubtless include the idea of teaching games, sports, and amusements with the deliberative objective of habituating their utilization

---

[36] Pope Pius XII, "Christian Conduct Towards Athletics," *Catholic Mind*, No. 54 (July 1956), pp. 409-417.

[37] Ross L. Finney, A *Sociological Philosophy of Education* (New York: The Macmillan Company, 1928), pp. 160-161.

[38] *Ibid.*, pp. 175-176.

in adult life. Such a philosophy might accord to tennis and chess at least as large and dignified a place in the school program as to solid geometry and freshman rhetoric; and it would certainly establish a close alliance between games of all kinds and the fine arts as recreational facilities. Such an educational policy would probably contribute in a very important way to the enrichment of life for the common people.[39]

It is possible that the above opinions by Finney are somewhat out of place and should be discussed a bit later when we consider the role of recreation and play in the educational pattern of the realist, but he comes so close to saying that games and sport should be required in the curriculum that we used the material at this point.

RATIONAL HUMANISM.   The position of the rational humanist, or at least that of Adler—one of its stronger proponents—on the subject of physical education is pertinent at this point in our discussion. In his essay *In Defense of the Philosophy of Education,* he presents the major divisions of the educational process as follows: (1) self-education and education by another; (2) types of habits established by education; (3) individual differences in relation to education; and (4) institutional or noninstitutional education. Under number 2—types of habits established by education—Adler divides habits basically into those associated with knowing and thinking *(intellectual)* and those associated with desiring and acting *(moral).* Then he explains how intellectual education can be further subdivided according to whether the objective is the achievement of habits of knowledge or habits of art. Adler concludes in the following manner:

A habit of knowledge is a habit of knowing *that,* whereas a habit of art is a habit of knowing *how.* Because every art is an intellectual virtue, every sort of artistic education is intellectual. There are as many subdivisions of artistic education as there are types of art, but principally there are three: (1) physical education, which cultivates the most basic arts, the arts of using one's own body well as an instrument; (2) vocational education, which cultivates all the useful arts, whether simply productive or coöperative; and (3) liberal education, which cultivates a special sort of useful art, the liberal arts, the arts of learning itself, the arts of thinking well, of using language well, and so forth.[40]

PERENNIALISM NEGLECTS PHYSICAL EDUCATION.   Brameld, in describing the educational position of perennalism (Catholic realism), does not mention physical education anywhere in a description of the elementary and secondary curriculum. "And what is 'right' content? Most important on the elementary level is 'reading, writing, and figuring,' with some consideration, in Hutchins' scheme, for history, geography, literature,

[39] *Ibid.*
[40] Mortimer J. Adler, "In Defense of the Philosophy of Education," in *Philosophies of Education, Forty-first Yearbook* of the National Society for the Study of Education (Chicago: University of Chicago Press, 1942), Part I, pp. 214-215.

science, and a foreign language." [41] Physical education is missing from the consideration of the secondary curriculum also. "One finds extraordinary unanimity in their proposal that almost all adolescents engage in a program of 'general education' or in trade and skill training." [42] Physical education may be implied here, as in Maritain's [43] presentation of the aims of education, but there can be no doubt of its place in the hierarchy of value.

HEALTH EDUCATION IN THE SCHOOL. What about the place of health education in the curriculum of the realist? Clark came to the conclusion that realism is dedicated to "the development of the maximum of physical vigor and health." [44] Bair, in his philosophical study, stated that the realist believed that "the physical education program should be based upon authenticated health knowledge and established forms of physical and recreational skills because they provide a basis for new experience." [45] Holbrook states that the realist "is interested in the processes which influence organic vigor and neuromuscular skill. . . . sees, knows and develops the clean, vigorous activity program which both reflects and conserves the cultural heritage and conforms to the social standards. . . . There would be a concern for the bio-physical nature of man." [46]

MC CLOY ON HEALTH. McCloy was concerned about "raising the level of personal and public health practice." He felt that much of the responsibility for such improvement fell to the health and physical education teacher where "the foundations for these practices are built up." He went on to say that:

Physical exercise alone has much to do with health, and lasting habits of participating in active sports and other health-producing practices must be inculcated. In the teaching of health it is the *doing* that must be stressed, not just the knowing. A school is somewhat like a country; it has a governing body, administering agencies, and citizens. School hygiene is the public health of the school organization, and it should be lived to the fullest extent by all. This implies joint projects of teachers, students, administrators, and janitorial staff. It implies teachers who live and foster this attitude. It implies research and investigation on how to make such education more effective. . . . It is health *education* that will lead the way toward a better civilization. [47]

[41] Theodore Brameld, *Philosophies of Education in Cultural Perspective* (New York: The Dryden Press, Inc., 1955), p. 328.

[42] *Ibid.*, p. 329.

[43] Jacques Maritain, "Thomist Views on Education," *Forty-first Yearbook* of the N. S. S. E. Part I, pp. 62-63.

[44] Clark, *Research Quarterly*, XV, 327.

[45] Donn E. Bair, "An Identification of Some Philosophical Beliefs Held by Influential Professional Leaders in American Physical Education" (Ph.D. dissertation, University of Southern California, 1956), p. 99.

[46] Leona Holbrook, "The Philosophy of Realism," a paper presented at Atlantic City, New Jersey, American Association for Health, Physical Education, and Recreation, March 19, 1961, pp. 7-8.

[47] McCloy, *Philosophical Bases for Physical Education*, pp. 134-135.

It should be pointed out that this stand regarding the importance of school health education is not typically essentialistic; in fact, it is very close to the position of the experimentalist. Of course, this is understandable when we recall that both pragmatism and realism (especially naturalistic realism) stem from a definitely naturalistic philosophical base.

BROUDY ON SCHOOL HEALTH EDUCATION. Broudy expresses himself very strongly about the position of the realist in connection with health education in the school. He leaves no doubt that the relationship should be clear-cut—the school should provide "an atmosphere conducive to both emotional and physical health." Furthermore, "knowledge about the principles of physical and emotional health is a proper ingredient of the curriculum." But at this point the relationship tapers off sharply. The community does have a responsibility to provide "clinical facilities for therapy, . . . but this does not mean that they are part of the school program or curriculum any more than are the boilers in the heating system." [48] Can there be any doubt about Professor Broudy's belief on this subject?

THE HOME SHOULD CARE FOR HABIT FORMATION. How then can we guarantee that our youth acquire desirable health habits which are obviously more than simply a question of knowledge? Broudy asserts that the home must have the complete responsibility for this, unless the country forms some system of youth organizations to accomplish this end. Even if we did try some system of lectures in the schools regarding proper attitude development toward health, Broudy states that "the health of adolescents is for the most part too good and their sources of energy are too great to make health problems real to them." [49] Similarly, sex education is certainly not a proper function of the school. As a final parting shot on this subject, Broudy explains that teaching of the means for securing the health values would be incomplete anyhow until the perspective from which they are to be viewed is also taught; this perspective, we are told, is found only in the humanities—in literature, art, religion, and philosophy.

THE CENTRAL PURPOSE OF EDUCATION. Consistent with Broudy's approach to the role of health education in the school is that taken by the 1961 statement of the Educational Policies Commission. Having stated that "the rational powers are central to all the other qualities of the human spirit," [50] that "this is the central purpose to which the school must be oriented if it is to accomplish either its traditional task or those

---

[48] Broudy, *Building a Philosophy of Education*, 2nd ed., p. 82.
[49] *Ibid.*, p. 163.
[50] Educational Policies Commission, *The Central Purpose of American Education*. p. 8.

newly accentuated by recent changes in the world," [51] and that "among the many important purposes of American schools the fostering of that development ['every citizen's rational powers'] must be central," [52] the school is urged to establish "certain conditions which are known to be basic to significant mental development." [53]

AN UNDERGIRDING FUNCTION. Obviously one of these conditions is that the child needs to possess physical health. Sickness or illness would prevent the child from learning. President Kennedy took this identical approach, when he said:

For physical fitness is not only one of the most important keys to a healthy body; it is the basis of dynamic and creative intellectual activity. The relationship between the soundness of the body and the activities of the mind is subtle and complex. Much is not yet understood. But we do know what the Greeks knew: that intelligence and skill can only function at the peak of their capacity when the body is healthy and strong; that hardy spirits and tough minds usually inhabit sound bodies.[54]

HEALTH KNOWLEDGE HAS A PLACE. For the realist, therefore, "there is certainly a basic core of knowledge that every human person ought to know in order to live a genuinely human life," [55] and this would include the learning of health knowledge. For the Thomist, or Catholic realist, "the essential hierarchy of values inherent in liberal education would be preserved, with the main emphasis, as to the disciplines, on philosophy"; [56] here the matter of health education would be foundational but not very high in the "essential hierarchy of values." This position is defined very clearly by Pius XII when he explains *dignity of the body*.

Sound doctrine teaches respect for the body, but not an esteem that is more than just. The maxim is this: care of the body, yes; cult of the body, divinization of the body, no, nor likewise divinization of the race, or the blood, or of their somatic presuppositions and constitutive elements. The body does not occupy the first place in man, neither the earthly and mortal body as it is now, nor the body glorified and spiritualized as it will be one day. The primacy in the human composition does not belong to the body taken from the earth's slime, but to the spirit, to the spiritual soul.[57]

PLAY DOES NOT BELONG IN CURRICULUM. Lastly under the aims and objectives of the educational philosophy of realism, the role of recreation in the school will be considered. Here again the position appears to be

---

[51] *Ibid.,* p. 12.

[52] *Ibid.,* p. 21.

[53] *Ibid.,* p. 15.

[54] Kennedy, *Sports Illustrated*, p. 16.

[55] John Wild, "Education and Human Society: A Realistic View," in *Modern Philosophies and Education*, ed. N. B. Henry (Chicago: University of Chicago Press, 1955), Part I, p. 34.

[56] Jacques Maritain, *Forty-first Yearbook*, Part I, p. 81.

[57] Pope Pius XII, *Catholic Newsletter*, No. 288.

clear-cut and decisive—work and play are sharply differentiated. "Play is all right on the playground at recess and after school, but it should not be imported into the regular curriculum." [58] Bagley strengthens this position when he indicates "that a fundamental fallacy of the Progressive movement lies in its assumption that work and play can be identified under the same psychological rubric." [59]

THE USE OF LEISURE.   It does not appear that the realist is anywhere nearly ready to accept the statement by Brightbill that "with the advance of science, and its concomitants, automation and enlightened medicine, it is no longer *work* but rather *leisure* which is the center of our culture." [60] The realist would agree that use of leisure is significant to the development of our culture, but he would be quick to point out that winning the "cold war" is going to take a lot more hard work and somewhat less leisure. This statement might be strengthened by pointing out how badly much of American leisure has been used as relief from work and for re-creative purposes.

A REALISTIC THEORY OF PLAY.   There have been many theories of play and recreation expounded in the past, and we would find it extremely difficult to state unequivocally that the realist believes very definitely in the surplus energy theory as opposed to the self-expression theory of play. All that can be done is to state that "the present knowledge and understanding of the function of play and recreation is admittedly somewhat limited," but that "the recent theories deal more with the direct causes of human behavior, taking into account self-expression as well as the primary causes of physiological, psychological, and environmental factors that motivate the individual's action." [61]

WHITEHEAD ON INTEREST AND INTELLECTUAL ZEAL.   Whitehead, in his essay, *The Aims of Education,* takes an interesting approach to the matter of joy, pleasure, leisure, and relaxation in life. Writing about the relationship between freedom and discipline in education, he states that "interest is the *sine qua non* for attention and apprehension." Subsequently he explains that:

Undoubtedly pain is one subordinate means of arousing an organism to action. But it only supervenes on the failure of pleasure. Joy is the normal healthy spur for the *élan vital.* I am not maintaining that we can safely abandon ourselves to the allurement of the greater immediate joys. What I do mean is that we should seek to arrange the development of character along a path of

---

[58] Brubacher, *Modern Philosophies of Education,* p. 238.

[59] William C. Bagley, *Education, Crime and Social Progress* (New York: The Macmillan Company, 1931), pp. 98-99.

[60] Charles K. Brightbill, *Man and Leisure* (Englewood Cliffs, N.J.: Prentice-Hall, Inc., 1961), p. 49.

[61] Allen V. Sapora and Elmer D. Mitchell, *The Theory of Play and Recreation,* 3rd ed. (New York: The Ronald Press Company, 1961), p. 110.

natural activity, in itself pleasurable. The subordinate stiffening of discipline must be directed to secure some long-time good; although an adequate object must not be too far below the horizon, if the necessary interest is to be retained.[62]

This is an unusual statement for an essentialist, but it is certain that Whitehead feels he is being very realistic. He is most desirous that his young countrymen develop an "intellectual zeal" that will result in a better England—a zeal that won't come through the juxtaposition of bits of inert knowledge. Whitehead indicates that "when we can point to some great achievement of our nation which has been won in the classroom of our schools, and not in their playing fields, then we may feel content with our modes of education." [63]

WHITEHEAD ON LIBERAL EDUCATION AND LEISURE. Whitehead believes that the ideal of technical education "is a commonwealth in which work is play and play is life" [64]—a most difficult state to achieve. It is possible to produce a nation of workmen, scientists, and employers who enjoy their work, but he feels it will develop only when a country's technological education is infused with a liberal spirit. By that he means that all those concerned with a country's progress must understand the why's and wherefore's of their efforts. Thus all men need enough liberal education, or general education as it is more commonly known today, for thought and for aesthetic appreciation. Any amount of such aristocratic education implies a society in which man enjoys leisure.

WHITEHEAD ON RELAXATION. The re-creation theory of recreation and the more recent biosocial approach to the theory of recreation (the idea of helping the organism to achieve balance) are suggested by Whitehead in his essay when he discusses the "enjoyment of relaxation" as one kind of intellectual enjoyment and the "enjoyment of creation" as the other. He emphasizes further that "to obtain the pleasure of relaxation requires no help. The pleasure is merely to cease doing. Some such pure relaxation is a necessary condition of health." [65] Speaking generally about the economy of a nation he explains:

To speed up production with unrefreshed workmen is a disastrous economic policy. Temporary success will be at the expense of the nation, which, for long years of their lives, will have to support worn-out artisans—unemployables. Equally disastrous is the alternation of spasms of effort with periods of pure relaxation. Such periods are the seed-times of degeneration, unless rigorously curtailed. The normal recreation should be change of activity, satisfying the cravings of instincts. Games afford such activity. Their disconnection emphasizes the relaxation, but their excess leaves us empty.[66]

---

[62] Whitehead, *The Aims of Education*, p. 42.
[63] *Ibid.*, p. 49.
[64] *Ibid.*, p. 53.
[65] *Ibid.*, p. 67.
[66] *Ibid.*

In a well-organized nation, literature and art would be a condition of healthy life, second in importance perhaps only to food and sleep.

BROUDY ON RECREATION'S VALUE.   A realistic approach to the value of recreation today is presented most interestingly by Broudy. He believes that recreation in the life of man has both intrinsic and instrumental aspects.[67] Play is the intrinsic aspect of recreation; it is difficult to define but quite easy to recognize. Although it isn't work, we often spend a great deal of energy on it. Adults should think of play as "carefree activity performed for its own sake." Broudy, while defining the play attitude as an unique mode of experience for man, deprecates the fact that the "play attitude" seems to be missing almost completely in organized sports. Because of this, sport is kept from being a truly recreational activity, and this is most unfortunate.[68]

There do appear to be both educational and health aspects in the play of children. When it comes to defining this phenomenon in the life of an adult, an explanation seems to be much more complex. Broudy believes that recreational activity should be "liberating," because of its carefree and flexible character. He feels that people can develop a number of potentialities for wholesome hobbies through recreation and that this may be the "salvation" for workers of a certain economic status. Lastly, he is most enthusiastic about the theory that recreation contributes to self-integration through the reduction of psychic tension caused by so many of life's typical stresses. He speaks of it as a "safety valve" that may prevent an "explosion" in the life of an individual.[69]

VERY IMPORTANT BUT EXTRACURRICULAR.   If play and recreation are so valuable to man, why shouldn't the school educate for leisure and include recreation education as part of the curriculum? In reply to this question, Broudy points out initially that general education is itself education for leisure. He criticizes the prevailing situation in which many people don't know how to acquire, use, and enjoy knowledge. Although games and sports are believed to have high recreational value and to provide badly needed exercise, Broudy appears content to call this area *recreation* and not *recreation education*. As important as education for leisure is, he believes that every student be required to receive instruction in one team game that can be played as an adult, two individual sports, ballroom dancing, one manual art or craft (e.g., painting), at least one card game, and one creative art (e.g., music, acting, etc.). Broudy asserts that it should not be considered part of the curriculum,[70] but it should be a graduation requirement that is extra-

---

[67] Broudy, *Building a Philosophy of Education,* 2nd ed., p. 164.
[68] *Ibid.,* p. 165.
[69] *Ibid.,* pp. 165-166.
[70] *Ibid.,* p. 167.

curricular![71] We are told that we can't be certain that students will prefer these activities above those of the tavern and cocktail lounge; we can provide milieu education and hope that it takes.

AN AMBIVALENT ATTITUDE TOWARD PLAY. It is especially difficult to gain perspective about recreational values since many sorts of value are possible through the medium of recreational activity. Some kinds of recreation improve a person's health; others may ruin it. Sport may build character, although this is difficult to prove. Unfortunately we appear to have commercialized it to such an extent that we have far too often removed the possibility of such development.[72] Broudy explains that we seem to have achieved an "ambivalent attitude toward play." He states:

On one hand, there is a Puritanical strain that condemns play as sinful, or at least, as frivolous. On the other hand, the tempo of our life is so rapid, competition so keen, that we need large doses of the trivial to relieve it. The attitude that sport is a serious business—a big industry and its stars national heroes—effects a neat compromise between our play impulses and our play inhibitions, for if play is serious business, it can be neither sinful nor frivolous.[73]

This approach seems to trouble him, and he is anxious to preserve the character of work and play by some distinction. As it has often been said, "Play is an indispensable seasoning to the good life!" Broudy would concur with this statement fully; he is anxious about educated man's ability to enjoy a wide variety of recreational values through participation in activities provided through his own resources as much as possible.

ART SHOULD BE A PART OF LIFE. An interesting approach to the cultural recreational pursuits of Americans is provided by Mannes who is as skeptical about this so-called acquisition of culture as Vance Packard is about America's return to religion. Miss Mannes believes that culture of all sorts needs to be woven "into the actual texture of our lives." [74] She explains what she feels a cultured individual needs as follows:

I think to make art a part of life, certain attitudes in our society must be changed, and one of them is the feeling that artistic expression is unmanly and that a boy who wants to be a dancer or a poet or a sculptor or a musician should be discouraged, not only for economic reasons but because these are not proper professions for a man.[75]

The important thing is that the creative instinct born in all men be

---

[71] *Ibid.*
[72] *Ibid.*, p. 169.
[73] *Ibid.*
[74] Marya Mannes, "They're Cultural, But Are They Cultured?" *The New York Times Magazine* (July 9, 1961), p. 14.
[75] *Ibid.*, p. 36.

freed so that it may work for the improvement of society and the people living therein. To do this we must develop an individual's senses to their highest capacity. Such an education must begin early in life and continue on as far into maturity as possible. But Miss Mannes displays her essentialistic beliefs concerning these bases for art of all types when she decries the artistic efforts of those who attempt to please the many "rather than instructing the few." In such cases, she feels, these teachers who may have become performers deny the existence of basic principles for all art. To these experimental, pragmatic individuals she explains that:

It must be evident by now that I hold to certain truths, that I believe in certain standards that are as timeless and immutable as the basic laws of nature and the composition of matter. . . . taste changes, fashion changes, and the face of beauty changes from age to age. But the laws that govern creation, whether of matter or of man or of art, do not change.[76]

Here is a plea for self expression but with discipline—a belief that "an awareness of the fundamental patterns of life is the measure of any real culture."

THE POSITION OF THE CATHOLIC REALIST.   It is very difficult to be absolutely unequivocal about the position of the naturalistic realist, the rational humanist, and the Catholic realist (supernaturalist) in regard to the place of play and recreation in the educational pattern, but it certainly appears to be safe to say that there is some vacillation. Debinski says that "recreation purely for the sake of recreation, and as an end in itself, is an outmoded philosophy."[77] But he does add that:

The moral, spiritual, and religious implications of recreation need to be more adequately explored, studied, and clearly understood by all who have an interest in this field of leisure time activities. Recreation cannot be treated as an entity in itself, but a contributing factor in the attainment of man's immediate and ultimate end."[78]

Sanders, an exponent of the Catholic realistic (supernaturalistic) position in educational theory, seems to be taking the position that a recreational game may be played for the achievement of both instrumental and intrinsic values when he states that:

Experiences may be practical or for pleasure, as one may play a game in order to return to a necessary task relaxed and refreshed, or merely for the pleasure

---

[76] *Ibid.*, p. 37.

[77] Benjamin Debinski, "Catholic Youth Work," in *Selected Papers presented at the 42nd National Recreation Congress* (New York: National Recreation Association, 1961), p. 188.

[78] *Ibid.*

of playing it. In the first case the game is a means to an end, in the second it is an end in itself.[79]

He does feel that the aesthetic quality of the experience will be lost "if one is told to play so that he can work better, or because he will be regarded as a good fellow, or because it is required, or because when he grows up he will make better business or professional contact through skill in playing games." [80] It does seem safe to argue that the realist (defined broadly) does not believe that recreational pursuits of all types are inherently an integral part of the educational pattern. The more essentialistic one's educational philosophy is, the more he sees a sharp distinction between work and play. This is not to say that each does not have a definite purpose in the life of man; it does mean that the aims of education are served when the student applies himself diligently to the basic curriculum of the school.

Methodology

What teaching methods shall the realist employ? Now that we have discussed quite carefully a number of realistic aims and objectives, the next step is to shift our emphasis to see how these goals agreed upon may be reached. It seems self-evident that aims and method should go hand in hand.

Offhand we would expect a realistic approach to the educative process in health, physical education, and recreation to make good, sound, common sense. Education should conform to reality, we are told, since there is a predetermined order in the universe and man's task is to align himself in the best possible relationship with it. We test truth by its correspondence with reality.

CONSIDERABLE VARIANCE IN METHODOLOGY. The educative process recommended by the realist will vary considerably depending on whether we are talking about the position of the naturalistic realist or that of the rational humanist and Catholic supernaturalist. There are, of course, many similarities between these processes or else they would not be considered under the heading of this chapter. The differences are mostly a matter of emphasis.

The naturalistic realist practices a problem-solving approach to classroom learning typically, but to someone like Broudy it is quite different than following a problem-centered concept only. Education has been conceived traditionally as "a simple transmission of information, conditioning of the pupil (shades of behaviorism!) so as to conform him to

---

[79] William J. Sanders, *The Public School and Spiritual Values, Seventh Yearbook* of the John Dewey Society (New York: Harper & Row, Publishers, Inc., 1944), pp. 182-183.

[80] *Ibid.*

his environment, and use of discipline in reinforcing both of these processes." [81] It is more than a matter of merely acquiring knowledge; we must learn how to use it practically for subsequent enjoyment of life.[82]

The approach to learning postulated by the rational humanist seems definitely more essentialistic than that described above. The concern is with the development of the intellect—the greater the amount of reasoning required to learn a subject, the more important is that subject in the curriculum. This doesn't leave very much room for physical, health, and recreation education unless we consider an answer to the question asked recently by the head of a philosophy department in a large state university.[83] He inquired of those present at a conference exploring the philosophical bases for physical education, "What ignorance do you liquidate?" To the extent that this question could be answered the physical educator (including health and recreation education) could claim a place in the educational curriculum. Proceeding from this premise we could presumably say that we liquidate ignorance about sound health habits, rules of various sports, and certain other knowledges which we hope that students will acquire. With this approach there would be two orders of knowledge: a logical or essential order and an order where the teacher starts with the child's interest and then works his way back to insure adequate coverage of the subject matter necessary for a complete treatment of the various knowledges to be covered.

The Catholic realist's approach is, of course, quite similar to that of the rational humanist. *The mind must master the essentials of the culture.* With the hierarchy of values that exists, the role of physical, health, and recreation education within the regular curriculum is definitely subordinate; the fact that it finds a place at all is because the Catholic sees the necessity of providing a vehicle through physical-recreation activity that is as healthy, refreshed, and rejuvenated as possible so that essential Christian education may take place. The elementary-school pupil is provided with "those experiences which are calculated to develop in him such knowledge, appreciation, and habits as will yield a character equal to the contingencies of fundamental Christian living in American democratic society." [84] Through what means this "habituation" takes place will be explained in the next few pages.[85]

---

[81] J. Donald Butler, *Four Philosophies,* rev. ed. (New York: Harper & Row, Publishers, Inc., 1957), p. 367.

[82] Cf., p. 137.

[83] This question was asked by Professor A. Castell at the University of Oregon in Eugene, Oregon on June 29, 1961.

[84] *National Catholic Educational Association Bulletin,* XXII (November 1925), 458.

[85] A definitive Catholic supernatural treatment of the place of physical, health, and recreation education is not available.

INTEREST SUBORDINATE TO EFFORT. What are some of the means whereby this learning may be effectuated? Pointing out that physical education and athletics "make a positive contribution when conducted along educational lines," Morland clarifies the educational process dictated by the essentialist. Interest, he relates, is "desirable but subordinate to effort." [86] The curriculum should definitely take precedence over interest. "Motivation is important but the lasting values are not to be sacrificed to immediate or 'felt' needs" is the stand taken also by the perennialist (Catholic realist). [87]

TRANSFER OF TRAINING. The theory of transfer of training is supported by the realist. This support is evidenced by a belief in the theory of identical elements and in the successful transference of disciplinary values. In the case of the rational humanist and the perennialist, transfer of training is strongly supported. When values are truly learned, they have a functional application in any situation.

A LOWER LEVEL OF LEARNING. In such things as physical education, of course, we are discussing what is considered a lower level of learning. As Wild explains it, man has a certain number of rights in this world which involve a correlated set of duties before the achievement of the rights becomes possible. Man's body is activated by a soul. His mental faculties apprehend reality. To live in society with some degree of success many of the rights expressed in the *United Nations Declaration of Human Rights* must be available to most men to a sufficient degree. [88] Thus the hierarchy of value for the education of man which places certain functions above others is explained as follows:

Now all these needs are essential. All should be satisfied. But the realist believes that nature also indicates a certain causal order among them. Thus, it is clearly the soul which normally moves the body and the mind which directs the soul. The lower support the higher and can even exist alone. From this, many infer that the lower are more valuable. But this is a mistake. Without activation and guidance from the higher functions, the lower lose all their *human* value. The body itself requires physical food which can exist perfectly well by itself. But what good is it to fill a body with excellent food when it is sick unto death? In the same way, what good is it to possess bodily health when the soul that animates it is diseased and corrupt? . . . The *value* of the lower functions depends upon their proper guidance from above. In this way, the higher levels of the hierarchy are causally more important and higher in value. [89]

How the above-mentioned transfer of training takes place is viewed

---

[86] R. B. Morland, "A Philosophical Interpretation of the Educational Views Held by Leaders in American Physical Education" (Ph.D. thesis, New York University, 1958), p. 294.

[87] *Ibid.*

[88] Wild, *Modern Philosophies and Education*, pp. 40-41.

[89] *Ibid.*, p. 41.

somewhat differently by the various types of realist. The naturalistic realist, whose theory of learning has been explained at great length through much of the fairly recent psychological investigation, is often a behaviorist and committed to a stimulus-response type of learning. When a new learning situation presents itself, it is quite apt to contain a number of identical elements that had appeared earlier in another learning circumstance. Such transferral would take place with skills as well as with knowledges. The rational humanist and perennialist strive to develop man's power to reason, and such reasoning ability can then be applied to similar situations, or any others for that matter. Such transfer, of course, must be positive and direct, and the teacher would be wise to make such a possibility known to the learner.

PURPOSEFUL DRILL IS BASIC.   Bair postulates that "learning is a process of acquiring objective knowledge by the scientific method." [90] If we hope to develop patterns of habit formation, drill is needed to perfect such responses at the lower learning levels. The perennialist would concur heartily in the need for purposeful drill as a necessary base upon which advanced learning can be superimposed. When learning a physical skill, drill is equally as important as when the learning of knowledges is desired. Such drill may well be varied and correlated with other teaching techniques. Obviously there is a strong relationship between drill and certain of the laws of learning (e.g., the law of use and disuse).

THE ROLE OF THE TEACHER.   The various aspects of the realist's educational process fall into place quite neatly as we recall the aims and objectives explained earlier in this chapter and the one immediately preceding. What about the role of the teacher as the educational realist sees him? Morland sees him as a "person of authority who transmits the truth and wisely guides immature minds." [91] McCloy was known to use such phrases as *positive teacher control.* Bair states that "the teacher should be the voice of science; clear, objective, and factual." [92] The teacher begins by making "an analysis of the skills to be learned, breaking them down into their elements and interrelations." [93] Such a teacher will find it perfectly legitimate to indoctrinate. There will be little opportunity for election of activities insofar as the regular program is concerned.

A REALISTIC PROGRAM.   The curriculum itself should be logically and sequentially arranged. It should take precedence over interest, although this factor should not be ignored. The scientific measurement approach to education is backed strongly by the naturalistic realist. The use of

---

[90] Bair, "An Identification of Some Philosophical Beliefs . . . ," p. 117.

[91] Morland, "A Philosophical Interpretation . . . ," p. 294.

[92] Bair, "An Identification of Some Philosophical Beliefs . . . ," p. 109.

[93] *Ibid.,* p. 120.

texts, tests, and grades are needed to convey to the student information about the caliber of his performance.[94] Clark points out further that the realist would tend to believe strongly in a health- and physical-education requirement throughout the formal educational system—or at least until certain objective standards of performance had been reached. Holbrook has indicated that the realist "is concerned with research, measurement, evaluation, and their application to physical education," and that he "relies upon tested and proven methodology and curricula." She believes that "there is no radical change to make in physical education under a philosophy of realism, but there would be continuing enlargement of systematic teaching which would lead to measurable results." [95]

The realist believes that the students have needs and that these needs must be met through planned activity. Often the student may not know what he needs, or he may know what he needs but may not be interested in its acquisition. The curriculum must stress the fundamentals presented in a logical and sequential manner. The teacher is the expert who makes decisions about what should be included, but there are certain limitations imposed because of the fact that the educational objectives are unwavering. The aim is for standardization of subject matter with a certain amount of leeway for experimentation in methodology by the teacher. Prizes and awards may be used by the teacher to stimulate students to achieve the greatest amount of excellence in their efforts.

REALISTIC APPROACH TO ADMINISTRATION. The realistic approach to administrative control is entirely predictable. The "boss" is the one who has the ultimate responsibility; so, he should make the decisions affecting the rest of the staff and the students. "Authority is therefore centralized in a line-staff pattern of control." [96] The administrator tends to function as a business executive who has been hired to make wise, clear-cut decisions when the situation warrants any action. The administrator may ask staff members for opinions; he may even have committees investigate certain problems and come up with recommendations. But the eventual decision is up to him. As Bair states, "As an administrator my decisions are dictated by the impersonal results of objective experimentation. However, I stand ready to modify procedures as more effective methods are established." [97] With this pattern of control the administrator is typically delegated a certain amount of responsibility commensurate with the authority granted him to get the job done. Of course, ultimate responsibility remains with the source that granted the power originally. In such a situation the teacher has little choice but to carry out the

---

[94] Clark, *Research Quarterly*, XV, 327.
[95] Holbrook, "The Philosophy of Realism," p. 8.
[96] Morland, "A Philosophical Interpretation . . . ," p. 295.
[97] Bair, "An Identification of Some Philosophical Beliefs . . . ," p. 106.

directions of his superior, no matter what his personal feelings may be at any given moment. The realist feels such administrative theory is compatible with life in an evolving democracy. Someone has to call the shots, bear the brunt of responsibility, and suffer the consequences or accept the rewards if the project at hand fails or succeeds as the case may be. The idea of taking a vote to get majority opinion before any departmental action is taken may sound good in theory, but it does not centralize the responsibilty on one pair of shoulders, and may well result in nothing but pooled ignorance concerning a controversial issue. Besides, it is humanly impossible in large organizations to take time to have a vote on everything. School boards, as one unit of control, must hire administrators, set policy, back up decisions made by administrators in line with such policy, and reward them if their successes on decisions are quite high.

Summary

AIMS AND OBJECTIVES. The realist believes that education of the physical should have primary emphasis in our field. He is concerned with the development of the maximum of physical vigor, and such development has priority over the recreational aspects of physical education. Many people, who believe in the same educational philosophy as he does, recommend that all students in public schools should have a daily period designed to strengthen their muscles and develop their bodily coordination. Physical education, of course, must yield precedence to intellectual education. The realist gives qualified approval to interscholastic and intercollegiate athletics, since they do help with the learning of sportsmanship and desirable social conduct if properly supervised. But all of these aspects, with the possible exception of physical training for some, are definitely extracurricular and not part of the regular curriculum.

The realist wants youth to be healthy. There is no question in his mind that the school should provide "an atmosphere conducive to both emotional and physical health." Furthermore, "knowledge about the principles of physical and emotional health is a proper ingredient of the curriculum." He believes that the community does have a responsibility to provide "clinical facilities for therapy, . . . but this does not mean that they are part of the school program or curriculum any more than are the boilers in the heating system." The home must have the complete responsibility for assisting youth to acquire desirable health habits—that is, unless we wish to establish some form of community youth organization to accomplish this end. Adolescents are typically too healthy and full of energy to be concerned with health problems.

Similarly, sex education is certainly not a proper function of the school. Is it not logical that teaching the means for securing the health values would be incomplete anyhow until the perspective from which they are viewed is also taught? This perspective is found only in the humanities— in literature, art, religion, and philosophy. The realist, therefore, believes that every person needs a basic core of knowledge in order to lead a human life, and this includes the learning of health knowledge. This is consistent with the central purpose of the school—the development of the individual's rational powers.

For the realist, work and play are typically sharply differentiated in life. Play serves a most useful purpose at recess or after school, but it should *not* be part of the regular curriculum. The use of leisure is significant to the development of our culture, but winning the "cold war" is going to take a lot more hard work and somewhat less leisure. The realist sees leisure pursuits or experiences as an opportunity to get relief from work while such recreation is serving a re-creative purpose in the life of man. The surplus energy theory of play and recreation makes sense to him. So does the more recent bio-social theory of play— the idea that play helps the organism to achieve balance. The realist feels that the "play attitude" is missing almost completely in many of our organized sports. Play and recreation are, therefore, very important to him. He believes that they can be "liberating" to the individual. People can develop their potentialities for wholesome hobbies through recreation. Furthermore, recreation can serve as a "safety valve" by the reduction of psychic tensions which are evidently caused by so many of life's typical stresses. Even though play should *not* be considered as a basic part of the curriculum, it does provide an "indispensable seasoning" to the good life. Extracurricular play and recreational activities and a sound general education should suffice to equip the student for leisure activities in our society.

METHODOLOGY.   Realistic methodology varies somewhat depending on whether the naturalistic realist, the rational humanist, or the Catholic realist is speaking. This is not meant to imply that there are not many similarities or overlapping points. The naturalistic realist practices a problem-solving approach to classroom learning typically. Education is more than a matter of merely acquiring knowledge; we must learn how to use it practically for subsequent enjoyment of life. For the rational humanist, the greater the amount of reasoning required to learn a subject, the more important is that subject in the curriculum. The Catholic realist, as well as the rational humanist, believes that there are two orders of learning: (a) a logical or essential order; and (b) an order where the teacher starts with the child's interest and then works his way back to insure adequate coverage of the subject matter necessary for a complete treatment of the various knowledges to be learned. Interest is desirable, but it must be subordinate to effort at many times.

The theory of transfer of training is supported by the realist. The rational humanist and the Catholic realist believe that transfer of training takes place through the transference of disciplinary values, which have a functional application in any situation.

The naturalistic realist is often a behaviorist and thereby committed to a stimulus-response type of learning. When a new learning situation presents itself, it is quite apt to contain a number of identical elements that have appeared earlier in another learning circumstance.

Drill is needed to perfect habit formation at the lower learning levels. Such drill may well be varied and correlated with other teaching techniques.

The realist, as an essentialist, is committed to a greater or lesser degree to the position that learning is a process of acquiring objective knowledge by the scientific method. Thus, the teacher should be the voice of science; clear, objective, and factual. He is a person of authority who transmits the truth and wisely guides immature minds. He analyzes the skills to be learned, and he breaks them down to their simplest components for the students.

A realistic teacher will find it legitimate to indoctrinate. Because the program is required, and because there is little opportunity for election, it is possible for the realistic teacher to arrange the curriculum logically and sequentially in advance.

The use of texts, tests, and grades is needed to convey to the student information about the calibre of his performance. Objective standards of performance are to be met. A realist is concerned with research, measurement, evaluation, and their application to physical education, and he relies upon tested and proven methodology and curricula. Prizes and awards may be used by the teacher to stimulate students to achieve the greatest amount of excellence in their efforts.

The realistic teacher is not averse to using various types of disciplinary measures. He feels that it is imperative that he control the conduct of his students so that necessary learning takes place. Parents and teachers can cooperate on this point. Eventually the student becomes free, and it is then up to him to discipline himself.

Strengths and Weaknesses

Once again it should be made clear that it is a most difficult task to list the strengths and weaknesses of a particular philosophical approach. This is especially true because the author wishes to remain as impartial as possible. Consequently, only a few of the strengths and weaknesses will be discussed, and then but briefly.

Generally speaking, realism seems to be *strong* because it encourages us to accept the world just as we find it. Things are the way we find them; our experience does not change them in the least. This would appear to be a straightforward concept that most people could understand without difficulty. Man lives in a world which is orderly and regular—a world of cause and effect.

In the field of education we see another example of what might be considered a strength of realism—whatever man has discovered to be true because it conforms to reality must be handed down to future generations as the cultural tradition. If man is to master all the subject matter which is to be passed on to succeeding generations, he must develop his intellect to its highest potentiality. If we realize that we *do not make reality* and that we *only discover it,* this tends to make us understand that we must get outside of ourselves as much as possible and establish contact with the world; only in this way can we hope to accomplish anything of consequence.

In our area of physical, health, and recreation education, realism would appear to be strong because it stresses that we have a unique function to perform—giving man an adequate physical basis so that intellectual life may be assured. At least this is the task of physical education, and it is not necessary to muddy the waters and make all sorts of claims about concomitant learnings—claims that can't be proved anyhow and to which many other educational areas make a contribution. In the struggle for survival "the stamina and strength which the defense of liberty requires . . . come only from bodies which have been conditioned by a lifetime of participation in sports and interest in physical activity." [98] Certainly this places physical education further down in a hierarchy of educational values, but at least we know exactly what our function is. No other area of education can make this particular claim, and this gives the realist in physical education an assured place, albeit a lower one by the very nature of the world itself.

This approach makes the issue among physical education, health education, and recreation more clear-cut. There does appear to be a marked trend toward moving away from each other anyhow; each has its own unique function—physical education can give strong muscle groups and an adequate circulo-respiratory system; health education can provide a healthy atmosphere and can provide knowledges about principles of emotional and physical health; and recreation can provide relaxation from work and carefree activity performed for its own sake, including all types of recreational interests. In other words, the three are allied fields.

Since aims and method seem to go hand in hand, realism would

---

[98] Cf., p. 143.

appear to possess certain strengths in its method. The main argument here revolves around the consensus which is possible. The student acquires knowledge and then uses it practically to make a better life for himself. He develops discipline by persevering when interest lags. These disciplinary values may be transferred to other aspects of life. With this approach the teacher assumes his rightful role of authority; he may develop the curriculum to a great extent in advance and then drill his students until they reach perfection, or as close to it as is humanly possible. The realist is not denying the importance of interest in learning; he is simply not giving it the primary role. He relies heavily on research and measurement to prove the wisdom of the chosen curricula and the methodology to insure mastery of the cultural heritage. These are strong arguments, and the realist believes in his position—a position which he feels we must implement if we hope to do something about the general weakening of the fiber of American youth.

Critics of realism as an educational philosophy would immediately raise as a weakness the question of the "academic artificiality" of learning which would seem to be evident in this approach. Broudy himself criticizes the older traditional approach and asks for much greater stress on problem solving. The critic cannot see the wisdom of placing such great emphasis on "cultural heritage" and its mastery. He points out that each child is a unique personality and cannot be forced into a typical educational pattern without hindering his maximum development. It would seem that far too much emphasis is placed on transmission of information.

The opponent of realism is quick to point out also that physical, health, and recreation education properly taught offers many truly educational advantages to the student, if the organism is seen as being truly unified. Approaching this task from a unified base offers much greater strength, and realism tends to dissipate this strength through divisiveness. It is pointed out by the experimentalist further that a teaching method not based primarily on interest has an almost insurmountable obstacle to overcome.

Another weakness of realism as seen by the experimentalist is that realism's authoritarian approach is not compatible with democratic principle. Staff growth is hampered in a situation where an administrator with ultimate responsibility makes all the important decisions for them as well as the students. The argument is that shared responsibility is not enough to guarantee maximum progress; shared authority promotes greater *esprit de corps* and a much more effective atmosphere in which to study and work. Succession from one administrator to another may be effected with a minimum of disruption; this means that progress toward goals is smooth and even. Initiative and self-reliance do not come as a result of a realistic pattern of administrative control.

Lastly, realism does not appear to place sufficient emphasis on society and the social implications of the educational process. As the experimentalist sees it, education is very definitely a social phenomenon and thereby one of the basic means by which society progresses and regenerates itself. Under a realistic system of education the authority given a teacher tends to prevent him from presenting all sides of an issue and then encouraging students to form independent personal conclusions. The growth of pupils may be hampered as they face an ever-changing environment.

PART FIVE

Idealism

CHAPTER TEN

Idealism in Philosophy
and Education

Idealism is the third leading philosophical position of the Western world in the twentieth century to be considered. There are others, of course, that might be included, such as existentialism, logical empiricism, ontological philosophy of education, and language analysis.[1] But their implications for education have not been generally recognized or fully exploited; hence, they have been mentioned, described very briefly,[2] and left until another time and place.

In this chapter we will consider idealism first as a philosophy and subsequently in regard to its implications for education. It may well be argued that idealism should have been introduced prior to realism, which has gathered strength increasingly in the latter half of the nineteenth century and in the twentieth century. As was explained at the beginning of Chapter 8, the justification for this order is that realism had a number of similarities to experimentalism in regard to the basic categories under consideration, and especially as to the involvement of the scientific method as the major means whereby the problem of education may be met most effectively.[3]

To recapitulate most concisely, naïve naturalism undergirds much

---

[1] For an interesting treatment of these philosophical positions and their implications for education, see N. B. Henry, ed., *Modern Philosophies and Education* (Chicago: University of Chicago Press, 1955).

[2] Cf., Chapter 3, pp. 39-42.

[3] Cf., p. 113.

of the philosophical thought in twentieth-century experimentalism and realism. Naturalistic belief holds that nature is reliable and dependable. Experimentalism stresses the importance of experience as the only means of discovering whether something is worthwhile. Realism, generally speaking, is the philosophical approach which accepts the world at face value. From the viewpoint of man, the world out there *is* exactly as he experiences it. It is as it seems to be, and our experiencing it changes it not one whit. Idealism, briefly, is defined as a world view which maintains that reality as a whole is best conceived in terms of ideas or thought. Many idealists would deny the existence of the material world save as it is dependent on man's mind or on the Universal Mind (an impersonal rational order). Translated into everyday terms, many men consider man to be composed of body, mind (brain), and spirit (soul). They believe in the reality of self and are also convinced that they have a soul which lives on after they die. Those who subscribe to the philosophy of idealism believe that man experiences a mind or spirit in himself; that it is a real entity; and that somehow (beyond their ability to describe it) the entire universe is essentially mind or spirit in its very nature.

In this chapter the metaphysics, epistemology, logic, and axiology of idealism will be explained in accordance with the sequence previously established in this book. In the second half of the chapter, society, school, and the individual, educational aims and objectives, and the process of education will be examined in the light of the philosophy of idealism.

Metaphysics

As we have indicated, idealists believe generally that mind (or spirit) as experienced by all men is basic and real and that the entire universe is mind essentially. For them, mind is the only true reality. In early modern history René Descartes described the first part of the position with his now famous statement, "I think, therefore I am." Here is a belief that one's own self is the most immediate reality in his conscious experience. For Descartes, also, "the experience of God is evidenced in the experience of each one of us by the fact that we have an idea of a perfect being."[4] This point is very important in understanding the knowledge process of the idealist.

THE NATURE OF MAN. A second metaphysical question has to do with the nature of man. Urban points out that we must make up our minds

---

[4] J. Donald Butler, *Four Philosophies,* rev. ed. (New York: Harper & Row, Publishers, Inc., 1957), p. 137.

whether we are high-grade monkeys or sons of God.[5] It is difficult to teach unless we know just what we are dealing with in our fellow man. According to the idealistic tradition, a man is more than just a body, more than one of many living in human society. He possesses a soul and such possession makes him of a higher order than all other creatures on earth. This soul is a link to the spiritual nature of all reality—the only true reality (as already stressed)!

THE NATURE OF BEING. Horne explains that the term *ontology* has been given to the subject which treats the problem of the nature of being. Somehow, we are told, *"to be* is to be experienced by an absolute self." [6] At this point in his explanation, Horne asks a series of four short questions—the answers to which give us some insight into this important philosophical position:

To what is the order of the world due? The order of the world is the problem of cosmology, and idealism holds that the order of the world is due to the manifestation in space and time of an eternal and spiritual reality.

What is knowledge? Knowledge is the problem of epistemology, and idealism holds that knowledge is man thinking the thoughts and purposes of this eternal and spiritual reality as they are embodied in our world of fact.

What is beauty? Beauty is the problem of aesthetics, and idealism says that the beauty of nature which man enjoys and the beauty of art which man produces is the perfection of the infinite whole of reality expressing itself in finite forms.

And what is goodness? Goodness is the problem of ethics, and idealism holds that the goodness of man's individual and social life is the conformity of the human will with the moral administration of the universe.[7]

In the following few pages we shall see a little more clearly what Horne means by these abstract concepts.

THE UNIVERSE IS BASICALLY SPIRITUAL. For many people it is difficult to understand just what the idealist means when he says that the world is basically spiritually constituted. How does the universe "think in me," as Bosanquet asserts?[8] It can evidently only happen because the individual is part of the whole, and it is man's task to learn as much about the Absolute as possible. Furthermore, if man finds it possible to interpret his world accurately, this would appear to be a positive indication that the universe is basically spiritual and not mechanical (as the naturalistic realist believes).

---

[5] Wilbur M. Urban, "Metaphysics and Value," in *Contemporary American Philosophy*, eds. G. P. Adams and W. P. Montague (New York: The Macmillan Company, 1930), Vol. II, 371.

[6] Herman H. Horne, "An Idealistic Philosophy of Education," in *Forty-first Yearbook* of the National Society for the Study of Education (Chicago: University of Chicago Press, 1942), Part I, p. 139.

[7] *Ibid.,* p. 140.

[8] Bernard Bosanquet, "Life and Philosophy," in *Contemporary British Philosophy*, ed. J. H. Muirhead (New York: The Macmillan Company, n.d.), Series 2, p. 61.

MONISM OR PLURALISM.   One of the most perplexing questions raised by the idealist is the problem of monism or pluralism. Is there just one God (or Spirit) of which all men's spirits are a part, or are there an infinite number of "individual finite minds" in existence? This matter may seem somewhat akin to the question, "How many angels can dance on the head of a pin?" But for the idealist the problem is very real, and we find a division of opinion and a search for synthesis. Some idealistic philosophers object most strenuously to the unity concept because of the destruction of the conception of individuality within the world. Furthermore, they simply can't conceive of such a "dilution" taking place within the "matrix" of the Supreme Reality. In addition, idealism's value concept as applied to the individual spirit would be destroyed if all spirits are, or become, part of the total Universal Mind.[9]

TYPES OF IDEALISM.   At this point it would seem only logical to present one philosopher's classification of the various types of idealism categorized somewhat in relationship to this problem of the one or the many:

1. *Spiritual Pluralism,* which interprets Reality as a Society of Spirits.

2. *Spiritual Monism,* which interprets Reality as the manifestation, or objectification, of a single Spiritual Energy.

3. *Critical (Kantian) Idealism,* which avoids offering a theory of Reality but makes clear that every form of experience, because of the universal and necessary principles of "Reason" in it, has a contribution to make to the theory of Reality.

4. *Absolute Idealism,* which attempts a synthetic, or synoptic, interpretation of Reality in the light of its various "appearances." [10]

Kant's so-called critical idealism developed from his careful analysis of man's acquisition of knowledge. He believed that one's conscious experience gives the world a unity. Sensations were described as *representations* within man. Through his power of reason, man receives twelve *conceptions,* which may be categorized according to quantity, quality, relation, or modality. "Out there behind it all," according to Kant, is the "thing-in-itself" that cannot be known by man. God placed moral law in the universe. Absolute idealism, the last of the four types of idealism listed by Hoernle, appears to be a synthesis or combination of spiritual pluralism and spiritual monism. In this belief the finite selves are unique, but still they are parts of a unified Ultimate Self.

THE PROBLEM OF EVIL.   The problem of evil within the world is a distressing one for many philosophers to explain, and this seems to be especially true for the idealist. Consider the question, "How can the

---

[9] J. A. Leighton, "The Principle of Individuality and Value," in *Contemporary Idealism in America,* ed. Clifford Barrett (New York: The Macmillan Company, 1932), p. 150.

[10] R. F. Alfred Hoernle, *Idealism as a Philosophy* (New York: Doubleday & Company, Inc., 1927), p. 306.

many be part of the One if they are evil and He is perfectly good?" The reply of the idealist might well be that evil is not self-sustaining; if in this world individuals have freedom to achieve and realize good, then evil as an alternative must be a necessary possibility. Hocking would have us believe that evil is the "seamy side" of good.[11] When we sin, it might be said that we have missed the target of good. Butler explains that "evil is not a real existent value; it is the negation of value." [12] In this theory the only reality is Ultimate Mind in which there exists no evil. Here evil has no "status," but is rather thought of as something that is past and gone. This is a great boon to a world that has seen much evil in the form of wars, pestilence, famine, and certain examples of man's inhumanity to man. Butler describes them as "immaturities sloughed off." [13] Other philosophers have asked questions about the evils in the world for which man doesn't seem to be responsible. These have been viewed by some as spurs used to awaken man and to stir him in such a way that he will strive for genuine achievement.

FREEDOM OF WILL.   Each of these philosophies that we have considered makes a case for man's freedom. He is seen as a free agent in this world; the crux of the matter revolves around the particular definition of the word *free*. The idealist would say that man has the freedom necessary to determine which way he shall go in this life. This freedom of will is seen as existing to the extent that an individual is a part of the whole of reality—within this sphere there is freedom of choice and action.

Epistemology

The theory of knowledge is vital to an understanding of the philosophy of idealism. It is obvious that we need substantial evidence that our ideas about the universe are true, and idealists claim that understanding the nature of knowledge will clarify the nature of reality. Greene, who calls himself a *liberal Christian idealist*, has explained how he views the "nature, limits, and criteria of human knowledge." Briefly, his reasoning is as follows: Man must experience something in order to truly know anything about it; yet, "primary experience alone can never suffice either to give us knowledge or to validate our alleged insights into the real." [14] The primary data that we receive through our senses must be interpreted. Furthermore, intuition defined as *immediate self-*

---

[11] William E. Hocking, *The Meaning of God in Human Experience* (New Haven, Conn.: Yale University Press, 1928), p. 178.

[12] Butler, *Four Philosophies*, p. 189.

[13] *Ibid.*

[14] Theodore M. Greene, "A Liberal Christian Idealist Philosophy of Education," in *Fifty-fourth Yearbook* of the National Society for the Study of Education (Chicago: University of Chicago Press, 1955), Part I, pp. 100-102.

validating insight is not acceptable, although there are probably times when certain individuals combine their insight and experience in such a way that they suddenly become aware of certain truths that they had not realized until that time. There is a middle position between naïve realism, a position that man knows reality merely by encountering it, and skeptical phenomenalism, a belief that man never actually encounters reality—only something which he constructs subjectively. This middle position, which Greene holds and classifies as critical realism, is one in which man actually encounters reality and reconstructs it for himself to the best of his human ability. Finally, we must be able to test a theory of knowledge, and Kant's idea of "correspondence" and "coherence" makes sense to Greene. First, we can accept any interpretations of reality that are based on reliable data (correspondence), and, secondly, such interpretations would be valid if they show a significant relationship to other judgments emanating from varied types of experiences (coherence).

OTHER IDEALISTIC THEORIES OF KNOWLEDGE.   We should examine other idealistic theories of knowledge in addition to that of Greene. Berkeley said that the world is meaningful to us only because our minds perceive it. Since, in man's experience, the world has quality and meaning, the Universal Mind must have put the meaning there.[15] Kant, known as a critical idealist, analyzed the knowledge process *without* making a radical leap beyond *our* world to comprehend reality. He theorized that the mind receives chaotic sensory stimulations passively; that they are made orderly by perception (categorized as space and time) which groups them into objects and events; and that a still further unity of conception is gained by a mind that is capable of linking causes and effects.[16] Kant believed that man can identify himself with this phenomenal world (of man's experience), but he did not envision a "Mind" (like Hegel and Fichte did) in the noumenal world beyond the "phenomenal sphere." [17]

HORNE'S IDEALISTIC PRINCIPLES.   As has been indicated, if we are able to comprehend the nature of knowledge, we can then obtain a better understanding of the reality of nature. Nature is the medium by which God communicates to us. Basically knowledge comes only from the mind —a mind which must offer and receive ideas. Mind is the "explainer" of the real. As Horne points out, matter "is a concept of mind." They are not "convertible terms" however.[18] In explaining his grounds for accepting idealism, several of his basic principles should be included for the light that they may shed on idealistic theory of knowledge. The first

---

[15] Cf., p. 33.

[16] Cf., pp. 33-34.

[17] The "noumenal world" is beyond man's ability to experience it (according to Kant).

[18] Horne, *Forty-first Yearbook,* Part I, p. 145.

of these ("Mind is the principle of explanation") has been touched on in a roundabout fashion already. Secondly, Horne explains that "mind is not matter." By this he means that matter occupies space, but mind does not; scientists can weigh matter, but this is impossible with mind. "The mind that thinks matter cannot itself be matter, and matter being unintelligent, cannot think itself." [19] Basically, therefore, they are "qualitatively different."

His third premise is that "mind comes from mind." Because mind and matter are "qualitatively different," it can be reasoned that a mind of an individual cannot be inherited from a body composed of matter. This leads to the belief that a finite mind emanates through heredity from another finite mind. Furthermore, it could be that all finite minds are "materializations" of an infinite mind—Universal Spirit. This belief is, of course, contrary to the theory of emergent evolution that looms so large in naturalistic and materialistic thought of today—the theory that mind does originate from matter.[20]

Horne's fourth principle is that "there can be no object without a subject." The basic premise here is that thought is the standard by which all else on the world is judged. Such thought serves as a unifying principle by which reality may be measured. This idea is explained as follows:

An object is always an object of thought. The subject is a thinker. The thinker thinks an object. Whatever the thinker thinks about becomes for him the object of thought. An alleged world of objects without a thinker to think them is a self-contradiction. The proposition that without a subject there is no object is true of all thinkers whatsoever. The world exists for the finite thinker only as he thinks the world. If he thinks the world exists when he is not thinking of it, it exists for him as this independent thing which he thinks it to be. The transition is easy in thought from the world as the object of finite thinking to the world as the object of infinite thinking. The world then would exist in itself as the object of infinite thinking just as it exists for us as the object of finite thinking. And because thinking the world and the will to have a world go together as phases of the mental process, man has a world because it fulfills his purposes to have a world. Even so, we may suppose, the world exists in itself as it is thought and willed, that is, ordered and sustained, by the universal mind whose thought the world is and whose purpose the world fulfills. This line of argument is epistemological. It holds that the kind of world we know suggests that it is itself the expression of a universal intelligence in whose image our own intelligence is cast.[21]

As difficult as this line of reasoning may be for us to follow, it is basic to the philosophy of idealism.

---

[19] *Ibid.,* p. 143.

[20] *Ibid.,* pp. 143-144.

[21] *Ibid ,* p. 146.

HOW MAN ACHIEVES KNOWLEDGE.   Idealistic philosophers differ in degree when they attempt to explain how man achieves knowledge. Calkins asserts that by direct observation (experience) she experiences "mental reality" and recognizes it as something "significantly different from what I observe as bodily process or physical reality." [22] Such knowledge of the reality of oneself may come from the self-satisfaction, exhilaration, or disappointment that an individual feels before, during, or after participation in recreational activities of all types. Enjoying the consummate violin artistry of a Fritz Kreisler; the feeling of exhaustion, and yet satisfaction, that an athlete experiences after a supreme effort; and the admiration that one feels after listening to someone like Bertrand Russell discuss the world's problems are all experiences which allow us to realize vividly our own reality, and perhaps the reality of something outside ourselves which is somewhat constricting and confining to us as individuals. And yet there is great similarity between the self and that which appears to be other than the experiencing self consciously taking part in the total experience. This outside agency is conjectured, therefore, as a greater self of which the experiencing individual is a part. An example of this might be as follows: a man stands at a certain vantage point overlooking a beautiful valley below; he sees a village, a winding river, and many people busily occupied with their daily tasks; a great sense of peace and well-being comes over him as he contemplates this scene fully realizing that his home and family are down there too (in other words, *he* is having this unique experience and he has a relationship to the people in that environment); and yet this man, and his family, and all those other people are finite selves who are a part of a greater self that is also achieving the values which are inherent in such a setting. Similarly, other idealists, believing that the reality of the self is a fact, assume that because of this the nature of the remainder of existence is implied—a greater Self! Any other belief, they assert, would make our world unintelligible and therefore pointless.

Truth for idealists is orderly and systematic. A test for truth is its coherence with knowledge that has been previously established. An individual, therefore, attains truth for himself by examining the wisdom of the past through his own mind. Everything that exists has a relationship to something else and is intertwined. Reality, viewed in this way, is a system of logic and order—a logic and order that has been established by the Universal Mind. Experimental testing helps to determine what the truth really is with the chips falling where they may.

---

[22] Mary Whiton Calkins, "The Philosophical Credo of an Absolutistic Personalist," in *Contemporary American Philosophy*, eds. G. P. Adams and W. P. Montague (New York: The Macmillan Company, 1930), Vol. I, 201.

Logic

In earlier chapters we have defined logic as the systematic study of certain general principles upon which correct thinking is based.[23] This involves the acceptance of basic propositions and a variety of subsequent interrelations which may be inferred from these statements. There is rather general agreement among the various philosophical positions that logic is primarily concerned with the methods of reasoning that a man may use as he attempts to find answers to his problems. Idealism, as does realism, places great emphasis of formal logic and its development because of the significance of mind and its various perceptions and conceptions.

For the idealist, formal logic, which got its start with the Greeks and was developed into a complete system by Aristotle, explains how man distinguishes sound from unsound reasoning. It is a particular kind of thinking that involves "the use of supposed truths as evidence in support of other supposed truths." [24] An intelligent person should be able to gather facts and determine what they mean. It appears to be true that a person must be trained, just like an athlete is trained and disciplined in his particular sport, in order to reason correctly. What a shame it is that so many educators, and especially persons in physical, health, and recreation education, never have, or take, the opportunity to study even elementary logic. There seems to be little doubt that we need clear thinking more than ever in the second half of the twentieth century.

TWO BRANCHES OF LOGIC. Idealists accept the traditional division of logic into two branches which are called *deductive logic* and *inductive logic* respectively. The aim in deductive logic is to reason by establishing a conclusive inference (or conclusive inferences) that is based upon true reason; hence, any inference based upon this reason (or these reasons) must be true. The process, therefore, moves from general premises to their necessary conclusion, or from the universal to the individual. When we use induction, or inductive logic, we reason from certain particulars to a general conclusion, or from the individual to the universal. The syllogism, which is used extensively for deductive reasoning, is an analysis of a formal argument in which the conclusion necessarily results from the given premises. It should be pointed out that modern scientific investigation relies very heavily on a thought process that is largely inductive, but it does revert quite often along the way to deduction as

---

[23] Cf., pp. 116-117. Traditional logic could well have been introduced under realism.
[24] Max Black, *Critical Thinking*, 2nd ed. (Englewood Cliffs, N.J.: Prentice-Hall, Inc., 1952), p. 5.

well. The materials of logic are the generally accepted truths that make up a lasting body of knowledge. They come from both everyday experience and scientific investigation.

SOME BASIC ELEMENTS OF LOGIC. It seems appropriate at this point to introduce to the student of physical, health, and recreation education a few of the basic elements of formal logic. For those who have already had a course in logic, this may seem very elementary; yet, it will serve as a very brief review. It may whet the appetite of others and perhaps encourage them to elect a course in logic or to study it on their own. As was mentioned earlier, idealism does stress formal logic heavily. For this reason it does fit here more appropriately than elsewhere.

A SYLLOGISM DEFINED. A fairly exact definition of a syllogism is that it is an argument which contains two premises and a conclusion. When the arguments contained in the premises are true, they infer a conclusion that is true as well. A syllogistic sentence contains four elements: a quantifier; a subject; a copula which relates the subject to its predicate; and the predicate itself.

DECLARATIVE SENTENCES. There are many different kinds of sentences in the English language, but logic includes only declarative sentences that make either true or false assertions about some phase of the world as we know it. Such declarative sentences may be either true or false, and it is important to know the difference. A sentence is negative when the word *no* or *not* modifies the verb (or copula). The sentence "All football players are gentlemen" is *affirmative,* while "Wrestlers are not hungry" is definitively *negative.* Here we are speaking about the quality of the sentences.

When we become concerned with the quantity of a sentence, then we encounter another basic classification of declarative sentences into those which are *universal, particular,* and *singular.* A universal sentence is one in which the subject refers to each and every entity in that classification (e.g., "*All* basketball players are tall."). A particular sentence's subject is qualified (e.g., "*Some* basketball players are tall."). The third type is called a singular sentence (e.g., "Wilt Chamberlain is tall."). A further distinction in syllogistic theory for purposes of simplification states that singular propositions are always to be interpreted as universal.[25]

FOUR POSSIBLE STANDARD SENTENCES. Now it is possible to state that in this logical system there are only four possible standard sentences. A declarative sentence is either affirmative, negative, universal, or particular. For purposes of discussion, universal-affirmative sentences are

[25] Avrum Stroll and Richard H. Popkin, *Introduction to Philosophy* (New York: Holt, Rinehart and Winston, Inc., 1961), pp. 14-17. Other excellent basic texts in logic are Morris C. Cohen, *A Preface to Logic* (New York: Holt, Rinehart and Winston, Inc., 1944), and Max Black, *Critical Thinking,* 2nd ed. (Englewood Cliffs, N.J.: Prentice-Hall, Inc., 1952).

called *A sentences;* universal-negative sentences are designated as *E sentences;* particular-affiirmative sentences are know as *I sentences;* and particular-negative sentences are called *O sentences.*

DISTRIBUTION. As we proceed along the way to an elementary understanding of syllogistic argument through the development of certain rules regarding the validity of a statement, it is important to understand the concept of distribution. The terms of all A, E, I, and O sentences are distributed in one way or another whether we are referring to the *subject term* or to the *predicate term.* For example, in the sentence, "All swimmers have webbed toes," the word *swimmers* is considered to be *distributed.* (Refers to all members of class denoted by term.) If we were to say, "Some swimmers are flexible," the term *swimmers* is described as *undistributed,* because only certain swimmers are being considered. Predicate terms are analyzed in the same way. The following rules summarize the distribution possibilities:

1. Universal-affirmative sentences (A) may have distributed subject terms, but the predicate term is always undistributed.
2. Universal-negative sentences (E) may have distributed subject terms as well as distributed predicate terms.
3. Particular-affirmative sentences (I) do not distribute the subject term or the predicate term.
4. Particular-negative sentences (O) do not distribute the subject term, but do distribute the predicate term.

Some typical sentences which explain, or are examples of, these four standard types are:

       D   U
1. All physical educators are good philosophers (A).
       D   D
2. No health educators are overpaid (E).
      U   U
3. Some recreators are true "missionaries" (I).
      U   D
4. Some coaches are not educators (O).

SYLLOGISTIC ANALYSIS. There are a few more terms which must be understood before we will be ready to determine the validity of any particular syllogism. As we said earlier, a syllogism contains two premises and a conclusion; furthermore, both premises must be true in order to get a valid conclusion. The terms *major term, middle term,* and *minor term* are used to give more exactness to premises and conclusion. Keep in mind that the two premises and the conclusion have a total of three subject terms and three predicate terms. Now consider the syllogism:

All realists are strong,
All weight lifters are realists,
Therefore, All weight lifters are strong.

Notice that of the total of six subject and predicate terms in this syllogism three are different. Furthermore, each of these different terms occurs twice, i.e., realists (M), weight lifters (S), and strong (P). The middle term (M) is that term which appears in both premises, but not in the conclusion. The major term (P) appears in the predicate of the conclusion and also in the first premise. The predicate of the conclusion is called the *major term* because it refers to the *largest class*. The minor term (S) is in the subject of the conclusion and is present also once in the premises. The major term contains the major premise, and the minor term contains the minor premise.

It is now possible to list the various rules to which a valid syllogism must conform.[26] At the same time it must be kept in mind that these rules hold *only* when syllogistic arguments are being considered. Several of these rules are known as *rules of quantity,* because they apply to the distribution of the subject and predicate terms. The remainder refer to whether the sentence is affirmative or negative and are known as *rules of quality.* Each rule will be illustrated with an example.

1. Two negative premises yield no valid conclusion.

> An example of a syllogism which violates this rule would be as follows:
> No swimmers are finned,
> No finned things are capable of walking,
> Therefore, no swimmers are capable of walking.

In this situation no suitable connection is made between the premises of the argument. There would have to be an affirmative premise showing that swimmers are indeed finned before a conclusion could follow logically.

2. If both premises are positive, the conclusion must be positive.

> An example of a syllogism which violates this rule would be as follows:
> All gymnasts are mortal,
> All mortals have muscles,
> Therefore, some muscled things are not gymnasts.

The difficulty in this case is that the conclusion is false, because it assumes information that has not been provided in the premises. We do know that mortals have muscles, but we are not in a position to conclude either that some muscled things are not gymnasts or that there are not some muscled things which are not gymnasts.

3. If one premise is negative, the conclusion must be negative.

> An example of a syllogism which violates this rule would be as follows:
> All ice-hockey players are skaters,
> Some Congolese are not skaters,
> Therefore, some Congolese are ice-hockey players.

In the particular situation described in this syllogism, many of the principles, or rules, of acceptable syllogisms are present. Even though both premises are

---

[26] Black, *Critical Thinking,* pp. 139-151.

true, the conclusion is false. Just because some are excluded from a particular group (i.e., skaters), we cannot infer that some must belong. In this case, all Congolese may not be ice skaters.

4. The middle term must be distributed at least once.

An example of a syllogism which violates this rule would be as follows:
  All New York Yankees are baseball players,
  All Detroit Tigers are baseball players,
  Therefore, all Detroit Tigers are New York Yankees.
Keep in mind the earlier rules that we have discussed. In this example it is baseball players, and it appears in the predicate term of both premises. But in universal-affirmative sentences (A) the predicate term is undistributed, and here it is not. The syllogism is not constructed so that the two premises are connected by an undistributed middle term. It must be kept in mind that valid reasoning has to go hand in hand with true premises to get a correct conclusion that makes sense. Remember *the fallacy of the undistributed middle!*

5. The major (minor) term cannot be distributed in the conclusion unless it is distributed when it appears earlier in the premises.

An example of a syllogism which violates this rule would be as follows:
  All football players are well paid,
  Some physical educators are not football players,
  Therefore, some physical educators are not well paid.
Here we have what may be called an *illicit process*. The predicate is undistributed in positive propositions, and it is distributed in negative ones. The conclusion above is an O sentence which does distribute its predicate term. As a result we find a conclusion which attempts to provide more information than is given in the premises.

In concluding these rules for the presentation of a valid syllogism, be certain to keep in mind that a syllogism cannot have more than *three* terms and that the conclusion cannot be particular unless *one* premise is particular as well.

Although we have devoted considerable space within this chapter to some of the rules of elementary formal logic, several more points should be made briefly before passing on to the axiology of idealism. In the first place, it should be clearly understood that it will take careful study to apply these rules to the conversation and written statements that we hear and read in everyday life. Unfortunately, ordinary English must be translated into the language of logic. Students are therefore advised to study the references listed regarding the many ways of transposing ordinary English into logical sentences that can then be analyzed by these rules.

As mentioned earlier, science, inductive approach, and man's own sensory experience with the world are basic to logic's materials. The idealist is vitally concerned with the development of knowledge. For him this is a problem of extending vision so that increasingly more relationships can be seen. The more intelligent a person is, the more he will see the complex interrelationships existing in the world. He will be better able to analyze and synthesize. Mentally he will be able to break wholes down into their constituent parts and then reassemble them again. The end result will be greater understanding and appreciation of the world in which we live.

Axiology

The value system of idealism will be quite familiar to the large majority of the readers of this text, because America is said to have an idealistic superstructure and a materialistic base. First, we will consider the question of idealistic values generally as expressed by leading authorities.

GREENE ON VALUES. Greene, whom we discussed earlier and who states that he has been "damned as a heretic both by Catholics and by Fundamentalist Protestants," believes "in the reality, the discoverability, and the importance to man of objective values—of truth, beauty, and goodness as pure essences, and of truths, beauties, and concrete instances of goodness as finite embodiments of these absolute values." [27] He sees values as being "embedded in reality itself." Man, to him, is a "purposive being" who "seeks to apprehend these Values." He believes that "man's life is good in proportion as his search for the value dimensions of reality is successful." [28]

THE WORLD HAS MORAL ORDER. In explaining the idealistic credo underlying his philosophy of education, Horne refers to a world in which there is moral order. He believes "that no man can flout the moral law and that in the end there is a return of the deed on the doer." There is a law of cause and effect in the moral world, and we see man's ethical convictions justified again and again. The very nature of absolute reality is good. If man sins, he is opposing the nature of reality. In the end, however, justice will be served. Nothing that man can do will disturb the moral order of the world. [29]

A VALUE STRUCTURE. Butler sums up the general theory of the idealist about the world's value structure by listing three basic propositions. [30] He states that the values so important to man are part of the context of existence. They are important because people are able to comprehend them and enjoy them. To realize value, however, man must be able to relate parts and wholes. Calkins explains that these whole and part rela-

---

[27] Greene, *Fifty-fourth Yearbook*, Part I, p. 97.

[28] *Ibid.*, p. 105.

[29] Horne, *Forty-first Yearbook*, Part I, pp. 149-150.

[30] Butler, *Four Philosophies*, p. 206.

tionships are basic; thus, the individual can broaden his experience (and thereby enjoy more values already existent in the world) by trying to relate and understand all aspects of life with totality.[31]

Ethically, Kant's representation of the idealistic position is one that has been accepted by many following in the same tradition. He saw individual man as a person and as an end in himself. According to this belief, man's potentialities are greater than any other type of existence known. Kant believed further that in each and every man there is an "innate imperative" that orders his conduct toward the good. Thus, man should follow the universal moral laws, he should do the right because it is important and necessary, he should work for the ideal society in which all men are treated as ends, and he will gain immortality if he fulfills the universal moral laws.

Aesthetically, the idealism of the eminent philosopher, Arthur Schopenhauer, offered clear insight into the nature of beauty. He analyzed art as "the flower of life." As he stated, "it repeats or reproduces the eternal Ideas, which are the direct and adequate objectivity of the thing-in-itself, the will." Its aim is to depict in tangible form "the knowledge of Ideas." Science never reaches a final goal, but true art is "everywhere at its goal." [32]

Schopenhauer was extremely pessimistic. He felt that man's greatest problem was his individuality; this meant that life involved an endless succession of such experiences as struggle and strife with subsequent satiety and boredom. Nevertheless, man could rise to a level of experience above "individuality" through the medium of art. In the visual arts, for example, he can achieve "knowledge of the object" (i.e., the Idea—Platonic Idea) and true "existence" for a moment as a "will-less subject" receiving impressions of the Ideas behind the phenomenal world. True genius *"understands the half-uttered speech of Nature,* and articulates clearly what she only stammered forth. He expresses in the hard marble that beauty of form which in a thousand attempts she failed to produce, he presents it to Nature, saying, as it were, to her, 'That is what you wanted to say!' " [33] To enjoy true beauty as may be accomplished in the musical art, mortal man, a product of the world's natural order, must lose his own individuality through enjoyment of the "copy of the Will itself."

Religiously, we shall examine certain of the beliefs of two philosophers of the twentieth century—Theodore M. Greene and William E. Hocking. Greene identifies himself as an " 'idealist,' then, only in the sense that I am in *general* sympathy with the long tradition of 'objective' idealism

[31] Mary Whiton Calkins, *Contemporary American Philosophy*, Vol. I, 210-211.

[32] Arthur Schopenhauer, *The World as Will and Idea* in *Master-Works of Philosophy* (New York: Doubleday & Company, Inc., 1946), p. 596.

[33] *Ibid.*, p. 600.

from Socrates, Plato, and Aristotle to Kant and the nineteenth- and twentieth-century 'objective' idealists in England, Europe, and America." [34] He goes on to state that he is "a professing Christian in the Protestant tradition." To explain this position further, he states:

This means that I believe in a God who, whatever else He may be, is a dynamic agent, a spiritual power of force, not to be equated with the most objective of values but rather to be conceived of as their ultimate ground and source. This belief is quite consistent with the characteristic idealist belief in 'objective' values but quite incompatible with the equally characteristic idealist insistence on the ontological ultimacy and self-sufficiency of values and with their frequent disbelief in a dynamic God of righteousness and love. [35]

Greene is saying that he grounds his religious values "ultimately in that dynamic Being who is worshipped as God in the Christian faith." He bases his faith further in man's search for the religious values of truth, beauty, and goodness. He believes in objective values, but he is not so dogmatic as to believe that man has infallible knowledge of values. As he explains, these values to skeptics are "wholly unknowable by men." This goes far beyond Greene's intermediate position.

Hocking's position is also that of objective, or absolute, idealism. He sees the Absolute as Intelligent Personal Self or Will. In keeping with this fundamental position, it is understandable why he sees axiology and religion as closely related. A man's religious convictions determine his values; in this connection Hocking believes that religion is as much a matter of ideas as well as of feelings. He sees two central values: (1) the experience of God in the self-consciousness; and (2) the experience of love for God. In the first, the worshiper has a kinship with God in working for a common purpose; in the second, it is an impulse or urge which "propels" man toward God. Other so-called secondary values are the "transformation of self" through a conscious relationship with Him; a certain "knowledge of truth" as a result of the worship experience; a possibility for increased creativity on the part of the individual through a "freeing" experience; the enjoyment of achievement vicariously through alignment with the force of God in the world; a deliberate actualizing of the self as it works to carry out God's purpose; and a general enhancement of all human relations based on the fulfillment of the purposes of true religion. [36] As Hocking states in *The Will as a Maker of Truth:*

In all these respects there is the strongest resemblance between the religious idea and human value. . . . Thus the birth of value and the birth of God-faith are alike. . . . Is it not possible that they are the *same* thing,—in both cases the work of an ultimate *good-will* toward our world? [37]

---

[34] Greene, *Fifty-fourth Yearbook*, Part I, pp. 93-94.

[35] *Ibid.*

[36] Hocking, *The Meaning of God in Human Experience*, pp. 360-420.

[37] William E. Hocking, "The Will as a Maker of Truth," in *Approaches to the Philosophy of Religion*, eds. D. J. Bronstein and H. M. Schulweis (Englewood Cliffs, N.J.: Prentice-Hall, Inc., 1954), p. 23. Taken from *The Meaning of God in Human Experience*.

Man enters the realm of religious conviction when he lives according to the premise that the highest values which he holds are in harmony with the ultimate purpose of the world. Such ideals and values are the goals really worth striving for in the universe!

Socially, the philosophy of idealism finds itself in what has occasionally been considered a contradictory position. Butler deplores the criticism that idealism has received for its lack of social consciousness —that it could have been more positive in its social theory. He explains that this may have arisen because both Russian communism and Dewey's pragmatism are considered to be reactions against the idealism of Hegel. But, Butler states that "it should be noted that this failure is not essential to the character of idealism. Because there are certain principles central in idealism which have necessary social bearings and others which offer great promise, if applied, for the positive realization of social value." [38] He is quick to point out, however, that, although the idealist's conception of society is that it is an "organism in which individuals participate," the individual is not subordinate to that society. Society provides the means whereby the individual may realize himself; both the individual and society are ends.

Greene speaks about the "essential conditions of a liberal society." His definition of liberalism implies that the rights and freedoms of man will be respected. Such a free man will possess the basic liberal virtues of "(a) serious concern, (b) intellectual and moral integrity, and (c) profound humility." As he sees it, possession of these virtues provides "the only possible basis for full and responsible social co-operation." The focus does seem to be on man more than society, however, as Greene refers to "the development of man's highest social potentialities," and he continues by stating that "the truly liberal goal of education can never be defined merely in terms of a society, actual or ideal; we must resist the temptation to absolutize any form of social organization and to make education *merely* a means to the furtherance of a social goal." Greene is pointing out very clearly that "education and democracy are *both* institutional means for the achievement of more ultimate human ends." [39]

In this same vein we find that Horne affirms the "ultimate worth of personality." He can think of "nothing higher or more valuable than selfhood, or personality." Very interestingly, Horne presents a schematic conception of the possible progression of the learner as follows:

. . . the learner may progress from the atomic organization of the naturalist to the selective nervous system of the realist, then to the behaving organism of the pragmatist, and then on to the growing, finite personality of the idealist. [40]

---

[38] Butler, *Four Philosophies,* pp. 217-218.

[39] Greene, *Fifty-fourth Yearbook,* Part I, pp. 111-113.

[40] Horne, *Forty-first Yearbook,* Part I, p. 154.

But it is not the civilization or the society that is, or seems to be, of greatest importance. He believes that it is true that civilizations do develop personalities, "but in a larger sense it is true that personalities make civilizations." In both the lower and higher types of civilizations, the great personality (or leader) shines through. "No civilization or culture of a people surpasses that of its greatest leader." Idealistic values achieved in the past may be lost through incompetent and uninspired leadership. *The important thing, however, is that in a purposeful, spiritual environment the individual personality develops; in this light, society appears to be a means to a higher goal.*

Society, School, and the Individual

As the reader will recall, the implications of idealism for education were omitted intentionally in the earlier discussion of the three other educational positions which along with idealism are considered by some to make up essentialistic educational philosophy.[41] The other three positions were, of course, naturalistic realism, rational humanism, and Catholic supernaturalism. Despite the importance of the realistic position for many today, and despite the fact that Hansen in describing "a new philosophical orientation for a new era" in which "traditional philosophic idealism, in all of its numerous variants, is probably obsolescent if not already obsolete," [42] there appears to be a great deal of the "idealistic superstructure" left in modern America. The influence of Protestant Christianity is still very great, and as indicated earlier it is undergirded by absolute or objective idealism, the various branches of which see the Absolute as Spirit, as Intelligence, and as Intelligent Personal Self or Will, respectively.

SOCIAL AND CULTURAL HERITAGE ARE PASSED ON. Idealism, as well as realism, takes the position that the institution of education is necessary, because man needs a culture in which to develop, and it is the function of education to see to it that the social and cultural heritage is passed on to each human born therein. Idealism believes further that education gives God the opportunity to reveal Himself to man so that man may know the Divine through such an education. Horne believes that we should educate in a social milieu, because it is the best place. "If we rightly educate there," we may expect "a transformed society, composed of transformed individuals." [43] Education is therefore formalized through a school system.

---

[41] Cf., pp. 122-123 et ff.

[42] Kenneth H. Hansen, *Philosophy for American Education* (Englewood Cliffs, N.J.: Prentice-Hall, Inc., 1960), p. 45.

[43] Horne, *Forty-first Yearbook*, Part I, p. 173.

EDUCATION AND FUTURE PROGRESS. The idealistic position is that schools are established and supported by a society that sees the need to preserve its particular culture and to plan for its progress in the future. Schools reflect the society in which they are established. The school is one influence, albeit a very important one, that makes a society what it is. In this approach the school has a social and a communicative function; it should also develop an individual's and the society's ability to reason and plan. The question of progress is seen differently depending on the philosophical orientation of the society. Idealists, with their great concern for individual personality, see history as more than the influence of outstanding leaders on other men and the culture. Horne sees "the great man himself as an expression of some immanent purpose in the world." For him the "principle of cosmic personality" is the real explanation of progress. It gives us "a spiritual, as distinguished from a material, interpretation of history." [44]

It is interesting to note further that idealists, according to Horne, see education's function as being much more than "mere preservation of the cultural heritage." In the first place, he suggests that the school can improve society by suggesting desirable lines of future growth. It can "educate for leadership and followership." Another function would be to "express appreciation for right social emphases and criticism of misplaced emphases." It "can assist in handling social problems in a scientific way." And lastly, it "can assist in transmitting the established values of the past." [45]

THE SUPREME IMPORTANCE OF INDIVIDUAL PERSONALITY. Idealists have traditionally shown a great concern for the moral and spiritual values in society. Although the school should work for an ideal social order, the reasoning behind this is so that timeless values may be brought into the lives of mortal man. According to a recent report of the Educational Policies Commission of the National Education Association, "the basic moral and spiritual value in American life is the supreme importance of the individual personality." [46] To bring about the realization of this fundamental value the Commission is in favor of plans of school organization and administration in which the curriculum meets the many needs, interests, and aspirations of students. This belief is summed up as follows:

In educational terms, this value requires a school system which, by making freely available the common heritage of human association and human culture, opens to every child the opportunity to grow to his full physical, intellectual, moral, and spiritual stature.[47]

---

[44] *Ibid.*, p. 175.

[45] *Ibid.*, pp. 176-178.

[46] Educational Policies Commission, *Moral and Spiritual Values in the Public Schools* (Washington, D.C.: National Education Association of the United States, 1951), p. 18.

[47] *Ibid.*, p. 19.

AN INTERMEDIATE POSITION.   Progressivists feel that the school "should dare to create a new social order." Hansen asks the question, "Does society determine what the school should be, and the school then simply follow the dictates of society?" [48] He answers his own question when he explains that this is the way that it has always been in the history of the world. Idealists appear to take an intermediate position in answering this question. They want to "preserve and transmit the established values of the past"; yet, they show great concern for future growth and the "handling of social problems in a scientific way." They insist that the best is yet to come.

EDUCATION'S TRUE FUNCTION.   Greene's liberal approach to idealism is one in which there is a division of labor between the school and the other agencies of society. He urges the school to leave "certain vital functions" to society's other important institutions. If the school becomes involved in too many tasks, Greene is afraid that it will be less efficient and will neglect its true function. This he visualizes as follows:

. . . the preservation, dissemination, and extension of man's knowledge of himself and his total environment, along with all the techniques of teaching and learning. [49]

In speaking of the role of the school in our society, he does see *three* major responsibilities. First, the school should teach "the basic structure and essential processes of a democratic community." Our young people need to acquire an understanding of, and a devotion to, the freedoms that we have in this evolving democracy. But he urges, secondly, that "there is nothing sacrosanct or absolute in any form of social and political democracy, including our own." Lastly, one of Greene's great concerns is that we infuse students with a passion for social justice. [50] Thus, it can be said that Greene believes that the school, as the only agency whose primary responsibility is education, should "stress knowledge and the development of the mind." [51] In fairness to his beliefs, however, it must be pointed out that he conceives the term *mind* as "man's *total* cognitive equipment."

Educational Aims and Objectives

It is a relatively easier task to discuss idealistic aims and objectives in education than was the case with realism in Chapter 8. There the positions of naturalistic realism, rational humanism, and Catholic real-

[48] Hansen, *Philosophy for American Education,* p. 187.

[49] Greene, *Fifty-fourth Yearbook,* Part I, p. 116.

[50] *Ibid.,* p. 133.

[51] *Ibid.,* p. 117.

ism (supernaturalism) had to be differentiated and subsequently united in summary form.

IDEALISM VERSUS REALISM. In relationship to the other essentialistic positions in education, idealism is considered by some to be "on the border line." [52] Whereas it may be said that idealism was responsible for a good share of educational change in the nineteenth century, this is not true when we consider certain educational innovations of the twentieth century. Because idealism does place great emphasis on freedom and development of the personality, however, there do seem to be certain features of idealistic philosophy of education which are quite close to progressivistic views. It is true also that idealists and realists disagree on many points. For example: idealism allows for more personal freedom; it views the world quite optimistically; it is inclined toward a monistic outlook of the universe; and its system of reality is based on God's spiritual mind. Yet despite all these dissimilarities, Brameld believes that:

. . . modern realism and modern idealism belong to a united front; they are engaged in a task so momentous as to require the talents and interests of both: the task of constructing the intellectual and moral foundations for a modern culture common to both.[53]

A MORAL IMPERATIVE ON EDUCATION. Idealistic philosophy of education stresses that the developing organism becomes what it latently is. All education may be said to have a religious significance, which means that there is a "moral imperative" on education. As man's mind strives to realize itself, there is the possibility of realization of the Absolute within the individual mind. Horne explains this approach somewhat more specifically by explaining that education's aim is to help the child adjust to "these essential realities that the history of the race has disclosed." [54] These "essential realities" (or spiritual ideals) are truth, beauty, and goodness—the permanent values of the race experience that must be inculcated.

THE IDEALISTIC EDUCATIONAL PLAN. The idealistic view urges very strongly that personality has ultimate worth. An understanding of this interesting concept offers us clear insight into the educational plan of the idealist. Horne clarifies this phase of the idealistic position as follows:

But the growth of the person, or the spirit, in man is even more marvelous [than the growth of the physical organism] . . . The person seems endowed with unlimited capacities for growth in the attainment of knowledge and

[52] John S. Brubacher, *Modern Philosophies of Education,* 2nd ed. (New York: McGraw-Hill Book Company, Inc., 1950), p. 309.

[53] Theodore Brameld, *Philosophies of Education in Cultural Perspective* (New York: The Dryden Press, Inc., 1955), p. 268.

[54] Herman Harrell Horne, *The Philosophy of Education,* rev. ed. (New York: The Macmillan Company, 1930), p. 102.

wisdom, in the production and enjoyment of the beautiful, and in the acquisition of the ideal virtues of understanding, sympathy, coöperation, forgiveness, and self-sacrifice.[55]

Further insight into the educational goals of the idealist may be gained from a description of the *idealistic pupil* who aims for the stars in everything he undertakes:

The idealistic pupil is characterized by that admirable trait, the will to perfection. Whatever he does, he does as well as he can. He is ambitious to deserve honors in scholarship. He wants to grow in knowledge and wisdom, to appreciate the aesthetic things in life, to deserve approbation, and to be a worthy person. He seeks to cultivate social responsiveness and responsibility and those skills and techniques necessary for effective action. He strives for perfection because the ideal person is perfect. His motives may be misunderstood by some of his fellows but he is not disturbed thereby and goes on his straight course the best he can. He has the secret satisfaction of having aimed high and striven hard. This type of pupil is not a trouble-maker for teacher or parent or police officer, though at times he may exhibit the defect of his quality and become fanatical, ecstatic, or visionary.[56]

A HIERARCHY OF EDUCATIONAL VALUES.   Our next step in this inquiry into the idealistic philosophy of education may well be into the realm of educational values. If we determine that the highest good in life is based on a particular view of human nature, it is then possible to enumerate the various objectives of living (and learning) into some sort of a hierarchy of values. The idealist is vitally concerned with man's effort to realize his absolute goal—the establishment of his likeness to the spiritual order.

HORNE'S BASIC VALUES OF HUMAN LIVING.   Again we must turn to Herman Harrell Horne for help, since he has enumerated what he has called "the requirements of human nature, . . . the characteristics of a truly-educated person," and "the educational objectives of the perfectly integrated individual" on a number of occasions. The following, then, is Horne's list of the basic values of human living: health, character, social justice, skill, art, love, knowledge, philosophy, and religion.[57]

If we were to scale some of these educational objectives as to their importance, *the most important one would be an understanding of worship* which brings man into a conscious relation with the infinite spirit of the universe. Secondly, the development of "character in the individual and justice in society" must be attended to in the best possible way. Very important also is a knowledge of how to produce and enjoy the beautiful; this is followed closely by knowledge about the structure of the universe. Although the idealist would be one of the first to argue

---

[55] Horne, *Forty-first Yearbook*, Part I, p. 154.
[56] *Ibid.*, pp. 156-157.
[57] *Ibid.*, p. 181.

that man cannot live by bread alone, still he is most anxious that a man attain the skill requisite to one's economic independence. And finally, in what must not be construed as a complete list of objectives in a hierarchical arrangement, we find *good health at the bottom*. Horne does say, however, that we can "yet esteem it highly as a basic value for all the others, enhancing the richness of each and all of them." [58] Education for the idealist can therefore be said to be *ideal-centered* rather than child-centered, or curriculum-centered, or society-centered.

A CULTIVATED VOCATIONALIST. Idealists differ somewhat in their beliefs about the importance of vocational education in comparison to liberal education, but it may safely be said that their typical position is more progressive in this matter than that of the other essentialists. Horne refers to the educated person as a "cultivated vocationalist," but he does place higher emphasis on the fact that he should become a "cultivated human being." [59] Greene stresses the importance of a liberal education, also. He calls "knowledge and the development of the mind" the "central concern" in the entire educational process, but he is quick to point out that he is referring to "man's total cognitive equipment" when he attempts to define "mind." [60] When he speaks about the total preparation of the individual, it may be stated that he is taking [what he himself calls] a liberal idealistic position. Many idealists would designate the following statement as perhaps too progressive for them:

. . . so-called 'liberal education' and 'vocational training' should be conceived of neither as hostile rivals nor as mutually exclusive enterprises but, on the contrary, as two essential and complementary aspects of the total preparation of the individual for his total life. . . . If these two equally essential preparations for life are thus divorced, a *merely* liberal education will indeed tend to be useless, and a *merely* vocational training, crass.[61]

ELIMINATE DISTINCTION. Greene takes a further stand on this question, which will prove most interesting to professionals in physical, health, and recreation. He urges strongly that the distinction between curricular and extracurricular activities should be eliminated forthwith; such an idea, he states, can only hurt the total personality development of the individual.[62] This belief very definitely represents a radical departure from the typical essentialistic position on this matter.

HORNE'S DEFINITION. It seems only appropriate to conclude this section on idealistic aims and objectives of education with Horne's classic definition of the educational process:

---

[58] *Ibid.*, p. 186.
[59] *Ibid.*, p. 161.
[60] Greene, *Fifty-fourth Yearbook*, Part I, p. 117.
[61] *Ibid.*, pp. 118-119.
[62] *Ibid.*, pp. 119-120.

Education is the eternal process of superior adjustment of the physically and mentally developed, free, conscious, human being to God, as manifested in the intellectual, emotional, and volitional environment of man.[63]

The Process of Education

Now that we have considered the relationship that should exist among school, society, and individual and the aims and objectives of education according to the idealist, we are faced with the questions which relate to the actual educational process. What kind of activities do students engage in according to these beliefs (and in what way) in order that the end result will be satisfactory and rewarding to all those who are concerned?

THE IDEALISTIC CURRICULUM. The idealistic curriculum should be based on (1) the child's needs and interests; (2) the worthwhile demands of society; and (3) the type of universe in which we live.[64] Furthermore, it should offer a "rounded view of man in his world, a taste for the best things in life, and the ability to take one's own practical part in the world." [65] To bring about the desired result, there are certain essential studies. Horne divides the curriculum into three parts: the sciences; the fine arts; and the practical arts. For Greene the essential curriculum is divided as follows: formal disciplines (language, logic, and mathematics); the factual disciplines (the natural sciences and increasingly the social sciences); the normative disciplines (certain branches of philosophy such as ethics and aesthetics, artistic and literary criticism, and religion); and the synoptic disciplines (history, geography, and the remainder of philosophy).[66]

GREENE ON CLASSROOM SKILLS. Greene believes that there are some *skills* (as he designates them) that can be directly taught in a rather formal classroom situation. These skills relate directly to the disciplines presented immediately above. The student should learn how to think clearly and consistently and to use the language. Secondly, he can be taught a great many facts about the natural and social sciences. Next, he should learn how to evaluate all the situations he encounters in the world around him according to a set of standards or values. Lastly, he needs to acquire the skill necessary to see the world and its people "on balance." This latter skill will help him to avoid narrowness of perspective.

---

[63] Horne, *The Philosophy of Education*, p. 285.

[64] Horne, *Forty-first Yearbook*, Part I, p. 159.

[65] *Ibid.*, p. 160.

[66] Greene, *Fifty-fourth Yearbook*, Part I, pp. 121-123.

ATTITUDE DEVELOPMENT CAN'T BE TAUGHT. But despite the fact that the above skills can be taught to a varying degree to the learner, depending on his native ability, Greene asserts that it is not possible to teach fundamental attitudes or values directly. How then is it possible to teach a passion for clear thinking and a love of language; or a respect and a keen desire for fact; or a respect for values and a desire to evaluate situations sensitively; or an understanding and abhorrence of a narrow-minded approach to the world which prevents one from seeing various relationships in broad perspective? The idealist's answer is that this type of attitudinal development must come about in children and youth indirectly "by example, inspiration, and contagion." [67]

THE IDEALISTIC TEACHER. The idealist believes, therefore, that the teacher's personality is tremendously important! Such a teacher, as the idealist pictures him, is central and is the key to the entire educative process; he determines the pattern of education, arranges the environment, conceive objectives, and organizes the arrangement of the subject matter. The various idealistic educational philosophers paint such absolutely magnificent pictures of the qualities that the idealistic teacher should possess that one cannot help but believe that such a teacher could accomplish a great deal working with children. In fact, although idealists say that their curriculum is ideal-centered, it may well be stated that it is teacher-centered to a certain degree as well. For example, Horne describes this personality as follows:

The idealistic teacher, like the idealistic pupil, pursues the method of perfecting and the ideal of a cultivated personality. The things that are dear to him are self-consciousness, self-direction, self-activity, selfhood, inner spiritual growth . . . The infinite and the eternal, though he does not fully comprehend them, mean more to him than the finite and the temporal. His mind seems to rise naturally to the heavenly places. Plato and Emerson inspire him. He is much interested in understanding others through social intercourse. He feels the need for his pupils even as they feel there is something satisfying about him, as though he answered their deepest questions and satisfied their highest cravings. . . . Thus, teacher and pupils grow together as he awakens the dormant powers in younger selves. The sense of comanionship in spiritual growth is dear to him. He is a life-sharer. [68]

Such a teacher would no doubt have a great influence on many of his pupils, but the true idealistic teacher (according to Horne) does not give children *the* answers to questions; he tells them what the *possible* answers are, and they must come to their own conclusions. Any other approach would negate the respect that an idealistic teacher should have for the child's personality and intelligence. He does point out the weak-

---

[67] *Ibid.,* p. 123.

[68] Horne, *Forty-first Yearbook,* Part I, p. 157.

nesses of other positions, but he would never superimpose his own will on the learner. It is presumed that "infinite time" may be necessary for all to see the truth as it really is.

EVER-BROADENING UNDERSTANDING.　Believing that "the organism already latently is what it is to become," the idealist's education begins with the "self" (the individual person); it is more than a behavioral process. "The mind is the source of its own reactions to the world." [69] As Butler indicates, "growth can only come through self-activity." [70] From an understanding of himself the student reaches out for an understanding of the world outside himself. Brameld explains the relationship of idealistic learning to the Gestalt theory as follows:

It follows that idealism often tends to respect and to stress subjective psychological ideas and processes. Introspection and tuition, for example, are more congenial to it than realism. Moreover, the capacity of the mind—in idealistic theory—to combine related parts into qualitative wholes of meaning suggests that idealism thus far anticipates the Gestalt approach to learning. [71]

But we cannot forget the importance of the "gradual acquiescence" of the learner (who has, to be sure, begun with himself) as he acquires a greater sense of understanding and a "feeling of oneness" with God. Once this relationship to Spirit is felt and appreciated, the result is a much greater self-understanding.

IMPORTANCE OF IMITATION.　In this theory of learning, imitation is natural and should actually be used as a method in the work of the school. Idealists place great emphasis on the influence of outstanding personalities on students at all levels. This is one of the ways by which youth grows to maturity, and it is a much more powerful influence than we realize at times.

INTEREST AND EFFORT.　Idealists believe further that interest is an extremely important factor in bringing about education, but they are not willing to rest their entire case on this one factor alone. Horne has said that "effort leads to interest," and this maxim of learning should not be forgotten. If this is true, a certain amount of discipline at particular stages of learning may be necessary. Horne is more interested in a free discipline as an end product. Mankind starting with freedom has laboriously gained disciplined accomplishment. It is possible for education to speed up this process in the young by beginning with a certain amount of coercion. The end result, of course, is a student who has developed his selfhood and who is able to achieve what it is in him to become. During this process it is fortunate that individual interests are typically not at odds with group interests. It is helpful also

---

[69] Horne, *The Philosophy of Education*, p. 170.
[70] Butler, *Four Philosophies*, p. 251.
[71] Brameld, *Philosophies of Education in Cultural Perspective*, p. 242.

that a certain amount of the subject matter included in the curriculum has formal disciplinary value. At this point it may be helpful to mention what Greene calls the "principle of flexible adaptation" to specific needs as part of the educational process.[72] Physical educators in recent years have known this principle as *the growth-and-development approach* in education. As the student matures, there are points along the way in which certain educational material may be introduced at an appropriate time in relationship to his developmental pattern. Such articulation of the various curriculum materials will tend to evoke the student's interest in the curriculum plan at hand.

A COMMON CORE OF KNOWLEDGE, SKILLS, AND ATTITUDES. As for the curriculum itself, we have mentioned above the various disciplines of which it should be composed and also the concept of the "cultivated vocationalist." The idealist feels that there should be sufficient objective content—a common core of knowledge, skills, and attitudes—to pass on the racial (social) inheritance. To construct a curriculum we must understand man and his ideal character as well as those characteristics which an ideal society should possess. The development of an idealistic curriculum would involve a "coöperative pooling of experience and knowledge" on the part of the teachers concerned.[73] It would be quite difficult for students to share in this process to any great extent inasmuch as the cultural heritage and the requirements of human nature (and the resultant hierarchy of educational values) have determined the objectives of living and learning. The ideals of man to be realized in the schools of American democracy must be achieved if we ever hope that his nature will be complete. These cannot be left to chance despite the concept of individual differences. One such ideal might be the Jeffersonian conception of democracy, which is explained as:

. . . the sound democratic principle of helping each individual, without regard to race, color, or creed, to make the most of himself, to rise as high in the scale of values as his native endowment permits. . . .[74]

This is explained by Greene as a "fusion of objective aristocracy and social democracy."

TEACHING METHODOLOGY. The teaching methodology employed by the idealistic teacher is not easily identified. Many might insist that they create their own teaching methods and do not wish to be bound by any particular approach. The typical idealistic teacher might stress drill as important, but he would be very careful that the repetition not become dull. He would stress that transfer of training may be explained through the whole-part relationship; thus, the teacher should be careful to point

---

[72] Greene, *Fifty-fourth Yearbook,* Part I, p. 127.
[73] Horne, *Forty-first Yearbook,* Part I, p. 159.
[74] Greene, *Fifty-fourth Yearbook,* Part I, p. 129.

out the similarities and relations between the parts and the whole. Lecture certainly has a legitimate place as a method for the idealist, but it should involve much more than mere repetition of facts and ideas. There should be ample opportunity for questions and answers (a sort of informal dialectic). Even the project method of the progressives would not be out of bounds for the idealist. It would be very important to allow for as much flexibility as possible and certain alternative courses from which the student may choose. Good teachers create suspense whenever possible; they encourage the students to make decisions; they avoid wholesale indoctrination if they are liberal; and they encourage active effort at all times.

Summary

Initially, from the standpoint of the metaphysics of idealistic philosophy, idealists believe generally that mind (or spirit) as experienced by all men is basic and real; the entire universe is mind essentially. One's own self is the most immediate reality in his conscious experience. Man is more than just a body; he possesses a soul. This makes him of a higher order than all other creatures on earth. Idealism holds that the world's order is due to a spiritual reality. If man is able to interpret his world accurately and, as part of the whole, makes every effort to understand the Absolute, this is evidence that the universe is basically spiritual.

Idealists differ in their beliefs about the question of monism or pluralism. Some interpret reality as a single spiritual energy, while others believe there is a society of spirits (spiritual monism as opposed to spiritual pluralism). Critical (Kantian) idealism refrains from offering a theory of reality; every experience makes a contribution to the theory. Absolute idealism attempts a synthetic interpretation of Reality based on the evidence (or "appearances").

There is disagreement also on the question of evil in the world. Evil is considered necessary by some if man is to have the opportunity to achieve good. Hocking says that evil is the "seamy side" of good. Butler says evils are "immaturities sloughed off." Still others view them as spurs to stimulate man to greater effort and higher achievement. Lastly, idealists see man as free but with certain limitations. They believe that he does determine whether his life shall be devoted to discovering the good or whether he shall be weak and succumb to evil.

According to idealistic epistemology, understanding the nature of knowledge will clarify the nature of reality. Greene agrees with Kant that we can accept any interpretations of reality that are based on reliable data. These interpretations are valid if they are related significantly to other judgments arising from a variety of experiences. Berkeley believed that Universal Mind gave the world quality and meaning because man has found it this way in his experience. Kant believed that man could identify himself with the world of experience, but he could not envision a "Mind" (like Hegel and Fichte did) in the world beyond man's experience. Nature is the medium by which God communicates to man, and knowledge comes from a mind which offers and receives ideas.

Horne believed that "mind is the principle of explanation." If "mind is not matter," then they are qualitatively different. "Mind comes from mind" and not from matter—a definite clash with the theory of emergent evolution. Lastly, because "there can be no object without a subject," Horne believed that "the kind of world we know suggests that it is itself the expression of a universal intelligence in whose image our own intelligence is cast."

Idealists differ in degree as they explain how knowledge is achieved. Calkins believed that she experienced "mental reality" by direct observation perhaps through emotional feeling. The "experiencing self" consciously takes part in the total experience, part of which is physical reality and part of which is "mental reality." Other idealists believe that the reality of the self is a fact. Because of this the nature of the rest of existence is implied—a greater Self. This, they say, is the only theory that makes the world intelligible.

There is logic and order in the world. Truth is true when it corresponds with previously established knowledge; it is orderly and systematic, because that is the way Universal Mind ordained it. Experimental testing helps us discover what God's truth is!

The logic of idealism explains how man distinguishes sound from unsound reasoning—the systematic study of certain general principles upon which correct thinking is based. Idealists accept the traditional division of logic into the two branches known as *deductive logic* and *inductive logic* respectively. The aim in deductive logic is to reason by establishing a conclusive inference that is based upon true reason, thereby moving from general premises to their necessary conclusion. Inductive logic involves reasoning from certain particulars to a general conclusion. The syllogism, used extensively for deductive reasoning, is an analysis of a formal argument in which the conclusion necessarily results from the given premises. Modern scientific investigation relies very heavily on a thought process that is largely inductive, but it does revert quite often along the way to deduction as well. The materials of logic are the generally accepted truths that make up a lasting body of knowledge. The idealist is most anxious that the development of knowledge takes place. As man's "vision is extended," increasingly more interrelationships will be seen. Clearer analysis and more comprehensive synthesis will result. In this way man will develop increasingly a greater understanding and appreciation of the Ultimate Mind.

Idealism's axiology, or value system, is comprehended almost instinctively by a great many Americans. As Greene has stated, an idealist believes "in the reality, the discoverability, and the importance to man of objective values—of truth, beauty, and goodness as pure essences." Furthermore, "man's life is good in proportion as his search for the value dimensions of reality is successful." According to idealistic credo, there is a law of cause and effect in the moral world; the very nature of absolute reality is good, and this is proved as man's ethical convictions are justified time and again.

Kant's representation of the idealistic position in ethics has been accepted by many. He believed that man's potentialities are greater than any other type of existence known. In each man there is an "innate imperative" toward the good. It is necessary for the individual and for the society that man does the right; he can earn immortality by fulfilling universal moral law.

Idealists desire an aesthetic appreciation of the true nature of beauty. Through art man can rise to a level of experience above "individuality." Through the various forms of art, man can attempt to express beauty by losing his individuality and receiving impressions of the Ideas behind the phenomenal world.

The religious values of the idealist emanate from a belief in God as a spiritual power of force who is the ultimate source of all objective value. Man has a duty to search for the religious values of truth, beauty, and goodness, although his knowledge of such value may never be infallible. The idealist feels an impulse to seek God; he believes that he and God are working for a common purpose. Man's highest values are in harmony with the ultimate purpose of the world.

Idealism may have been criticized for its lack of "social consciousness," but Butler feels that such criticism has been unjust. Society provides the means whereby the individual may realize himself. Individual man is not subordinate to society; both the individual and society are ends. Idealists are concerned with "the development of man's highest social potentialities," but it is clear that democracy is a means for the achievement of man's ultimate end. "The ultimate worth of personality" is realized through a purposeful, spiritual environment.

The implications of the philosophy of idealism for education are that such an institution is necessary for complete development of the individual and that only through this means can the social heritage be passed on to each succeeding generation. Schools are established and supported by society to plan for its progress in the future as well. They can and should "educate for leadership and followership" as society meets the various social problems of the time.

Idealists believe strongly that the school has a responsibility to inculcate in its students a knowledge of the moral and spiritual values which are inherent in the world. A sound curriculum will open "to every child the opportunity to grow to his full physical, intellectual, moral, and spiritual stature."

There should be a division of labor between the school and the other agencies of society. The school should not overburden itself and attempt to do everything. Greene stresses that the school should teach youth about the structure and processes of democracy and the freedoms that may be enjoyed by all in an evolving democratic community. There is a great need to emphasize the concept of social justice and all that this implies.

In regard to idealistic aims and objectives for education, in some ways idealism may be said to be on the border line between progressivism and essentialism. It places great emphasis on freedom and development of the personality; it views the world quite optimistically because its system of reality is based on God's mind; and it does allow for experimentation with seemingly progressive teaching method. Basically, however, modern idealism and modern realism are united in an essentialistic approach to education through which the child is helped to adjust to the "essential realities that the history of the race has disclosed"—the spiritual ideals of truth, beauty, and goodness.

The idealist has enumerated the various objectives of living and learning into a fairly definite hierarchy of values. The highest good in life is based on a view of human nature which will allow man to realize his absolute goal—the establishment of his likeness to the spiritual order. Horne's list of the requirements of human nature, or the basic values of human living, include health, character, social justice, skill, art, love, knowledge, philosophy, and religion. Of these, the most important would be an understanding of worship which brings man into a "conscious relation" with "the infinite spirit of the universe."

Idealists differ somewhat about the relative importance of vocational education in comparison to liberal education. Horne's ideal is a "cultivated vocationalist," but still higher emphasis is given to the concept of a "cultivated human being." Greene believes that liberal education and vocational training are complementary—that both are equally essential in the preparation for life. He emphasizes further that for total personality development of the individual the distinction between curricular and extracurricular activities should be eliminated as soon as possible.

The process of education necessary to bring about the aims and objectives of the idealist involves certain essential studies. Horne believes that these include the sciences, the fine arts, and the practical arts. Greene's classification is comprised of the formal disciplines, the factual disciplines, the normative disciplines, and the synoptic disciplines.

Certain skills relating to the above disciplines or sub-divisions of the curriculum can be taught directly in a formal classroom setting, but fundamental attitudes and values come about indirectly "by example, inspiration, and contagion." (Greene) The idealist believes, therefore, that the teacher's personality is tremendously important. He determines the pattern of education, but he does not give students *the* answers to all questions; he tells them what the *possible* answers are, and they must come to their own conclusions.

Education for the idealist is more than a behavioral process. From an understanding of himself the student reaches out for an understanding of the world outside himself. Idealism stresses the subjective psychological processes of introspection and intuition which take place within the individual. The mind blends related parts into qualitative wholes of meaning. Greater self-understanding results from increased comprehension of God.

Believing in the importance of interest, idealists take the position that "effort leads to interest" and that discipline may be necessary at certain stages. Some subject matter has formal disciplinary value. Educational material should be introduced, however, when it is most appropriate to the child's stage of growth and development. A common core of knowledge, skills, and attitudes are basic to the transmission of the social heritage. Students have only a very limited role to fulfill in curriculum construction.

Idealists do not wish to be confined to any particular teaching methodology; they want to create their own teaching methods as the educational process develops. Drill has a place, but should be varied so that learning does not become dull. Lectures, question and answer periods, and a variety of other techniques would be acceptable. Students should take part actively and make decisions whenever possible.

CHAPTER ELEVEN

Idealism in Physical, Health, and Recreation Education

The powerful force of a realism that is strongly materialistic has threatened America's idealistic superstructure to such an extent that it has been said that "traditional philosophic idealism, in all of its numerous variants, is probably obsolescent if not already obsolete." [1] As disturbing as the above statement might be to an idealist, he would probably concur in the belief that it is necessary for America to build (or rebuild) its spiritual core to meet the challenge of the second half of the twentieth century.

The idealistic outlook and its implications for physical, health, and recreation education is, according to Brubacher, part of the over-all essentialistic position. [2] The educational philosophies of naturalistic realism, rational humanism, and Catholic realism (supernaturalism) and their implications for this specialized area were considered in previous chapters. [3] These three educational philosophies, grouped together under the heading of realism, typically accept education of the physical as the unique contribution of physical education. Idealism is much more complex to analyze, since it cannot be said that it stands completely either for education of the physical or education through the physical. Brubacher places it "somewhat on the border line" [4] between progressivism

---

[1] Kenneth H. Hansen, *Philosophy for American Education* (Englewood Cliffs, N.J.: Prentice-Hall, Inc., 1960), p. 45.

[2] John S. Brubacher, *Modern Philosophies of Education* (New York: McGraw-Hill Book Company, Inc., 1950), pp. 309-314.

[3] Cf., Chapters 8 and 9.

[4] Brubacher, *Modern Philosophies of Education,* p. 309.

and essentialism, but he does state further that "there is a measure of absolutism in idealistic philosophy of education which seems more properly to align it with essentialism." [5] This writer believes that the individual professional should find his place on a spectrum through careful self-examination.

Aims and Objectives

Horne's classic definition of idealistic education was given in the foundational chapter immediately preceding this one.[6] He stated that "education is the eternal process of superior adjustment of the physically and mentally developed, free, conscious, human being to God, as manifested in the intellectual, emotional, and volitional environment of man." According to this approach it is necessary to determine what the highest good in life is, based on a particular view of human nature. In this hierarchy of educational values, the highest, or absolute, aim is the establishment of man's likeness to the spiritual order. Thus the most important educational objective would be an understanding of worship which brings man into a "conscious relation" with "the infinite spirit of the universe." The other "educational objectives of the perfectly integrated individual" may then be listed in a fairly straightforward descending order of importance. If education, then, is idea-centered (or ideal-centered), and if these ideas, eternal and unchanging, shape the pattern of the world, they necessarily become educational essentials. This does not mean, however, that physical education and vocational education are unimportant, but it does mean that they will undoubtedly occupy "lower rungs on the educational ladder." [7]

PHYSICAL EDUCATION AS A TERM. It was explained earlier that the experimentalist is most dissatisfied with the name *physical* education, whereas the realist would have no objection at all to the use of this term to describe this specialized area's function within the total educational pattern. If the idealistic physical educator were to examine himself and this philosophical tendency, he would probably be forced to admit that the term *physical education* is *at least partially acceptable* to him. Idealists speak of the organic unity of an individual and refer to man as a *unitary being*. They find themselves in a most difficult position, if they accept a dualistic theory of the nature of man which divides him into mind and body. They have therefore accepted a monistic approach, because they believe that it is necessary for mind to be active ceaselessly

[5] *Ibid.*, p. 310.
[6] Cf., Chapter 10, p. 192
[7] Brubacher, *Modern Philosophies of Education*, p. 310.

as it attempts to comprehend the world. They marvel at the growth and development of the physical organism as well and realize how necessary a healthy body is for the acquisition of life's higher values. Hence, from one standpoint, the name *physical education* is quite acceptable and descriptive of the role that physical, health, and recreation education fills within the educational pattern.

From another standpoint, however, this term is *not acceptable at all.* According to the idealistic view, personality has ultimate worth, and the growth of this personality is paramount. The achievement of a "cultivated personality" is dependent "partly on our inherited disposition, partly on the training and experiences we have had, and partly upon our choices, based upon reflection, of ideals to follow."[8] Many physical educators, raised in the idealistic tradition, believe fervently that physical, health, and recreation education (including competitive sport) has a truly significant role to play in the development of personality and character. For this reason, many are, and should be, dissatisfied with the term *physical education* as being descriptive of the function of the area within education.

PLATO ON PHYSICAL EDUCATION. A discussion of the implications of idealism for physical, health, and recreation education that did not return to a consideration of the contributions of Plato (427–347 B.C.) to thought on this matter would be seriously lacking. Burke points out that "the definitive element of Idealism is its viewpoint that reality lies essentially in the realm of mind and spirit."[9] The field of physical, health, and recreation education owes much to a major work written by Cahn in 1941.[10] In great detail he presented the contributions of Plato to thought in our specialized area. He believed that a system of physical education was closely related to the sociological influences of that period in the history of ancient Athens.

Plato's beliefs concerning physical education were seemingly determined by his conception of the answer to the purpose of life. Man's function is to live as closely as possible with the divine laws which govern the universe. A reasonable man would use physical education activities to assist him in the development of a good life. It serves:

. . . to harmonize the conflicting psychological elements of reason, desire, and spirit; develops an intelligent courage acting with reason and intelligence in

---

[8] Herman H. Horne, "An Idealistic Philosophy of Education," in *Forty-first Yearbook of the National Society for the Study of Education* (Chicago: University of Chicago Press, 1942), Part I, p. 156.

[9] Roger Burke, "Idealism and Physical Education," in *The Philosophic Process in Physical Education,* E. C. Davis (Philadelphia: Lea & Febiger, 1961), p. 33.

[10] L. Joseph Cahn, "Contributions of Plato to Thought on Physical Education, Health, and Recreation" (Ed.D. dissertation, New York University, 1941).

the face of fears, hopes, and pleasures; engraves habits of right thought and action into the good character; develops organic strength; and insures training in the necessary life skills.[11]

Such a physical-education program was vitally concerned with the individual's goals in life; moreover, any program of education which neglected it was markedly deficient. Plato's aesthetic ideal envisioned the harmony of a beautiful soul united with a beautiful form—a somewhat different concept than the Roman *mens sana in corpore sano.*[12] As Cahn saw it, "the Platonic ideal is more subtle and graceful; it suggests a keener intellect, combined with a poised power capable of acting quickly with the dignity of ease and beauty."[13] An individual who endeavored to approximate this ideal would certainly agree with Socrates when he said, ". . . what a disgrace it is for a man to grow old without ever seeing the beauty and strength of which his body is capable."[14]

CHRISTIANITY INFLUENCED PHYSICAL EDUCATION ADVERSELY. It is not our purpose at this point to trace idealistic influence on physical education in any detail historically, but it may be said that early Christian idealism furthered the dualism of mind and body—a concept which has had detrimental effects on physical education ever since. Furthermore, the doctrine of original sin, with the possibility of ultimate salvation if asceticism were practiced, negated the fostering of the Greek ideal for well over a thousand years. It was not until the period of the Renaissance and the advent of certain humanistic educators that a rebirth of the Graeco-Roman ideal to any extent became apparent.

Despite the tremendous negative influence which Christianity has exerted on physical education in the past, there is considerable evidence that this situation has been improving gradually in the United States in the past hundred years. Leaders in the Young Men's Christian Association movement just after the middle of the nineteenth century realized that physical education and athletics were very attractive to young men. Their objectives mentioned the improvement of physical status (as well as spiritual, mental, and social status). An idealistic concept of physical education became apparent as man was viewed as an organic unity. Athletic activity in YMCA gymnasia was believed to exert a definite influence on the development of Christian character.[15]

IDEALISM IN AMERICAN PHYSICAL EDUCATION. Early physical-education leaders such as Dudley Allen Sargent and William Gilbert Anderson

---

[11] *Ibid.,* p. 157.

[12] Juvenal, *Satires,* X, 356.

[13] Cahn, "Contributions of Plato . . . ," pp. 289-294.

[14] E. N. Gardiner, *Greek Athletic Sports and Festivals* (London: Macmillan & Co., Ltd., 1910), p. 130. Socrates is cited at this point.

[15] Elmer Johnson, "A History of Physical Education in the Young Men's Christian Association" (Ph.D. dissertation, University of Southern California, 1954), pp. 47 and 89.

may be said to have developed the thread of idealism present in American physical education as well. Sargent, with his various testing devices whereby the individual might assess his own ability and development, had a great influence on physical education in the United States. He fostered the concept of self-realization through diligent application to the necessary prerequisites.[16] This concept of self-realization was evident to a marked degree also in a statement by Anderson when he wrote:

The object of life is the complete development of all the moral possibilities of man. These possibilities are sevenfold. Man is capable of development physically, and morally. A man who neglects one or more of these natures is one-sided, and the man who develops each one of these natures nearest to its utmost possibility of development comes closer to attaining the object of life.[17]

BURKE ASSESSES IDEALISM IN THE TWENTIETH CENTURY. Idealism in the twentieth century is assessed very cogently by Burke when he enumerates some of the characteristics of this philosophical tendency as (1) reaffirmation of the principle of dualism between body and mind; (2) the belief that values and moral standards are enduring and unchangeable; (3) the concept that a liberal education is paramount because through it a man learns to appreciate life's true values as well as the ability to reason correctly; and (4) the realization that man, actually a part of the Divine, is much more than an animal or some sort of a mechanism.[18] Burke explains further that idealism would definitely favor physical education to a considerable degree because of the status accorded it in Greek idealism; because of the transfer of training theory which implies that attitudes of sportsmanship and fair play learned through desirable athletic competition can and do transfer to life situations; and because idealistic emphasis on striving for perfection through achievement of the values of truth, beauty, and goodness does not completely negate physical fitness and sound health—merely places them somewhat lower in a hierarchy of desirable aims and objectives in life.[19]

Now that we have discussed the purpose of this chapter generally, and also somewhat specifically in regard to some of the historical implications of idealism for physical education, it is time to consider some of the viewpoints on this matter as it has appeared in fairly recent literature and research.

WORK OF MARGARET CLARK GANNETT. Special mention should be made again of the truly significant contribution made by Margaret Clark

---

[16] Donn E. Bair, "An Identification of Some Philosophical Beliefs Held by Influential Professional Leaders in American Physical Education" (Ph.D dissertation, University of Southern California, 1956), pp. 52-54.

[17] William G. Anderson, *Methods of Teaching Gymnastics* (New York: Hinds and Noble, 1896), p. 49.

[18] Burke, *The Philosophic Process in Physical Education*, pp. 51-52.

[19] *Ibid.*, pp. 53-54.

Gannett in 1943 when she attempted the philosophical interpretation of a program of physical education in a state teachers college.[20] This appears to have been the first philosophical research of its type in the history of American physical education. Mrs. Gannett realized that physical education needed philosophical treatment, and, furthermore, she dared to treat physical education philosophically. As is so often the case with pioneering ventures, her complex analysis received little recognition by the field of health, physical education, and recreation. She would probably be one of the first to recognize the limitations of her study. This writer wishes, however, to pay tribute to her effort and to those from whom she received guidance.

Mrs. Gannett came to the conclusion that the philosophy of idealism, chiefly, characterized the program which she interpreted. She explained these similar and unique emphases as follows:

The idealistic characteristics of the program are found to be, in summary, that it employs the ideas of leaders in education; it provides opportunities for choice and the development of judgment; it uses various data; it provides means for building wholeness of mind and body, and skill and beauty of body; it recognizes the supreme worth of personality; and finally, it helps to realize the values of life which Idealism stands for, among which are the development of strong, healthy bodies; good habits of mental and physical health; skill, success and fun in physical activity; achievement in successful teaching of physical education to children; and the conservation and enhancement of personality.[21]

VOICES FOR IDEALISM. Those who feel that idealism is on the wane and that consequently its influence on physical, health, and recreation education is not worthy of much attention may be reflecting their own opinions, but they are obviously not fully aware of the many voices that are being raised in its behalf recently.

For example, it may be pointed out that during World War II every effort was made to continue a competitive athletic program for as many young men as possible. It is true that pragmatism (experimentalism) can take some credit for this retention. Because of its value pragmatically, it is probably also true, as Bair indicates, that "the retention of competition as a persistent value indicated an idealistic measure of stability relating to programs of physical education." [22]

When the Korean conflict came along so soon, physical educators apparently did not see the need to revert to an emergency fitness pro-

---

[20] Margaret C. Clark, "A Philosophical Interpretation of a Program of Physical Education in a State Teachers College" (Ph.D. dissertation, New York University, 1943).

[21] *Ibid.*, p. 318.

[22] Bair, "An Identification of Some Philosophical Beliefs . . . ," p. 58.

gram that would of necessity sacrifice program enrichment. In the 1951 report of the National Conference for the Mobilization of Education stress was placed on physical-education opportunities which would bring about organic and moral development of the individual. The importance of successful experience in a variety of motor activities was considered highly desirable. Such statements undoubtedly show idealism's continuing influence on our educational programs.[23]

A DUAL INFLUENCE AND ECLECTICISM. Bair's study, in which he made an effort to identify some of the philosophical beliefs held by influential professional leaders in American physical education, was completed in 1956. Although there would be a division of opinion regarding his grouping of the four philosophies included into what he defines as *naturalism* and *spiritualism,* his findings have significance for us as we consider idealistic influence. In his concluding statement he summarized his results briefly as follows:

On the basis of present indicated beliefs, most professional leaders appear to be providing a predominantly naturalistic direction to American physical education. The study revealed some evidences of strong spiritualistic beliefs which suggested a dual influence and lack of general agreement in some areas of physical education.[24]

The evidence clearly points to the persistent, pervading influence of idealism. A careful examination of Bair's findings, however, does show an eclecticism which would be considered by many to be philosophically indefensible. This writer hastens to say again that we should not expect our leaders to be *purely* anything—that is, wholly and purely idealistic, or realistic, or experimentalistic. But in the second half of the twentieth century we will need increasingly logical, consistent, and sequential philosophical positions on the part of individuals and segments of our field. As professional educators, we can settle for no less!

INFLUENCE OF THE YMCA. The Young Men's Christian Association has exerted a significant influence throughout the world on health, physical education, and recreation. This influence has emanated from an idealistic base, the tenets of which were expressed clearly:

The conceptions of the various faiths and philosophies regarding the human body are as numerous as sand is plentiful on the beach. There are all shades of opinions—from the conception 'the body is divine' to the other extreme, 'the body is evil.' The YMCA is neither a religion nor a philosophy. It is a movement which from the very beginning has left no doubt as to how it regarded the human body: as a living reality, as a part of the great whole—

---

[23] *Highlights from the National Conference for the Mobilization of Education* (Washington, D.C.: The American Association for Health, Physical Education, and Recreation, 1951), p. 8.

[24] Bair, "An Identification of Some Philosophical Beliefs . . . ," p. 161.

mind, body, spirit. Just as the Movement itself achieved such success in the age of the urban civilization, so also this conception was so sound that it has proved and maintained its value right up to the middle of our own century.[25]

In 1960 the theme of the World YMCA Consultation on Health and Physical Education, held at Rome in connection with the Olympic games, was *Health and Physical Education—YMCA Practice and Purpose.* At this important meeting, delegates from twenty-one national YMCA's in all five continents heard discussions from outstanding leaders of the movement concerning purpose and practice. Steinhaus explained that "the concept of the mind-body-spirit unity of man is today a basic tenet of all sciences dealing with man, and also of education." Because of this, he stated his belief that "every impact of man on man or of programme on man invariably does influence in some way man's body, man's mind, man's spirit." [26] Steinhaus means in this statement that a physical activity leaves its influence on the whole man, and there is a strong inference that the leader has a great deal to do with whether this influence is for good or for bad.

LIMBERT EXPLAINS CENTRAL EMPHASIS.   Paul Limbert, secretary general of the World Alliance of YMCA's, speaking at the Rome consultation also clarified, however, the reason for the hierarchy of values in Christian idealism in the following statement:

The central emphasis of Christian faith is not on development of the individual as such but on *equipment for service,* both to God and man. Focus on the development of physical strength or athletic prowess runs the risk of self-centeredness; that which should be a means to an end becomes an end in itself, an 'idol.' Too much attention to personal development as such tends toward pride and self-righteousness.[27]

FRIERMOOD LISTS FIVE OBJECTIVES.   In another important paper presented at Rome, Harold T. Friermood, U.S. national YMCA secretary for physical education, assessed the role of physical education as an integral part of the YMCA program. He listed the five objectives for physical education which appeared in a publication resulting from a two-year study in the United States:

1. Development of health and physical fitness
2. Education for leisure
3. Personality adjustment (learning to live with self and others)
4. Development of responsible citizenship and group participation
5. Development of a philosophy of life based on Christian ideals.[28]

---

[25] "Physical Education, Sport, and Recreation," *World Communique* (January-February 1961), p. 3.

[26] *Ibid.,* p. 9.

[27] *Ibid.*

[28] *A New Look at YMCA Physical Education* (New York: Association Press, 1959). As mentioned in Friermood's mimeographed article.

Pointing out that "people are more important that the program tools," he explained that "things can happen in the life of a person that are just as significant for him in the gymnasium, in the locker room, or on a hike as in a bible class." [29]

AVOID OVEREMPHASIS. R. W. Jones of the United Kingdom, director of the UNESCO Youth Institute, sounded a warning at Rome concerning "growing specialization" in sport. He explained his feeling that overemphasis in international sport would tend to have deleterious effects on personality growth as follows:

The growing specialization tends to reduce the interest of people who are concerned for the whole personality of the participant. The mechanics become more important than the competitors. The rules are becoming more important than the participant. More notice is being taken of making sport a spectacle for the spectator than the effect of the play on the player. [30]

THE FELLOWSHIP OF CHRISTIAN ATHLETES. Organized Christianity has taken the role of sport much more seriously in recent years as well. One important indication of this interest has been the recent establishment and rapid development of the Fellowship of Christian Athletes. This organization was an idea in the mind of a sophomore physical-education major at Oklahoma State University in 1947. Subsequently Don McLanen and a Presbyterian minister, Dr. Louis H. Evans, formed an advisory board in May of 1955. From this small beginning, and with the help of Branch Rickey of baseball fame, this group has made remarkable gains. [31] The main office of the Fellowship of Christian Athletes, Inc. is located in Kansas City, Missouri. It "exists to serve Christ and the Church. Its concern is to draw athletes in particular and youth in general into the realm and experience of vital Christian commitment within the Church." [32] Reverend Gary Demarest has offered some key phrases which help us see the goals of this movement:

The hero worship accorded coaches and athletes by millions of youth and adults . . . is inherently neither good or evil but a medium out of which either may come.
To the man for whom the spiritual and moral dimensions of life are central, the nature of this responsibility is critically important.
It is the belief of the FCA that a coach can better fulfill the moral and ethical demands of his calling by keeping the influence and example of this national group of concerned and committed athletes before his players. [33]

[29] *World Communique* (January-February 1961), p. 9. Quoting H. T. Friermood.
[30] *Ibid.*, p. 10.
[31] Gary Demarest, "Hero Worship Harnessed," *Journal of Health, Physical Education, and Recreation* Vol. XXXI, No. 5, (May-June 1960), 30-31.
[32] *The Fellowship of Christian Athletes*, (January 19, 1962). Pamphlet made available through the courtesy of Robert Stoddard, Acting Executive Director.
[33] Demarest, *Journal of Health, Physical Education, and Recreation*, Vol. XXXI, No. 5: 30-31.

It is interesting to note the ecumenical nature of this movement. **Dr.** Samuel Shoemaker stresses that "loyalty to one's own church is stressed in the movement, but one is exposed to a great many who belong to other households of faith." [34] Vance Morris, assistant football coach, Excelsior Springs, Missouri, writing in the FCA publication *The Christian Athlete,* states a fundamental idealistic tenet in a recent article, when he encourages athletes to strive "for that same perfection that we seek on our athletic teams in our individual lives." [35]

JAARSMA SOUNDS A WARNING.   Although athletics are recommended as a source from which good can come, there are many Christian educators who are most concerned about the ever-present possibility of overemphasis. Professor Cornelius Jaarsma, Grand Rapids, Michigan (where Calvin College is located), states that "in selecting a physical education program the teacher must remember not to over-emphasize competitive games." [36] His first concern in this matter is that a certain percentage of the student body will be left out of an activity that is important in their over-all development, whereas "others may become demoralized by repeated failure." Secondly, he stresses that interscholastic athletics may become a real stumbling block as we work toward the aim of a fine physical-education program for all. As he sees it, ". . . though it may benefit the participants directly and others indirectly, it constantly threatens to usurp the center of the stage." [37]

PHYSICAL EDUCATION DOES HAVE A PLACE.   Jaarsma, of course, is concerned primarily with the Christian school as a setting for learning. He explains how "in Christian education the learner is viewed as a child in Christ, the goal is a formed personality as a son of God, and the body of subject matter is the learning material appropriate to the subject and the goal." [38] Now what about the role of physical education? Although Jaarsma has been careful to restate that "subject matter is the principal medium for development in the school," he does believe that "physical education falls within its legitimate scope":

This is true because, as we have urged many times, the total personality of the child is involved in the learning process. . . . Indeed, it is so necessary for total personality development that some form of it should be required of every adolescent. A well-directed program of physical education will provide a variety

[34] Samuel M. Shoemaker, *Fellowship of Christian Athletes: Answer to America's Youth.* A sermon distributed in pamphlet form by the Fellowship of Christian Athletes, Kansas City 6, Missouri.

[35] Vance Morris, "Striving for Perfection," *The Christian Athlete,* No. 4 (December 1961), 10.

[36] Cornelius Jaarsma, *Human Development, Learning & Teaching* (Grand Rapids, Mich.: Wm. B. Eerdmans Publishing Co., 1961), p. 105.

[37] *Ibid.,* p. 106.

[38] *Ibid.,* p. 226.

of activities that help to form worthy ideals and habits of body care that produce self-esteem and responsibility.[39]

STEEN STRESSES VALUES. Steen, director of physical education at Calvin
College, bears out this idealistic philosophy of physical education as
he describes the program at this institution. Emphasizing the concept
of the unitary nature of man, he states his belief that physical education
offers physical values, mental values, guidance toward ethical standards,
and desirable recreational skills and attitudes.[40] These beliefs appear to
be borne out, with some exceptions, in a study conducted by Lozes in
which she discovered that "the philosophy of physical education, as
proposed by the eleven church-related institutions visited, stressed the
integrational, recreational, and physical purposes of physical education,
and gave less emphasis to the social and mental purposes." [41]

MORAL AND SPIRITUAL VALUES IN EDUCATION. The whole question of
moral and spiritual values in education has been a persistent problem
in America. Because of differences in religious belief, and the seeming
impossibility of achieving any consensus as to what might be included
in a course on comparative religion, public schools have remained almost completely secularized in this important matter insofar as direct
teaching is concerned. It is generally understood, however, that the
school does attempt to *teach* morals indirectly in a definitely incidental
manner. Those who don't believe this matter can be handled effectively
in such a seemingly haphazard fashion have found other means to meet
this need. Those of us concerned with public education, and in this
case especially with physical, health, and recreation education, should
understand how some educators believe this problem can be solved to
a degree through the medium of our specialized area.

PHYSICAL EDUCATION CONTRIBUTES. As far back as 1929, several important educational leaders expressed themselves in an idealistic manner
on this subject. Henry S. Pritchett, a former president of the Carnegie
Foundation for the Advancement of Learning, stated that "for the sake
of every youth whom school and college sport touches, the desired moral
and social values that it can yield must be made realities." [42] In the
same year Professor Matthias of the University of Munich explained
that we should "consider Physical Education as it affects the body, and

---

[39] *Ibid.*, pp. 105-106.

[40] Barney Steen, "Physical Education at Calvin College," *The Banner*, XCVI, No. 35
(September 1, 1961), 11 and 19.

[41] Jewell Helen Lozes, "The Philosophy of Certain Religious Denominations Relative to Physical Education" (Master's thesis, Pennsylvania State University, 1955),
p. 103.

[42] H. W. Carson Ryan, Jr., *The Literature of American School and College Athletics*,
Bulletin 24 (New York: The Carnegie Foundation for the Advancement of Teaching,
1929), p. vii.

then consider the effects as they manifest themselves upon the soul experiences of man." [43] Also in 1929, Professor Kennedy of Princeton said:

It will always be difficult to frame a definition of sportsmanship that will be completely accurate and comprehensive, for sportsmanship is so subtly rooted in the reactions of the human spirit, so various in its possible gestures, and so intricately interwoven with the elements of individual character and personality that it is by its very nature not susceptible of being caught and held in any net of words.[44]

GENERAL RESPECT FOR RELIGIOUS BELIEFS. Despite the many materialistic influences of the twentieth century, a strong idealistic current has persisted in the United States—a country which is largely Christian, although sprinkled with members of other faiths. Traditionally the American public school has shown a respect for religious beliefs. Our Constitution and Bill of Rights are stated in such a way that religious ideals are recognized as a part of the culture, although it should be stated quickly that each person may worship God as he sees fit. The fact that there are more than 240 different religious groups is ample evidence that this right is generally recognized. Yet, conversely, although a person does have a right to be agnostic or avowedly atheistic, he had better not be a presidential candidate once having declared such a position.

A NATIONAL REPORT ON VALUES. In a country such as this with such a strong religious base, it is little wonder that the question of moral and spiritual values would be such a recurrent theme when educational policy is being considered. This is true despite the fact that global warfare tends to lessen ethical sensitivity and that moral and spiritual values must be inculcated indirectly in our public schools because of misunderstanding and distrust. It was no accident that the Educational Policies Commission of the National Education Association and the American Association of School Administrators published a report on moral and spiritual values in the public schools. Classroom teachers were concerned about their role in this matter and asked that a study be made to develop ways of improving the teaching of such values. The Commission listed a number of values on which the American people are agreed. Idealists will rejoice in the assertion that the "basic value of human personality" is "fundamental to all that follow." As the report states, "the basic moral and spiritual value in American life is the supreme importance of the individual personality." [45] A complete listing of these values follows:

---

[43] E. Matthias, *The Deeper Meaning of Physical Education*, trans. Carl Schrader (New York: A. S. Barnes and Company, 1929), pp. 5-6.

[44] Charles W. Kennedy, "Self-Control and Chivalry Through Sport," *Sportsmanship* (June 1929), p. 5.

[45] Educational Policies Commission, *Moral and Spiritual Values in the Public Schools* (Washington, D.C.: National Education Association, 1951), p. 18.

1. The supreme importance of the individual personality.
2. Each person should feel responsible for the consequences of his own conduct.
3. Institutional arrangements are the servants of mankind.
4. Mutual consent is better than violence.
5. The human mind should be liberated by access to information and opinion.
6. Excellence in mind, character, and creative ability should be fostered.
7. All persons should be judged by the same moral standards.
8. The concept of brotherhood should take precedence over selfish interests.
9. Each person should have the greatest possible opportunity for the pursuit of happiness, provided only that such activities do not substantially interfere with the similar opportunities of others.
10. Each person should be offered the emotional and spiritual experiences which transcend the materialistic aspects of life.[46]

SPORT HAS A PLACE. This report of the Educational Policies Commission goes on to say that all of the resources of the school should be used whenever possible to teach the above-mentioned moral and spiritual values. Of interest to us in physical, health, and recreation education is that the members of the Commission believe that sports have a vital role to play in such instruction, and that "the teacher of sports is usually one of the most influential members of the school community in the shaping of moral and spiritual values." [47]

A CONTINUING EMPHASIS ON VALUES. That there has been a continuing emphasis on the moral and spiritual values that may be gained by the individual through participation in physical-education activities is readily noticeable from an examination of the literature in recent years. Of course, idealists cannot take all the credit for this; the experimentalist would argue that "values are man made in an effort to serve man's own ends. They are derived from experience and represent instruments which make possible effective functioning within our environment." [48] An idealistic value system comes into the picture only when the individuals concerned believe that their value system is grounded on objective values of truth, goodness, and beauty that "are embedded in reality itself." The man who seeks diligently to apprehend these values (and to help others do the same) is leading a good life insofar as his own quest for these values succeeds, and presumably insofar as he helps others to realize these values for themselves (in his role as a teacher).

RESICK ON VALUES. Resick appears to be following in the idealistic tradition when he explained how physical education activities could conceivably contribute to each of the ten values listed in the report of the Educational Policies Commission. A particularly idealistic strain is evident when he writes about "spiritual enrichment." He explains that

---

[46] *Ibid.*, pp. 18-30.
[47] *Ibid.*, pp. 68-70.
[48] Bair, "An Identification of Some Philosophical Beliefs . . . ," p. 174.

"the word spiritual here denotes the highest level of the capacity of the human spirit." [49] And then he gives his approval to a statement that "the prime value of the game is the spiritual lift it affords through the liberation of powers and its secondary value is the feeling of physical well-being that ensues." [50]

WILTON'S STATUS SURVEY.   In 1956, Wilton completed a most significant study in which he made a comparative analysis of certain statements made by important leaders in American physical education in relation to the moral and spiritual values which they felt their subject afforded.[51] He accepted the listing of moral and spiritual values offered by the Educational Policies Commission and subsequently made comparisons between these values and the statements attributed to the outstanding physical educators. Because youth is interested in play and sport proficiency, Wilton reasoned that the play leader has a unique opportunity "to encourage proper moral and spiritual growth." [52] His hypothesis was that statements discovered would show that physical educators agree that their subject "should be charged with the responsibility of improving young people" and "that teaching for the improvement of moral and spiritual values should be a planned part of physical education." [53]

It may well be argued by some that these values described could be considered experimentalistic (or pragmatic) ethical values as well. The term *moral values* would probably satisfy the experimentalist and at the same time not offend the idealist. But "spiritual values" as defined by Wilton definitely coincide with idealistic philosophy of education:

Spiritual values usually take effect in terms of the individual's inner feelings. They give strength to precepts of morality *above reasoned social action* [italics inserted by E.F.Z. to emphasize the distinction between experimentalism and idealism]. Though consistent with religion, they are not exclusively dependent upon it for its sanction; thus, their practice in the exercises of the public school is approved.[54]

Idealists may gather strength from Wilton's summary and conclusions that the seventeen leaders picked by a jury of experts ratified his hypothesis that physical-education experiences "are of real value in the development of moral and spiritual values." [55] Under *the pursuit of*

---

[49] M. C. Resick, "Moral and Spiritual Values in Physical Education," *The Physical Educator* Vol. XII, No. 1, (March, 1955), 5.

[50] John S. Brubacher, *et al.*, *The Public Schools and Spiritual Values* (New York: Harper & Row, Publishers, Inc., 1944), p. 90. As cited by Resick.

[51] Wilton M. Wilton, "A Comparative Analysis of Theories Related to Moral and Spiritual Values in Physical Education" (Ed.D. thesis, University of California, Los Angeles, 1956).

[52] *Ibid.*, pp. 1-2.

[53] *Ibid.*, p. 2.

[54] *Ibid.*, p. 6.

[55] *Ibid.*, p. 278.

happiness (value number 9), the leaders believed that "creative experience, noble achievement, true friendship, and spiritual satisfaction are encouraged by physical education." He found further that *spiritual enrichment* (value number 10), a term not associated with physical education typically, was enhanced greatly according to the opinions of the outstanding leaders. As Wilton points out in his concluding statement:

Lofty thoughts and ideals can and must be made important by the coach or physical education teacher. Creative expression, honored ritual, great men, brotherhood, group causes, are true examples of the avenues through which physical education can tap deep appreciations of a spiritual nature. Honesty, teamwork and fair-play are the essence of good sportsmanship, and therefore may be classified as factors in spiritual growth. The leaders concur that the physical education teacher must be a person of impeccable character.[56]

OBERTEUFFER EXPLAINS IDEALISM. Writing on the subject of idealism in physical education, Oberteuffer emphasized many of the tenets of this position heretofore mentioned. Stressing initially that man "is real but is real only when the mind and soul are included," and that he should be perceived as a whole, as an organic unity, Oberteuffer pointed out that this unity is *"the most powerful concept* ever to bear upon what we do in physical education. It traps us completely . . . denies us forever the doubtful privilege of not caring what happens to our charges as long as they grow strong, or perform well." Starting from such a base, he stated that the idealistic curriculum will not be child-centered, or subject-matter centered—but ideal-centered." Then he criticized certain modern trends and emphases in physical education. For example, he questioned the wisdom of testing "a million children with a dynamometer" without at the same time developing "a solid program of total development to orient the test scores with some kind of relationship to things which are really important." He discussed the matter of the individual's interests and the moral imperative which is part of idealistic philosophy. Decrying twentieth century exploitation of the college athlete, he indicated that we cannot be "satisfied with scores instead of character," and that we should leave competitive sport to a large degree in the hands of the boys. It is sportsmanship and ethical choice that are important. Bodily development is a means to an end leading to truth, beauty, and goodness. Creative expression on the part of the individual is a worthy means whereby the idealist hopes to achieve his educational goals. As Oberteuffer concludes, "self-activity leading to self-development involving the total self is to the idealist the important thing." [57]

[56] *Ibid.,* p. 285.
[57] Delbert Oberteuffer, "Idealism in Physical Education," in *Philosophies Fashion Physical Education,* Elwood Craig Davis, ed. (Dubuque, Iowa: Wm. C. Brown Company Publishers, 1963), pp. 16-24.

MABEL LEE'S POSITION. Before concluding this section treating the implications of idealism for physical education, the views of one more physical educator should be considered—the venerable Mabel Lee, former director of physical education for women at the University of Nebraska. Morland has classified Miss Lee as an essentialist—of this there appears to be little doubt.[58] Our premise here is that many of her beliefs were indeed idealistic. It is for this reason that she herself might say, "so most probably I am an essentialist in some respects and a progressivist about others." [59] Let us consider some of her statements briefly. In speaking about "fitness and the good life," she says that the "physically inadequate" will never receive the "spiritual uplift" from outdoor living.[60] She stresses the need for physical reserve in life when she states, "whether of the body or of the spirit, burdens are more easily borne if there is a physical reserve. 'Build thee more stately mansions, O my soul,' is meant for both the body and the spirit." [61] We need "fitness to enjoy life to its fullest, physically, emotionally, or spiritually." [62] She and her co-author concur with a list of values which includes "the value of spiritual and ethical character." [63] In speaking about public relations, Morland summarizes her belief that "it will take the combined efforts of the entire profession if the deeper meaning of physical education is to be realized by those who have such a large voice in determining the success of future programs." [64]

MORLAND'S ANALYSIS OF LEE. Stressing the "importance of disciplined work," Lee criticizes those who advocate "false philosophies" such as "physical education that is purely recreational in nature." The best type of teacher, she asserts, "will insist upon disciplined training of the body. Such training has a spiritual as well as a physical value." [65] Morland points out Lee's belief that "good posture, for instance, is considered as having direct spiritual, social, economic, and health value." [66] On the question of the philosophy of awards, Lee believes that the Greeks had the right idea. She states that "even parents are coming to realize that it is poor training to motivate children to favorable action by the

[58] Richard B. Morland, "A Philosophical Interpretation of the Educational Views Held by Leaders in American Physical Education" (Ph.D. dissertation, New York University, 1958), p. 499.

[59] Communication from Dr. Mabel Lee, February 1, 1962.

[60] Mabel Lee and Miriam M. Wagner, *Fundamentals of Body Mechanics and Conditioning* (Philadelphia: W. B. Saunders Company, 1949), p. 1.

[61] *Ibid.*, p. 2.

[62] *Ibid.*, p. 3.

[63] *Ibid.*, p. 19.

[64] Morland, "A Philosophical Interpretation . . . ," p. 424.

[65] Lee and Wagner, *Fundamentals of Body Mechanics and Conditioning*, p. 259.

[66] Morland, "A Philosophical Interpretation . . . ," p. 416.

hope of reward other than the spiritual recompense that comes from the satisfaction of having acted favorably."[67]

Dr. Lee sums up her beliefs about herself when she says, "I know I am an idealist, or I would not feel as strongly as I do against women teachers drinking and smoking . . . but I also know I am a realist or I would not all these years in my professional work . . . have seized upon every opportunity to present my idealistic views on the subject to young women in our profession."[68] From her many statements it is not possible to classify Dr. Lee as a pure idealist by any means. Her self-avowed eclecticism seems to hit the mark, but the balance is shifted very definitely to the side of essentialism. In the statement above she appears to equate idealism with high ideals and realism with practical common sense. Only in the past few years have any of our outstanding leaders begun to consider philosophy in a formal sense. Hence it appears that Morland's study is most helpful in that it arrived at philosophical classification from the delineation of practices.[69]

IMPLICATIONS FOR HEALTH EDUCATION. And now what about the implications of idealistic philosophy of education for health education? This is quite difficult to analyze, and there has been very little philosophical interpretation in this area which is rooted in medicine, public health, and education. There have been many disagreements by various leaders in regard to aims and objectives, curriculum content, and teaching methodology.

CAHN ON PLATO. Cahn, in delineating the thought of Plato on health, refers to health as a " 'dynamic equilibrium' between all inner and outer forces with the object of having an individual at harmony with himself and society."[70] Any program designed to maintain and improve health should result from the application of a logical approach to everyday health problems—a continuous, never-ending process both for individual man and the community in which he lives. We should never think of man and society as separate; a program of health education must be continually aware of this union.

A SEEMING CONTRADICTION. A very helpful statement of the idealist's position in the matter of health and health education comes from Horne. He begins by omitting it under a discussion of "the essential studies"[71] except where it might be included incidentally under biology, but then mentions health first in a list of nine basic values of human living.[72]

---

[67] Mabel Lee, *The Conduct of Physical Education* (New York: A. S. Barnes and Company, 1937), p. 494.

[68] Communication from Dr. Mabel Lee, February 1, 1962.

[69] Morland, "A Philosophical Interpretation. . . ."

[70] Cahn, "Contributions of Plato . . . ," p. 289.

[71] Horne, *Forty-first Yearbook*, Part I, p. 162.

[72] *Ibid.*, p. 182.

In another work he mentions health (or implies the presence of sound health) by his first three answers to the question, "Are we educated?" He states that the truly educated individual should be "physically fit," should live "near the maximum of his efficiency," and should have "a body which is the ready servant of his will."[73] How can we explain this seeming contradiction? The answer is that we must reconsider the idealist's aim of education, which for Horne is as follows:

> We might put good health at the bottom of the hierarchy [of educational values], and yet esteem it highly as a basic value for all the others, enhancing the richness of each and all of them. At the top of the scale would come worship as bringing man into conscious relation to the infinite spirit of the universe.[74]

IDEALISTIC STRESSES.   In Margaret Clark Gannett's philosophical interpretation of a program of health, physical education, and recreation, she concluded that certain "idealistic stresses" were noted and that these were the concept of "building wholeness of mind and body, . . . the development of strong, healthy bodies, . . . good habits of mental and physical health, . . . and the right start in the teaching of health, safety, and physical education to children."[75]

DOWNEY'S 1956 STUDY.   In 1956 Downey completed a study in which he attempted to identify the philosophical beliefs of certain teacher educators in the field of health education.[76] One of the questions he asked was, "What are the dominant emphases in the basic beliefs of these educators with special reference to idealism, pragmatism, and realism?" He devised a *Teacher Education Beliefs Indicator for Health Education* and used it as a tool. He validated his instrument for accuracy and then established criteria which would "indicate influences and possible directions in the field." Although the chief influence being exerted in teacher education was pragmatic, a lesser influence was connected with the idealistic view especially in relation to methods, directed teaching, field experiences, and facilities and equipment. It is notable that there seemed to be disagreements in regard to the objectives and values of health, as well as in the role of the teacher educator. This gives some credence to the belief that idealistic views still exert a certain amount of influence. The results of this study in regard to methodology will be presented later in this chapter.

LIMBERT ON HEALTH.   Paul Limbert, speaking at the Fifth World

---

[73] Herman Harrell Horne, *This New Education* (Nashville, Tenn.: Abingdon Press, 1931), pp. 125-236.

[74] Horne, *Forty-first Yearbook*, Part I, p. 186.

[75] Clark "A Philosophical Interpretation . . . ," pp. 310-311.

[76] Robert J. Downey, "An Identification of the Philosophical Beliefs of Educators in the Field of Health Education" (Ph.D. dissertation, University of Southern California, 1956).

YMCA Consultation on Health and Physical Education in Rome, September 12–14, 1960, pointed out that "the YMCA's emphasis on health and physical education is rooted in a Christian understanding of man and his world." He asked the question, "How could the objectives of health and physical education in the YMCA be rephrased to show more clearly how this programme is grounded in Christian faith?" He continued by asking YMCA leaders to work for a larger measure of integration in the individual by promoting "more intensive study of the body, leading to scientific knowledge: anatomy, body chemistry, hygiene, physiology, etc.; and attention to sex characteristics and habits, leading to a greater understanding of the place of sex in human life, with implications for hygiene." [77] Commenting at this consultation, Thomson stated that "the contribution which physical exercise makes toward good health is recognized." [78] In this connection Cureton quoted John Dryden's words as follows:

> Better to hunt in the field for health unbought,
> Than fee the doctor for a nauseous draught;
> The wise for cure on exercise depend,
> God never made his work for man to mend. [79]

Writing about the physical values to be derived from a program of physical education, Steen speaks about "the healthful gifts produced by large muscle activity" and that exercise "helps prevent bodily injury, aids in medical restoration, and promotes desirable emotional releases." Furthermore, he states that "adequate diet, rest, health habits, and emotional stability are part of healthful living, but they are not complete without exercise." [80]

BENNETT DESCRIBES MORMON POSITION. The Church of Jesus Christ of Latter-Day Saints, of all the various religions and denominations therein, appears to be taking the strongest position in regard to the care of the body. In describing this position at the Cincinnati convention of the American Association for Health, Physical Education, and Recreation in April, 1962, Bennett stated that:

The Mormon faith teaches that the spirit and body are the soul of man. It looks upon the body as a non-evil component of the eternal soul of man and anticipates literal resurrection after death. Thus, the body must be treated with respect and intelligence and maintained at a high level of efficiency. The body should be kept free from impurities and substances deleterious to its best

---

[77] Paul M. Limbert, "Physical Education as an Integral Part of YMCA Programme," a paper presented at the Fifth World YMCA Consultation on Health and Physical Education, Rome, September 12-14, 1960. Summarized in *World Communique* (January–February 1961).

[78] *World Communique* (January–February 1961), p. 9.

[79] *Ibid.*

[80] Steen, *The Banner,* XCVI, 11.

functioning. (Mormons abstain from coffee, tea, smoking, and alcoholic beverages). Mormon scripture treats man as a whole being with mind, muscle, heart,
nerve, and spirit all important in the education and training to achieve the
'abundant life' promised by Christ to men.[81]

THE SERVICE PROGRAM.   Despite all these statements which emphasize
the beliefs of idealists concerning the importance of a healthy body, it
still appears evident (as Horne has indicated) that "good health is at
the bottom of the hierarchy" of life's many values. Yet, as he also indicated, it is esteemed very highly by the idealist as a basic value. Could
this perhaps be the reason why the required program of health and
physical education in American schools and colleges has been known as
the *service* program? In this conception it provides a service to man by
its contribution to his health thereby enabling him to pursue higher
educational goals.

THE ROLE OF SCHOOL RECREATION.   Lastly under the aims and objectives of the educational philosophy of idealism, the role of recreation
in the school will be considered. The position here is not clear-cut and
decisive because of the somewhat borderline status on the spectrum
which idealism occupies. As was explained earlier in this chapter, however, idealistic philosophy of education does belong more correctly on
the essentialistic side of the spectrum because of its concern with educational essentials. The importance of recreation and play in idealistic
philosophy of education has perhaps not been fully understood or appreciated in the past. Their role in the development of the personality
and the perfectly integrated individual is looming larger with each
passing year. It is for this reason that a person subscribing to idealistic
philosophy of education should reassess the contributions that recreation and play can and do make in the education of man. That there is
a great need for educational research along these lines is self-evident.

THE PUBLIC IMAGE IS BLURRED.   Another difficulty that we encounter
at this point is that it is often difficult to differentiate between physical
education and recreation. One reason for this is that the public in the
early twentieth century, and today for that matter in many instances,
still thinks of physical education as being synonomous with physical
recreation and vice versa. This belief has caused untold hardship for
the physical educator who attempts to explain that it is just as difficult
to teach his subject well as almost any other subject in the curriculum.
People think typically that his task is to give a few exercises and then
roll out the ball. The recreator has experienced great hardship also
because he has difficulty explaining that his program involves more than

---

[81] Bruce L. Bennett, "Religion and Physical Education," a paper presented at the
Cincinnati Convention of the American Association for Health, Physical Education,
and Recreation, on April 10, 1962.

physical recreation—that it consists of meeting the child's social, communicative, aesthetic and creative, and learning (hobbies) interests as well. Of course, in the context of this book we are considering the role of the physical-, health-, and recreation-education teacher in schools and colleges. Thus, we believe that this person should be responsible for *physical* recreation only in a direct way. In an indirect way, he should meet all the other recreational needs and interests of boys and girls by working cooperatively with the recreation administrator (either within the school system or in the community) at all times.

A COMPATIBLE THEORY OF PLAY? One other matter should perhaps be clarified at this point; however, it is extremely difficult to state that this or that theory of play seems to coincide identically with idealistic philosophy of education.[82] We should be able to get some help in this connection by reviewing very briefly the idealistic view. In the first place, the ultimate worth of personality is paramount, and the highest virtue is respect for that personality. Idealists marvel at the growth of man's physical organism, but they are even more amazed by the growth of man's spirit. As Horne has stated it so beautifully and yet so concisely:

. . . our philosophy dares to suggest that the learner is a finite person, growing, when properly educated, into the image of an infinite person, that his real origin is deity, that his nature is freedom, and that his destiny is immortality.[83]

In the light of such a statement embodying man's uniqueness among all the creatures of the world—and because of his infinite possibilities for growth and for the acquisition of the ideal virtues, as well as the concept of the unity of the organism—it would seem that idealists might view very closely any theories of recreation and play which grant educational possibilities to these activities of man. This is not to say that instinct-based theories of play would be automatically eliminated.

THE SELF-EXPRESSION THEORY OF PLAY. Sapora and Mitchell devoted an entire chapter to the underlying theory of play and recreation. The *five* traditional theories of play described are the surplus energy theory, the re-creation theory, the relaxation theory, the instinct-practice theory, and the catharsis theory. Each one considered individually seems to have merit, but none seems to provide the whole answer. It is quite possible that we will never have a completely satisfactory explanation. It is certain, however, that there will continue to be research conducted along these lines. The newer self-expression theory of play explained in detail in Sapora and Mitchell borrows from the traditional theories and yet combines, refines, and clarifies. It begins by listing what appear to be facts which are basic to a modern theory of play. They are: (1) that

---

[82] Cf., p. 192.
[83] Horne, *Forty-first Yearbook,* Part I, p. 154.

man is an active, dynamic creature; (2) that the physiological and anatomical structure of the organism predispose it to certain kinds of activity; (3) that the physical fitness of the organism has an effect upon the type of activity it engages in; and (4) that the psychological inclinations of the individual predispose him toward certain types of activity.[84] From this underlying reasoning the self-expression theory is developed, since this is postulated as the chief need in man's life—to achieve the satisfaction and accomplishment of self-expression of one's own personality. Here is an explanation that seems to consider quite fully the conception of man as an organic unity—a total organism. Many aspects of it seem compatible with idealistic philosophy of education, and yet it appears much more progressive than the dualistic theory of work and play of the strict essentialist which characterizes play only as a relief from work, as a means of using up surplus energy, and as a means of recreation, so that the individual may again be ready for the many types of work in which most men become involved.

OTHER PERTINENT FACTORS. The preceding explanation is, of course, all very interesting. It gathers still further strength when other points of analysis are offered (some of which do not seem to be antithetical to idealism) as follows: (1) the role of habit in play, which indicates that "throughout life the individual is inclined toward those activities which are habitual to him"; (2) the role of social contact in habit formation; (3) the role of the physical environment as a limiting factor in the choice of recreational activity; and (4) the role of universal wishes, which implies that all mankind may have "universal motives or common desires" such as "the wishes for new experience, for security, for response, and for recognition," not to mention "the wish for participation and for the esthetic." [85]

We may ask at this point how these wishes differ from instincts. You may think that we are right back again where we started. It does appear that the naturalistic realist might regard these "wishes" as instinctive, and the pragmatic experimentalist would tend to view them as being determined as a result of experience. The idealist, however, would probably revert to the theory of human nature which he holds and consequently look for those aspects of this self-expression theory which seem promising to him.

RECREATION AND THE ETERNAL VALUES. You will recall that idealists believe generally that mind (or spirit) as experienced by all men is basic and real, and that the entire universe is mind essentially. Mind is the true reality. They believe further that man possesses a soul and

---

[84] Allen V. Sapora and Elmer D. Mitchell, *The Theory of Play and Recreation,* 3rd. ed. (New York: The Ronald Press Company, 1961), pp. 89-91.

[85] *Ibid.,* pp. 92-98.

is therefore of a higher order than all other creatures on earth. Without going again into the problem as to whether a particular idealist is a spiritual monist or pluralist, each of these various positions grants man freedom of will to determine which way his life shall go. Without reviewing again idealistic theories of knowledge acquisition and logic (to which the reader may wish to refer at this point in the preceding chapter), we shall conclude this discussion by explaining that the idealist believes man is a purposive being who is striving to achieve the values which are embedded in reality itself. To the extent that the idealist can realize the eternal values through the choice of the right kinds of play and recreation without flouting the moral order in the world, he will be progressive enough to disregard a dualistic theory of work and play—a theory that has plagued us in the United States right down to the present day.

PLATO ON PLAY. As we now turn to some of the specific statements displaying idealistic beliefs regarding the values of play and recreation, we shall examine first, albeit very briefly, the essence of Plato's contribution to thought on this matter. In the first place, "Plato had no intention of allowing play to be left to whim and fancy. Play or recreation of any sort, from children's games to behavior at banquets, was a serious matter for the legislature." [86] To make certain of this, he recommended that children should be under the very careful supervision of teachers at a very early age. He felt that "the characters of future citizens are formed through their childhood games," and that "play must be, therefore, most carefully utilized and supervised by the state." [87] Cahn made one other extremely important point which Plato believed about recreation which coincides with certain present-day theories about its place in life as follows: "Recreation, the activity of leisure, is a necessary alternate with toil to balance the daily life to permit the growth of the integrated man within society." [88]

MIXED MOTIVES. Earlier in this chapter, the implications from idealism were explained. It was pointed out that early Christian idealism furthered the concept of the dualism of mind and body and that this has exerted a detrimental influence on physical education ever since. The same observation may be made about this influence on the development of physical- and social-recreation interests at least, but it is very evident that attitudes toward all types of recreational activities, as well as sports and games, have been improving steadily with some exceptions throughout the twentieth century. It is not completely clear in some instances whether such affairs are being tolerated, are being exploited for the

---

[86] Cahn, "Contributions of Plato . . . ," p. 98.
[87] *Ibid.*, pp. 289-294.
[88] *Ibid.*

attraction that they hold for youth and adults, or whether their contribution to the achievement of integrated personality is being fully realized. Let us now examine some of the statements in the literature to help us make up our minds.

THE METHODIST CHURCH AND RECREATION. Bennett describes briefly the history of the Methodist Church's attitude toward recreation.[89] A specific list of "sinful amusements" was repealed in 1924, when the church reverted "to Wesley's original prohibition which is printed in the most recent Methodist *Discipline* (1960)." Members were urged to refrain from "the taking of such diversions as cannot be used in the name of the Lord Jesus." Despite such prohibitions, Bennett does go on to say that such regulations were not actually carried out or even endorsed by all concerned. He refers to a statement that appeared in 1920 as follows:

While we are aware that improper amusements are a 'fruitful source of spiritual decline' we also believe that the social and recreational instinct is God-given, and, if properly guided, will strengthen rather than injure the spiritual life. The church must no longer allow her youth to 'go into nearby villages and buy themselves the victuals of social life,' but, rather, should say 'Sit down and eat' of the clean, wholesome things provided by the church, which seeks to build a social and recreational life that is spiritual and a spiritual life that is social and recreational.[90]

BENNETT ON RECREATION'S ROLE. Bennett, himself a Presbyterian, believes strongly that recreation under religious sponsorship can serve to help the American people improve moral and ethical standards, but, with the exception of The Church of Jesus Christ of Latter-Day Saints (Mormon) which does view "the body as a non-evil component of the eternal soul of man and anticipates literal resurrection after death," he believes that Protestant churches are unsure of their role in this area and that the quality of recreational leadership and opportunity provided varies greatly within individual churches.[91]

LOZES'S SURVEY. There are distinct signs, however, that specific denominations are becoming increasingly aware of the role that recreation can play in the promulgation of the Christian idealistic way of life. In 1955, Lozes completed a study of the philosophy of certain religious denominations relative to physical education (interpreted broadly) and the effect of this philosophy on physical education in certain church-related institutions. She visited and interviewed administrative personnel at eleven church-related institutions of higher learning and received additional information by written inquiry to thirteen other church-

---

[89] Bennett, "Religion and Physical Education," pp. 3-5.
[90] *Ibid.* As quoted by Bennett.
[91] *Ibid.*

related institutions. Interestingly enough, "the purpose which the largest number of presidents, or their representatives, and also the largest number of physical education directors stated was to provide recreation for the students." [92] In the main, also, it was felt that the religious denomination did have a definite influence on the physical-education program. Presidents tended to emphasize the physical, the integrational, and the recreational purposes of physical education, while the physical-education department heads stressed the recreational purposes, integrational purposes, physical purposes, mental purposes, and social purposes in that order. The majority of presidents (by a vote of six to five) and eight of the physical directors believed that physical education was equal in importance to other college subjects. Of interest to our discussion at the moment was the statement by Lozes that "there did not seem to be a mind-body philosophy peculiar to a particular religious denomination unless it might be the lower hierarchy of the physical faculties mentioned by two Catholic institutions!" It was indicated further that the relatively lower status of physical education "seemed to be due to academic influence more than to religious influence." [93]

AN INCREASED AWARENESS OF RECREATION'S ROLE. In 1956, the Christian Education Commission of the Church of the Brethren published an entire volume entitled *Recreation and the Local Church.* A publication such as this shows an increased awareness of the role that recreation can play in the life of a Christian. Clemens, Tully, and Crill make it very clear that:

For the Christian there is a simple but significant standard: In the light of what I know and am learning about Jesus, my foremost companion, does this activity fit the pattern He would have me live during this generation?

Leisure to the Christian can become power, for in it he can deepen his fellowship with God, increase his knowledge and wisdom through education, regain strength through play and recreation and extend himself and God's Kingdom through service to his fellow men." [94]

WILTON'S ANALYSIS OF THEORIES. Wilton's study completed in this same year made a comparative analysis of theories related to moral and spiritual values in physical education.[95] His definition of "experience in physical education" is definitely progressivistic:

Physical education experience is defined as that area of the school's curriculum which conducts education through physical activity. Its basic purposes are considered to be the same as those of other school departments. It attempts to benefit the student in as many phases of adjusted living as possible; it must

---

[92] Lozes, "The Philosophy of Certain Religious Denominations . . . ," pp. 97-104.

[93] *Ibid.,* p. 103.

[94] Frances Clemens, Robert Tully and Edward Crill, eds., *Recreation and the Local Church* (Elgin, Ill.: Brethren Press, 1956), p. 28.

[95] Cf., pp. 214-215.

therefore produce adequate emotional and social growth along with proper physical development and acquisition of play skills.[96]

Such a definition as this, while strongly progressivistic and also definitely experimentalistic, would not be incompatible with a "liberal idealistic approach" in the opinion of the author. In order to analyze the definition critically, it would be necessary to have it amplified still further and to know more about the writer's specific basic philosophical and subsequent educational beliefs. The assumption made is that if physical education includes instruction in and opportunities for practice of play skills it includes a certain amount of physical recreation as well. When Wilton tells us, therefore, that seventeen leaders in physical education see this activity as including spiritual enrichment value, he is seemingly subscribing to what is typically an idealistic tenet. In speaking about current practice in interscholastic and intercollegiate sport, he states further that:

Evidence taken from the writings of the leaders used in this study tends to justify the assumption that spiritual growth can be the outcome of properly conducted physical education; hence play leaders are obligated to make goals which will lead to an appreciation of *moral and spiritual values.*[97]

The last statement in Wilton's study is progressivistic to the core and would bring joy to the hearts of idealists and experimentalists alike:

Any teaching for growth in moral and spiritual values is contingent upon one major consideration—real, genuine *interest in* and *respect for* the individual student.[98]

CHRISTIAN RECREATION. Boyd discussed the subject "Recreation and the Faiths—The Southern Baptist Church Recreation Philosophy at Work" at the 42nd National Recreation Congress held in Washington, D. C., September 25–29, 1960. Expressing the opinion that "recreation is the hardest area in which to include our religious principles," he stated further that:

Failure to carry religious principles into leisure makes spare time a purely selfish possession rather than another opportunity for Christian development. Making our recreation Christian also carries with it a responsibility to choose wisely what we will do with all of our spare time.[99]

DIVIDED JEWISH OPINION. Bennett has indicated that "it seems apparent that physical education and sports are rather distant from the heart of

---

[96] Wilton, "A Comparative Analysis of Theories . . . ," p. 5.

[97] *Ibid.,* p. 288.

[98] *Ibid.,* p. 293.

[99] Robert M. Boyd, "The Southern Baptist Church Recreation Philosophy at Work," in *Selected Papers presented at the 42nd National Recreation Congress* (New York: National Recreation Association, 1961), p. 184.

Jewish religious life," and that "the Jewish rabbis and synagogues have somewhat reluctantly recognized the need for the Jewish Centers which have largely supplanted the earlier Young Men's Hebrew Associations." [100] Yet it would seem that there is a difference of opinion on this matter depending on whether the position is being stated by an Orthodox, Conservative, or Reform Jew. Speaking at the AAHPER convention in Cincinnati, April 9, 1962, Rabbi D. J. Silver, a Reform Jew, spoke beautifully on the use of leisure in a truly idealistic vein. Explaining how the Jews had "architected the Sabbath as a day of leisure," he emphasized that this should be "pleasure with a purpose." He urged that we "think of the whole man and his role in society." He asked the recreators assembled not to "destroy the uniqueness of man"; to "put the whole of the world before the child and before the adult"; and to "fire the child with enthusiasm for life and learning." His message was a distinct challenge in that he pointed out how recreation could serve to carry out God's purpose for man on earth. [101]

HISTORICAL BACKGROUND. Turning aside from some of the statements of certain religious groups regarding the role of recreation in the educational process, we will now very briefly trace the development of the play and recreation movement in the United States with a cursory examination of some of the changing views of leisure down through the ages. It has been stated by Martin and Esther Neumeyer that "no systematic theories of leisure or play developed until toward the end of the nineteenth century. Yet the views held, at least by certain classes and individuals, affected both the amount and the uses of leisure." [102] They continue by listing five of the changing views as follows:

1. *Military Conception*—gymnastics, sports, games, and related activities were considered fundamentally as means to an end, because the focus of attention in the long run was upon the military objective rather than the activities themselves. [103]

2. *Sports and Physical Training*—there developed a special interest in sports and games among the Greeks and Romans that was somewhat divorced from the ultimate military value. The greatest achievement of the Greeks in athletics and sports was the development of the Olympic games, which eventually became international in scope. [104]

3. *Cultural and Art View*—the Athenian ideal of a citizen was that not only of a soldier and an athlete, but an artist, philosopher, and statesman as well.... But the physical side was not all. The Athenians utilized their leisure in

---

[100] Bennett, "Religion and Physical Education," pp. 2-3.

[101] Rabbi D. J. Silver, a paper presented at the American Association for Health, Physical Education, and Recreation Convention, Cincinnati, Ohio, April 9, 1962.

[102] Martin H. Neumeyer and Esther S. Neumeyer, *Leisure and Recreation—A Study of Leisure and Recreation in their Sociological Aspects*, 3rd ed., Copyright ©. (New York: The Ronald Press Company, 1958), p. 50.

[103] *Ibid.*, p. 51.

[104] *Ibid.*, pp. 51-52.

philosophical disputations, in cultivating the arts of painting, sculpture, drama, and music. . . . The Greeks, however, never completely got away from the notion that all activity had a purpose beyond itself.[105]

4. *Puritanical Attitude*—church leaders assumed a strong reactionary attitude toward recreation, but this hostile view was by no means confined to the church . . . intellectual and political leaders during the Middle Ages and years later joined hands with the religious forces to suppress sports, games, and other forms of entertainments.[106]

5. *Recognition of the Values of Play*—the recognition of its value began during the Middle Ages, but it was not until the modern era that the more favorable attitude became widespread. A series of inventions, reform movements in religion, politics, and education, the spirit of scientific inquiry, intellectual interests, and the developments in social thought produced gradual but effective changes in attitudes and conduct.[107]

In the United States recognition of the values of play and recreation has been largely a twentieth-century phenomenon. Playgrounds have developed to a point where they are an integral part of American urban life. The whole recreation movement catering to the needs and interests of all ages has been a fascinating chapter in a developing leisure economy. A former mayor of Detroit, for example, payed a backhanded compliment to this field when faced with a transportation strike by his remark that "transportation is as important to this city as water, sewage disposal, and recreation." Recreation programs are now in effect year-round and include activities designed to meet social, aesthetic and creative, communicative, and learning (hobbies) interests, as well as physical-recreation interests. At present, recreation is clearly one of the major social institutions in American life.

HORNE ON RECREATION.   Our concern in this section of this chapter has been primarily how play and recreation fits in with idealistic philosophy of education. In conclusion we shall present a few more statements which show evidence of idealistic import. As stated previously, Herman Harrell Horne has been a leading figure in idealistic philosophy of education in this century. That he sees an important place for recreation in the education of man is obvious from a consideration of his stated beliefs. "The ideal suggests the integrated individual in an integrated society growing in the image of the integrated universe." [108] Many of the characteristics of an educated person listed by Horne show the importance of all types of recreation in the educational pattern that he envisioned as follows:

---

[105] *Ibid.,* pp. 54-55.
[106] *Ibid.,* p. 55.
[107] *Ibid.,* p. 56.
[108] Horne, *Forty-first Yearbook,* Part I, p. 186.

1. He is physically fit.

. . . . .

3. He has a body which is the ready servant of his will.

. . . . .

8. His social interests are constantly widening.

. . . . .

19. He loves nature.

. . . . .

25. His is a happy life.

. . . . .

26. He can enjoy a vacation.

. . . . .

30. He can make something with his hands.

. . . . .

32. He can play with children and have a truly fine time.[109]

. . . . .

VALUES IN RECREATION. Discussing values in recreation in his book *Recreation in the American Community*, Danford stated that "the development of a higher level of moral and ethical behavior is the problem of every man, woman, and child in this nation." [110] He stated that:

There is nothing inherently good or bad about a game. Games possess no innate qualities which automatically are transferred to the boys and girls who participate in them. The leader has to dig for these values and he gets them chiefly in two ways: (1) by planning for them just as carefully as he plans for the development of skills; and (2) by setting an example himself of upright conduct. These situations which arise constantly in the play experience of youth and adults represent a great opportunity for the leader to give his players some understanding of Christian ethics and of what democracy means in terms of human relationships.[111]

JAY B. NASH AND CREATIVE RECREATION. Jay B. Nash, one of America's great leaders in recreation and physical education, felt very strongly about the values of recreation and its place in our evolving democratic system of education. If we were asked to categorize him as to his philosophical position, we would have to call him a liberal or progressive idealist. His most recent book *Philosophy of Recreation and Leisure* abounds with his progressive and idealistic beliefs. One of the concluding chapters of this inspirational work is entitled *Recreation: A Way of Life*. Nash brings this chapter to a close as follows:

When recreation is thought of as a complement to work, hence a need for all men, it will assume the stature it deserves. When it is recognized that our age is witnessing a humane and psychic disintegration, possibly more profound,

---

[109] Horne, *This New Education,* pp. 125-136.
[110] Howard G. Danford, *Recreation in the American Community* (New York: Harper & Row, Publishers, Inc., 1953), p. 116.
[111] *Ibid.,* p. 117.

possibly more world-wide than any previous age has known, and when it is realized that the cause of this can be laid at the door of the materialistic philosophy of life, then will creative recreation take on significance—possibly spiritual significance. Recreation can and even may become a way of life.[112]

SPIRITUAL VALUES IN OUTDOOR EDUCATION.   Outdoor education and school camping are gradually assuming an increasingly important role in the education of America's youth. In 1959 Moseley completed a study of the philosophies of camp directors and of the opinions of campers as related to the spiritual values derived in the field of camping. Some of her findings have definite implications for the promulgation of idealistic philosophy of education. She reported that:

> . . . an emphasis was definitely placed on the thesis that life in the out-of-doors is a means of gaining a greater appreciation and understanding of God. The directors mentioned the inspiring beauties of nature and the opportunities of affiliating the wonder of these beauties with the omniscient presence of God.[113]

She found further that directors wanted a "counselor who is qualified to bestow upon the camper an intense desire to be the best type of person he or she knows how to be. The counselor should set the example and encourage the camper to follow." [114] Campers, however, felt a need for improved religious services, a devotional period at the end of the day, and an opportunity to feel "close" to God.[115] In conclusion, a statement of philosophy associated with the role of spiritual values in the modern day camp was presented along with various methods by which these aims and objectives might be achieved.[116]

BRIGHTBILL AND IDEALISM.   In concluding this section on the implications for recreation education from idealistic philosophy of education, one more fine contemporary statement of a philosophy of leisure must be mentioned. Brightbill's *Man and Leisure: A Philosophy of Recreation* explores the problem of man's "new leisure" and offers his beliefs about how man "can have a personally satisfying and full existence through *recreative living.*" [117] An analysis of this work leads the present writer to the conviction that there is a definite kinship between Nash's progressive idealism and the philosophy of Professor Brightbill, although Bright-

---

[112] Jay B. Nash, *Philosophy of Recreation and Leisure* (Dubuque, Iowa: Wm. C. Brown Co., 1960), pp. 208-209. Published originally by The C. V. Mosby Company in 1953.

[113] Mary Louise Moseley, "A Study of the Philosophies of Camp Directors and of the Opinions of Campers as Related to the Spiritual Values Derived in the Field of Camping" (M.Ed. thesis, Woman's College, University of North Carolina, 1959), p. 43.

[114] *Ibid.*

[115] *Ibid.*, pp. 43-44.

[116] *Ibid.*, pp. 45-50.

[117] Charles K. Brightbill, *Man and Leisure: A Philosophy of Recreation* (Englewood Cliffs, N.J.: Prentice-Hall, Inc., 1961), p. vi.

bill offers much that will appeal to the realist and experimentalist as well. Idealistic phrases which caught our attention are:

It is the eternal *search* for these ideals and not their attainment that seems to provide the satisfaction . . .[118]

And although his behavior often appears to deny it, man also has great love for humanity, which is blanketed—difficult as it may be to define—by his love of God.[119]

Also, our deepest religious needs, peace of mind, and sense of spiritual purpose often seem to come from relating ourselves to that which is beautiful in life, from gearing our existences to the totality of things and from using our powers to create and express those needs which emanate from the mysteries of life.[120]

Brightbill, as a professor of recreation at the University of Illinois, is, of course, tremendously interested in the wise use of leisure. He sees such a way of life as vital in the "enveloping Western civilization" of today's world. He defines this need as "a social proposition" that "summons *action.*" Speaking about the role of leisure in education, Brightbill states that:

Education for leisure, as education for anything else, is not something that can be accomplished quickly or easily. It must begin early in the home and be given large attention during the flexible, youthful years in the school and community[121]

In concluding his philosophy of recreation he re-emphasizes the great and unique role that recreation can fulfill in the future, and he warns that mankind is faced with what amounts to a "recreational imperative":

Latent in leisure are tremendous potential forces for good that are ready and awaiting that time when our social thinking and action mature to unleash them for the benefit of all humanity. Recreative living is living 'to whom it may concern.' It should concern everyone, for it is the GREAT proposition made to mankind and his society, neither of which have any other choice except to use it well or perish.[122]

Methodology

What teaching methods shall the idealist employ? Now that we have discussed a number of idealistic aims and objectives carefully, the next step is to shift our focus and direct our attention to the means whereby these goals may be reached. It should be readily apparent that objectives and method must concur to the highest degree possible. As we indicated earlier, it is often possible to get a certain amount of consensus about

---

[118] *Ibid.,* p. 3.
[119] *Ibid.,* p. 11.
[120] *Ibid.,* pp. 16-17.
[121] *Ibid.,* pp. 279-280.
[122] *Ibid.,* p. 283.

long range objectives between conflicting educational positions. The truth of this statement appears obvious when we consider, for example, the seven cardinal aims of education published originally in 1918. The difficulty arises when any attempt is made to list them in order of importance, and when the necessary teaching methods are discussed whereby specific objectives may be achieved.

PLATO AND TEACHING METHOD. We can get considerable help on idealistic teaching method initially from Cahn's analysis of the contributions of Plato to thought on physical, health, and recreation education. In the first place we are told that for Plato "method was the tool used to carve out the good life." [123] Furthermore, it should "at all times . . . be subordinate to the objectives" of idealistic philosophy. The various activities of the physical-education program are used as a means to an end—that end being the effort of the individual to achieve the good life. This can be accomplished by the wise teacher who so arranges and presents the activities that they:

. . . harmonize the conflicting psychological elements of reason, desire, and spirit; develop an intelligent courage acting with reason and intelligence in the face of fears, hopes, and pleasures; engraves habits of right thought and action into the good character; develop organic strength; and insure training in the necessary life skills.[124]

So, for Plato, the teacher should not concern himself necessarily with outlining the various aspects of the curriculum in great detail, nor should he be especially conscious of using one technique as opposed to another. The teacher should use his reason and should base his selection of a particular activity or teaching technique on the basis of sound scientific investigation which has demonstrated validity and, of course, proper psychological methodology. Although, for example, a play attitude is especially good with children, the instructor should not forget that time-proven proverb that the "hard is the good." Life presents many problems to developing youth, and the teacher should be as logical as possible in devising the means whereby youth can be prepared for what lies ahead in maturity.

IDEALISTIC TEACHING METHOD. In her philosophical interpretation of a program of physical education in a state teachers college, Clark presented much both directly and indirectly which gives further insight into the problem of teaching method and technique as viewed by the idealist. She concurred that "there are many ways of accomplishing the ends of education." [125] This is borne out by Butler who stated that "idealists are likely to insist that they are creators and determiners of

[123] Cahn, "Contributions of Plato . . . ," p. 157.
[124] *Ibid.*
[125] Clark, "A Philosophical Interpretation . . . , " p. 3. Abstract of thesis.

method, not devotees of some one method." [126] Whereas the experimentalist "waxes ecstatically" about the concept of "learning by doing," Horne does not appear quite so upset about the "spectator versus participant" controversy that rages about the heads of those who sit in the stands watching interscholastic or intercollegiate contests. He states:

Three things must be noted here. The first is that the contrast between the spectator and participant is perhaps overdrawn. The role of the spectator is not always passive; he is not entirely indifferent to what is going on; he has an interest in what he is observing. This is even true of the prisoner watching the rain. It is especially true of spectators at athletic contests with favorites of their own; muscles are taut and fatigue results. The spectator is really more than a spectator, he is a restrained participant.[127]

CLARK ON THE TEACHER'S ROLE. Clark believed further that the teacher has a most significant role to play in the education of youth and that this is especially true in idealistic philosophy of education. The word *guidance* was used a number of times in such ways as "students, under guidance, choose objectives, activities, textbooks, topics for reports, and the like"; and "that data about students, both objectively and subjectively derived, are used for individual guidance and group planning; . . . ." [128] She mentioned that "the lives and works of great leaders are used to enrich the lives and works of a younger generation." In physical, health, and recreation education this would apply to the lives and practices of great athletes and coaches, as well as to outstanding teachers and recreation leaders. Children are great imitators, and idealistic educators make full use of this teaching aid to encourage youngsters to strive for high attainment in athletic competition. As Horne pointed out, "The child through imitating others, becomes aware of his own capacity for a wide variety of acts that he otherwise would have believed were beyond his powers." [129]

OTHER IDEALISTIC STRESSES. A few remaining idealistic stresses according to Clark give still further insight into recommended teaching method. The idealist places great emphasis on the development of certain life values that stimulate desirable personality growth. One of these is a strong, healthy body. Such a body is developed and maintained only through vigorous exercise of a regular nature throughout life. Secondly, "good habits of mental and physical health" are necessary. It is essential to make "the right start in the teaching of health, safety, and physical

---

[126] J. Donald Butler, *Four Philosophies* (New York: Harper & Row, Publishers, Inc., 1957), p. 258.

[127] Herman Harrell Horne, *The Democratic Philosophy of Education* (New York: The Macmillan Company, 1932), pp. 165-166.

[128] Clark, "A Philosophical Interpretation . . . ," p. 3. Abstract of thesis.

[129] Herman Harrell Horne, *Philosophy of Education*, rev. ed. (New York: The Macmillan Company, 1927), p. 180.

education to children." Lastly, they should become skillful, have a reasonable amount of success, and get a lot of fun through physical activity.[130] The idealistic physical educator, anxious to develop these "life values," should give careful consideration to interest, effort, and discipline as educational techniques. Interest is, of course, most important, but the idealist has discovered that it alone will not suffice to accomplish all the educational objectives necessary. It must often be supplemented by discipline in such a way that the student will respond with the effort needed to get the job done, whatever the responsibility may be. Furthermore, when discipline is invoked to cause the student to respond with effort, he may well discover in a short while that his interest has been aroused.[131] Approaching the task of education from the standpoint of interest only appears to be an extremely slow and costly method.

IDEALISM IN COACHING. Many coaches make use of an idealistic dictum when they point out to aspiring young athletes that they will have to make certain sacrifices if they hope to be successful and worthy team members. Such sacrifices include refraining from smoking, avoidance of alcoholic beverages, regular hours of sleep, correct dietary habits, keeping profanity to a minimum, and reasonable dating practices so that there will be time to study. The idealist strives for ideals—very high ideals—and because of this he works for the maximum of efficiency as he achieves personal excellence.

Although the idealistic teacher should be an active, energetic individual who uses a variety of methods to instruct his charges, it is most important that he develop the self-activity of his students. Hocking pointed out that the teacher or coach must eventually step into the background as his boys achieve maturity. After all, his goal is not glory for himself but to help the participants achieve their inherent selfhood.[132] As Butler has stated it, ". . . they are souls who are capable of a genuine initiative, and their responses are the struggles of that initiative coming to life and flowering into full bloom." [133] We must confess that it is easy for the coach, subject to all sorts of personal and exterior pressures, to fall prey to the influences of a materialistic culture that all too often seems to demand a winning team at almost any cost. But the coach with a truly idealistic philosophy will struggle with all his might and main to keep from succumbing to the demands of the public—a most difficult ideal to achieve.

THE PRINCIPLE OF SELF-ACTIVITY. Butler explains the need for the teacher to work for this principle of self-activity and offers sound advice to the idealistic physical educator as follows:

---

[130] Clark, "A Philosophical Interpretation. . . ."
[131] Horne, *The Democratic Philosophy of Education*, p. 174.
[132] William E. Hocking, *Human Nature and Its Remaking* (New Haven, Conn.: Yale University Press, 1918), pp. 277-278.
[133] Butler, *Four Philosophies*, p. 251.

Self-activity leading to self-development, according to idealists, is not an abstract process having little relation to bodily or temporal factors. To develop the self certainly includes development of the body and fully embraces physical education [Horne, *Philosophy of Education*, Rev. Ed., p. 95]. But, of course, development of the body is limited to developing and strengthening what is given the individual by birth. Education cannot add to the nerve cells of the brain, but it can fully develop capacities for which potentiality is given in the individual (*Ibid.*, pp. 41-42).[134]

IMPORTANCE OF INFORMAL DIALECTIC. Despite what has been said about the idealistic educator not being a devotee of any particular teaching method, and because of the belief that true education takes place when there is self-activity on the part of the student, it may seem strange to say that the lecture and discussion appears to be most popular. Butler is very careful to explain, however, that an "informal dialectic" should be taking place in the class a good share of the time.[135] By this he means that the teacher should not imply that there is only one way of thinking about some problem, or only one way of performing some skill in the gymnasium. This does not mean that the student shouldn't be told what appears to be the best way at the moment in the light of experimental research, but it does mean that the player should feel completely free to raise questions and even to offer suggestions for change. This, of course, should not take place to the extent that a "stalemate" occurs, nor should it result in an "ill-prepared pooling of ignorance."

OTHER IDEALISTIC PRACTICES. It is interesting to note that Downey in his identification of the philosophical beliefs of leading educators in the field of health education found that certain idealistic practices predominated in the areas of method, directed teaching, field experiences, and facilities and equipment. In regard to teaching method, a significant number of the respondents indicated that they were practicing "the use of discussion with some lecturing and experimenting." [136] They believed that there should be greater use of this type of teaching method throughout teacher education as well.

BUTLER'S SUMMARY. Butler's summary of idealistic teaching method applies largely to classroom situations which physical, health, and recreation educators meet a certain percentage of the time:

Teaching methods should be used which create a slight feeling of suspense for the student—suspense to be resolved only by his own decision or active effort.

---

[134] *Ibid.*, p. 252.

[135] *Ibid.*, p. 259.

[136] Robert J. Downey, "An Identification of the Philosophical Beliefs of Educators in the Field of Health Education" (Ph.D. dessertation, University of Southern California, 1956), p. 26.

Questioning and discussion lend themselves admirably to this purpose, but there is also much place for solid instruction, as in lecturing, and for pupil activity, as in projects employing constructive and creative work.[137]

There are, however, certain implications which can be drawn from the above statement that will aid the instructor in the gymnasium or the coach on the field. The matter of creating a slight feeling of suspense that will lead the student to make decisions for himself and act accordingly is a practice that we see all too rarely in much teaching of physical education. The rigidly formal physical-education class, the stereotyped, dull team practice, or the gymnasium activity which is often merely poorly organized informal recreation would not be the type of teaching method that would gladden the heart of the truly idealistic teacher of physical, health, and recreation education.

METHOD IN CHRISTIAN IDEALISM. At this juncture we shall turn to a brief consideration of teaching with more of a Christian idealistic emphasis. Limbert, speaking at the Fifth World YMCA Consultation in Rome in 1960, felt that the leader should emphasize the concept of "equipment for service, both to God and man." [138] Jones, director of the UNESCO Youth Institute, was troubled by "the growing specialization that tends to reduce the interest of people who are concerned for the whole personality of the participant. The mechanics become more important than the competitors." [139] Steinhaus stressed the idea that "every impact of man on man or of programme on man invariably does influence in some way man's body, man's mind, man's spirit. This is the most important truth which I would bring to your attention." [140] Friermood continued with this idealistic emphasis when he postulated that "the chief considerations are how the tools are used in serving human needs and in helping persons see clearly and be guided by the Christian principles fostered by the organization." [141] This concept of the importance of the leader in developing individual personality growth was reiterated further by Limbert as he explained how method must be broadened and widened as follows:

The leader must not only be able to teach specific skills and impart technical knowledge, he must be alert to opportunities for developing related interests, leading into deeper understandings which involve a wide range of human experience.[142]

---

[137] Butler, *Four Philosophies*, p. 262.

[138] Paul M. Limbert, "Physical Education as an Integral Part of YMCA Programme," a paper presented at the Fifth World YMCA Consultation on Health and Physical Education, Rome, September 12-14, 1960. Summarized in *World Communique* (January- February 1961).

[139] R. W. Jones, in *World Communique, op. cit.,* p. 10.

[140] *Ibid.,* p. 9.

[141] *Ibid.*

[142] *Ibid.*

Christian education definitely places firm emphasis on the need for the Christian physical educator and coach to so arrange his teaching and/or coaching that ethical conduct is fostered:

> The development of ethical conduct is more easily taught at the elementary and secondary levels but is part of the value of physical education in college. The attributes of team work, perseverance, courage, respect for law and order are part of all Christian education, but games and sports contribute to their development through direct and dramatic means.[143]

AN IDEALISTIC ADMINISTRATIVE PATTERN. Before concluding this section on teaching methodology, some brief consideration should be given to the matter of whether there is such a thing as an idealistic pattern of administrative control that might follow logically and consistently from the idealist's approach to working with people. There are many who would say immediately that to venture any opinions on this question would be skating on very thin ice indeed. Of course, the anticipation of such criticism does not remove any blame from the writer's shoulders if he does make some remarks about this subject. Although you may not agree, it does seem that an idealist serving as an administrator should be guided by his basic beliefs. As we have indicated several times before, philosophy has a choice of either getting on the battlefield or retreating from it forever and leaving its work to newer disciplines. To press this analogy perhaps a bit too far, the idea of staying on the field as a litter bearer for language analysis seems to be far too ignominious a task for such a noble warrior of the past.

At any rate we might say that the idealistic educator finds himself faced with a predicament that he will have to resolve himself when it comes to working out a logical and consistent pattern of administrative control. On the one hand, idealism has been considered as part of what might be called *essentialistic* philosophy of education. Brubacher has stated that it is, however, "on the border line" in relationship to the other essentialistic positions. Brameld, also, has seen them as belonging to a united front. Because of the moral law or natural law in the universe, and because education's aim is to help the child adjust to these essential realities that the history of the race has disclosed, idealists feel it is necessary to preserve and transmit the established values of the past. On the other hand, idealistic philosophy of education places great emphasis on the freedom, growth, and development of the personality. Despite his "will to perfection," the idealist is increasingly concerned with social responsiveness and responsibility and those skills and techniques necessary for effective action. If we hope to develop the correct attitudes in children, then they must come indirectly by example, inspira-

---

[143] Barney Steen, "Physical Education at Calvin College," *The Banner*, XCVI, No. 35 (September 1, 1961), 11.

tion, and contagion. This leads us to the view that the personality of the teacher is tremendously important." The ideal teacher has great respect for the student's personality and intelligence; he does not super-impose his will on others. The teacher does not demand respect; he earns it by his manner and bearing. The teacher is a friend, a good friend to the pupils in his classes. He has a keen desire to show students what fine democratic living is like, because he realizes that they in turn will develop attitudes that will help to democratize other people in other groups with whom they will some day come in contact. Is it too much, therefore, to suggest that there are many implications here for the idealistic administrator—to hope that true democracy in educational administration will some day become a reality despite the line-staff pattern of control which appears to be a hallmark of essentialistic educational philosophy?

Summary

AIMS AND OBJECTIVES. The idealist in physical, health, and recreation education believes in education of the physical, and yet he believes in education through the physical as well. Physical education is important, but it does "occupy a lower rung on the educational ladder." The idealist believes that a reasonable man would use physical-education activities to assist him in the development of a good life.

The idealist is, of course, extremely interested in individual personality development and self-realization. He believes that man should develop all of his "natures" nearest to their utmost possibility of development. For him, physical education means more than merely a sound mind in a sound body; the ideal is more subtle and graceful, suggesting "a keener intellect combined with a poised power capable of acting quickly with the dignity of ease and beauty." Desirable objectives for physical education would include the development of responsible citizenship and group participation. In competitive sport, the idealist believes that the transfer of training theory is in operation with the development of desirable personality traits. Sports participation, however, should always be a means, not an end.

For the idealist, health is a basic value of human living, and the truly educated individual should be physically fit with a body that is the ready servant of his will. But even though health is a basic value for all the others, it must be placed at the bottom of the hierarchy of educational values. Worship must be placed at the top, because through it man is brought "into conscious relation to the infinite spirit of the universe." Thus, physical education and health education would not be included in a listing of the essential studies of the curriculum except where health would be included incidentally under biology.

Despite some of the above statements, the idealist does stress the necessity for "building wholeness of mind and body, . . . the development of strong, healthy bodies, . . . good habits of mental and physical health, . . . and the right start in the teaching of health, safety, and physical education to children." There is no question in his mind but that educators should work for a larger measure of integration in the individual by promoting "more intensive study of the body, leading to scientific knowledge: anatomy, body chemistry, hygiene, physiology, etc.; and attention to sex characteristics and habits, leading to a greater understanding of the place of sex in human life, with implications for hygiene." But such knowledge is made available to boys and girls, and young men and women, as a "service" program in the schools—a service is provided to man, and through this contribution to his health he is enabled to pursue higher educational goals.

The idealist believes that the role of play and recreation in the development of personality and the "perfectly integrated individual" is looming larger with each passing year and that it has not been fully understood or appreciated in the past. For this reason it seems quite logical to many idealists that education should reassess the contributions that recreation and play do make in the education of man. That there is a need for educational research along these lines is self-evident. Some idealists believe further that we should examine very closely any theories of play and recreation which grant educational possibilities to these activities of man. The self-expression theory of play suggests that man's chief need in life is to achieve the satisfaction and accomplishment of self-expression of one's own personality. Here is an explanation that seems to consider quite fully the conception of man as an organic unity—a total organism. The idealist believes that man is a purposive being who is striving to achieve those values which are embedded in reality itself. To the extent that he can realize the eternal values through the choice of the right kinds of play and recreation without flouting the moral order in the world, he should be progressive enough to disregard a dualistic theory of work and play. Recreation has developed to the point where it is now clearly one of the major social institutions in America. All mankind today is actually faced with a "recreational imperative." Idealism appears to be swinging to the position that recreation can make a contribution to the development of an "integrated individual in an integrated society growing in the image of the integrated universe."

METHODOLOGY. The idealistic teacher would probably not wish to be known as the devotee of some particular teaching method. Plato himself felt that the teacher should not be concerned necessarily with outlining the various aspects of the curriculum in great detail, nor should he be especially conscious of using one teaching technique over another. It can be said that the teacher should use his reason and should base his selection of a particular activity or teaching technique on the basis of sound scientific investigation which has demonstrated validity and, of course, proper psychological methodology. An idealistic teacher, therefore, would like to feel that he is the creator and determiner of his own method. But he would be quick to point out that method, as "the tool used to carve out the good life," should be "subordinate to the objectives" of idealistic philosophy.

Initially, in physical education, the idealistic teacher realizes that the "development of the body is limited to developing and strengthening what is given the individual by birth. Education cannot add to the nerve cells of the brain, but it can fully develop capacities for which potentiality is given in the individual."

Students, under careful guidance, should be most actively involved in the educational process and should "choose objectives, activities, textbooks, topics for reports, and the like." The instructor cannot forget, however, the time-proven proverb that "the hard is the good," and should curb the highly desirable play attitude when suitable progress toward educational goals is not resulting.

The teacher should gather as much data as possible about the students and should use it for group planning as well as individual guidance. It is important for the idealistic teacher to make "the right start in the teaching of health, safety, and physical education to children"; the pupils should become skillful, have a reasonable amount of success, and derive a lot of fun through physical activity.

The idealistic teacher through his personality should exert a highly beneficial influence on his students. He can use "the lives and works of great leaders to enrich the lives and works of a younger generation." Children are great imitators, and idealistic educators can make full use of this teaching aid to encourage youngsters to strive for high attainment. In the classroom an "informal dialectic" should be carried on a good share of the time. The teacher should not imply that there is only one way of thinking about some problem or, for that matter, of performing some skill in the gymnasium. There is a place for lecturing and experimenting as well as the use of discussion. Good idealistic teaching method would "create a slight feeling of suspense for the student—suspense to be resolved only by his own decision or active effort."

Interest is most important, but the idealist has discovered that it alone will not suffice to accomplish all the educational objectives necessary. When discipline is invoked to cause the student to respond with effort, he may well discover in a short while that his interest has been aroused.

The rigidly formal physical-education class, the stereotyped, dull team practice, or the gymnasium activity which is merely poorly organized informal recreation would not be the type of teaching method that the truly idealistic teacher would employ.

The idealistic coach will point out to aspiring young athletes that they will have to make certain sacrifices if they hope to be worthy and successful team members. The teacher-coach should eventually step into the background as his boys achieve maturity. The glory of the coach is definitely secondary; the goal is to help the participants to achieve their inherent selfhood. The coach with a truly idealistic philosophy will do all in his power to keep from succumbing to the materialistic demands of the public—a most difficult ideal to achieve. The coach is above all an educator who does more than impart technical knowledge; he should serve human needs and lead young men and women into deeper understandings involving the breadth of human experience. As Steinhaus has said, ". . . every impact of man on man or of programme on man invariably does influence in some way man's body, man's mind, man's spirit." It is the duty of the idealistic teacher to live according to his highest ideals and to help others realize the good life for themselves as they strive for total personality development and excellence within a many-sided nature.

Strengths and Weaknesses

As indicated at the end of similar earlier chapters, it is a most difficult task to enumerate, as well as to evaluate, the strengths and weaknesses of a particular philosophical position. If an author wishes to remain impartial, such an evaluation is doubly difficult. Despite these problems, however, an attempt will be made to discuss a few of the apparent strengths and weaknesses of the idealistic position briefly.

Generally speaking, idealism is strong because it is a complete all-inclusive philosophy embodying a theory of reality, a theory of knowledge acquisition, a system of relating ideas, and a system of values. The idealist sees ultimate meaning existing in a unified universe. Furthermore, idealism envisions a very important place for man in the scheme of things. The central point of this philosophical position is man who believes (whose intuition tells him) that he is a real being. In addition, it gives man a feeling of importance, because he is pictured as being unique—something higher than all other creatures on earth. This can be classified as a strength, since it is most comforting to man to know, because of the character of knowledge which actually reveals something to him about the nature of reality, that he has a place in God's Kingdom —a cosmos that is actually God thinking.

From an educational standpoint, idealism is strong because it gives us a single conception of the pupil—a unified, developing organism that has the potentiality to "become what it latently is." If it is, as Plato said, a "world of eternal unchanging ideas" which are the fabric of ultimate reality, such ideas become absolutely essential to the educational process. Here is the security of a set of educational values which must be realized in the life of the individual to the best of his ability. Continuing education in life is squarely up to the person involved; he is part of an educational system in which his personality and selfhood are fully recognized. Furthermore, he has the potential to work for the continuance of society, as well as his own personal development, through the use of his own reason. He has the security of knowing that all education of the right type has the approval of his church. In fact, there is a "moral imperative" on education to encourage man to strive for knowledge of truth and goodness, although the infinite, Absolute idea will never be fully realized on this earth. There is the strong hope, however, that individual man's spirit will be immortalized by ultimately becoming part of God's spirit.

In the area of physical, health, and recreation education, the idealistic philosophy of education has significant strength as well, although it appears quite obvious that its potential has never been fully realized. Because of the concept of the unity of the organism, it is quite apparent to us from the scientific advances made by the field of psychology that physical, health, and recreation education offers many opportunities for the development of man's physical and social aspects, not to mention his spiritual nature. *There is, of course, an educational hierarchy which necessarily places physical and health education on a lower level, albeit an indispensable rung of the ladder.* Yet we can take comfort from the position of the idealist which seems to allow room for both education *of* the physical as well as education *through* the physical.

The athletic coach can gather some strength from idealism because of the transfer of training theory which implies that attitudes of sportsmanship and fair play learned through the right kind of competition in sport can and do transfer to other more important life situations. Man is encouraged to develop all sides of his nature and to strive for perfection insofar as this is ever possible. The coach, of course, must always be an educator first and keep the welfare of his team members paramount. Furthermore, if they are to develop their true individuality, the coach as a teacher must be willing to step into the background. Thus, a high standard is set for both athlete and coach; they must be willing to sacrifice for the attainment of sport's highest goals. When Christian idealism is added to this concept, the paramount goal becomes "equipment for service" both to God and man. If teachers of sports are able to live up to these ideals, they can make a significant contribution to the basic moral and spiritual value structure of American life.

The importance of recreation and play to idealistic philosophy of education has not been fully appreciated in the past either. To the extent that the idealist can realize the eternal values through the choice of the right kinds of play and recreation without flouting the moral order in the world, he will use this source as a powerful, positive force to deepen his fellowship with God and will extend himself and God's Kingdom through service to his fellow man. Creative recreation can assume a "spiritual significance" in holding back the world's materialistic forces.

Looking at idealism negatively, however, it must be confessed that there are a number of *weaknesses.* In the first place, the idea of a soul—a spiritual entity quite different from material body—is quite romantic and difficult to comprehend. Because idealism is a most complex approach, there is a great and ever-present danger of many misconceptions. Opponents would ask how mere man can be capable of actually interpreting reality. How can he know that values are embedded throughout the universe? It does appear that it would be easy for fallible man to insulate himself from reality by faith—a faith that could well be a snare and a delusion!

In the educational realm, it is quite difficult to accept the argument that an individual must be guided by values based on the authority of past experience—an experience which often appears to be hopelessly outdated in a changing environment. How, for example, can we justify telling the student that he must persevere even though his interest has waned—or, for that matter, was never stimulated initially? The transfer of training theory often leaves much to be desired as well. Furthermore, to many it is a deadening experience to be told that the "developing organism becomes what it latently is." What challenge is there for man to accept the position that only God knows what truth and goodness really is? It is man's lot to strive for a perfection that is never attainable. If his ideas in life and in education work well, then he will know that they are true because God made the world that way. This means that there is room for freedom of will, but the choice has really been spelled out in advance and in great detail.

Although idealism offers much hope to the teacher of physical, health, and recreation education, especially if he works for the realization of the Greek ideal, he finds only lip service given to the concept of the unity of body and mind in today's schools. The current stress on physical fitness does appear to be largely materialistic and pragmatic. In addition, it is very disconcerting to a dedicated professional to be told that he "belongs on a low rung of the educational ladder" by the very nature of things.

Idealism does appear to be slipping in a coldly materialistic world. The very nature of most people seems to make the idea of sacrifice and dedication to a priori, antecedent ideals most difficult to achieve. All around us we find coaches under pressures to win at almost any cost, and when it is suggested that their primary function is to build character, they are quick to respond, and quite correctly, that they may lose their jobs and future chances for advancement if they don't win a good share of the time. And quite often it is these very coaches, who may have put their ideals aside, who end up as directors of the entire programs of physical, health, and recreation education in schools and colleges. Why does this happen? Quite possibly because they are the people who can bring to fulfillment the unspoken materialistic goals of the alumni and the public, and perhaps the educational administrators. The cynic would say that idealism appears very weak in the face of such a materialistic outlook which uses the medium of physical, health, and recreation education to such a questionable end.

And what happens to the development of desirable personality traits and the development of a philosophy of life based on Christian ideals through sports participation? Can it be proved that there is transfer of training from the game situation to a life situation? Even if it were true, what kind of example do we see being set even by some who have professed that their lives are motivated by Christian idealism? When a college football coach breaks a contract to take another post that may seem more desirable, the offended university officials are quite upset, although they rarely test the legality of the contract. But what about moral obligations of this professed Christian idealist? They are usually cast aside, and rationalization is used as a device to justify the move. The squad members, many of whom are probably prospective coaches themselves, learn by example in such situations—the wrong example!

In the area of play and recreation, idealism is plagued further by persistent retention of a dualistic theory of work and play. If there are educational opportunities available through the medium of recreation, why do Christian idealists especially, as well as many from the Jewish faith, continue to deny such possibilities? The challenge of active and creative recreation may well be the salvation of an American economy and way of life facing the pressing problem of automation. What *will* many people do if the time ever comes when they are paid *not* to work?

There is no doubt but that idealism has much to offer, but this is only true if the individual can accept the initial premises on faith. This is most difficult for many in the twentieth century marred by monstrous examples of man's inhumanity to man and with no scientific, factual evidence of God's concern for man. Faced with such a situation, man has in many instances turned to naturalistic humanism, existentialism, atheism, agnosticism, or seemingly just plain indifference.

Systematic Philosophies and Some Persistent Problems of Physical, Health, and Recreation Education

Systematic Philosophies
and Some Persistent Problems
of Physical, Health,
and Recreation Education

Introduction

Up to this point we have laid the groundwork for the physical, health, and recreation educator's search for a consistent and logical philosophy. We have discussed very briefly philosophy of history as a possibility; orientation to philosophy as a discipline; and a brief history of the ideas and problems of philosophy as some necessary prerequisites prior to a consideration of philosophy of education. Then we considered specifically naïve naturalism and the three great philosophical positions in the Western world. These were experimentalism, realism, and idealism, although this was not necessarily their order of historical development. Naturalism was considered more as a pervasive influence underlying modern naturalistic realism or pragmatic naturalism (called *experimentalism*). The metaphysics, epistemology, logic, and axiology of each of these philosophical tendencies was explained concisely prior to a consideration of their influence on philosophy of education. The educational philosophy of each was subdivided into the following topics: (1) society, school, and the individual; (2) educational aims and objectives; and (3) the process of education. Finally the implications of these educational philosophies for physical, health, and recreation education was discussed in considerable detail.

CONSTRUCT ONE'S OWN PERSONAL PHILOSOPHY. The main thesis of this text is that each physical, health, and recreation educator has a responsibility to examine himself and to construct his own personal philosophy, so that he may be an effective professional person. At first glance the average person may not see the need for such a disciplined approach.

He may well argue that he hasn't the time to be bothered with any sort of a detailed analysis and that he is already practicing his profession quite effectively. His argument quite often is that he possesses a certain amount of common sense and that this has proven quite effective. This is a fairly difficult argument to overcome, especially if the individual has achieved a certain amount of success through his efforts. The method is quite sound, because problems of an everyday nature can be met by using this common sense. He is operating on the basis of certain underlying opinion—a theoretical group bias. To this extent, therefore, it may be said that all practitioners do have a philosophy of education.

ACHIEVEMENT OF UNIFIED PHILOSOPHY. The premise here, of course, is that any such person may increase his influence and effectiveness by the achievement of a unified philosophy—one that is as consistent and logical as possible in reference to the individual's background and experience. The contention is that the common-sense system of deciding problems breaks down when extended planning is necessary, and certainly some extended planning appears to be vital as we face the many persistent and recurring problems of the second half of the twentieth century. We might through analogy liken the individual using the common-sense approach to an automobile moving along in second gear with the attendant stresses caused by continual progress in such a manner. In fact, a careful analysis of such "progress" might even indicate that the car is swaying from side to side all over the road. The question is how can we get the car to shift into high gear or possibly even overdrive and follow a straight course. This appears to be the case with the individual as well. We contend that the field of physical, health, and recreation education needs a great many more people who are truly operating in high gear rather than in second or even, as often appears to be the case, in low.

HOW CAN WE IMPROVE ON COMMON SENSE? Thus the difference between a philosophical approach as compared to a common-sense approach is one of degree. If we were to consider the question as to whether our field has made progress in the past 100 years, it is quite possible that a strong case could be assembled for the negative position. This is not to say that a strong case could not be made for the affirmative position as well. If this assumption is true, the question then is how can we improve on common sense.

PHILOSOPHICAL SYNTHESIS. The scientist improves on common sense by all kinds of experimentation. His task is to select a particular problem which can be defined narrowly and precisely. After a precise problem definition has been accomplished, he begins his experimentation, striving for as much reliability and objectivity as is possible under the circumstances. Conversely, the philosophic method of improving on common sense moves in a quite different direction. Instead of refining and delimiting, he becomes all inclusive by drawing from a wide variety of sources available in order to effect the best possible philosophical synthesis. In such a situation the professional is endeavoring to bring common sense and tradition into alignment with the results of available scientific experimentation, so that the philosophic process may be furthered as best possible.

THE REASON FOR PHILOSOPHY OF EDUCATION.   No matter where you may travel on the North American continent, teachers and parents alike seem to be sharply divided as to what should be included in the school curriculum. With the advent of the "cold war" and the so-called space age, the question as to how our children should be educated for these social conditions is asked almost daily. Shall education be "progressive," "somewhat progressive," or should it deal exclusively with the "essential studies" that are time-proven? Health, physical education, and recreation (including interscholastic athletics) are right in the middle of this controversy. If we teach more mathematics, science, and foreign languages, then something may get crowded right out of the curriculum. Some are anxious to include subjects which have lasting value and give the child mental discipline, while others seem to hold values more tentatively and want to offer a curriculum that is based to a considerable extent on the interests as well as on the needs of the child. If we end up by seeking a common denominator, those with a more authoritative approach to education are certain that youth will not be adequately equipped to meet the demands of the future.

TWO MAJOR METAPHYSICAL POSITIONS.   When we consider the nature of existence from a metaphysical standpoint, there appears to be two major positions. Either we are confronted by a dynamic, changing world with evolving goals not yet fully realized, or we are part of a universe in which there are certain basic unchangeable aspects of reality which have emanated from a supernatural source or are simply present in the universe because of the nature of things—in the latter case, it is a question of moral or natural law and order.

TWO VIEWS OF MAN.   Looking at man himself, we again find two opposing positions. According to one viewpoint, man is regarded as an evolving organism in a changing world; any constancy that seems apparent in human nature is only relative. The other belief involves man as the possessor of a spiritual entity that somehow has a definite relationship to the Great Spirit or God. Human nature itself is unchanging, and man has freedom to choose between good and evil as he traverses this mortal sphere en route to possible immortality.

THREE MAJOR THEORIES OF KNOWLEDGE ACQUISITION.   When it comes to the question of epistemology, or theory of knowledge acquisition, there appears to be three major theories however. They all revolve about whether man can truly know reality or whether such knowledge makes any practical difference. One theory is that man can know reality through his intelligence. When we acquire knowledge through this means and find that it corresponds with actual reality, we have discovered truth and can then transmit knowledge through a prescribed curriculum. A second belief that came later is that there are "two worlds," so to speak. There is a world that can be known by man through his senses and another world, the knowledge of which is forever impossible to man. A third view has gradually emerged which disregards the approach of the other two to the problem of knowledge acquisition. This position involves the matter of environmental adaptation; if something works, then it is true and knowledge results.

ONE OR MANY PHILOSOPHIES OF EDUCATION. The whole question seems to resolve itself into whether there *is* one philosophy of education or whether *many* philosophies of education are possible. However you may view what often appears to be a hopeless impasse, because the democratic setting of life on this continent allows the promulgation of many different philosophies of education. Facing such a situation, the educational philosopher's task becomes actually quite complex. He can analyze and delineate the various positions to the best of his ability. Where possible, he may attempt a synthesis and try to resolve or at least to reduce the many philosophical discussions and arguments which are everywhere evident. Quite often his task seems to be almost hopeless, because he can't even get opposing factions to agree on a set of ground rules by which the game may be played.

THE ROLES OF SCIENCE AND OF PHILOSOPHY. Quite often we hear it said that science has the task of determining the facts in any given educational situation. Because of this ability, educational science can tell us what the aims of education are at a given time in a particular school system. But it remains for the educational philosopher to assess these findings and to tell us whether these aims are good ones or the best ones. Unfortunately, or perhaps fortunately, it is not possible for the educational philosopher to separate himself completely from the educational process he is attempting to evaluate. This is a bias, of course, that the educational scientist must try to avoid assiduously. Educational research may assess historical development, it may describe the present status or norm, and it may devise experimental projects to give us particular answers to certain problems. The educational philosopher has the task of analyzing and synthesizing these findings and then speculating about those values which education ought to pursue (in the light of his own bias!). Even though his conclusions may appear to be quite theoretical, it is possible that he may be able to clarify educational thought so that ineffectual practice may be eliminated.

A DIVISION OF LABOR. And so today we find educational philosophy playing a more limited role than its progenitor which was the queen of sciences. Instead of educational philosophy discovering all the facts, it now treats the assumptions underlying these facts and assesses the educational values which appear to be related to these facts. The relationship of the broader field of philosophy to the specific field of educational philosophy becomes immediately apparent; the former looks at all of life, and the latter carries out any implications from the principles or generalizations which may be established in the special field of education. The philosopher in physical, health, and recreation education refines this process still further by applying his reasoning power to this specialized area of the educational system. Some would disagree with this division of labor, and indeed even with the premise that there is such a thing as educational philosophy, but it is our contention that such philosophizing is necessary as the complexity of relationships in the world continues to multiply.

THE POSSIBILITY OF AN EDUCATIONAL SPECTRUM OR CONTINUUM. If philosophy of physical, health, and recreation education is going to take its place on the battlefield of ideas in the educational sphere in the latter half of the twentieth century, it is going to have to put on its armor, pick up its weapons, and come out swinging! For too long our field has been buffeted about by the public and our educational confreres because, very frankly, we haven't known what we were talking about—or at least we haven't truly understood our philosophical foundations. We are not suggesting that this approach is going to be a panacea for all our ills, and that our problems are going to cease when individuals consider their own philosophical positions more carefully and seriously. But, the main thesis of this book is that we will be in a much better position to meet our persistent, recurring problems intelligently when we know where we stand, and we can discuss conflicting philosophies more logically and consistently than we have been able to do up to this time. To accomplish this goal we recommend that each individual professional who is concerned examine himself to the best of his ability and find his place on a somewhat loosely knit educational-philosophy spectrum in accordance with some of the ideas expressed previously under the leading philosophical tendencies. The following spectrum chart should help to give some orientation in this direction. In attempting to do this, keep in mind that *progressivism* is greatly concerned about such things as pupil freedom, individual differences, pupil interest, pupil growth, no fixed values, and that education is life now. The essentialist believes that there are certain educational values by which the individual

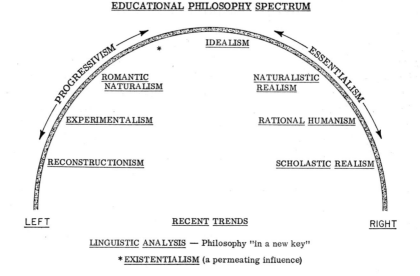

EDUCATIONAL PHILOSOPHY SPECTRUM

PROGRESSIVISM

IDEALISM

*

ROMANTIC
NATURALISM

ESSENTIALISM

NATURALISTIC
REALISM

EXPERIMENTALISM

RATIONAL HUMANISM

RECONSTRUCTIONISM

SCHOLASTIC REALISM

LEFT   RECENT TRENDS   RIGHT

LINGUISTIC ANALYSIS — Philosophy "in a new key"

*EXISTENTIALISM (a permeating influence)

must be guided, that effort takes precedence over interest and that this girds moral stamina, that the experience of the past has powerful jurisdiction over the present, and that the cultivation of the intellect is most important in education. These beliefs attributed to each broad position are, of course, only representative and not inclusive. There is reason to believe, however, that a person should be able to delineate his own position generally under one broad category or the other. The remainder of this chapter will now be devoted to an examination of some of the persistent problems facing our field. This will be carried out within the framework of a philosophical context, and every effort will be made to delineate at least how the progressive educator and the essentialistic educator view these recurring problems which are plaguing us at the present and will probably continue to cause us greater or lesser concern in the years that lie ahead. We should keep in mind that there is every likelihood that there are not two best answers to these problems. Because of this, we should continue to work for consensus as experimental evidence and experience indicate that any such consensus is possible. In the next chapter we shall consider the matter of possible consensus at some length.

Wherever possible an effort will be made to explain how the varying, more refined educational positions listed in the educational-philosophy spectrum chart (and explained at some length in the preceding chapters) view these broad problems in the light of the specific philosophical foundations. Readers will understand that many of these judgments are subjective and are made in the hope that the author's powers of perception are quite sound, *and* that it is possible for him to be relatively unbiased. The reader will, of course, have to use his own judgment to decide if the author's assumptions are valid. We can only say that every effort has been made to be fair and impartial.

Progress in Physical, Health, and Recreation Education through the School

The question often arises whether progress has been made in physical, health, and recreation education through the agency of the school or through some other agency concerned with organized instruction. Obviously, any judgment made will be to a large degree subjective, even though the author has high intentions for his philosophical analysis and has made every effort to be as scientific as possible. Any analysis and fusion of the past and the present, which this effort undoubtedly is, cannot escape controversy and struggle. The author recognizes that it is literally impossible for him to raise himself above the conflict, because he is actually in the middle of the battlefield.

Furthermore, it is a judgment that you may have already made for yourself, or that you are in the process of making, or that you will eventually make for yourself to the best of your ability. Your judgment could well be determined by the mood you are in because of your personal situation or by the prevailing mood of the times. The man or woman who thinks profoundly in the light of the occurrences of the twentieth century cannot be blamed for being pessimistic or skeptical at best. Some people are typically more optimistic than others, and the future may look considerably brighter to them. Your considered philosophy will have a great deal to do with the type of progress you may look for in the future. One thought does seem appropos: we wouldn't even be pondering about our future if the 102 Separatists, known as the *Pilgrim Fathers,* had been so pessimistic in the early seventeenth century that they had decided that the Mayflower had no chance of making the trip across the Atlantic to these shores. So avail yourself of that phenomenon known as *second wind,* and let's continue this quest a little further.

Values in Physical, Health, and Recreation Education

ARE VALUES OBJECTIVE OR SUBJECTIVE? First, we must decide for ourselves whether values are objective or subjective. In other words, do values exist in the world whether man happens to be present to realize them or not? Or is it man who ascribes value to his various relationships with other people and with his physical environment? If physical, health, and recreation education is inherently valuable to youth, it should be included in the curriculum whether students or parents recognize this value or not. If, on the other hand, it should somehow be proved that physical education has no instrumental value, and that children don't want it and parents see no need for it, then it should be eliminated according to the subjective theory of value.

Another aspect of the question of values relates to their qualitative aspects. We might say that some things are desired by the individual, but other expressions of want may be desirable also because society has indicated its approval. It is undoubtedly true that a continuous appraisal of values goes on. If a value in physical education is considered good in and of itself, such a value has intrinsic worth. A value that serves as a means to an end has become known as an instrumental value. Aesthetic value constitutes another gradation of value in which intense emotion and appreciation are involved. Our specialized area of education seems to offer many opportunities for the realization of aesthetic values unless too narrow an interpretation is made and such values are limited only to the fine arts and literature.

A HIERARCHY OF EDUCATIONAL VALUES.   The question of a hierarchy of educational values is ever present in our society. We have seen in previous chapters how certain essentialistic philosophies of education holding to a more objective theory of educational value tend to allow the construction of a gradation of various values. Premeditated values rank higher on the scale. If such values seem to coincide with eternal values inherent in the universe, they are considered still more valuable and are rated even more highly. So-called instrumental values may also be ranked according to their usefulness to man in his living pattern. Physical education might be considered important by the idealist, but it would not take precedence over an aspect of the curriculum which invokes man's rational powers to help him to achieve still higher goals. To the experimentalist, on the other hand, competency in self-defense or swimming might on a given occasion rate at the very top of the educational hierarchy if such competency were necessary to save a life. There appears to be no question that the role of physical, health, and recreation education in the educational pattern will vary depending on the final or ultimate aims of education to which the individual subscribes. Specific educational objectives must be chosen in the light of these ultimate goals.

THE THREE MAJOR POSITIONS.   Specifically, there appear to be three major philosophies of physical, health, and recreation education in regard to educational values. They are experimentalism, or perhaps pragmatic naturalism, which emphasizes the concept of total fitness rather than physical fitness alone; realism, which typically accepts education *of* the physical as the primary emphasis in the field; and idealism, which is basically an essentialistic position that stresses education of the physical and yet believes in education through the physical as well. The delineation of these three positions does represent progress, but it doesn't tell us anything about the possibility of consensus and where we go from here.

Politics and Nationalism

A second persistent problem that the teacher of physical, health, and recreation education faces in the building of his own personal philosophy is that of the influence of politics and nationalism on his field.

THREE TYPES OF POLITICAL STATE.   Students with a fundamental grasp of the history of education know that the kind and amount of education has varied throughout history depending on whether a particular country was a monarchy, an aristocratic oligarchy, or a type of democracy. Some democratic societies have made significant efforts to allow individual development through the medium of education, whereas other totalitarian states have suppressed the needs and desires of individuals and made them conform to a rigid educational pattern.

SEPARATION OF CHURCH AND STATE.   Whereas in a totalitarian state there is but one philosophy of education permitted, certain other types of government allow pluralistic philosophies of education to flourish. Under the latter type of arrangement the state could conceivably exercise no control of education whatsoever, or it could take a greater or lesser interest in the education of its citizens. When the state does take an interest, the question arises as to whether the state, through its agency the school, the family, or the church, shall exert the greatest amount of influence on the child. When the church feels very strongly that the central purpose of education is religious, it may decide to educate the child itself in its own way. In a society where there are many different religious affiliations, it is quite possible that the best arrangement is for the church and state to remain separate.

THE PHENOMENON OF NATIONALISM.   The phenomenon of nationalism merits consideration. It has been defined as a fusion of patriotism with a consciousness of nationality. Obviously, it is a relatively simple matter to promote nationalism the more totalitarian a state is, and, conversely, it is quite difficult for strong nationalism to develop in a somewhat pluralistic state. People living in a democratic society could not be satisfied with nationalism in education that was dictated by a minority. But if it is possible for nationalism in education to emanate from the goals of a free people, this would then be quite satisfactory. In this way the citizens of a democracy believe that such an influence might work for the common good. Democratic educational objectives always protect the rights of the individual, and when such interests are occasionally submerged in the interests of nationalism, the very structure of democratic life is endangered. A democracy which is far enough advanced to consider sharing its culture with other groups is well on the way to a concept of internationalism which may well lead to the idea of "one world" that some believe is the only method of insuring world peace.

IMPLICATIONS FOR PHYSICAL EDUCATION. Experimentalism in education, and specifically in our area, can flourish only in a type of democratic society, whereas essentialism may be promoted in all three types of society. The realist can and does function under various philosophies of state, but the idealist may run into difficulty in a political system where the individual and his needs and desires rank high. Thus, in a progressive system the state will tend to be more positive in its attitude toward the education of the individual toward more socialistic goals. The more totalitarian a state becomes, however, the more control it takes over the educational system and the end results it desires for each child. Obviously, it is extremely difficult to promote nationalism in health and physical education when it must emanate from the goals of a free people.

Economics

Professionals in physical, health, and recreation education rarely give much consideration to the influence of economics until they begin to feel the "pinch of economy moves" and find that some segments of the society consider their subject-matter area to be less important than others and decide that it should be eliminated, or at least sharply curtailed. Such a move often comes as a shock, and it is frequently rationalized by our claim that we are being used as a lever to pry more funds from a recalcitrant and pleasure-seeking public that would not wish to see its spectacles discontinued.

HISTORICAL BACKGROUND. But there is much more to the question of the influence of the economic order on the educational system. This problem has been with man from the time of primitive societies. The Greeks developed a surplus economy of a type, and it was during this time that great educational advances were recorded for the freemen who made up approximately one-quarter of the population. Down through the centuries in certain sections of the world there have gradually emerged types of economies vastly different from earlier agrarian societies. Education has prospered when there was a surplus economy and declined when the economic structure weakened. Thus, it may be said that educational cycles of rise and decline seem to have coincided with economic cycles. Despite these developments, formal education has rarely if ever given the study of economics an important place in the general education curriculum throughout history. Similarly, it has been traditional to regard vocational areas of study with less esteem than the liberal art or humanities.

AIMS VARY ACCORDING TO ECONOMY. Educational aims will tend to vary depending on how people make their money and create surplus economies. There is not much time for schooling in the typical agrarian society, because people have to work long and hard. If commerce is added to the agrarian base in a country, education will advance considerably as people will ask more from it to meet the needs of the various classes. Modern industrial economy has made still further demands on education and has produced the necessary monies whereby it might be obtained.

INDUSTRIAL CIVILIZATION AND WEALTH DISTRIBUTION. Advancing industrial civilization has brought many advantages to man, but it has created many problems as well. One of these has to do with specialization in function—some people manage and other people labor, and this results in an uneven distribution of wealth. Of course, there has always been specialization of function of one sort or another in societies, and the leaders have invariably seemed to end up with the lion's share of the good things of life. The labor movement is striving mightily to reverse this trend to a degree, and this has had a definite effect on the educational structure of the society involved. The people with more money have been able to afford longer periods and different types of education for their children. It is not difficult to understand why the social-welfare-state concept has been popular with the middle and lower economic classes, and, incidentally, why the Democratic party, traditionally the party of the people, has more registered voters in the United States than its rival. This discussion has, of course, oversimplified the problem, but the trend of development is there.

THE CLASSLESS SOCIETY. It is true further that essentialistic education has tended to preserve the culture of the past and would not strive for the same sort of change—certainly not at the same rate—that progressivistic education would tend to do. If it is inevitable that there will always be classes of society sharply divided, and that those who work with their hands will be considered inferior, the only hope for the masses is probably in increased educational advantages made possible through continued technological advancement and automation. Much has been written in the United States about the possibility of a classless society, and certainly many of the advantages of the good life are increasingly being made available to all. Some educational philosophers predict the day when all people will profit from a general education and thereby have the opportunity to understand more than ever before what is happening in the world and what role as individuals they can hope to play. One of our goals in the United States has been to recognize talent in any person no matter what his economic status may be and then to give him an opportunity to realize his potential. One of the unfortunate outcomes of this trend has been that the cream has been skimmed off many of our less fortunate communities, and we have developed no means to put it back again.

IMPLICATIONS AND INTERRELATIONSHIPS.   Education of the physical has a good chance for improvement under either trend of economic development—even or uneven distribution of wealth. In largely agrarian societies, much physical fitness would be gained through hard work, whereas in industrial societies some means would have to be developed whereby all would maintain a minimum level of physical fitness. In the social-welfare state, where a person would enjoy a relatively longer period of educational opportunity, society would have to decide to what extent it can or should demand physical fitness of all its citizens. This type of state would be more concerned about meeting the health needs of people through democratically approved taxation to governmental agencies and to schools and through donations of interested individuals and groups to private agencies dedicated to the improvement of national health. Both nationalism and internationalism are exercising a good influence on health standards as well.

Recreation education for school-age youth, and for other age groups as well, depends a great deal on the educational philosophy prevailing as to how much support will be provided for these activities in the educational system. There is not much use of education for leisure unless a surplus economy exists. In the United States, it seems evident that automation will force our society to prepare people for improved use of leisure. If uneven distribution of wealth exists, the wealthy will have the most expensive recreational pursuits, and the rest of the people will have less time to spend on play and recreation.

Methods of Instruction

As we have seen in our previous discussion, the educational curriculum has been influenced by a variety of political, economic, philosophical, and scientific factors. In curriculum construction, therefore, a primary task is to determine which subjects should be included because of the recurring interest that has been shown among educators for their inclusion at some level of the educational system. Shall curriculum construction be based on the philosophy of state and its function, on the demands of nationalism, on whether it will help man to make a better living, on the need for reduction of tension in a troubled world, on the nature of man, or according to the way he learns best? Or is there perhaps a predetermined set of values in the world which in a sense dictates what educational aims should be? We must ask ourselves further whether the educator's task is to transmit the cultural heritage, to help youth develop skills for problem-solving, or to provide a miniature society in which students may enjoy living at its best, so that they will have an example to put into practice in their after-school days. If we view the curriculum as a means of discipling the mind, we will tend to stress certain time-proven subjects. If, on the other hand, we want to help youth develop a number of habit patterns that will be effective in his social environment, certain other subject-matter areas or experiences will be included. The curriculum has developed and expanded at a fantastic rate in the United States, and many people insist that this growth must be halted and, still further, that this trend should be reversed so that the essential subjects can be taught adequately.

This question has a direct bearing on our field of specialization. Is it curricular, extracurricular, or co-curricular? At the risk of oversimplification once again, we will state our belief that your answer to this question may well depend on your position on the educational-philosophy spectrum pictured earlier in this chapter. Thinking about our entire field of physical, health, and recreation education (and this includes safety and driver education, as well as intramural and interscholastic athletics), the experimentalist will see it as *curricular:* the realist will see it as *extracurricular* with the possible exception of a daily physical-training period; and the idealist would be willing to grant the field *co-curricular* status at the present time.

THE INFLUENCE OF CONTENT ON METHOD. Having taken this stand, we must come to a decision about the influence that content has on method. Shall physical, health, and recreation education (or whatever part of it you would include) be taught formally, semiformally, or informally? Our primary concern as teachers is, of course, how we can motivate the student to learn, so that it will occur most easily and will be remembered and/or truly learned. Looking at it another way, we might wonder how the teacher can effectively get the student to perform a physical skill most efficiently in keeping with his potential. Or from still another standpoint, what is the best way for the teacher to arrange the learning situation, so that the student may modify his ways of behaving and truly understand what he is doing? In offering some answers to these questions from the standpoints of progressivism and essentialism, we should keep in mind that teachers generally, no matter what their educational philosophy, have been increasingly sensitive to change in the psychological theory about how learning takes place.

IMPLICATIONS FOR OUR FIELD. Experimentalistic teachers seem to be characterized by a broad social outlook, great consideration for the learner, well prepared teachers, and a minimum of inherited technique as such. By involving the student in purposeful activity just as soon as possible—his basic concern is with aims that emerge out of the educative process—he guides his students in such a way that they will use their reasoning abilities in the realization of the technical, associated, and concomitant learnings available to them as they learn the various skills of physical education and physical recreation. The reader should keep in mind that the position of the utopian reconstructionist in this matter is still further to the left on the educational-philosophy spectrum described earlier than that of the experimentalist.

Idealistic teachers have progressed with their analysis of teaching method to the point where they take their stand near the center and slightly to the right on this spectrum (or continuum, if you prefer it that way). They regard method as definitely subordinate to objectives. An idealist, for example, is apt to state that he follows no one method wholly, but that he determines his own method as he progresses toward the realization of his immediate educational objectives. He believes typically that students, *with careful guidance,* should choose their objectives, activities, topics for reports, and perhaps even their textbooks. Interest is most important, but it alone will not suffice to accomplish all the necessary educational objectives. He wants to help the student develop fully any capacities for which he may have potential. The truly idealistic coach will eventually step into the background, since his goal is not self-glory but to help the participants achieve their inherent selfhood as they gain maturity. Such a teacher is anxious to have his boys learn more than mere physical skills; opportunities for the development of related interests should not be overlooked.

A consideration of the characteristics of a realistic teaching method takes us further to the right on the essentialistic side of the educational-philosophy spectrum. Generally speaking, learning is a process of acquiring objective knowledge by the scientific method, but one essentialist stresses that education is more than a matter of merely acquiring knowledge since it must be used practically for subsequent enjoyment of life. The naturalistic realist practices a problem-solving approach, while, for the rational humanist, the greater the amount of reasoning required to learn a subject, the more important that subject is in the curriculum. Realists support the theory of transfer of training, and they believe that interest is desirable but subordinate to effort; for this reason one finds prizes and awards being used to stimulate students to achieve the greatest amount of excellence in their efforts. They drill students to perfect patterns of habit formation, especially at the lower learning levels, in a curriculum that is logically and sequentially arranged. There is little opportunity for election of activities insofar as the regular program is concerned. As a person of authority, the realistic teacher finds it legitimate to indoctrinate and to use required texts. Quizzes and examinations are needed, and objective grades give students an honest appraisal of their progress and relative position in regard to others. The physical-education period should be organized in such a way as to guarantee muscle development, improvement of circulo-respiratory efficiency, and increased coordination.

The Role of Administration

The American people have always had faith in education as the guardian of a democratic government, as probably the best assurance of a forward-looking society, and as an open door for every person to realize his potential abilities. Education has become a tremendous public business with the typical community using a good share of its property-tax money for the upkeep of schools. Many millions of people have some direct connection with public education, and this number would be increased sharply if private education figures were included. The business of education is still growing. Many opportunities still need to be provided for a large segment of our population to realize the ideals of a democracy. The school has been a truly remarkable social experiment, and it should always keep in line with social needs.

IMPORTANCE OF SOUND ADMINISTRATION. There is a definite need for sound administration conducted in a businesslike manner in such a large organization as the modern school. Many problems present themselves continually to administrators in an unending chain of details. The well-prepared and ethical school administrator is responsible for the efficient performance of this myriad of duties. It is important for him to be ever mindful that his position and its resultant functions exist as means to an end. There is an ever-present need for more and better qualified administrators.

DEFINITION. When the term *administration* is used in the educational field, we associate it with such words as superintendence, direction, management, planning, supervision, organization, regulation, guidance, and control. In common usage we think of it as the process of directing people in an endeavor, and this function is carried out by many people in physical, health, and recreation education as well. The typical approach to administration is to ascertain those principles and operational policies upon which we can base our own theory and practice. Administration, in its simplest form, could probably be likened to a football coach blowing his whistle to call the players together at the beginning of practice. To carry the parallel further, we realize that the coaching of a football team involves different types of activity. The more complex the activity, the more specialization becomes necessary. Thus, the administrator must devote long hours to planning, organization, and coordination, in addition to this function of directing on the basis of the plan thus evolved.

A PHILOSOPHY OF ADMINISTRATION. Traditionally, departments seem to have operated on the basis of a group of often unexpressed major and minor principles. Such principles of physical, health, and recreation education seem necessary to the formulation of operational policies. The department may even function in such a way that a philosophy is clearly evident. Moreover, certain over-all principles of education often exist beneath the specifics of the professional field. Still deeper, a consistent and logical philosophy of life and/or religion should be the foundation upon which at least the administrator or the majority of his department rests. Unfortunately, emergencies and practical considerations, as well as individual personalities and varied administrative patterns, force a department constantly to make exceptions to its prevailing philosophy. At times the program takes on the appearance of a patchwork that bears little resemblance intrinsically to any departmental philosophy. For these reasons, it seems logical to draw some inferences for administrators from progressivistic and essentialistic educational philosophy, and more specifically from experimentalism, idealism, and realism.

The experimentalistic approach to administration is in keeping with the aims and objectives of this philosophical tendency. The administrator makes every effort to conduct the affairs of the department as a democratic undertaking in which all the various individuals concerned have the opportunity to share in policy formation as well as the rest of the operation; thus, all departmental policy is decided through democratic procedure. Authority accompanies responsibility within the framework of this general approach. The administrator endeavors to create an atmosphere in which all can grow and make a full contribution to the progress of the department. He views administration as a developing social science. Such is the experimentalist's position.

The idealistic approach to administration, admittedly in a number of cases quite progressive, faces a problem immediately: it is committed to essentialistic philosophy of education, but it does place great emphasis on freedom, growth, and development of personality. Correct attitudes come indirectly "by example, inspiration, and contagion"; hence the personality of the teacher and the administrator is tremendously important. In keeping with idealistic tradition, greater teachers and leaders have respect for the personalities of those under them. Thus, we can assume that the idealistic administrator would not superimpose his will on others. He should not demand respect; he should earn it by his manner and his bearing. He would like to be a friend to all and show them what fine democratic living is like. Such an approach will develop attitudes that will help school personnel to democratize other people in other groups and classes with whom they come in contact. The idealistic administrator, therefore, will make true progress when *true democracy* (very difficult to define, of course) in educational administration becomes a reality despite the line-staff pattern of control which is a hallmark of essentialistic educational philosophy.

The realistic approach to administrative control appears to be entirely predictable: the administrator is the one who has the ultimate responsibility; so, he tends to function as a business executive who has been hired to make wise, clear-cut decisions when the situation warrants any action. He may ask staff members for opinions, and he may also have committees investigate certain problems and make subsequent recommendations. The eventual decision, however, is up to him. Of course, ultimate responsibility remains with the source that granted the power originally. Staff members have little choice but to carry out the directions of their superior. The realistic administrator may believe that administration is an art, or he may even believe that his decisions are dictated by the impersonal results of objective experimentation. He does maintain that such a theory of administration is compatible with life in an evolving democracy, because there will always be a few chiefs and many Indians. He asserts that responsibility must be centralized in one man. Policies of an over-all nature may be set by a higher body from which the source of power emanates, but administrators must make decisions for the operational unit beneath this higher body in accordance with these policy directives. This is a realistic approach, and the realistic administrator believes that it works in education as well as in other similar business enterprises.

Professional Preparation

With the development of a complex public-school system in the United States, it was quite natural that attention turned to the quality and type of teacher hired for so important a task as the education of the coming generation. Improvement in the quality of general professional education came slowly in the period from 1860 to 1890, but by the end of the nineteenth century the normal school was a well-established part of the American educational system. The twentieth century has witnessed a number of significant developments in teacher education, but primarily for secondary and elementary school teachers. In the period from 1900 to 1930, some 575 colleges and universities added professional education courses to their curricula in order to qualify their graduates for state certification which had been inaugurated in more than half of the states by 1925.

PROFESSIONAL PREPARATION FOR PHYSICAL EDUCATION. Professional preparation for physical education, which started with Lewis's Institute in 1861, has undergone a vast transformation in the past 100 years. Down through the years of the twentieth century many leaders have urged that a stronger cultural education was necessary for prospective physical-education teachers. They have expressed further, a desire for an improved background in the foundation sciences. Until somewhat more recently there had been a definite trend toward increasing the numbers of hours required in general professional education courses. A number of studies have indicated a lack of standardization in course terminology. In an attempt to rectify what appeared to be a confusing situation, separate curricula in school health and safety education, and also in recreational leadership, were gradually developed. There seems to be a trend toward specialization of function which may take the various subdivisions of physical, health, and recreation education further apart. Through a variety of media, the field has made a significant effort to promote self-evaluation.

It appears to be possible to delineate between progressivism and essentialism in this area of professional preparation. The essentialist, typically, is suspicious of the value of professional education courses. Within this group the idealist would be inclined to stress the need for more study in the humanities, while the realist (the naturalistic realist especially) tends to believe that increased emphasis in foundation science courses is needed.

The matter of the use of the competency approach divides the field to a certain extent. Can we be reasonably certain that our graduating students will be able to function satisfactorily as intelligent citizens and competent professionals unless we have a more effective means of assessing their ability as determined by specific competencies developed through selected experiences with subject matters as resource areas? The essentialist is not particularly disturbed with the present passing-courses-to-graduate approach, while the progressivist is more concerned about what is happening to the individual as this process goes on. The progressive idealist tends to share this concern.

Many realists, both naturalistic and scholastic, feel that we should stop the tendency in the direction of generalization of function. This would mean lessening the emphasis in our curricula on school health and safety education (including driver education), recreation education, and education for coaching. The *progressivist* believes typically that we should include all these functions under one roof.

Another development that is bound to have an influence on our developing professional curricula is the current political nationalistic concern for physical fitness, or "physical" fitness if you are progressivistic enough to prefer it that way. The realists are making a strong bid for more objective measurement of physical fitness, while the experimentalistic progressivist, and a number of idealists, are disturbed by this trend and wish to keep the emphasis on individual evaluation.

There is a certain amount of consensus between the progressivists and the essentialists on the matter of developing standards for accreditation of colleges and universities offering professional preparation. The progressivist backs the concept of self-evaluation and would resent the strict application of fixed standards. The essentialists wish to eliminate the inadequate institutions summarily unless they raise their standards within a fixed period of time.

The Healthy Body

That the condition of his body has always been a concern for man is certainly a truism. Early man found that a certain type of fitness was necessary for life. Because he has had the experience of his forefathers upon which to base his judgments, modern man has been more successful than his prehistoric brother in making an adjustment to his environment. His success is dependent, however, on complicated procedures in the various phases of dentistry and medicine. Life in a society that is becoming increasingly automated has tended to make men and women weak, flabby, and poorly conditioned from the standpoint of circulorespiratory efficiency. In addition, he is finding it increasingly difficult to adjust his elemental emotions to civilization's stresses. As a result he often cracks under the strain and occupies a hospital bed—a victim of a so-called psychosomatic ailment.

A study of past and present civilizations indicates further that the sociological influence of whether a society was at war or at peace has had a direct bearing on the emphases in personal and community health. Freedom from disqualifying defects, strength, and endurance are important to men who want to win wars. When a particular war is over, the society is then able to focus its attention again toward the mastery of its own environment at home.

During the twentieth century there has been outstanding progress in public health, although it is profoundly disturbing that so many people in the world are not able to profit to the greatest extent by these advances. In the United States the federal government has played a gradually increasing role in the promotion of public health despite the ever-present concern of many that such assistance from the national level can be carried too far. In the 1920's after World War I, the public became concerned about the frightening draft statistics, and it was realized that many of these defects would not have turned up if proper preventive measures had been taken during the school years of the draftees. Since this time, the development of school health education in its many phases has been a matter of concern to many.

Despite a certain amount of progress, we find some conflicting ideas as to the definition of health and the place of health instruction in the school curriculum. This disagreement appears to stem to a considerable extent from differing educational philosophies. We still find prevalent a persistence of the dualistic concept of man and a resultant dichotomy of physical and mental health despite the seeming agreement by many that man is a unity. The average citizen uses the terms *health* and *health education* loosely. What then are the implications for school-health education from the standpoint of the educational philosophies of experimentalism, idealism, and realism?

IMPLICATIONS FROM EDUCATIONAL PHILOSOPHY. The experimentalist begins with a naturalistic undergirding and stresses that a standard of rugged health should apply to girls as well as to boys. He would agree further that the child needs health instruction and that such instruction is an important part of the curriculum. To the experimentalist, in fact, it is one of the primary objectives of education, and the success of the school health education program depends on the degree of cooperation among home, school, and community agencies. He would take the position that a natural program of health, physical education, and recreation may be administered as a unified program within a school system for all children and young people within the school district during the time when school is in session.

Today an educated person must understand the difference between health and disease, and he should know how to protect and improve his own health, that of his dependents, and that of the community both large and small. To be truly effective, health education should be concerned with the development of attitudes that will assist the individual to lead a rich, full life. This means more than providing a health service so that students can maintain minimum health needed to pursue intellectual work with the least amount of strain. Health should be defined positively. A school health education program that will bring about such an outlook should be composed of three distinct, yet most closely related, divisions as follows: healthful school living (development of an environment that facilitates students' optimal growth and development); health instruction (programs definitely organized to promote specific learnings in the area of health); and health services (provision for (a) the care of emergency sickness or injury, (b) specific procedures for the prevention or control of communicable diseases, (c) health appraisal, and (d) health counseling).

The idealist views human health from a spiritualistic base. Although Herman Harrell Horne omitted health education in a discussion of the essential studies in the curriculum except where it might be included incidentally under biology, he does mention health first in a list of nine basic values of human living. This seeming contradiction is explained by Horne as follows: health can be placed at the bottom of the hierarchy of educational values, and yet it is a basic value for the other educational aims since it enhances the richness of each and all of them.

Christian idealists typically refer to the importance of health and health education without necessarily indicating its place in their educational hierarchy. They believe, for example, that study of the body leads to valuable scientific knowledge which can be useful in preserving health. Mormons, however, appear to take the strongest position in regard to the care of the body, because their faith teaches them that the spirit and body are the soul of man. They conceive of the body as a nonevil component of man's eternal soul and look forward to literal resurrection after death on earth. Thus, it would seem that the idealist values a program of health and physical education highly as a *service* program which, through its contribution to man's health, enables him to pursue still higher goals in education and in life.

The realistic position in regard to the place of health is not as clear-cut since some educators view it from a naturalistic standpoint, while others add revelation and theological considerations to their position. The naturalistic realist, for example, encourages the development of the maximum of physical vigor and health. For the Thomist, or scholastic realist, the essential hierarchy of values inherent in liberal education would be preserved, with the main emphasis, as to the disciplines, on philosophy. Here the matter of health education would be foundational but not very high in the essential hierarchy of values. The primary concern for the Catholic is the spiritual soul, not the body as it is on earth or as it will be ultimately.

Harry Broudy's position on the place of health education in the school appears to be such that many realists would find themselves in substantial agreement with it. He believes that the school environment should be healthy and that knowledge about the bases of emotional and physical health belongs in the curriculum. But at this point the relationship tapers off sharply, because other agencies should take up the task. The community, for example, does have a responsibility to provide clinical facilities for therapy. The home should bear the basic responsibility for helping youth to acquire desirable health habits. How could education hope to treat the matter of sex education adequately?

In fact, Broudy even questions whether adolescents are not for the most part so healthy that health problems could ever be presented in such a way as to seem real to them. For the realist, therefore, health knowledge is necessary so that the individual can live a truly human life. At this point the educator's responsibility ceases!

Physical Education and Recreation for Women

The role of woman in physical education and physical recreation has been a persistent problem of greater or lesser import since some form of historical record has been available; so, we may safely assume that it caused some concern even before that time. The great Aristotle believed that women had been fitted by nature for subjection to the male of the species, because they had no ability for self-direction. Generally speaking, he felt that they were weaker, less courageous, and incomplete. Plato, on the other hand, held a different view. He believed that women should have all types of education similar to the pattern he prescribed for men, including the highest type of liberal education and even preparation for warfare. Women's physical education, therefore, was hampered not only by the concept of the place of physical education in the particular society, but also by the place that women held in society and by the ideas that men and women have had about the limitations of women because of their anatomical structure.

WOMEN'S EMANCIPATION.   Certainly one of the significant sociological trends of the twentieth century has been woman's emancipation. It had been erroneously concluded in most societies throughout history that women simply did not possess the intellectual capacity to profit from the so-called higher types of education. As a result of this belief, they were given no intellectual function, and, on the whole, their duty has been to bear children and manage the home. This concept has changed considerably in the United States through such influences as the expansion of the American frontier, the Industrial Revolution, and a democratic theory of state which fostered equalitarianism. This emancipation has taken place in certain countries, not necessarily democratic in nature, to an even greater degree in the areas of sport and science.

THE SAME SET OF EDUCATIONAL VALUES?   We have now arrived at the point where we must ask ourselves whether the same set of educational values in physical, health, and recreation education that applies to men applies to women as well. Immediately we encounter the issue as to whether the two sexes are actually so different, and, if so, in what ways? From an anatomical standpoint, the differences are apparent at once. However, this matter is so important for the future of the world that it demands much more serious consideration by the male of the species than it has gotten for perhaps several thousand years (in the so-called Western world at any rate). In our opinion there are far too many men physical educators who are all too willing to ignore the efforts of women physical educators and to let them go their own way. The assumption seems to be that men really have nothing at stake in this matter. Nothing could be further from the truth! Incidentally, there is another group of male coaches and athletic administrators who seems to be all too willing to go along with the prevailing situation in girls' and women's physical education in the United States because there is very little conflict among the sexes for the after-school use of equipment and facilities.

WOMEN'S ROLE HAS CHANGED STEADILY. The study of history has shown us, as we have indicated above, that women have traditionally been considered as inferiors in comparison to men. A steady change in woman's role seems to have taken place, however, despite the fact that a larger view of cultural sociology reminds us continually that the truly important functions of life must be continued. We cannot escape the fact that women have a unique function to fulfill—that of continuing and protecting life. And yet our changing way of life and the increasing tempo of civilization have come upon us so fast, relatively speaking, that there is a considerable amount of uncertainty and confusion despite the onset of a recent conservative trend. Perhaps the question is whether we can shape the thinking of our society so that we can concentrate to a greater extent on individual differences rather than on the time-honored sex-difference approach. In this way it is conceivable that all individuals in America, regardless of sex, may have the opportunity to develop to the maximum of their potentialities in keeping with the pattern of evolving democracy.

RELATIVE OR INTRINSIC VALUES. But this day-dreaming could well be a bit too experimentalistic for the United States at present; so, we must return to a more realistic assessment of the present situation in regard to values in physical, health, and recreation education. This means that some women physical educators see educational aims as relative and experimental, whereas others look upon them as objective and intrinsic in the universe. For this latter group, therefore, the intrinsic values are most important, and it is logical to construct a hierarchy of values which has direct application to the educational system.

THE SAME THREE MAJOR PHILOSOPHIES. With this in mind, it seems reasonable to state that the same three major philosophies of physical, health, and recreation education apply to women, and that these approaches are modified by certain sociological influences concerning women's role in society and the educational pattern that they should follow. These three philosophical tendencies have been delineated at some length earlier in this chapter under the discussion of values and at considerable length under earlier appropriately designated chapters.[1]

SOCIETY'S NORM FOR WOMEN.　No matter which of the three philosophical tendencies a woman physical educator aligns herself with, she finds herself also confronted with the image that our society has of the role of a woman. Women physical educators are most anxious, and probably rightly so, to preserve the correct image for themselves and for their students. Many have been able to accomplish this, but in so doing they have not necessarily lived up to the highest goals of any of the particular philosophical positions for our field. The norm projected by society for women tends to be retrogressive and not progressive. Such a norm is certainly not in the vanguard, and it has been modified by many societal influences not all necessarily good. For example, most women are concerned about their appearance, but it is often the result of artificial contrivances, and they are rarely physically fit. It is difficult for a man to write about these matters (and this particular man would be the first to admit that male physical educators have similar problems), but women physical educators are not, generally speaking, setting a standard in this regard, and students are great imitators. In this connection, it probably doesn't make much difference from which philosophical base you are operating. The desired amount of physical fitness is simply not there!

COMPETITIVE SPORT FOR WOMEN.　An ancillary problem is the matter of competitive sport for women. There is no doubt that athletic competition for boys and young men has been and is being carried to unwarranted extremes in many institutions. The leading women in our profession reacted violently to many of these excesses by the men, and, to their credit, saw to it that similar problems did not arise in the programs for girls and women. In so doing, they were able to set quite a good, and in many cases an excellent, standard in the other phases of the total program. But in their zeal to meet the needs of the average girl, they have negated one of the basic tenets of our democracy—giving every girl, insofar as possible, the opportunity to develop to the maximum of her potential. The accelerated youngster has been slighted and has turned elsewhere, if possible, for her competitive athletic experience and coaching. In most cases it has not been possible for her to reach her potential. If competitive sport experience in an educational setting has value, and all of the philosophical tendencies grant this to a greater or slightly less extent, then it is the duty of the woman physical educator to make these values available to girls and young women, and as soon as possible in the years that lie ahead. The excuse that such a development would immediately place the average woman physical educator in the same untenable position that the average male physical educator

---

[1] Cf. Chapters 5, 7, 9 and 11.

is in might be true to a certain extent, but only if the women allow it to develop that way. Second best is not good enough for the United States. We must work for the ideal and guarantee that it is under educational auspices. It can be done; the division for girls' and women's sports of the AAHPER is moving in the right direction, and it needs the support of the entire field. As educators it is our responsibility to bring all the advantages to young people that our field offers; girls and women are no exceptions. They have the right to enjoy an outstanding, well-balanced program of physical, health, and recreation education.

Dance in Physical Education and Recreation

The role of dance in physical education and in physical recreation has been a persistent problem in our field throughout its history; in fact, dance in certain primitive societies was believed to serve the function of restoration and preservation of bodily health. As both an art and a social function, dance will probably always be with us and will reflect the dominant influences of the age which is being described. People have danced for personal pleasure, for religious purposes, for expression of the gamut of emotions, and for the pleasure of others in all ages. Consequently, the statement that it is possible to distinguish the pulse beat of a civilization by an analysis of its dance forms can be well substantiated.

In the twentieth century, despite the advancement of modern dance and its acceptance in modern education as witnessed by the development of dance-education–teacher-preparation programs across the country, there still remains a great deal to be done in this area. A body of research knowledge is lacking. A certain amount of curriculum standardization for prospective teachers seems desirable, and an improvement of the interaction between the teacher and the professional performer would add further strength to the development. The various public-school levels need an integrated and articulated curriculum as well. Further analysis must be made of the reasons why modern dance especially, and many of the other dance forms, seem unacceptable to the majority of the male physical-education teachers. Square dancing and social dancing continue to be popular throughout many parts of the country with the masses, and a certain amount of folk dancing remains. Tap dancing and ballet appear to be on the wane.

IMPLICATIONS FOR DANCE FROM EDUCATIONAL PHILOSOPHY. At this point we must ask ourselves what implications we can draw from the major educational philosophies regarding the place of dance in education. This is apt to be a controversial subject and is in need of careful investigation by educators competent and knowledgeable in both educational philosophy and the dance. A few tentative opinions will be expressed which will hopefully offer an avenue of approach to those who are most vitally concerned. They are based on the assumption that occasionally an outsider (in this case to the dance) might be able to offer some insight because of a different vantage point.

In the first place, it can be stated that rightly or wrongly the public and educators in general view dance as physical movement and associate it with physical education, sport, physical recreation, exercise, and the like. Therefore, we might find that dance would be equated with physical education and thereby be considered curricular, co-curricular, extra-curricular, or completely outside the educational sphere. Carrying this analogy further, the progressivist might view dance as curricular, or at least co-curricular. The essentialist would tend to see dance as extra-curricular or completely outside the sphere of education. It should be pointed out, however, that the naturalistic realist, although an essentialist basically, could conceivably see it as serving a useful function within education. This can be explained through the desire of the naturalistic realist to allow the student an opportunity for the expression of natural instincts, and because modern dance especially promotes a type of animal fitness.

EXPERIMENTALISM. Secondly, we may be able to be somewhat more specific in relation to the major philosophical tendencies of experimentalism, realism, and idealism. The experimentalist, for example, would see the various dance forms being introduced in an articulated curriculum in such a way as to conform to the child's growth-and-development pattern and thereby contributing to his total fitness for life in our society. As an integral subject, or phase, of physical, health, and recreation education, dance activities tend to bring natural impulses into play. The dance teacher within an experimentalistic pattern evaluates the needs, interests, and abilities of the student and is concerned with the progress of the individual in relation to his environmental adjustment. She believes that a reasonable level of dance skill in the various forms according to the individual's potential can be a fine aesthetic experience. She sees vigorous dance activities making a valid contribution to the "physical" fitness of the student and believes that such activity should be available to boys as well as to girls. Believing that education for leisure is basic to the curriculum, she sees participation in dance as a worthwhile leisure activity allowing man to use his free time creatively and helping him to insure desirable individual growth. Furthermore, dance as a natural activity can promote sound mental and physical health, thereby helping the student to acquire skills resulting in a rich, full life. Obviously, the methodology to be employed in the teaching of dance will be identical with that of experimentalistic teaching in other phases of the total physical-, health-, and recreation-education program.

REALISM.   The realist would tend to see dance as an activity which promotes education of the physical—that is, if it is vigorous enough. To him this is more important than any recreational aspects of dance participation. Dance has value as it is able to contribute to the beauty and utility of life and if it helps pupils develop their muscles and bodily coordination. To the extent that it furnishes an adequate physical basis for intellectual life, it should be included as part of regular physical training. But since it is part of physical education, it must, therefore, yield precedence to intellectual education.

Many realists would concur in the belief that social- and square-dancing skills are important for use in later life, but they are extra-curricular and should be taught after the regular school day is over. One reason for this is that play and work cannot be identified under the same psychological rubric. This does not mean that dance cannot serve a useful function in life. It can help man be re-created in his leisure, and it helps the organism to achieve balance among the various pursuits of his daily living. Normal recreation should provide for change in activity, and such play should be as carefree as possible. For this reason, dance, and other physical-education and physical-recreation activities, should not be overemphasized and too highly organized. Dance can assist in the reduction of any psychic tensions that life's activities and stresses may create. Lastly, dance forms should be in keeping with the fundamental laws which were basic in the creation of the universe. Realistic educational teaching methodology should be employed in teaching dance just as in other physical-education activities.

IDEALISM.   The idealist in dance education should perhaps be an ambivalent creature who sees dance as making a contribution to both education of the physical and education through the physical. Despite this belief, however, she would tend to view dance, and other physical-, health-, and recreation-education activities, as occupying a lower rung on the educational ladder. An idealistic dance teacher sees dance education as one part of the total program which aims to assist man to develop a good life through the development of the physical, aesthetic, and perhaps religious aspects of his nature. Idealistic emphasis typically strives for perfection through the achievement of the enduring values of truth, goodness, and beauty. Therefore, dance's importance would have to be judged on the basis of the contribution it can make to the realization of these values for each individual.

The idealist stresses the need for building wholeness of mind and body and would wish to see her students develop beautiful and skilled bodies. The supreme worth of personality is readily apparent to the idealistic dance teacher, and she would teach her subject so that good habits of mental and physical health result. She would not wish the student dancer to become too self-centered, and dance should very definitely be a means to an end, and not an end in itself. This would be in keeping with her emphasis on a well-balanced program of physical, health, and recreation education for all students. Furthermore, she sees dance as an activity which affords the performer a spiritual lift through the liberation of powers and because of the physical well-being it engenders. It should be a creative experience that helps to provide a physical reserve for life's many physical and spiritual burdens. The progressive idealist sees the traditional attitude against dance of many major religious groups in modern history as being uninformed and unappreciative of the true role of dance as taught in an educational setting. To the extent that the idealistic dance teacher can help students realize the eternal values through choice of the right kinds of dance experience without flouting the moral order in the world, she will be progressive enough to disregard a dualistic theory of work and play. Such dance experience even *under* religious sponsorship can actually serve to help the American people improve moral and ethical standards. Dance experience can aid the individual to offset the psychic disintegration taking place in the world by providing creative experience which can be spiritual in nature. It can assist man to relate himself to that which is beautiful in life and can be one of many forces in leisure which has unique potential for the good of humanity.

The Use of Leisure

Earlier in this chapter we discussed the influence of economics on physical, health, and recreation education as a persistent historical problem. An historical analysis of this problem indicated quite clearly that education prospered when there was a surplus economy and declined when the economic structure weakened. Furthermore, educational aims varied depending on how people made their money and created these surplus economies. It has been an unfortunate outcome of our advancing industrial civilization that many problems have arisen even though the technological advances have brought many advantages to man. Citizens in the Western world now have more leisure than ever before, but the promotion of the concept of education for leisure depends a great deal on the prevailing educational philosophy and whether it will allow sufficient support for the inclusion of such programs in the educational system. When people achieve leisure, the question arises as to what they *should* do with it. We will attempt to answer this through an analysis of the major trends in Western educational philosophy.

DEFINITIONS.   A few definitions seem to be in order. The word *leisure* is used to explain the time that a person has free from his work and that he does not need for his sleep and basic survival activities. There have been many definitions of *play,* which indicates the difficulty of trying to analyze its meaning. It is not necessary for our purposes here to delineate too carefully; so, we will accept the definition that play is an instinctive form of self-expression through pleasurable activity which seems to be aimless in nature. The term *recreation* seems to have developed a broader meaning than *play,* although they are quite commonly used interchangeably. Typically, recreation embodies those experiences or activities that people take part in during their leisure for purposes of pleasure, satisfaction, or education. Recreation is a human experience or activity; it is not necessarily instinctive, and it may be considered as purposeful.

THE TWENTIETH CENTURY.   The twentieth century in the Western world has been characterized by the greatest surplus economy that the world has ever seen. We have witnessed a vast new development in the United States and Canada that may be called an organized recreational pattern. The outlines of this pattern had been barely discernible at the end of the nineteenth century, but in the past fifty years the development of public- and voluntary-agency recreation has been absolutely phenomenal. Further social and economic changes have taken place; professional associations have developed; professional preparation for recreational leadership has mushroomed; and city-supported recreation programs along with community centers in schools form a network across our fifty states.

WHAT THE FUTURE MAY HOLD.   Now we face the second half of the twentieth century with a good deal of fear. Behind us are all sorts of wars, depressions, and examples of man's inhumanity to man, as well as much that gives us hope for the future. We are, however, in the middle of a "cold war" which could spell utter devastation for mankind, and yet we look ahead idealistically, realistically, pragmatically, existentially, materialistically, or what have you? On the home front we watch the rises and declines of the economy apprehensively. We try to comprehend the peaceful and the shooting revolutions going on all about us. We hear that automation may bring about a situation where people will be paid *not* to work. Education for leisure would seem to warrant serious consideration in the face of such a development. History shows that no civilization has survived for long when the people had too much free time. Can we continue our unprecedented development as a country where most people will find happiness and satisfaction despite the fact that we are increasingly crowding people together in heavily populated cities and suburbs? To answer these questions in relation to the use of leisure, we should examine our philosophical positions with their implications for education. What we decide as professionals will exert a considerable influence on the place of physical, health, and recreation education in our educational system.

EXPERIMENTALISM. The experimentalist does not like the "fractionating" that is taking place within our field in the educational system; so, he would immediately wish to protest against the idea of a separate discussion of recreation education. He is much more concerned with a unified approach whereby the three specialized areas of school health, physical education, and recreation education would provide a variety of experiences involving knowledges and understandings that will enable the individual to live a richer, fuller life through superior adjustment to his environment. He would argue that education for the worthy use of leisure, both from a theoretical and a practical standpoint, is basic to the curriculum of the school—a curriculum in which pupil growth, as defined by the experimentalist, is all important. Secondly, play shall be conducted in such a way that desirable moral growth will be fostered. Thirdly, overly organized sport competition is not true recreation, since the welfare of the individual is often submerged in the extreme emphasis which is so frequently placed on winning. The experimentalist makes it quite clear that it is a mistake to confuse the psychological distinction between work and play with the traditional economic distinction that is generally recognized. All citizens should have ample opportunity to use their free time in a creative and fruitful manner. He would not condemn a person who watched others perform with a high level of skill in any of our cultural activities as long as the individual kept such viewing in a balanced role in his life. Furthermore, he would view with favor a carefully planned program of interscholastic sports that is built on a sound physical-education and intramural athletic base.

REALISM. The realist typically takes an essentialistic position when the role of recreation education in the school is considered. Work and play are usually quite sharply differentiated. Play serves a most useful purpose at recess or after school, but it should not be part of the regular curriculum. He would agree that the use of leisure is significant to the development of our culture, but he would also be quick to point out that winning the "cold war" is going to take a lot more hard work and somewhat less leisure. He sees leisure pursuits or experience as an opportunity to get relief from work while it serves a re-creative purpose in the life of man. The surplus-energy theory of play and recreation makes sense to him. So does the more recent bio-social theory of play—the idea that play helps the organism to achieve balance. He would tend to deprecate the fact that the "play attitude" seems to be missing almost completely in many organized sports. Recreational play is, therefore, very important to the realist; it should be "liberating" and arranged in such a way that people can develop their potentialities for wholesome hobbies through recreation. As he sees it, recreation can serve as a "safety valve" by the reduction of psychic tensions which are evidently caused by so many of life's typical stresses. Even though play should not be considered as a basic part of the curriculum, we should not forget that it provides an "indispensable seasoning" to the good life. Extracurricular play activities and a sound general education should suffice to equip the student for leisure activities in our society.

IDEALISM. The idealist is by virtue of his basic philosophical position an essentialist, although a number of educators could be classified as progressive idealists because of their serious concern with individual personality and its development. Thus, the position of the idealist in regard to the role of recreation in the school and in adult life is not clear-cut and decisive. It might be said that the importance of recreation and play in idealistic philosophy of education has perhaps not been fully understood or appreciated in the past. Their role in the development of the personality and the perfectly integrated individual is looming larger with each passing year. It is for this reason that a person subscribing to idealistic philosophy of education should reassess the contributions that recreation and play can and do make in the education of man. That there is a need for educational research along these lines is self-evident.

Another difficulty that confronts us is differentiating between physical education and recreation. In the context of this book we are considering the role of the physical-, health-, and recreation-education teacher in schools and colleges. This person should perhaps have the responsibility for *physical* recreation only; the meeting of all the other recreational needs and interests of boys and girls should be his responsibility only indirectly as he works cooperatively with the recreation administrator (either within the school system or in the community) at all times. It is undoubtedly most unfortunate that the typical physical educator has such a workload that he must spread himself much too thinly and usually falls down on certain aspects of his job. In addition, he usually does not have the broad background of interests necessary for a recreation administrator.

It would seem that idealists might view very closely any theories of recreation and play which grant educational possibilities to these activities of man. The self-expression theory of play suggests that man's chief need in life is to achieve the satisfaction and accomplishment of self-expression of one's own personality. Here is an explanation that seems to consider quite fully the conception of man as an organic unity—a total organism; thus, many aspects of the theory seem compatible with idealistic philosophy of education. Idealists believe that man is a purposive being who is striving to achieve those values which are embedded in reality itself. To the extent that the idealist can realize the eternal values through the choice of the right kinds of play and recreation without flouting the moral order in the world, he will be progressive enough to disregard a dualistic theory of work and play—a theory that has plagued us in the United States right down to the present day.

There are distinct signs that specific Protestant denominations are becoming increasingly aware of the role that recreation can play in the promulgation of the Christian idealistic way of life. In the United States such recognition has been largely a twentieth-century phenomenon. Recreation has developed to the point where it is now clearly one of the major social institutions in American life. If, as Horne believes, "the ideal suggests the integrated individual in an integrated society growing in the image of the integrated universe," then all types of recreational experience and activity can seemingly make a contribution to the realization of this ideal. We are warned that mankind is faced with a recreational imperative. Idealism should re-examine its traditional position to discover if play and recreation, including education for leisure, are not valuable enough to become a basic component of our educational curriculum.

Amateur, Semiprofessional, and Professional Sport

The last persistent problem we shall consider, and certainly one of the most disturbing and perplexing ones, is that of amateur, semiprofessional, and professional sport and its relationship to our educational system as well as to our entire culture. We hope that the reader will be able to comprehend the ramifications of the enormous problem somewhat more clearly than previously. Here is a *persistent* problem that will undoubtedly plague the physical educator-coach throughout his career. And yet sport is part of the very lifeblood of our field and offers the possibility of great benefits and satisfaction to the participant and coach alike. It is a great cultural influence which offers the possibility of good or bad to our society. How we allow or help it to develop depends to a considerable extent on us—on how we use it for the service of man.

WHY PEOPLE PLAY GAMES.   People engage in games and sport for many reasons. The motivation behind such participation is so complex that there is really no general agreement on the matter. Do we take part in these activities for fun, for recreation, for self-expression, for health, for exercise, for competition, or for what? Or do we do it for a variety of reasons, some stronger at times than others?

THE TWENTIETH CENTURY.   The twentieth century has been characterized by a phenomenal growth in competitive athletics in America at all levels both within and without the public educational system. Women's sports were controlled quite carefully to avoid the excesses that crept into the men's programs. A type of semiprofessionalism has gradually been recognized tacitly by collegiate bodies, but the AAU has clung quite rigidly to the classic amateur ideal. In the early 1960's a great struggle developed between the NCAA and the AAU over the matter of athletic control. Some one group is going to win this struggle, but not before the United States suffers further embarrassment or many fine young athletes are hurt in one way or another.

Your outlook on this problem will depend a great deal on your philosophy of education. Initially, we must recognize that the essentialist will look at past history and will tend to believe that the classic definition of amateurism has considerable merit. He will be apt to wish to retain the good from the past and to change the *status quo* very slowly if at all. The progressivist believes that there are no fixed values and that changing times demands new methods. He appreciates the contributions of the past, but doesn't regard them as sacrosanct and hopes that we can learn from the lessons of the past. He would be willing to accept a new approach to this perennial problem in sport if it worked; his attitude would be that we will never know the answer to this problem unless we try out some of the proposed solutions using a problem-solving approach.

OVEREMPHASIS IS GENERALLY CONDEMNED. None of the three leading positions in educational philosophy condones overemphasis in competitive sport in education. The experimentalist believes that physical-education classes and intramural sports are more important to the large majority of students than interscholastic and intercollegiate sports. He can, however, give full support to team experiences in competitive sports, because they can be vital educational experiences if properly conducted. The *realist* is concerned with the adequate training and development of the body itself for all students. He gives qualified approval to competitive sport, because he believes that it contributes to the learning of sportsmanship and desirable social conduct. Competitive athletics are extracurricular and should come after the official school day is over. The use of leisure for play activities is important, but, unfortunately, this play attitude is quite often missing from highly organized sport. The idealist definitely favors sport because of the status accorded such activity in Greek idealism. He believes in the transfer of training theory which implies that attitudes of sportsmanship and fair play learned through desirable athletic competition can and do transfer to life situations. But the coach should be careful not to let his boys become too self-centered as they strive for a high level of performance. Sport should be a means to an end, not an end in itself. Extreme specialization may warp the personalities of all concerned.

Athletic competition is accepted to a greater or lesser degree in American education as an integral or ancillary phase of that process. Moreover, competitive sport has become a vital phase of our way of life. Teachers of physical, health, and recreation education have a great stake in the answers that are given in the coming years to this matter of amateur sport. The materialistic image of today's professional in sport does help very much; in fact, it is decidedly harmful. The professional sportsman should be encouraged to devote his life to a social ideal—the idea of service to his fellow man through his contributions to all aspects of his own sport and to the highest ideals of sportsmanship.

RE-EVALUATION IS NEEDED.   In education, some re-evaluation involving straightforward thinking and willingness to compromise appears to be absolutely necessary, so that athletic competition at a high level may continue to be an important phase of our American way of life. Such re-evaluation is absolutely necessary at the national and international levels as well. We must answer the question as to whether we are now ready to accept a tripartite division into amateurism, semiprofessionalism, and professionalism with safeguards for all involved. Has our way of life truly changed sufficiently to warrant such a change?

Conclusion

We have now come to the end of Part Six in which we have delineated the position of each of the three leading philosophical tendencies toward eleven important, persistent problems in our field. You may feel that there are other problems that should have been included, or perhaps that some of these should have been omitted. As has been stressed time and again, it is up to you to examine yourself and to formulate your own opinions. You should decide whether the school should reflect society, or whether it should endeavor to reconstruct it. Only you can make these decisions for yourself.

It is not enough to know your own position and to work for it however. You must be fully aware of the other positions in order to appreciate the opinions and attitudes of many of your colleagues in your own specialized area, in general professional education, and in general education. Together all of you should be searching for consensus wherever possible because of the national and international significance of such agreement. A discussion of this topic follows in Part Seven.

PART SEVEN

Consensus and Summary

CHAPTER THIRTEEN

The Possibility of Consensus

The Importance of a Continuing Search for More Agreement

The search for, and the possibility of, consensus among the conflicting philosophies of education in the Western world is a most interesting topic to discuss. Some might omit it in this type of exposition and dismiss the omission without a further thought. We were sorely tempted to avoid the issue in just this way, because it appears to be so important for teachers of physical, health, and recreation education to examine themselves and delineate *their own* individual philosophies insofar as this might be possible. We have been floundering around for so long that even the attempt to delineate our own positions would represent a vast improvement over the present status of philosophical thought in our field. These words are not meant to be derogatory to our specialized field; they apply equally well to the entire field of education.

EDUCATION AND ATTITUDE DEVELOPMENT. But such delineation of one's own philosophy, as truly basic as it is to one's professional advancement, is not enough in light of the world situation today. We cannot, and dare not, be an island unto ourselves as we tried to be in the past. Competition between and among nations seems destined to continue for a considerable time to come, and the concept of the United Nations, although a reality to a degree, is still in many ways only a dream. A large part of the responsibility for establishing attitudes desirous of world peace, according to Brubacher, rests with the schools, and he believes that educators will have to be capable of rising above their divisions in educational philosophy if we ever hope to accomplish this purpose.[1]

DIFFICULTY OF ACHIEVING CONSENSUS. Of course, this is the same problem that we face here at home in our own schools and colleges insofar as this matter of consensus is concerned. In any given school system you are quite apt to find individuals at all points on the educational-philosophy spectrum. School administration and curriculum development can be a very trying experience under such conditions, especially if you discover belatedly that you and your immediate superior are, philosophically speaking, at opposite poles. Fortunately, you both speak the same language, although at times you may wonder even about this. One can imagine the difficulty of debate in the United Nations between the U.S. and the U.S.S.R. where the languages are *completely* different and where each participant comes from a completely different environment.

MORE AGREEMENT IN PRACTICE THAN IN THEORY. Strangely enough, in order to disagree a certain amount of agreement is necessary. We must agree on the issues and on an interpretation of the rules for debate. Furthermore, we realize that we aren't striving for complete agreement on all issues anyhow. Fortunately, whether we are talking about the situation at home or abroad, it is well to remember that there tends to be much more agreement in practice than in theory. This is a most comforting thought to keep uppermost in our minds, if possible, when we come to an impasse and further debate seems futile.[2]

METHODS OF ACHIEVING GREATER CONSENSUS. There are actually a number of methods available by which greater consensus can be achieved. One way is to do everything in our power to break down the communication barriers—a formidable but perhaps not an impossible task. The study of semantics, the language analysis movement in philosophy, and the developing social science of human relations in administration will make significant contributions toward the improvement of communication in the years to come. The development of a truly international language, which could be taught in all countries in conjunction with the mother tongue, would be an enormous aid to such a development as well.

A most promising way to achieve greater consensus also is through the continuance of scientific investigation especially along the lines of the psychology of learning. There is no doubt that the twentieth century is the age of science, and that people are developing an increasing re-

---

[1] John S. Brubacher, *Modern Philosophies of Education*, 2nd ed. (New York: McGraw-Hill Book Company, Inc., 1950), p. 326.

[2] *Ibid.*, p. 327.

spect for any scientific findings. This is not to say that the results of scientific endeavors will find immediate acceptance, but any change warranted can be expected to come in a reasonable period of time. Change and possible consensus may be a matter of learning for some and a matter of relearning for others.

Where disagreements cannot be resolved, we shall probably have to resort increasingly to compromise or perhaps to the employment of majority rule. The crucial question is whether we should insist on *our* way when we believe so strongly that we are right. We may wonder how far we can go in this matter of compromise and still live with our consciences. In the practical implications of conflicting educational philosophies, this is certainly most difficult and trying at times. In the "cold war," failure to compromise may bring on the next war which could well be the last war!

Some Common Denominators in Education

It is interesting to note that there are some common presuppositions or denominators among the different educational philosophies. Greene makes this quite clear as follows:

In the first place, different philosophical points of view, 'schools,' or positions are not mutually exclusive in all respects. On the contrary, all, of necessity, share some common presuppositions, and each finds itself in considerable agreement with one or more of its presumptive rivals. More significant, then, than any specifiable type or types of philosophy is the larger pattern of partly contrasting, partly overlapping, *emphases and trends* of contemporary belief on ultimate matters.[3]

What then are some of these areas of practical agreement—these common presuppositions or denominators in general education? Initially, there is agreement that the safety of the child is basic, and that every precaution should be taken to protect him from the everyday hazards of life. The school, moreover, has a responsibility to provide a health-service facility—that is, someone should be available to provide first aid and to assist in the detection of early symptoms of illness and possible communicable disease. This service would include such things as advising parents that their child should have his eyes examined by a physician or that he should be vaccinated for the protection of his health. There is agreement, also, at least within the borders of a state, that all boys and girls must be educated for a certain period of time before they can leave school to seek employment. Furthermore, each state has its own

---

[3] Theodore M. Greene, "A Liberal Christian Idealist Philosophy of Education," *Fifty-fourth Yearbook* of the National Society for the Study of Education (Chicago: University of Chicago Press, 1955), Part I, p. 91.

requirement concerning the educational background and experience that a teacher must have before he is hired to teach, although there is no such thing as standardization of requirements among the various states, and there are many loopholes provided for emergencies.[4]

A CERTAIN AMOUNT OF AGREEMENT. There is a certain amount of agreement as well in connection with the aims and objectives of education, although it must be admitted that such a listing, without a discussion of the educational methodology to be employed or of any hierarchy of educational values, is not as meaningful as it might be. As far back as 1918, a commission of the National Education Association published the famous *Cardinal Principles of Education,* which were extremely well received by all factions. They included the following headings: (1) Health; (2) Command of the Fundamental Processes (of communication and computation); (3) Worthy Home Membership; (4) Vocation; (5) Civic Functions; (6) Worthy Use of Leisure Time; and (7) Ethical Character.[5] Since this time there have been a number of other proclamations by the Educational Policies Commission of the NEA and other groups concerned with this matter. The most recent statement, *The Central Purpose of American Education,* re-emphasizes the goals expressed in 1918 as well as the further statement in 1938) and then goes on to state a central purpose, which is not meant to be thought of as exclusive. Such clarification is bound to cause confusion, but, for what it is worth, the central purpose is expressed as follows:

The purpose which runs through and strengthens all other educational purposes —the common thread of education—is the development of the ability to think. This is the central purpose to which the school must be oriented if it is to accomplish either its traditional tasks of those newly accentuated by recent changes in the world. To say that it is central is not to say that it is the sole purpose or in all circumstances the most important purpose, but that it must be a pervasive concern in the work of the school. Many agencies contribute to achieving educational objectives, but this particular objective will not be generally attained unless the school focuses on it. In this context, therefore, the development of every student's rational powers must be recognized as centrally important.[6]

There are some additional areas of agreement that should be mentioned, although it must be confessed that the ice is getting rather thin in spots. An example of this would be the question of the extent of involvement with controversial social issues. Here we might find a willingness to admit that a particular issue existed, but above and

---

[4] Brubacher, *Modern Philosophies of Education,* p. 328.

[5] Commission on the Reorganization of Secondary Education, *The Cardinal Principles of Education,* U.S. Bureau of Education Bulletin 35 (Washington, D.C.: National Education Association, 1918), pp. 11-15.

[6] The Educational Policies Commission, *The Central Purpose of American Education* (Washington, 6 D.C.: National Education Association, 1961), p. 12.

beyond such an admission there are relatively few high schools, either public or private, where a completely free discussion could be held without the possibility of repercussions to the administrator or school board by some of the parents of the children involved. We might say, also, that there is consensus that the student should be free to arrive at a solution, but (let's face it!) he'll have to be quite careful how he expresses himself in certain areas of religion, politics, or problems of a social nature.

We might say further that there is general agreement that the race experience ought to be the common heritage of all. But then we are not certain as to how much race experience should be included in the curriculum, or what should be emphasized, or how it should be taught. As to teaching method, problem-solving has common approval and so does the belief that there is a time and place for drill. Even here, however, it is extremely difficult to explain exactly what is meant. This holds true as well with the idea that there is a need for motivating instruction and that interest will be maintained when classwork is geared to present experiences. And, for example, when and to what extent are teachers who subscribe to one or the other of the philosophical positions ready to allow students to share in classroom management when they appear to be ready for such involvement.[7]

Some Common Denominators in Physical, Health, and Recreation Education

One common denominator in our specialized field stands out more clearly than any other—the belief of the large majority that regular physical education periods should be required for all school children through grade ten or eleven at least. Upon this we have consensus, and it gives us a talking point.

A second point of agreement is evident in the matter of health and health education. It is vitally important that a child develops certain attitudes toward his own health in particular and toward community hygiene in general. Furthermore, certain basic health knowledges should be taught somewhere and at some time in the curriculum.

We can find consensus also on the worthy use of leisure time. It is understood that in America many people are presumably enjoying a greater amount of leisure than has ever been available before with the possible exception of the final years of the Roman Empire.

Professionals within the field would argue to a man that physical vigor is important. Beyond this we cannot go, however, since there would be no general agreement among the men, or between men and women,

---

[7] Brubacher, *Modern Philosophies of Education,* pp. 329-331.

about what constitutes physical vigor. This may seem like an unfair statement, but we believe it is true. We have no national standards for physical fitness, only national norms which give us present status—nothing more. It would be next to impossible to get an agreement on national standards for boys and girls, and perhaps this is a good thing. This you must decide for yourself.

Even the role of competitive sports for boys and girls is an area in which there is some agreement. We feel generally that boys and girls at some stage of their development should have an experience of this type. But we can find no general agreement beyond this—beyond what is actually a meaningless statement unless we clarify it further. This is, however, a starting point, and this much is encouraging.

The matter of remedial exercise for physical defects that can be corrected offers us another opportunity for a bit of agreement. We would all agree that something should be done about the youngster with what appears to be an abnormal development of his musculature. But, once again, there the agreement stops short. We don't know who should look after this, or when or where.

The area of character and personality development has come in for much discussion in the past. We know this is important; other teachers and all parents are concerned as well. We don't agree on the role of the teacher of physical, health, and recreation education in this matter.

There are undoubtedly a number of other specifics upon which we could achieve a greater or lesser amount of agreement, but at least we do have consensus on what has been mentioned to this point. We submit that the time is long overdue when our field should be able to present to the American public far greater agreement on what it is that we do.

Your immediate reaction may be that we need more research to make our case to the public. This is most assuredly true, and such research should cover all facets of our field and not merely physiological research, as vitally important as this is. And we need to be better informed about research in allied fields which has implications for physical, health, and recreation education. Furthermore, we are abysmally ignorant about periodical literature and research findings in other countries in the world.[8] It is equally true that many of us do not make use of the knowledge that is available and has been published. We could probably achieve much greater consensus if people in the field only kept abreast of current research findings. We can well be proud of the special supplement of

---

[8] Fortunately, Dr. Henry Montoye, now of The University of Michigan, developed the *Index and Abstracts of Foreign Physical Education Literature* (1955), Vol. I in cooperation with Dr. R. R. Schreiber, Executive Secretary, Phi Epsilon Kappa Fraternity, 3747 North Linwood Avenue, Indianapolis 18, Indiana. Professor Herbert Olson, Michigan State University, East Lansing, is now the editor.

the May, 1960 *Research Quarterly* of the American Association for Health, Physical Education, and Recreation entitled *The Contributions of Physical Activity to Human Well-Being*. This outstanding project of the Association's research council summarizes and gives conclusions on available research findings concerning the contributions of physical activity to physical health, social development, psychological development, skill learning, growth, and rehabilitation.[9] Such statements as these, if read and assimilated, will go a long way toward helping us to achieve a greater amount of consensus which is sorely needed.

Issues that Stand in the Way of Greater Consensus

It is not our intention to devote much space at this point to the issues that stand in the way of greater consensus. These have undoubtedly been apparent to you as you have read the discussion of the twelve persistent problems immediately preceding this chapter, as well as the earlier chapters treating the implications for physical, health, and recreation education from the major philosophical positions. And from the standpoint of this particular chapter treating the possibility of consensus, the issues begin presumably at the various points where the limited amount of consensus that has been achieved ceases.

Hopefully, you will agree that there is a vital need for a greater amount of consensus. To achieve such agreement there will have to be full and free discussion of the issues. To help you accomplish this, we have included a fairly complete listing of debatable topics in Appendix I of this text. There will undoubtedly be other issues that you will wish to state in the form of debating topics. We suggest that you hold a series of, say, ten debates as part of the laboratory work in the course for which this text may be used. As you debate these issues, and it can be a fascinating experience, do not hesitate to accept responsibility for either side of the issue. There is a much greater chance of achieving consensus, if you truly understand the other fellow's position and can express it to his satisfaction. This will tend to make you a bit of a Sophist, but have no fears about this. It never hurts anyone to understand *all* the aspects of a question.

Concluding Statement

Within our field we find much confusion and vacillation. Many professionals are using common sense but little foresight and philosophical analysis. Hence we find a considerable number of people taking a very

---

[9] "The Contributions of Physical Activity to Human Well-Being," *Research Quarterly*, XXXI, No. 2 (May 1960), Part II.

narrow approach, which, in turn, damages our professional status and gives the public a hazy conception of what our aims and objectives are. Without destroying our individual philosophies, we can do much to sharpen our image in the minds of the consumer—the American public.

Today we hear much about the pursuit of excellence in American education, but we are not always certain about what is meant by this demand. Do we mean that we want to develop outstanding students? Or do we want all students, regardless of their inherent potential, to be motivated by a desire for excellence insofar as this is possible for each individual? Or is it perhaps that we believe excellence is necessary in order to preserve our way of life?[10] We can, quite possibly, answer all three of these questions in the affirmative. But, as Brubacher has pointed out, it is the answer to the third question that is crucial in the second half of the twentieth century—the preservation of our tradition of freedom:

Obviously we are the inheritors of a great tradition, a great national purpose. At our best we need not take second place or a back seat where freedom is involved. Yet, somehow we must get, not just fired up, but incandescent about freedom. It may be a dire way to put it, but one can fairly easily imagine our longing for freedom if we were once to lose it. The Babylonian exile would be nothing compared to it. That we should lose it, that there should even be a slight risk of losing it, may seem absurd on first thought. On second thought, however, it may seem much less so. What was it Lincoln said at Gettysburg? 'Four score and seven years ago our fathers brought forth on this continent a new nation, conceived in liberty . . . We are now met on a great battlefield of that war to see whether that nation or any nation so conceived and so dedicated can long endure.' As recently as this past winter President Kennedy declared in his state of the union message to Congress, "We shall have to test anew whether a nation organized and governed such as ours can endure." These are serious words. None of us is entitled to take them at less than their face value. Certainly students and faculty of the nation's colleges and universities should know better than most people that freedom can only be won by being constantly rewon! [11]

---

[10] John S. Brubacher, "Higher Education and the Pursuit of Excellence," an address delivered in Huntington, West Virginia, at Marshall University, April 25, 1961, p. 3.
  [11] *Ibid.*, p. 17.

CHAPTER FOURTEEN

Building Your Own Personal Philosophy

Introduction

Building your own personal philosophy, as you undoubtedly realize, can be adventurous and extremely exciting. It can also be very rewarding despite the fact that it will be time-consuming and will require painstaking effort. Much care has been taken in the preceding pages to avoid bias and prejudice in presenting the various aspects of the major philosophical tendencies to you. At this point some might feel that the author should use, or at least is entitled to use, a few pages to tell you what *he* really believes. It is possible that you may feel that you know already.

It would be all too simple to attempt to build a strong case for one particular approach at this time. You might even forgive me for trying to do it. The really important issue right now, however, is for you to continue the development of your own philosophy based upon your own experience and reflection. Besides, as Greene has explained it so well:

No philosopher worthy of the name is a pure exemplification of any school or type, the wholly appropriate recipient of any handy philosophical label. He may prefer, and merit, some one label in reference to any other presently available, but if he actually functions as a philosopher he is devoting his life to the development and articulation of *his own* more or less distinctive beliefs, even if these fall primarily, or even wholly, within the confines of a historical school or tradition.[1]

---

[1] Theodore M. Greene, "A Liberal Christian Idealist Philosophy of Education," in *Modern Philosophies and Education, Fifty-fourth Yearbook* of the National Society for the Study of Education (Chicago: University of Chicago Press, 1955), Part I, p. 91.

Five Possible Stages of Development

You may find that you have been in the *ostrich stage* up to now—that is, you may have buried your head in the sand and refused to allow yourself to become aware of the conflicting philosophies within education or within your specialized field of physical, health, and recreation education.

Or perhaps you have climbed the ladder (in this instance a *five-runged step ladder*) a bit further and are at the *cafeteria stage,* which involves selecting some of this and some of that which looks appetizing for your philosophical fare. This eclectic approach has a great deal of appeal initially, but there appears to be strong evidence that it is generally regarded as philosophically indefensible. It may, of course, be one stage in an individual's development, but it is to be hoped that the devoted educator will soon make his way higher. Wegener explains this situation as follows:

Eclecticism implies that one holds ideas and principles drawn unsystematically from a variety of sources, and organizes them loosely so that they tend to form a mosaic of diverse conceptions rather than a genuine integration of thought. *Eclecticism* is frequently a forerunner of a unified philosophy—it is a preliminary stage of development. *Eclecticism* in its relationship to a *systemic* or *coherent* philosophy is analogous to the relationship of mixture and compound in chemistry. One is merely a mixture of elements, while the other achieves a new unity.[2]

There is every reason to believe that a person will be attracted by certain elements of the various approaches. But we must be extremely careful not to lift anything out of context and insert it somewhere else where it simply does not belong. Such an approach is merely a resting place along the way, and, if not followed by continued growth, will prevent the individual from reaching his highest potential in the final analysis.

The third rung of the ladder is a popular place. Furthermore, there has to be a lot of room here to hold all the people who have gotten this far and no further. We have designated this as the *fence-sitter stage* or level. Here we find people who have matured a bit more and have found, perhaps unconsciously to a degree, that they are inclining in one direction or another. But beyond that they are unwilling to go! Why? Maybe they're too lazy intellectually or physically, if such a distinction may be made. Perhaps they're somewhat afraid of the consequences of a determined stand; we are told that all too many people

---

[2] Frank C. Wegener, *The Organic Philosophy of Education* (Dubuque, Iowa: William C. Brown Co., 1957), p. 31.

today tend to be organization men who don't wish to rock the boat for fear of the consequences. Then again, there are often other reasons not disclosed.

In time we fervently hope that you will rise to the fourth rung on this philosophical ladder. This we will call the *Stage of Early Maturity*. At this point the individual educator has wrestled with himself and his environment and has achieved a quality of unity or harmony which is characteristic of a philosophical position that is reasonably logical and consistent in its various departments. He is able to justify his convictions (which may earlier have been only persuasions) intellectually to the extent that scientific knowledge, and perhaps faith, can assist him. As a result he has developed strong attitudes that are reflected in the moral ardor of his personal and professional life. It is probably not necessary to say that there is plenty of room on this rung of the ladder! Beware of the strong possibility of intolerance and fanaticism at this point.

Hopefully, as we mature still further, we will achieve wisdom as well as mere knowledge. If we do, we may arrive at the *Stage of Philosophical Maturity*. This level of professional development can come from a broad, sound experience, diligent study, and ordered reflection. It is at this point that we realize the supreme importance and need for agreement on a nation-wide and a world-wide basis. Our world has reached a stage where the need for peaceful strife is infinitely greater than the types of struggles that have taken place in the past as well as in the present. At this level on the ladder, we most certainly realize the unique aspects of our own position and the importance of a continuing search for truth, however we may define it. And yet we should be tolerant of others and their beliefs, realizing that a sincere effort should be made to increase the boundaries of the areas of consensus. After all, it is quite possible, and seemingly quite probable, that only one position is truly right.

Conclusion

No matter which stage of philosophical development you may be at presently, you may find it necessary to retrace the various steps that have been recommended to assist the teacher of physical, health, and recreation education to build his own personal philosophy logically, consistently, and systematically. Obviously, there is no hard and fast progression to which you *must* adhere. The steps which have been suggested in the various chapters of this text seem reasonable and should at least serve as a point of departure. Keep in mind that the philosophic quest is a never-ending one. You won't suddenly, at some advanced stage of your development, find *all* the answers to the problems which have been perplexing you. But you will be leading a greatly enriched life that may truly be an "adventure of ideas," as Whitehead has so aptly expressed it. Each of you *should* earn the right to be an influential person in your chosen field at least within your own sphere of operation, and perhaps much further. The field of physical, health, and recreation education has a truly unique contribution to make in the lives of men. Whatever your philosophical position may be, understand it fully, and it will enable you to live up to the highest standards of your profession. Ours can be a proud profession, if each of us strives to help people realize all the values that life has to offer.

Appendix A

Debating Procedures

The value of competitive debating in the professional preparation of teachers of physical, health, and recreation education has not been generally recognized. After using this classroom technique for a number of years at both the undergraduate and graduate levels of instruction, the author has become thoroughly convinced that it can be an extremely interesting and beneficial experience for all concerned. The eagerness and anticipation shown for forthcoming debates by several classes of male physical-education seniors at The University of Michigan would be enough to convince the most hardened skeptic. Listening to these young men continuing the debate topic after class as they go down the hall to their next class was music to the ears of this instructor.

A COMMUNICATIONS PRO. Teachers in general, and especially teachers in our field, are going to spend the rest of their lives defending their beliefs and making as strong a case as possible for the various phases of their work. Teachers of physical education and athletic coaches are usually extroverted individuals who love to talk in the gymnasium or on the athletic field. But when they are forced to break away from the vernacular and speak somewhat more formally in the classroom, at a teachers' meeting, or at a local service-club luncheon, they often find the transition somewhat difficult. Giving students the opportunity to organize their thoughts in a logical sequence, to present them in front of a group of their peers, and then to refute the arguments of an opponent under a certain amount of pressure can be one of the finest experiences that a professional student can have in his undergraduate career. It has been interesting to note that many graduate students, even those who have taught for several years, seem to need this experience equally as much as do the undergraduates.

A PROCEDURAL PATTERN. We are not recommending that any such debates should be overly formalized, but there are certain rules which should be established. Typically, there is a chairman appointed in advance, and there are two teams with each team generally consisting of two speakers. A schedule of debates can be established and mimeographed for distribution early in the semester. One debate a week should be sufficient. This will give each student an opportunity to debate twice and to be a chairman once. If possible, it seems advisable to have a student be on the affirmative team once and on the negative once. Coeducational debating is even more interesting than dividing the sexes, although for certain topics such a division provides for natural rivalries between the sexes. Students can be allowed to select the topics, and, if possible, they should be coordinated with current lectures and discussions. The teacher can use his judgment to prevent one team from being stacked against another, as unevenness of ability tends to destroy interest in the actual debate. It is fun sometimes to hear a student debating against a position which everyone knows he accepts in everyday life. The quality of the debate depends, of course, on the ability of the speakers and the preparation which they have made. Typically, the quality of the debates improved markedly during the semester, as students learn from their own experience and that of their classmates.

Usually in a debate each team has two constructive speeches and two rebuttal speeches. This procedure was modified for the typical fifty-minute class period by eliminating one of the rebuttal speeches from each team's format. The suggested time schedule, therefore, would be as follows:

1. First affirmative—7 minutes.
2. First negative—7 minutes.
3. Second affirmative—7 minutes.
4. Second negative—7 minutes.
5. Negative rebuttal—5 minutes.
6. Affirmative rebuttal—5 minutes.

Such a format would consume approximately thirty-eight minutes of a fifty-minute class period, allowing a bit of time at the beginning of class for organization and some time at the end for the gathering of analyses from the class members. These analyses serve a most useful purpose, since most students are anxious to have a critical appraisal of their efforts. Such appraisals may be gathered by the instructor upon the completion of the debate and read anonymously, even though signed. At this point the teacher may also give his assessment of the efforts of both teams.

The students not involved in the debate may serve as judges as well by recording their decisions on each appraisal sheet. The team that debates best should win. If the affirmative does what the proposition requires, it should win. The decision should be based on whether the affirmative has shown that it is advisable to adopt the proposed plan, or whether the negative has refuted the plan. It should be stressed that the judges (the students and the teacher) can base their final vote only on the material presented by the debaters—material which seems to be reasonable proof.[1]

If a team violates the rules of debate, there is a penalty of a sort. If, for example, one side introduces new constructive arguments during its rebuttal period, the judges are obligated to ignore any such evidence. Hence, this side has merely wasted its time thereby weakening its total case.

A sample of a recommended appraisal sheet (regular 8½"x11" mimeograph paper torn in half) is as follows:

JUDGES' APPRAISAL SHEET

Date: Dec. 10, 196–

Debate Topic: Resolved that departments of physical, health, and recreation education should claim that their programs develop desirable personality traits.

Affirmative—Jim Beale

1. I like your sense of humor.
2. You seem to be off the topic much of the time in your discussion of personnel.
3. Your points are good, but you take too long to develop them. They lose their punch.
4. Lots of illustrations, but what are they illustrating?
5. Your affirmative talk would be greatly improved if you had a few dynamic points to make and showed more organization.

Rebuttal

1. This was much better than your opening talk. You had a few good arguments to use against Garth, and you spoke easily with a fair amount of emphasis.

Loser—**B**⁻ Grade

Negative—Garth Poston

1. I like the way you established your stand at the outset.
2. Your start was good, but you seemed to run downhill in your discussion on recreation.
3. There were times when I wasn't sure which side you were on.
4. The citing of several good studies to prove your case would have been better than listing a large number briefly.

Rebuttal

1. Good delivery—you had everyone sitting up and listening! But I think we could do without the snide remarks at your opponent.

Winner—**B** Grade

---

[1] Certain of this material has been adapted from Musgrave, George McCoy, *Competitive Debate,* 3rd ed. (New York: The H. W. Wilson Company, 1957), chaps. i and iii.

The efforts of the other two participants can be recorded by the judges on the other side of the appraisal sheet. Obviously, if the usual debate format has been shortened, only one speaker will be rated on his effort at refutation. Each team usually decides for itself who will give the rebuttal speech, but both team members get together on which points they will stress.

The actual proposition to be debated should be worded as a proposed policy, and the affirmative is required to support a definite, specific action by a person or group. The topic should not be one-sided, and it should be interesting to the majority of the listeners. Be careful to insure that the topic expresses one main idea clearly.

The affirmative should make a sensible definition of the various terms included in the topic. This does not mean that the negative must accept this definition. They may give their own interpretation, but they should do this at the first opportunity. If they seem to agree on the affirmative's interpretation of the question at the outset, they can't object to it later on. The judges have to accept the interpretation that makes the most sense to them.

The next obligation of the affirmative is to demonstrate that the proposed policy or plan would be desirable if adopted. They can't be expected to prove that the necessary approval for any plan could be obtained. They should be careful to stay within the limits of the topic and not to recommend too much, since the burden of proof rests with them. The negative has to show the loopholes and defects of the plan. If they can show that the disadvantages of such a proposal outweigh the advantages, they have a good chance to win. Remember that any counterplan offered by the negative must be proved to a certain extent as well.

Logic and evidence are important in debating. Judges may not agree themselves with a team's arguments, but they have an obligation to assess fairly how well the various speakers make their points. The debaters, also, should be scrupulously honest in the presentation of their facts. If a speaker quotes any remarks of his opponent, they should be accurate.

The first affirmative speaker addresses his audience, explains the proposal or plan, lists its advantages over the present situation and discusses each, and then summarizes his position by enumerating them again. He may include a few crucial questions that his opponent should answer.

The first negative speaker then lists his team's objections to the proposed plan and discusses each of the claimed defects. It may be well to summarize the defects briefly after discussing them. Then he may wish to refute the various advantages that the first affirmative speaker has given for the plan. Obviously, he should attack his opponent's strongest points first. Finally, he can conclude his talk by reiterating the disadvantages that he mentioned at the outset.

The second affirmative speaker has a somewhat more difficult task than his teammate. Initially, he may reiterate the advantages offered by the proposed plan by listing them in order. But then he has to try to repair the damage that the first negative speaker has done by rebuilding his arguments. After this, he may wish to refute some of the disadvantages mentioned by the previous negative speaker. If he has time, he should conclude by restating the advantages of his proposal again in as favorable a light as possible.

The second negative speaker follows the pattern of the second affirmative speaker almost exactly, except that he is, of course, on the other side. He lists the objections, strengthens them if necessary, lists them briefly in outline form, refutes the claimed benefits of the plan, and finally summarizes the defects once again.

The speaker chosen for the rebuttal speech plays a key role. The negative rebuttal speaker tells about the defects of the affirmative proposal and then tells how the advantages explained by the affirmative speakers have been refuted. If his teammate immediately preceding him left anything important out of his argument, this speaker fills in the gaps. Following this, he explains how his team negated the purported advantages of the affirmative plan. Lastly, he lists the disadvantages of the affirmative plan as strongly as he can.

The *affirmative rebuttal speaker,* the last speaker of the debate, begins by outlining the advantages of the proposed plan over the presently prevailing situation. He tells how the points made by the negative speakers were refuted and fills in any possible loopholes in the affirmative team's arguments. He then summarizes the benefits of the new proposition, explains how the alleged defects were refuted, and finishes by listing the advantages of the new plan strongly. The final talks of each side should combine refutation and summarization; the only time anything new should be added is when some direct question has been left unanswered.

Twenty-five Suggested Debatable Topics

1. Resolved that physical education should be required at all educational levels.
2. Resolved that the field of physical education should change its name to sports education.
3. Resolved that community recreation programs should operate on a self-sustaining basis.
4. Resolved that sex education should be taught coeducationally as part of high-school health-instruction programs.

5. Resolved that the board of education is the best agency to administer a community recreation program.

6. Resolved that the program of professional preparation for teachers of physical, health, and recreation education should be lengthened to five years at the college level.

7. Resolved that the city child should receive a longer and more intensive program of physical, health, and recreation education than the country child.

8. Resolved that interscholastic and intercollegiate athletic programs should generally receive less emphasis.

9. Resolved that parks and recreation should be combined under one administrative head in the community.

10. Resolved that body-building through weight-training should be an integral part of every physical-education program.

11. Resolved that post-season tournaments and play-offs should be available for all high-school and college athletes.

12. Resolved that women's physical education should be given greater emphasis.

13. Resolved that coaches should have a specific rule prohibiting smoking and drinking by varsity squad members.

14. Resolved that the budgetary account for intramural sports and voluntary physical-recreation activities should approximate the size of the account for interscholastic athletics.

15. Resolved that departments of physical, health, and recreation education should claim that their programs develop desirable character and personality traits.

16. Resolved that a student's scholastic average should have no bearing on his athletic eligibility.

17. Resolved that military training is not an adequate substitute for required physical education.

18. Resolved that contact sports should be eliminated from high-school programs because of the athletic injury problem.

19. Resolved that interschool athletic competition should be abolished at the junior-high-school level.

20. Resolved that athletic competition at the college level shall no longer be considered amateur sport.

21. Resolved that summer playground programs are typically far too heavily oriented to physical-recreation activities.

22. Resolved that health instruction belongs in every high-school curriculum as a required subject.

23. Resolved that a minimum set of physical-fitness standards should be required for graduation from all levels of public education for students free from serious medical defects.

24. Resolved that a varsity team member should be excused from required physical-education classes during his sport's regular season.

25. Resolved that community recreation programs should promote intercommunity sports' competitions.

Appendix B

Several Recommended Types of Examinations and Term Papers

The following is a three-hour final examination that was used on several occasions in an undergraduate philosophy course in physical, health, and recreation education. It can be adapted in a number of ways or individual questions may be used.

UNIVERSITY OF _____

Final Examination—May 196__

Time: 3 hours   Intramural

PHRE 450

Philosophy of Physical, Health, and Recreation Education

Preliminary Instructions:
In planning this examination it seemed to be eminently practical to conduct this your last examination in physical, health, and recreation education in a

different way. The idea is to give you the opportunity to extemporize, to correlate, to explain, and to justify your various ideas and beliefs.

Imagine that you have just boarded a train going from Chicago to Des Moines. It's dinner time; so, you decide to go to the diner. The steward seats you next to a dignified, prosperous looking gentleman and across from an elderly couple. During the course of the table conversation you mention that you are planning to teach physical education and coach in a high school in the fall. You learn that the man next to you is a self-made industrialist who owns a small factory in the Chicago suburbs. The couple across the table own a farm near Des Moines. They are returning home from a short vacation with relatives in Chicago. They ask you some questions. One answer leads to another question, and so on. You are actually involved in a defense of your field.

Remember the need for keeping in mind the background and interests of the people to whom you are talking.

1. "So you're going to be a physical-training instructor? Well, I hope you run a better program than I had in school. We spent most of our time (what there was of it!) marching, doing calisthenics, and jumping around on iron horses (or whatever they called them). It was pretty dull. Do you still do that sort of thing in your classes?"   *(From the businessman)*

2. "Do you coach basketball too? Seems to me it's kind of foolish having kids running up and down a gym floor bouncing a ball. I figure my boy would be a lot better off helping me around the farm after school. I'm not as young as I used to be, and he'll get all the exercise he needs working around home."   *(From the farmer)*

3. "My daughter Sally doesn't talk very much about her 'phys-ed' class in school. They don't get to use the gym very much especially after school. Besides, there are always too many girls on the floor. She hates to take showers there too, because there's not enough time; there's not enough privacy; and she can't get her hair dry. Honestly, I wish someone would help her stand a little straighter. She's tall and stoops over all the time. I keep telling her she's round-shouldered, but I can't make much impression on her. No one seems to pay much attention to that. Don't they teach you about that? Why don't they help her with what she needs?"   *(From the farmer's wife)*

4. "There's a lot of talk about federal aid to education lately. Frankly, I'm not convinced that it's such a good idea anyhow. Would they be using any such money to build gymnasiums and swimming pools rather than the classrooms which are really needed? Something has got to be done about taxes; they're killing me!"   *(From the businessman)*

5. "I read in the paper the other night that Des Moines is using over two mills of its tax money for recreation. They've started a lot of those so-called community centers in the schools at night. What's behind this evening business? Are the taxpayers going to have to foot the bill for all those people to play? Why should older folks with no young children pay for that?"   *(From the farmer)*

6. "My sister's little boy is playing in some baseball league where they seem to do nothing but try to copy big-league baseball players. She says that the coach yells at the kids all the time. When they win, he

isn't satisfied; when they lose everyone acts as though someone died. Do you think youngsters of his age should be encouraged to play a ball game under those conditions?"   *(From the farmer's wife)*

7. "Doesn't seem to me that we Americans can be very healthy. Somebody must be keeping all those companies that advertise on television in business. Why during the last war they rejected over one-third of our young men for service. And then my son Jim tells me they sometimes see football movies during their health classes. Frankly, he can't get very interested in watching the teacher draw pictures out of the book of the heart and lungs and all that stuff on the board. Why don't they teach him to eat proper food and not to smoke so much? Why don't they teach him something really useful in those health classes?"
(From the businessman)

8. "This high-school football seems to be nonsense to me. Jim Thompson's boy down the road hurt his knee last year, and they had to operate on it. The insurance didn't pay all the bills either. The boy wasn't able to help Jim with the haying last summer. No one seems to be helping him make it strong again either. Jim's beginning to wonder if his leg will ever be right again. I went to see one of those games last fall. One fellow hurt his shoulder real bad, a couple more were helped off with their ankles sprained or something, and another boy had three teeth knocked out. It doesn't seem to me that it's worth it. What do you think?"   *(From the farmer)*

9. "Last time I went to see Dr. Johnson I asked him about Sally going in those running races last year at the track meet. He said that people don't need strenuous exercise to be healthy. A person would think a doctor knows what he is talking about. Wouldn't you think so?"
(From the farmer's wife)

10. "A committee of the workers in my plant have been after me to hire a recreation director. I can't see why what they do on their own time is my business. I'm having enough trouble keeping the place in the black now. Besides, they'd probably be coming to work tired all the time. If they do go ahead with their plan to form a recreation committee, why can't my personnel man tell them what to do?"
(From the businessman)

11. "I was reading in the paper the other day that the President says the average kid isn't rugged enough. But I don't see them doing much about it as far as most of the youngsters are concerned. Why don't they send them out to work on the farms and the roads when school's out? We'll make them rugged. But, oh no, nowadays kids don't want to do anything that's hard. What's this country coming to anyhow?"
(From the farmer)

12. "At the parent-teachers' meeting last spring I heard they were going to have to pay Miss Jones $6,200 to keep her next year. I think she's a good teacher, but that's an awful lot of money. Why my oldest boy Bob is only making $63 a week working in town, and he has to support a family. He doesn't get all summer off either." *(From the farmer's wife)*

13. "My son Jim got all A's and B's in his subjects last year, but a C in 'phys-ed' kept him off the honor roll. Why I was fit to be tied, and

so was his mother. I can see giving the kids a little exercise to keep them from getting flabby, but who ever heard of giving the same sort of a grade for playing games?"   *(From the businessman)*

14. "My brother who lives in the city has a boy who has been doing a lot of running. He's a good one too. Some fellow from the university came over to see him about a month ago. He wants Joe to go to school there; he says it won't cost the boy a cent, right down to his spending money. My brother hasn't been doing too well lately, and it would be a big help to him. But Joe would like to be a doctor, and this fellow says his grades aren't good enough. He wants him to enroll in the 'phys-ed' course instead. Does that sound right to you?"
                    (From the farmer)

15. "My husband and I were shocked when Sally told us the things they were talking about in her health class. Can you imagine that they were actually talking about sexual relationships and intimate parts of the body. Sally said she was so embarrassed she didn't say a word. Those are things that a mother tells her daughter about. I called that teacher up and gave her a piece of my mind. Do you know what she said? She said that the school has to help with the job, because many parents aren't up on their facts. What do you think of that for an answer? Well, young man, I suspect we'd better let you eat your dinner. It's getting cold, and the train is due in the city in about five minutes!"
                    (From the farmer's wife)

A second type of final examination that has been used is of take-home variety. This may also be assigned as a term paper in a philosophy or principles course. The plan is to ask the student to submit his or her own personal philosophy of life and/or religion, philosophy of education, and philosophy of physical, health, and recreation education. This is, of course, a highly personal matter, and care should be taken to preserve the anonymity of each paper. We suggest a brief outline for the student to follow, although we never insist that any format be followed rigidly. Typically, the student presents in his own words the metaphysics, epistemology, logic, and axiology of the philosophical tendency to which he subscribes; some of the basic concepts of his philosophy of religion; the general orientation of his educational position including aims and objectives and educational methodology he would employ; and the implications for physical, health, and recreation education from his particular educational philosophy. The importance of logic and systematization is stressed, insofar as this may be possible for the individual.

The following paper is a sample selected from many such papers that have been submitted and is presented with the permission of the author. We do not wish to imply that we are necessarily agreeing with *this* philosophical position, but it was thought that one sample would be helpful. Space does not permit the presentation of papers representing each of the beliefs discussed in the text.

MY PHILOSOPHY

by
George B. Lewis
Dearborn, Michigan

Philosophy of Life and Religion

For a man to state his philosophy of life, he must first realize that it is not an easy task. A true philosophy cannot be arrived at through several timely remarks. A philosophy embodies many facets of life and should be arranged in an orderly fashion. It is not something to be gathered at a particular moment; it is the revelation of years of living during which certain principles have been formulated and followed either knowingly or otherwise. It may be likened unto a type of superstructure within the life of a man. It reaches out through his physical and spiritual makeup to fashion him into the type of person he really is.

I might compare a philosophy of life to a gigantic building—let us say a hospital—which is symbolic of the stages in complete sorrow or joy. Within this site one may discover many wings containing rooms in which the varying emotions of joy and sorrow are experienced daily. Leading to these rooms are many and varied corridors. A philosophy of life may well correspond to these hallways which are the physical facilities leading to areas of activity. These hallways, though not physical and tangible, are facilities through which man travels the pathways of life. This entire physical structure must have a firm foundation in order to be truly serviceable. A philosophy must also have a foundation which reaches deep within the life of man to be considered sound. Such a foundation varies in the life of each human being both in depth and in type.

For me, this basis of life is a religious belief which is deeply rooted, thereby enabling me to live the kind of life which I envision as a good life. Ideally, religion means to me, very simply, a way of life. I have accepted as a fact that this world as we have known it down through the ages was created by a Power more almighty than a human could ever conceive. This belief was doubtlessly instilled in me through childhood experiences in my church and in my family. This, I believe, is the basis for everyone's early religious convictions. Our particular religious faith is even chosen for us by our family. These beliefs may be altered as time passes, and reasoning becomes a greater influence in our lives.

In my case this influence was Protestantism. I was taught early that my religion was based on the Doctrine of the Trinity. This, of course, is explained by the concept of the Father, Son, and Holy Ghost. This philosophy of religion held even greater significance for me as I grew older.

After my high-school years life became quite realistic. There were many complexities of which I had never dreamed. I began to realize what had been meant by the educational term *life adjustment*. Somehow up to this point I had managed to keep my head above water. Now, with an eye toward the future and an ear tuned to the past, I began to wonder where I was going now that I had arrived at this plateau.

This problem was answered for me through the presence of something intangible which influenced my every thought and action, and I wondered if this might not be true for every person. This conclusion solidly substantiated my belief in the Trinitarian Doctrine of God, the Creator of all, Jesus Christ, the Son of God through whom God demonstrated to man His omnipotence, and the Holy Spirit, that force and still, small voice within man which leads him in time of trouble and inspires him in his everyday life. One other step occurred in my religious life. I committed myself to the Presbyterian Church. This, I believe, was in some ways inconsequential; however, a man has to be happy in his religious affiliation. My convictions as to the physical and spiritual makeup of a church are compatible with those of the Presbyterian Church. I prefer a religious service which appeals to the intellect as well as to the emotions. And I prefer a church which is not wholly dominated by its pastor. The Presbyterian Church is governed by a general assembly; yet, each individual church is governed by its own session which is elected by the congregation. This type of organization appeals to me because of my convictions regarding democracy. The Presbyterian Church has a strong church school which exerts an influence on the life of an individual from the nursery through the rest of his life. The church-school curriculum is geared toward making church life and family living as compatible as possible. Church school is also a preparatory exeperience for adjustment to public school life.

The Presbysterian Church is active not only in spreading Christianity throughout our nation and other nations of the earth, but is also deeply concerned with the formal education of people in all walks of life. It is gravely concerned with the plight of persons not so fortunate as to be as well nourished, clothed, and sheltered as we in most sections of the United States. For these, and many other reasons, I call myself a Presbyterian. Perhaps I could be equally as happy as a member of some other church of the Protestant faith. I have often wondered whether we, who believe in Protestantism, are so far apart in our creed that there is a need for so many denominations. Through some sort of a unified effort, I believe we could arrive at certain goals in a much more orderly and effective fashion.

With a basis established in my life in the form of a religious belief, it follows naturally that many other basic beliefs have arisen from this central idea. I feel that within man there is a soul which is God's Holy Spirit and that this governs his thought and actions. I cannot conceive of this soul eventually ending up in any other state than immortality. Even though our physical bodies, the earthly homes for our real selves—the soul—will wear out in time, I believe that our souls continue to live in a state which has been determined by our earthly thoughts and actions. I believe that good and evil are present on this earth, at least in the choices made by man. I believe, also, that each person has been created as an individual with a power to think and reason. How he uses this power is a matter of grave personal concern, and I choose to believe that this is where the influence of a Being more powerful and more perfect than man makes His presence known—not forcibly, however. Each person must be the aggressor; he must feel this need and seek guidance which he receives, if he so wills, in the form of the *good* thought or action. I do not feel that a person is to be condemned for a wrong choice occasionally. Even Simon Peter, Jesus' leading disciple, is reported to have denied his Lord thrice. Evil or wrong may be erased through truthful repentance and prayer.

I have been influenced by a quotation each Sunday morning that appears on the cover of our church bulletin and order of service. It says, "Enter to worship, depart to serve." I interpret this thought as meaning that our church life should carry over into our daily lives in our dealings with other people. The church is *not* a place to go each Sunday morning for social and possible economic reasons. The sanctuary must serve only as an assembly facility for the worship of God. Those ideas and truths which touch our lives through this facility must be reflected in our daily living. I believe they are reflected most widely if we develop a sincere love for our fellow man. This feeling must encompass our relationship with all mankind as well as with our immediate families. A man who is more concerned with himself than with others cannot truly call himself a Christian in my estimation. Such a man could actually be embarking on the road to self-destruction, as he could soon develop a type of pride and self-love that could well place him above reproach.

This thought of love of mankind leads directly into my beliefs on the family relationship of man. To be truly effective, I believe a man must realize the satisfaction derived from a happy marriage and, if God so wills, the privilege of parenthood as well. Another step toward the ideally happy life would be to know the pleasure of being the father of a boy and a girl. I have been blessed with this situation, and not a day passes that I do not feel grateful. I believe a man should seek a mate whom he respects and who shares a similar background. If both persons share similar religious beliefs and mutual respect is present, the years will be accompanied by a deep devotion which has a carry-over value into our daily dealings with others.

A philosophy cannot be painted all black or all white. Life is not all sublime happiness. Man is confronted daily with tasks and problems which must be solved. How he meets and adjusts to these situations largely determines his state of happiness. Most people are in a constant pursuit of happiness in addition to other endeavors. The accompanying state of mind varies with each person depending on the values he stresses in his daily living. Believing that man must have a general plan for his earthly life, I feel as well that he should not project so far into the future that he neglects the present. The little things accomplished in the present go a long way toward fulfilling one's role in life. What is this role? It varies with each human being. I do not believe that I am any less a Christian, or even less effective, because I am a physical educator and a football coach rather than a minister or a missionary. Each person has an interest and a potential to exploit, and through sincere effort he can be happy and successful in his chosen career. In this career, be it physician or ditch-digger, or be it missionary or professional athlete, we must be guided not by a self-love but by a genuine love of mankind. And in so doing, each person we meet will be enriched, and not harmed, through this chance relationship. Through this type of devotion to mankind comes a satisfaction in life which is not so likely to be influenced by materialistic gain. I feel our needs will somehow be met through on honest effort on our part to be humanly compatible, stressing those values which are consistent with our individual philosophies. In simpler terms, to me, happiness is a by-product of the Christian way of life. It evolves as we share a full life with our neighbor.

In concluding this section of my philosophical statement, I wish to stress that man, being human, needs something specific on which to base his beliefs as well as his spiritual guidance through prayer and worship. This has been presented to us in the form of the Ten Commandments, a moral code to live by; and the teachings of Jesus, a human created in the image of God, as portrayed in the New Testament scriptures.

Philosophy of Education

Although a man's philosophy of life may be theoretical in nature, it should be practical in that it is workable for him and for those with whom he comes into contact. With this thought, I should like to share certain of my beliefs on education in general.

I believe the education of the child has its beginnings long before we in the school system have our first opportunity to attempt to mold this young mind. Education, then, has its origin in the home. A child blessed with loving parents, in the deepest meaning of the term, is well on his way to becoming a willing "receptacle" for truth and knowledge. Religious influence and parental influence lay the bases for a profitable school experience.

A child's education is also affected by the type of persons he is able to lay claim to as *his* teachers throughout this educational process. This, I believe, is equally as important as the actual subject matter. A dedicated teacher, well versed in his field and mature in mind and action with the fire of enthusiasm about him, will kindle interest in the minds of his pupils. This interest plus effort results in knowledges and attitudes gained. Of course, heredity has played its part in this process already, but the environment, which the educator controls to a considerable extent, is a key factor in the educative process. I see no reason why this process should not be repeated each year in the formal education of the student. It is unfortunate that each teacher with whom the student comes in contact will not be the ideal teacher; however, I feel that it is a common occurrence for a student to say that he was influenced immensely by some educator in his life.

As to the curriculum itself, I think it should be as enriched as the resources of the community will allow. Some people look at certain courses and remark, "Of what practical use are they? Let's rid our curriculum of such fads and frills as ————." I say, "Each course, each seeming fad and frill, has some value, and since each individual personality is different, there is someone who will appreciate and grow intellectually in some way through having experienced this course or activity."

I do believe that we are stressing some courses today to such an extent that others are being neglected. I am thinking specifically of mathematics and science. These courses are due their rightful place in our curriculum, but I do not wish to see them receive emphasis out of proportion to the social sciences or the humanities (especially English). I feel that communication should be the backbone of educational progress. To speak and write fluently is basic to the transmission of knowledge. The times have placed a great burden on education, but it is not as though it were the first time a crisis has occurred. Throughout history, periods marked by relative stability have changed through some upheaval usually caused by man's creative thought and action. At the present it is how to best cope with the age of the missile. I agree that we must advance in this field through the encouragement of outstanding minds in mathematics and science. But we should not lose sight of the fact that to know is to understand, and true understanding of ourselves and others is a crucial need today.

Sometimes I wonder what great beliefs would be engendered through a completely honest effort to help all people understand their neighbors in other lands. We should stress other languages, other customs, and other ways of life. From the early primary years through college, international understanding should be an objective of our schools. I am assuming once again that we can develop teachers who can really do a selling job.

Finally, I feel that the education of an individual is a never-ending process. I believe that we should do everything possible to salvage each human mind. Maturity often brings intellectual curiosity, and perhaps even a friend, as well as a teacher, will be able to ignite the flame that will make a mediocre mind more competent. Through the educative process, a human mind can develop the power to perceive those values—the eternal values—which can benefit the individual and the society in which he lives.

Philosophy of Physical, Health, and Recreation Education

A basic principle governing my approach to physical education is the belief that man's body and mind cannot be considered as entities in relation to education. Education of the whole person, while no original thought with me, is one of my fundamental guides in building a philosophy of physical education.

Each boy and girl should have directed physical activities, even in the early primary years. I believe the program should be broad and varied—once again in line with my general education philosophy. This program should at all times be geared to the total readiness of the child. Each student should have the benefit of finding out where his physical interests lie. Sincere effort by the learner may uncover a vast new field for him, which he may formerly have labeled undesirable through lack of understanding. The physical educator, with his knowledge and experience, should guide the student along this path in his total educational development. He, as an educator, must understand all aspects of the individual and his nature. He must strive to live those ideas which he stresses. The wonderful world of athletics, including those engaged in it professionally, sets an example for more youngsters than any other single area of life, in my opinion. Believing this, and realizing the many intangibles to be gained through group physical participation, I consider my position in life a truly gratifying one. In addition to teaching physical actvity, I feel that the physical educator should seek every opportunity to stress healthful living. I do not believe, however, that we should take time too frequently from the activity program for health instruction.

At times I feel somewhat authoritarian in my approach. Along with the total physical-education program, I still visualize the necessity for purposeful gymnastics, calisthenics, and, more recently, weight-resistance exercises. This type of thinking gradually lost favor after the turn of the century, but somehow in times of national stress many of us leap on the bandwagon of physical fitness, which should probably be referred to as *total fitness*. I am perturbed when I see a gymnasium with no provision for these activities. I don't want these activities to supplant the program as we know it today, but I do feel very definitely that they have value. I have always considered the ideal physical-education program to be one in which no one aspect was stressed unduly. If a certain phase of the program become unwieldy, then, in my opinion, the program is in need of revision. I believe this should be true in all facets of life, although I am interested in excellence. It takes honest self-evaluation occasionally to demonstrate this imbalance to ourselves.

I believe it is highly important that each person find some physical activity in which he can experience some success. Success in physical activity will undoubtedly encourage participation in carry-over sports in the postschool years in community recreation programs.

I believe that regular "cleansing" of the body through physical activity might well replace nerve medicines, the variety of tranquilizers, and the many patent medicines which now evidently play such a key role in the American way of life. A good portion of the adult population in America needs to re-experience the values to be gained through regular physical activity.

Conclusion

I believe each man must approach his philosophy of life with caution. I feel that a person cannot really label himself as 100 per cent in agreement with one specific philosophy. If I were to name a philosophy in which my beliefs may be mainly categorized, I would choose *idealism*.

In my opinion, a philosophy is not a stable phenomenon. I believe that a central idea, a basis for life, remains fairly constant. In my case, I feel this constant to be my religious belief. As the years pass, and as knowledges are gained, my viewpoint will probably vary accordingly. For this reason I believe that each man needs to sit quietly from time to time and review the basic ideas guiding his life. This should not be done for personal gain, but for the service that it is possible for an individual to offer others. My conception, therefore, of the beautiful, full life is one in which self-love is not the dominant factor. Life, the good life, must be outgoing, guided by a central idea, and dedicated with a sincere devotion to all mankind.

A professional educator is usually concerned about the knowledges, skills, and competencies that a prospective teacher may have acquired through his experience with him. These are often difficult to measure. Attitude development sometimes seems almost impossible to ascertain. A course in the philosophy of physical, health, and recreation education cannot help but be concerned with the study of values as it applies to life and to education. The teacher might wish to experiment with *several types of pre-tests* that could be administered to a class at the beginning of a semester and then repeated again at the end. One interesting scale for measuring the dominant interests in personality (relating to values) has been developed over the past thirty years. It is called *Study of Values* by Allport, Vernon, and Lindzey and is available through the Houghton Mifflin Company in Boston. The six categories of values included are as follows: theoretical; economic; aesthetic; social; political; and religious. Women, for example, are more religious, social, and aesthetic than men. Educators tend to rate higher in the theoretical, aesthetic, and social values, and correspondingly lower in the other three categories.

Another more traditional type of pre-test and post-test could be developed by an instructor and used to measure what changes if any had occurred in the individual student's beliefs. Ideally, such a test might be administered to a class on the occasion of their first session together. The instructor should be careful to point out to the students that this particular test has absolutely nothing to do with the grades that they will get for the course eventually. They might be asked to put their initials only on the back of the test for later identification purposes by them only. Then the instructor could tabulate the results in a general way and report back to the class the second time they meet. He might say to them that eighteen students appeared to be largely idealistic in their beliefs, fifteen could be identified mainly with either naturalistic realism or scholastic realism, fourteen seemed to be typically experimentalistic, and eight were so evenly divided among the three positions that no distinction could be made. *Such a test could be administered again at the end of the course.* On this occasion, the students might be asked to complete the test and *then* to identify their own pre-tests (which might be spread on a few tables upside down so that they could find their own initials). After each student makes his own comparisons, the instructor could then question them to ascertain generally what changes were made in the course of the semester. We have found that the results are usually very interesting. Actually, it isn't necessary to make such a test very long. A series of ten or fifteen questions can be read, assimilated, and answered in about thirty minutes. Questions might cover such topics as metaphysical position, theory of value, definition of education, definition of religion, content of physical-education program, teaching methodology preferred, place of health education, and theory of recreation. A few sample questions are as follows:

Instructions: Read the statements below carefully and indicate by an (X) that statement in each question which seems closest to your own personal belief. Keep in mind that how you answer these questions will have no influence on your grade, and that it is important for your own professional development that you make every effort to reflect your own belief as accurately as possible.

I. Metaphysical Position

a. ____ Nature is an emergent evolution. The world is characterized by activity and change. Rational man has developed in the process of organic evolution, and the world is yet incomplete.

b. ____ Mind as experienced by all men is basic and real. The entire universe is mind essentially. Man is more than just a body; he possesses a soul, and such possession makes him of a higher order than all other creatures on earth.

c. ____ "The world exists in itself, apart from our desires and knowledges. . . . The universe is made up of real substantial entities, existing in themselves and ordered to one another by extramental relations. . . . To be is not the same as to be known. . . ." Man lives within this world of cause and effect, and he simply cannot make things happen independent of it.

II. Definition of Education

a. _____ "A philosophy holding that the aim of education is the acquisition of verified knowledge of the environment and adjustment to the environment; recognizes the value of content as well as of the activities involved in learning. and takes into account the external determinants of human behavior."

b. _____ Through education the developing organism becomes what it latently is. All education may be said to have a religious significance, which means that there is a moral imperative on education. As man's mind strives to realize itself, there is the possibility of realization of the Absolute within the individual mind. Education should aid the child to adjust to the basic realities (the spiritual ideals of truth, beauty, and goodness) that the history of the race has furnished us.

c. _____ The general aim of education is more education. "Education in the broadest sense can be nothing less than the changes made in human beings by their experience." With such an approach, ends become means in a continuing process as students receive experience in coping with an ever-changing environment.

III. Values in Physical Education

a. _____ I am much more interested in promoting the concept of total fitness rather than physical fitness alone. I believe that physical education should be an integral subject in the curriculum. Students should have the opportunity to select a wide variety of useful activities, many of which should help to develop social intelligence. The activities offered should bring natural impulses into play. To me, physical-education classes and intramural sports are more important to the large majority of students than interscholastic or intercollegiate sports and deserve priority if conflict arises over budgetary allotment, staff available, and use of facilities. I can, however, give full support to team experiences in competitive sports, because they can be vital educational experiences if properly conducted.

b. _____ I am extremely interested in individual personality development. I believe in education of the physical, and yet I believe in education through the physical as well. Nevertheless, I do see physical education as important but occupying "a lower rung on the educational ladder." I believe that desirable objectives for physical education would include the development of health and physical fitness, education for leisure (outside of the regular curriculum usually), personality development, and development of responsible citizenship and group participation. In competitive sport, I believe that the transfer-of-training theory is in operation in connection with the development of desirable personality traits, but sports participation should always be a means not an end.

c. _____ I believe that education of the physical should have primary emphasis in our field. I am concerned with the "development of the maximum of physical vigor," and such development has priority over the recreational aspects of physical education. Many people, who believe in the same educational philosophy as I do, recommend that all students in public schools should have a daily period designed to strengthen their muscles and develop their bodily coordination. Physical education, of course, must yield precedence to intellectual education. I give qualified approval to interscholastic athletics, since they do help with the learning of sportsmanship and desirable social behavior if properly conducted. But all these things, with the possible exception of physical training, are definitely extracurricular and not part of the regular curriculum.

IV. Values in School Health Education

a. _____ I believe that man should be a rugged animal, and this standard should apply to girls as well as to boys. Health, as I see it, is a primary objective of education, and the child needs health instruction. The success of the school-health-education program depends on the degree of cooperation among home, school, and community agencies. An educated person must understand the difference between health and disease, and he must know how to protect and improve his own health, that of his dependents, and that of the community. As I see it, the program of school health, physical education, and recreation education may be administered as a unified program within a school system. I believe that natural types of exercise promote sound mental health. All these aspects of the total program may be coordinated because they are related in many ways. Through unity, these subdivisions, which are basically related, could probably serve the needs of school children and youth much more effectively than is the case so often at the present. To be truly effective, school-health education must be concerned with helping the individual to lead a rich, full life. This means more than providing a health service so that students can maintain minimum health needed to "pursue intellectual work with the least amount of strain." Health should be defined positively—as that quality which enables us *to live most and serve best.*

b. _____ I believe in "the development of the maximum of physical vigor and health." There is no question in my mind but that the school should provide "an atmosphere conducive to both emotional and physical health." Furthermore, "knowledge about the principles of physical and emotional health is a proper ingredient of the curriculum." I believe that the community does have a responsibility to provide "clinical facilities for therapy, . . . but this does not mean that they are part of the school program or curriculum any more than are the boilers in the heating system." I assert that the home must have the complete responsibility for assisting youth to acquire desirable health habits—that is, unless we wish to establish some form of community youth organizations to accomplish this end. "The health of adolescents is for the most part too good and their sources of energy are too great to make health problems real to them." In a similar vein, sex education is certainly not a proper function of the school. Is it not logical that teaching the means for securing the health values would be incomplete until the perspective from which they are viewed is also taught? This perspective is found only in the humanities—in literature, art, religion, and philosophy. In summary, therefore, every person needs a basic core of knowledge in order to lead a human life, and this includes the teaching of health knowledge. This is consistent with the cental purpose of the school—the development of the individual's rational powers.

c. _____ I believe that health is a basic value of human living and that the truly educated individual should be physically fit, should live "near the maximum of his efficiency," and should have "a body which is the ready servant of his will." But even though I believe health is a basic value for all the others, I would have to place it at the bottom of the hierarchy of educational values. Worship must be placed at the top, because through it man is brought "into conscious relation to the infinite spirit of the universe." Thus it (health) would not be included in a listing of the essential studies of the curriculum except where it would probably be included incidentally under biology. However, I am interested in "building wholeness of mind and body, . . . the development of strong, healthy bodies, good habits of mental and physical health, . . . and the right start in the teaching of health, safety, and physical education to children." There is no question in my mind that educators should work for a larger measure of integration in the individual by promoting "more intensive study of the body, leading to scientific knowledge: anatomy, body chemistry, hygiene, physiology, etc.; and attention to sex characteristics and habits, leading to a greater understanding of the place of sex in human life, with implications for hygiene." But such knowledge is made available to boys and girl, and young men and women, as a service program in the schools—a service is provided to man, and through this contribution to his health he is enabled to pursue higher educational goals.

V. *Values in Recreation (Education)*

a. _____ I am inclined to favor the adoption of the name *recreation education* for the field. I see advantages in a unified approach whereby the three specialized areas of health, physical education, and recreation (in schools) would provide a variety of experiences that will enable the individual to live a richer, fuller life through superior adjustment to his environment. I believe that education for the worthy use of leisure is basic to the curriculum of the school—a curriculum in which pupil growth, as defined broadly, is all important. Secondly, play shall be conducted in such a way that desirable moral growth will be fostered. Thirdly, overly organized sport competition is not true recreation, since the welfare of the individual is often submerged in the extreme emphasis which is so frequently placed on winning. I believe it is a mistake to confuse the psychological distinction between work and play with the traditional economic distinction that is generally recognized. All citizens should have ample opportunity to use their free time in a creative and fruitful manner. I do not condemn a person who watches others perform with a high level of skill in any of our cultural recreational activities, including sports, as long as the individual keeps such viewing in proper proportion in regard to the amount of time spent on life's many other activities.

b. _____ As I see it, work and play are typically sharply differentiated in life. Play serves a most useful purpose at recess or after school, but it should *not* be part of the regular curriculum. I believe that use of leisure is significant to the development of our culture, but I realize today that winning the "cold war" is going to take a lot more hard work and somewhat less leisure. I see leisure pursuits or experience as an opportunity to get relief from work while it serves a re-creative purpose in the life of man. The surplus-energy theory of play and recreation makes sense to me. So does the more recent bio-social theory of play—the idea that play helps the organism to achieve balance. I feel that the "play attitude" is missing almost completely in many organized sports. Play (and recreation) is, therefore, very important to me; I believe it should be liberating to the individual. People can develop their potentialities for wholesome hobbies through recreation. Furthermore, recreation can serve as a "safety valve" by the reduction of the psychic tensions which are evidently caused by so many of life's typical stresses. Even though play should *not* be considered as a basic part of the curriculum, we should not forget that it provides an "indispensable seasoning" to the good life. Extracurricular play and recreational activities and a sound general education should suffice to equip the student for leisure activities in our society.

c. _____ I believe that the role of play and recreation in the development of personality and the "perfectly integrated individual" is looming larger with each passing year and that it has not been fully understood or appreciated in the past. For this reason it seems quite logical to me that education should re-assess the contributions that recreation and play do make in the education of man. That there is a need for educational research along these lines is self-evident. I believe further that we should examine very closely any theories of play and recreation which grant educational possibilities to these activities of man. The self-expression theory of play suggests that man's chief need in life is to achieve the satisfaction and accomplishment of self-expression of one's own personality. Here is an explanation that seems to consider quite fully the conception of man as an organic unity—a total organism. I believe that man is a purposive being who is striving to achieve those values which are embedded in reality itself. To the extent that we can realize the eternal values through the choice of the right kinds of play and recreation without flouting the moral order in the world, we should be progressive enough to disregard a dualistic theory of work and play. Another difficulty that confronts us is differentiating between physical education and recreation. It would seem appropriate for the physical-, health-, and recreation-education teacher in schools and colleges to have a responsibility for *physical* recreation only; the meeting of all the other recreational needs and interests of boys and girls is his responsibility only indirectly as he works cooperatively with the recreation administrator (either within the school system or in the community) at all times. Recreation has developed to the point where it is now clearly one of our major social institutions. I believe that recreation can make a contribution to the development of an "integrated individual in an integrated society growing in the image of the integrated universe." Mankind today is actually faced with a "recreational imperative."

An instructor may well wish to ascertain what *knowledges* have been mastered by the student. For this purpose, quizzes and examinations may be given upon completion of various chapters or parts of the text during and at the end of the semester (or whatever calendar plan is in vogue). Essay questions, multiple-choice questions, completion questions, and matching questions can be developed as desired from the material by the individual instructor.

Glossary

Note: Many terms of a theological nature are omitted, because they are defined elsewhere. Certain philosophical terms are defined also at the end of the chapter designed to introduce the reader to philosophy.

Absolute: The term used to denote that which is final and complete within itself; it is frequently used as another term for God.

Absolutism: The doctrine that fundamental reality is fixed and unchanging; it refers also to the existence of power that is unconditional.

Abstract: A term which has no application to a particular, concrete object.

Aesthetics: The subdivision of that branch of philosophy known as axiology (theory of values) which treats the theories of the essential character of the beautiful.

Agnosticism: The belief that knowledge of the ultimate origin of the universe is impossible.

Altruism: The belief that man is best fulfilled on earth by devoting himself to the best interests of others.

Analysis: In philosophy, a procedure whereby an effort is made to come to some conclusions and to solve problems by reflective thought involving resolution to fundamental issues or parts.

Animism: The belief that all living things have souls; in some instances plants and stones, etc., are said to contain souls existing in a separate state.

Anthropomorphism: The conception of God as a being possessing human qualities.

A posteriori: This describes the type of reasoning which arrives at principles by generalizations from facts; hence, this describes that knowledge which is derived through sense-experience.

A priori: This describes the type of reasoning which assumes certain self-evident principles initially and then makes subsequent deductions independent of experience.

Asceticism: A practice of self-denial by means of which an individual hopes to discipline himself in order to reach higher spiritual levels.

✓ *Atheism:* The disbelief in a God or supreme power underlying the cosmos.

✓ *Atomism:* The theory that nature is composed of minute, indivisible, and indestructible particles.

✓ *Authoritarianism:* The theory that advocates obedience to indisputable authority (such as the Church) which certifies basic knowledge to man.

Axiology: The branch of philosophy which treats the general theory, nature, and kinds of value.

Axiom: In logic an axiom is a statement of a self-evident truth which has universal recognition.

Beauty: A term used to describe one or more characteristics or qualities in a person or thing which give pleasure and appeal to the aesthetic sense of the beholder.

✓ *Behaviorism:* The doctrine that generalizations about man's behavior should be based completely on an observation of his external behavior.

Categorical Imperative: A term used by Kant to describe the nature of moral law as he interpreted it; man should act in such a way as his reason indicates in order to arrive at universal laws of conduct.

Category: The arrangement and classification into a system of the objects of knowledge and thought; hence, a category becomes a fundamental concept or principle.

Causation: Those positive and/or negative conditions which produce an effect or event.

Concept: A mental image of a unifying nature which is formed by generalizing from particulars.

Cosmology: A subdivision of that branch of philosophy known as metaphysics which treats theories about the origin, nature, and development of the cosmos.

✓ *Creationism:* A theory concerning the origin of the universe which states that a Creative Cause was and is at work; hence, a category under cosmology (a subdivision of metaphysics).

✓ *Cynicism:* A type of philosophy founded in Greece about 400 B.C. which was characterized by the holder's exaltation of independence from the material world, its pleasures and conventions; hence, there was a strong tendency toward asceticism.

―――*Deduction:* A method of reasoning and/or problem solving which involves the drawing of inferences from the general to the specific.

p. 19 ✓ *Deism:* A belief in God as the Personality who established natural and moral laws, but who is quite separate from the universe (contrary to the position of Christianity).

Dialectic: A subdivision of logic; the process of reasoning which involves systematic analysis of conceptions which conflict in order to arrive at the truth.

✓ *Determinism:* A belief that individual behavior and natural events are predetermined because of antecedents; hence, man does not have complete freedom of will.

Dichotomy: A division of a class into two subheadings or entities (e.g., that man has a body and a soul).

Dilettantism: A superficial approach to some branch of knowledge or phase of life.

Dogma: A doctrine which has been stated formally and laid down authoritatively.

Double Aspect Theory: The theory that fundamental reality has two aspects—mind and body.

Dualism: The theory that the universe was founded on the basis of two irreducible elements such as good and evil, which are in opposition to each other.

Eclecticism: The practice of combining a variety of theories from different philosophical schools into a body of fairly compatible beliefs.

Egoism: The belief that furtherance of the individual's own interests is an acceptable approach for moral action; this motivation of conduct is a category under ethics.

Emergence Theory: The theory that mind is a relative newcomer on the world scene and will undoubtedly develop further in the many centuries that lie ahead; hence, it is not the same as the body.

Empiricism: The theory that man's knowledge originates in experience and not from theories about facts; hence, knowledge is a posteriori and comes from sense experience.

Epicureanism: A hedonistic approach to living whereby man seeks to satisfy his desire for a variety of sensual pleasures.

Epiphenomenalism: The theory that the mind functions as part of the brain and that it does not influence occurrences; hence, it does accompany bodily activity.

Epistemology: That branch of philosophy which treats the nature and possibility of the acquisition of knowledge.

Essentialism: The educational belief or position that there is a fundamental core of knowledge and ideals that should be transmitted to all students while maintaining high achievement standards; individual freedom is seen as a goal rather than a means.

Eternity: A never-ending state of time such as implied by the concept of immortality.

Ethics: That branch of philosophy which investigates the norms and correct patterns of conduct.

Evil: Anything including moral badness which negates man's happiness or welfare—the opposite of good.

Evolutionism: The metaphysical theory that the cosmos evolved and is evolving of itself and toward a definite end.

Experimental reasoning: A scientific problem-solving approach used to answer "unknowns"; after a hypothesis is postulated, primarily inductive but also deductive reasoning is used to gather and test data prior to arriving at conclusions.

Experimentalism: A term used synonomously with pragmatic naturalism and instrumentalism to describe the progressive educational philosophy initiated by John Dewey; it is characterized by naturalistic education based on change and novelty using a problem-solving approach to educational problems.

Fallacy: Reasoning which is illogical, inconsistent, or incomplete.

Fatalism: The theory that all events are predetermined, as are the acts of men; hence, volition on the part of man is negated. This doctrine is not synonymous with determinism.

Existentialism
p. 29, 40-41

fundamentalism

Free will: The belief that man is capable of true initiative in a world which offers him freedom of choice insofar as his actions are concerned.

Generalization: The forming of a principle or law or proposition which covers all instances of the items or phenomena being referred to.

Gestalt: A German word meaning *form* or *shape*. The term is used in psychology to describe the theory that formed patterns of sensations or reflexes are responsible through interrelation for the occurrence of events. The whole is therefore greater than the sum of its parts, and the parts receive their character because of the total configuration.

God: A term interpreted in various ways; in philosophy and modern religion it usually means a Supreme Being, the infinite Spirit, or the Creator of the universe. There are various arguments and beliefs about the existence of God. Some religions believe in more than one god.

Good: That which is considered to be beneficial to man, and which is right and fitting in the moral order of the universe (pragmatism denies built-in moral order). A term used frequently in ethics.

Hedonism: An ethical doctrine which states that man should guide his ethical conduct on the basis of the personal pleasure such conduct will bring him. It must be kept in mind that there are many different conceptions of pleasure.

Humanism: A position in which concern for man's welfare is central; stresses the importance of man in working out his own destiny. (There are a number of ancillary definitions.)

Hypothesis: A supposition or tentative explanation suggesting the correct disposition or resolution of a problem.

Idea: A concept or percept existing in the mind as the result of apprehension.

Ideal: A model or standard of perfection or excellence serving as a goal; often conceived however in its relationship to idealism.

Idealism: A term which describes a philosophical position of long standing that envisions a rational order in the universe, since all reality is basically idea or spirit; it is the opposite of materialism and is sometimes used to connote an ideal system or doctrine. There is also an idealistic philosophy of education.

Illusion: A condition in which man's senses do not react in typical fashion— a false perception.

Immanent: When applied to God, this means that He operates within or is actually present in the cosmos.

Immortality: The belief that a human's soul will exist after death throughout eternity.

Imperative: A command which may not be evaded. (See Categorical Imperative.)

Individualism: A theory that the freedom of an individual should not be curtailed, as such freedom is most important to society's development; some would go so far as to state that the individual's welfare should be the chief aim of society.

Induction: A method of reasoning and/or problem solving which involves the forming of generalizations from specific instances; hence, the opposite of deduction.

Inference: That which appears to be a reasonable conclusion based on certain premises.

Infinite: The quality of being without limits as to space or duration.

Instrumentalism: A term coined in the field of educational philosophy around 1930 to describe progressivism in education—the pragmatic naturalism of John Dewey in which theories are put to the test of experience experimentally; thought is instrumental in improving conduct; a term often used interchangeably with experimentalism at one time, which has now been superseded by it and pragmatic naturalism.

Interactionism: The theory that explains mind and body as separate entities within reality, although each may have a direct influence on the other.

Interest Theory: A belief under the nature of value of the branch of ethics that the existence of value depends on interest shown by the individual concerned; hence, if something is desired, it has value.

Introspection: To look (or the act of looking) within one's own mind or thought processes.

Intuitionism: A theory in both metaphysics and ethics that self-evident truths and moral values respectively may be gained through immediate, intuitive awareness or insight.

Logic: The branch of philosophy which treats the exact relating of ideas; known also as the science of inference and proof.

Materialism: The theory that matter is the ultimate reality in the cosmos and which denies the presence of spiritual substance; speaking ethically it is an ethical doctrine that places individual well-being uppermost.

Mechanism: The theory that there are natural laws in the world which operate in machine-like fashion regardless of man and his desires.

Meliorism: The theory that man can and should work to improve his situation in the world even though it is not possible to know anything final about the goodness or evil of existence.

Metaphysics: The branch of philosophy which considers theories about the nature of reality.

Monism: The theory that the cosmos, or ultimate reality, is unified and qualitatively of one type of matter or energy (as opposed to dualism).

Mysticism: The belief that man can know ultimate truth intuitively through direct insight.

Naturalism: A term that describes an early philosophical position that has persisted to the present day; the philosophical theory which emphasizes that the physical nature of the universe is self-explanatory and denies any teleological system; also a philosophy popularized by Rousseau that served as a foundation for progressive education.

Natural Law: A "higher law" considered universally valid and derived from the nature of man; a principle in ethics which man may derive through his reason alone.

Nature: The sum total of all phenomena or physical experiences in the universe; sometimes referred to as those forces which control the physical universe.

Noumenon: An object which is apprehended rationally (i.e., nonempirical).

Ontology: That subdivision of the branch of philosophy known as metaphysics which treats and inquires into the nature of being or reality.

Optimism: The belief that this is the best of all possible worlds in which reality is essentially good, and this goodness shall win out over any and all evil.

Pantheism: A doctrine that makes God and the universe identical; in other words God is immanent in nature.

Parallelism: A belief under the nature of man in the branch of metaphysics which treats the problem of the relation of body and mind; the theory is that mind and body are corresponding aspects of reality but separate.

Perfectionism: The belief that ultimate perfection of the individual and the society is possible and should, therefore, be a goal.

Pessimism: A belief engendered by observation of life in this world which sees more evil than good and which questions the desirability of struggle against the elements and forces present; people with this attitude frequently seek an escape mechanism. (The opposite of optimism.)

Phenomenon: An object which is known empirically (i.e., through the senses) and not through intuition or thought.

Philosophy: The "love of wisdom" (lit.); a science which investigates the facts, principles, and problems of reality in an attempt to describe, analyze, and evaluate them.

Pluralism: The belief that reality is composed of a number of ultimate substances such as mind, matter, energy, process, etc.; all are real and may be either quantitative or qualitative.

Polytheism: The theory that there are many gods who may, or may not, have an effect on the destiny of man.

Positivism: A belief popularized by Comte that man can only know that which can be proved through the sense-experience of scientific method; this would eliminate metaphysical speculation.

Pragmatism: The philosophical theory that truth may only be known through the logical and physical consequences of experiences embodying the theory to be tested; applied to education it means that we learn truly only by involvement or doing.

Proposition: A statement or expression of anything in declarative form which may be true, doubtful, or false.

Rationalism: The philosophical theory that knowledge may be derived through man's reasoning power as opposed to the application of sense-experience.

Realism: A term used to describe so many different, but related, positions, that it is difficult to classify; there does appear to be general agreement on the objectivity, or independent reality, of the world apart from the conscious mind of man which attempts to know it. It is in direct opposition to idealism on this point. In education, its aim is that man should acquire verified knowledge of the world in order to adjust in the best way to his environment.

✓ *Relativism.* Metaphysically, this theory is that no measurement standard has complete objectivity since all things including truth are relative in space, motion, and time. This has definite implications for epistemological theory, since knowledge, not being intrinsic, depends on comparison with other data.

Revelation: The belief that the Deity has communicated to man in a variety of ways relative to His will.

Scholasticism: The main Christian philosophy of the Middle Ages, which embraced all activities of the medieval schools; it is based on tradition and revealed religion—a method as well as a system of thought.

Skepticism: The belief that absolute truth and knowledge are not available to man, although partial knowledge may be possible.

Soul: An essence or substance that is possessed by man and which is enduring after mortal life on earth is over; the "vital principle" of an organic body; it is believed by some that this part of man is also part of God.

Speculation: The contemplation about a subject in regard to its different aspects and relations; there is the implication that such theorization is taking place without sufficient scientific evidence to support any conclusions reached.

Spiritualism: In philosophy, the belief held by most idealists that the ultimate nature of the universe is spirit; God, in this interpretation, would be absolute Spirit, while humans are finite spirits.

Stoicism: Originally a school of early philosophy; it is now interpreted as a belief wherein man practices devotion to duty and remains impassive to pleasure or pain.

Summum bonum: A Latin phrase meaning the highest or supreme good; usually applies to the highest goal for man's conduct as being intrinsically good.

Syllogism: Describes a type of deductive reasoning invented by Aristotle in which certain judgments called major and minor premises result in a particular conclusion only if they are true.

Teleology: The study of whether the universe is purposeful as opposed to a theory or mechanism; the past and present may be interpreted by the future.

Theism: A religious philosophy which is unitarian in regard to the nature of God; He is seen as distinct from humans and is regarded as immanent rather than external to the world.

Transcendentalism: The belief, when applied to God, that He is beyond and apart from the world or universe.

Utilitarianism: The belief that the right act for a human is the one which will result in the greatest amount of happiness in the world; it has subsequently been interpreted as meaning the greatest amount of "intrinsic good" and has also found an interpretation in pragmatic ethics.

Utopia: Means literally the land of nowhere; generally conceived as the ideal society, perhaps of the future.

Virtue: A quality ascribed to men who lived their lives according to reason in the days of Aristotle; with the Romans it meant strength of character; now it generally applies to qualities of moral excellence such as the Christian virtues.

Will: Man's conscious process at work resulting in a decision—voluntary action (i.e., conation).

Bibliography

Chapter One

Philosophy of History

✓Adams, Brooks, *The Law of Civilization and Decay*. New York: Vintage Books, 1955.

✓Berdiaev, N. A., *The Meaning of History*. London: Geoffrey Bles, Ltd., 1949.

*Boodin, John E., "Philosophy of History," in *Twentieth Century Philosophy*, ed. Dagobert D. Runes. New York: Philosophical Library, Inc., 1943.

✓Bury, J. B., *The Idea of Progress*. New York: Dover Publications, Inc., 1955.

✓Collingwood, R. G., *The Idea of History*. New York: Oxford University Press, Inc., 1956.

*Davis, H. W. C., *The Study of History*. Oxford: The Clarendon Press, 1925. A lecture.

✓Day, Edmund E., "Primary Elements of the American Tradition." Washington, D. C.: U.S. Department of Agriculture, 1942. An address.

Field, Guy C., *Some Problems of the Philosophy of History*. London: H. Milford, 1938. A lecture.

✓Gardiner, Patrick, *The Nature of Historical Explanation*. London: Oxford University Press, 1952.

Gustavson, C. G., *A Preface to History*. New York: McGraw-Hill Book Company, Inc., 1955.

✓Hegel, G. W. F., *Reason in History*. New York: Liberal Arts Press, 1953.

*MacKinnon, D. M., *On the Notion of a Philosophy of History*. London: Oxford University Press, 1954. A lecture.

*Mandelbaum, M. H., *The Problem of Historical Knowledge*. New York: Liveright Publishing Corp., 1938.

*Maritain, J., *On the Philosophy of History*, ed. J. W. Evans. New York: Charles Scribner's Sons, 1957.

*Meyerhoff, H., ed., *The Philosophy of History in Our Time*. New York: Doubleday & Company, Inc., 1959.

✓Ortega y Gasset, J., *Toward a Philosophy of History*. New York: W. W. Norton & Company, Inc., 1941.

*Pringle-Pattison, R. S., "The Philosophy of History," in *Proceedings* of the British Academy, London, England, 1921–23.

✓Spengler, Oswald, *The Decline of the West*. New York: Alfred A. Knopf, Inc., 1926. Authorized translation.

✶ Taggart, F. J., *Theory and Processes of History*. Berkeley and Los Angeles: University of California Press, 1941.

✓Toynbee, Arnold J., *A Study of History*, abridgement of Vols. I–VI by D. C. Somervell. New York: Oxford University Press, Inc., 1947.

✓ von Schlegel, F., *The Philosophy of History*. London: G. Bell & Sons, Ltd., 1915.

✓ Woody, Thomas, *Life and Education in Early Societies*. New York: The Macmillan Company, 1949.

Chapter Two

Orientation to Philosophy

Beck, L. W., *Philosophic Inquiry: An Introduction to Philosophy*. Englewood Cliffs, N. J.: Prentice-Hall, Inc., 1952.

Black, M., *Critical Thinking*, 2nd ed. Englewood Cliffs, N. J.: Prentice-Hall, Inc., 1952.

Blau, J. L., *Men and Movements in American Philosophy*. Englewood Cliffs, N. J.: Prentice-Hall, Inc., 1952.

Brinton, C., *Ideas and Men: The Story of Western Thought*. Englewood Cliffs, N. J.: Prentice-Hall, Inc., 1950.

Bronstein, D. J., Y. H. Krikorian, and P. P. Wiener, eds., *Basic Problems of Philosophy*, 2nd ed. Englewood Cliffs, N. J.: Prentice-Hall, Inc., 1955.

Brubacher, John S., *Modern Philosophies of Education*, 2nd ed. New York: McGraw-Hill Book Company, Inc., 1950.

Butler, J. Donald, *Four Philosophies*, rev. ed. New York: Harper & Row, Publishers, Inc., 1957.

Castell, A., *An Elementary Ethics*. Englewood Cliffs, N. J.: Prentice-Hall, Inc., 1954.

Durant, Will, *The Story of Philosophy*, rev. ed. New York: Garden City Books, 1938.

Frank, Phillip, *Philosophy of Science: The Link between Philosophy and Science*. Englewood Cliffs, N. J.: Prentice-Hall, Inc., 1957.

Frost, S. E., Jr., ed., *Masterworks of Philosophy*. New York: Doubleday & Company, Inc., 1946.

Gamertsfelder, W. S. and L. D. Evans, *Fundamentals of Philosophy*. Englewood Cliffs, N. J.: Prentice-Hall, Inc., 1936.

Hospers, John, *An Introduction to Philosophical Analysis*. Englewood Cliffs, N. J.: Prentice-Hall, Inc., 1953.

Joad, C. E. M., *Guide to Philosophy*. New York: Dover Publications, Inc., 1946.

Martin, S. G. *et al.*, *A History of Philosophy*. New York: Appleton-Century-Crofts, Inc., 1941.

Runes, Dagobert D., *The Dictionary of Philosophy*. New York: Philosophical Library, Inc., 1942.

Russell, Bertrand, *A History of Western Philosophy*. New York: Simon and Schuster, Inc., 1945.

Woody, Thomas, *Life and Education in Early Societies*. New York: The Macmillan Company, 1949.

Windelband, Wilhelm, *A History of Philosophy*, rev. ed. New York: Harper & Row, Publishers, Inc., 1901, Vols. I and II.

Wright, W. K., *A History of Modern Philosophy*. New York: The Macmillan Company, 1941.

Chapter Three

Brief History of the Ideas and Problems of Philosophy

Adams, George P. and Wm. P. Montague, eds., *Contemporary American Philosophy*. New York: The Macmillan Company, 1930, Vols. I and II.

Ayer, A. J., *Language, Truth, and Logic*. London: Victor Gollancz, Ltd., 1936.

Barrett, William, *Irrational Man: A Study in Existential Philosophy*. New York: Doubleday & Company, Inc., 1958.

Beck, L. W., *Philosophic Inquiry: An Introduction to Philosophy*. Englewood Cliffs, N. J.: Prentice-Hall, Inc., 1952.

Black, M., *Critical Thinking*, 2nd ed. Englewood Cliffs, N. J.: Prentice-Hall, Inc., 1952.

Blau, J. L., *Men and Movements in American Philosophy*. Englewood Cliffs, N. J.: Prentice-Hall, Inc., 1952.

Brinton, C., *Ideas and Men: The Story of Western Thought*. Englewood Cliffs, N. J.: Prentice-Hall, Inc., 1950.

Bronstein, D. J., Y. H. Krikorian, and P. P. Wiener, eds., *Basic Problems of Philosophy*, 2nd ed. Englewood Cliffs, N. J.: Prentice-Hall, Inc., 1955.

Brubacher, John S., *Modern Philosophies of Education*, 3rd ed. New York: McGraw-Hill Book Company, Inc., 1962.

Butler, J. Donald, *Four Philosophies*, rev. ed. New York: Harper & Row, Publishers, Inc., 1957.

Castell, A., *An Elementary Ethics*. Englewood Cliffs, N. J.: Prentice-Hall, Inc., 1954.

Cohen, Morris R., *A Preface to Logic*. New York: Holt, Rinehart & Winston, Inc., 1944.

————, *Studies in Philosophy and Science*. New York: Holt, Rinehart & Winston, Inc., 1949.

Collins, James, *The Existentialists*. Chicago: Henry Regnery Co., 1952.

Dewey, John, *Intelligence in the Modern World*, ed. Joseph Ratner. New York: Modern Library, Inc., 1939.

————, *Reconstruction in Philosophy*. New York: Mentor Books, 1951.

Durant, Will, *The Story of Philosophy*, rev. ed. New York: Garden City Books, 1938.

Faguet, Emile, *Initiation into Philosophy*. New York: G. P. Putnam's Sons, 1914.

Feibleman, James, *The Revival of Realism*. Chapel Hill, N. C.: The University of North Carolina Press, 1946.

Frank, Phillip, *Philosophy of Science: The Link between Philosophy and Science*. Englewood Cliffs, N. J.: Prentice-Hall, Inc., 1957.

Frost, S. E., Jr., ed., *Masterworks of Philosophy*. New York: Doubleday & Company, Inc., 1946.

Gamertsfelder, W. S. and L. D. Evans, *Fundamentals of Philosophy*. Englewood Cliffs, N. J.: Prentice-Hall, Inc., 1936.

Hospers, John, *An Introduction to Philosophical Analysis*. Englewood Cliffs, N. J.: Prentice-Hall, Inc., 1953.

James, William, *Essays in Pragmatism*. New York: Hafner Publishing Co. Inc., 1948.

_____, *Pragmatism: A New Name for Some Old Ways of Thinking*. New York: David McKay Co., Inc., 1931.

Joad, C. E. M., *Guide to Philosophy*. New York: Dover Publications, Inc., 1946.

Krikorian, Yervant H., ed., *Naturalism and the Human Spirit*. New York: Columbia University Press, 1944.

Martin, S. G. *et al.*, *A History of Philosophy*. New York: Appleton-Century-Crofts, Inc., 1941.

Nagel, Ernest, *Sovereign Reason*. New York: Free Press of Glencoe, Inc., 1954.

Pap, A., *Elements of Analytical Philosophy*. New York: The Macmillan Company, 1949.

Perry, Ralph Barton, *Present Philosophical Tendencies*. New York: George Braziller, Inc., 1955.

Popkin, R. H. and A. Stroll, *Philosophy Made Simple*. New York: Garden City Books, 1956.

Runes, Dagobert D., *The Dictionary of Philosophy*. New York: Philosophical Library, Inc., 1942.

Russell, Bertrand, *A History of Western Philosophy*. New York: Simon and Schuster, Inc., 1945.

Schneider, Herbert W., *A History of American Philosophy*. New York: Columbia University Press, 1946.

Toulmin, S. E., *The Philosophy of Science*. London: Hutchinson & Co. (Publishers), Ltd., 1953.

Wahl, Jean, *A Short History of Existentialism*. New York: Philosophical Library, Inc., 1949.

Wiener, Phillip P., *Evolution and the Founders of Pragmatism*. Cambridge, Mass.: Harvard University Press, 1949.

Wild, John, ed., *The Return to Reason*. Chicago: Henry Regnery Co., 1953.

_____, *Introduction to Realistic Philosophy*. New York: Harper & Row, Publishers, Inc., 1948.

Wittgenstein, L., *Philosophical Investigations*. New York: The Macmillan Company, 1953.

Windelband, Wilhelm, *A History of Philosophy,* rev. ed. New York: Harper & Row, Publishers, Inc., 1901, Vols. I and II.

Wright, W. K., *A History of Modern Philosophy*. New York: The Macmillan Company, 1941.

Chapter Four

Naturalism in Philosophy and Education

Hobbes, Thomas, *The English Works of Thomas Hobbes*, coll. and ed. Sir William Molesworth, Bart. London: John Bohn, 1889, Vols. I–X.

Huxley, Thomas Henry, *Science and Education*. New York: Appleton-Century-Crofts, Inc., 1896.

Krikorian, Yervant H., ed., *Naturalism and the Human Spirit*. New York: Columbia University Press, 1944.

Lange, Frederick A., *History of Materialism*, trans. E. C. Thomas. Boston: James R. Osgood and Co., 1877, Vols. I–III.

Lucretius, *Of the Nature of Things*, trans. W. E. Leonard. London: J. M. Dent & Sons, Ltd., 1921.

Rousseau, Jean Jacques, *Émile*. London: J. M. Dent & Sons, Ltd., 1943.

_____, *Social Contract*, in *Social Contract: Essays by Locke, Hume, and Rousseau*, ed. Sir Earnest Barker. New York: Oxford University Press, Inc., 1948.

Spencer, Herbert, *First Principles of a New System of Philosophy*, 2nd ed. New York: Appleton-Century-Crofts, Inc., 1896.

_____, *The Synthetic Philosophy*. New York: Appleton-Century-Crofts, Inc., 1900, Vols. I–XIII.

_____, *Education: Intellectual, Moral, and Physical*. New York: Appleton-Century-Crofts, Inc., 1889.

Chapter Five

Naturalism in Physical, Health, and Recreation Education

Brightbill, Charles K., *Man and Leisure*. Englewood Cliffs, N. J.: Prentice-Hall, Inc., 1961.

Butler, J. Donald, *Four Philosophies*, rev. ed. New York: Harper & Row, Publishers, Inc., 1957.

Groos, Karl, *The Play of Animals*. New York: Appleton-Century-Crofts, Inc., 1898.

_____, *The Play of Man*. New York: Appleton-Century-Crofts, Inc., 1901.

McCloy, C. H., *Philosophical Bases for Physical Education*. New York: Appleton-Century-Crofts, Inc., 1940.

_____, "A Half Century of Physical Education," *The Physical Educator*, XVII, No. 3 (October 1960), 83–91.

Spencer, Herbert, *Education: Intellectual, Moral, and Physical*. London: C. A. Watts & Co., Ltd., 1949. Originally published in 1861.

Williams, J. F., *The Principles of Physical Education*, 7th ed. Philadelphia: W. B. Saunders Co., 1959.

Note: Prior to the publication of this text, a significant doctoral dissertation was completed by Mary Margaret Frederick at Springfield College under the direction of Dr. Reuben Frost, director of the School of Physical Education. Students who are interested in the philosophy of naturalism as expounded by Jean Jacques Rousseau, and the implications of this philosophical tendency for physical education should refer to this work. It is available in microcard form through Microcard Publications, School of Health, Physical Education, and Recreation, University of Oregon, Eugene, Oregon. The bibliographical reference is as follows:

Frederick, Mary Margaret, "Naturalism: The Philosophy of Jean Jacques Rousseau and Its Implications for American Physical Education," D. P. E. dissertation, Springfield College, 1961.

Several of the important conclusions reached by Dr. Frederick are as follows:

p. 213—The writer believes that Rousseau's philosophy of naturalism contained three ideas which greatly influenced American physical education. These were:

1. Rousseau's insistence on the natural and spontaneous movements for proper growth and development.
2. Rousseau's promulgation of the unity of mind and body.
3. Rousseau's belief in the value of the individual.

p. 214—In the opinion of the writer, the four primary beliefs, which are significant in Rousseau's *Émile,* advocated by Wood, Hetherington, Williams, and Nash, and far-reaching in modern physical education were:

1. Wood's program of naturalism.
2. Hetherington's "New Physical Education" program which stressed the possibilities of character development.
3. Williams' theory of the importance of experience and need for self-expression.
4. Nash's belief in the need of the individual to be creative and to experience emotional development.

Chapter Six

Experimentalism in Philosophy and Education

Berkson, I. B., *Preface to an Educational Philosophy.* New York: Columbia University Press, 1940.

_____, *Education Faces the Future.* New York: Harper & Row, Publishers, Inc., 1943.

Bode, Boyd H., *Conflicting Psychologies of Learning.* Boston: D. C. Heath & Company, 1929.

_____, *Progressive Education at the Crossroads.* New York: Newson & Company, 1938.

_____, *How We Learn.* Boston: D. C. Heath & Company, 1940.

Brameld, Theodore, *Ends and Means in Education: A Midcentury Appraisal.* New York: Harper & Row, Publishers, Inc., 1949.

————, *Patterns of Educational Philosophy: A Democratic Interpretation.* New York: Harcourt, Brace & World, Inc., 1950.

————, *Philosophies of Education in Cultural Perspective.* New York: The Dryden Press, Inc., 1955.

————, *Toward a Reconstructed Philosophy of Education.* New York: The Dryden Press, Inc., 1956.

Brubacher, John S., *Modern Philosophies of Education,* 3rd ed. New York: McGraw-Hill Book Company, Inc., 1962.

————, ed., *Eclectic Philosophy of Education,* 2nd ed. Englewood Cliffs, N. J.: Prentice-Hall, Inc., 1962.

Brubacher, John S. *et al., The Public School and Spiritual Values.* New York: Harper & Row, Publishers, Inc., 1944.

Burton, W. H., *Introduction to Education.* New York: Appleton-Century-Crofts, Inc., 1934.

Butler, J. D., *Four Philosophies,* rev. ed. New York: Harper & Row, Publishers, Inc., 1957.

Childs, John L., *Education and the Philosophy of Experimentalism.* New York: Appleton-Century-Crofts, Inc., 1931.

————, *Education and Morals: An Experimentalist Philosophy of Education.* New York: Appleton-Century-Crofts, Inc., 1950.

————, *American Pragmatism and Education.* New York: Holt, Rinehart & Winston, Inc., 1956.

Counts, George S., *Education and the Promise of America.* New York: The Macmillan Company, 1946.

Curti, Merle, *The Social Ideas of American Educators.* New York: Charles Scribner's Sons, 1935.

Dewey, John, *Democracy and Education.* New York: The Macmillan Company, 1916.

————, *Reconstruction in Philosophy.* London: University of London Press, Ltd., 1921.

————, *Human Nature and Conduct.* New York: Holt, Rinehart & Winston, Inc., 1922.

————, *Experience and Nature.* Chicago: The Open Court Publishing Company, 1925.

————, *The Quest for Certainty.* New York: Minton, Balch & Co., 1929.

————, *How We Think,* new ed. Boston: D. C. Heath & Company, 1933.

————, *Art as Experience.* New York: Minton, Balch & Co., 1934.

————, *A Common Faith.* New Haven, Conn.: Yale University Press, 1934.

————, *Experience and Education.* New York: The Macmillan Company, 1938.

————, *Logic, the Theory of Inquiry.* New York: Holt, Rinehart & Winston, Inc., 1938.

————, *Intelligence in the Modern World,* ed. Joseph Ratner. New York: Modern Library, Inc., 1939.

————, *Education Today,* ed. Joseph Ratner. New York: G. P. Putnam's Sons, 1940.

————, *Problems of Men.* New York: Philosophical Library, Inc., 1946.

Dewey, John and James H. Tufts, *Ethics.* New York: Holt, Rinehart & Winston, Inc., 1908.

Dewey, John *et al., Creative Intelligence.* New York: Holt, Rinehart & Winston, Inc., 1917.

Edman, Irwin, *John Dewey: His Contribution to the American Tradition.* Indianapolis: Bobbs-Merrill Company, Inc., 1955.

Feibleman, James, *An Introduction to Peirce's Philosophy.* New York: Harper & Row, Publishers, Inc., 1946.

Geiger, George R., "An Experimentalist Approach to Education," in *Modern Philosophies and Education,* ed. N. B. Henry. Chicago: University of Chicago Press, 1955.

Hook, Sidney, *The Metaphysics of Pragmatism.* Chicago: The Open Court Publishing Company, 1927.

————, *Education for Modern Man.* New York: The Dial Press, Inc., 1946.

Horne, Herman Harrell, *The Democratic Philosophy of Education.* New York: The Macmillan Company, 1932.

James, William, *Pragmatism.* New York: David McKay Co., Inc., 1907.

————, *A Pluralistic Universe.* New York: David McKay Co., Inc., 1909.

————, *Essays in Radical Empiricism.* New York: David McKay Co., Inc., 1912.

————, *The Will to Believe.* New York: David McKay Co., Inc., 1912.

————, *Talks to Teachers.* new ed. New York: Holt, Rinehart & Winston, Inc., 1946.

————, *The Philosophy of William James Drawn from His Own Works.* New York: Modern Library, Inc., n.d.

Johnson, Glen. *Some Ethical Implications of a Naturalistic Philosophy of Education.* New York: Bureau of Publications, Teachers College, Columbia University, 1947.

Kilpatrick, William H., *Education for a Changing Civilization.* New York: Appleton-Century-Crofts, Inc., 1926.

————, *Philosophy of Education.* New York: The Macmillan Company, 1951.

————, *The Educational Frontier.* New York: Appleton-Century-Crofts, Inc., 1933.

Mayhew, K. C. and A. C. Edwards, *The Dewey School.* New York: Appleton-Century-Crofts, Inc., 1936.

Ratner, Joseph, *The Philosophy of John Dewey.* New York: Holt, Rinehart & Winston, Inc., 1929.

Raup, R. Bruce *et al., The Improvement of Practical Intelligence: The Central Task of Education.* New York: Harper & Row, Publishers, Inc., 1950.

Sayers, E. V., and W. Madden, *Education and the Democratic Faith.* New York: Appleton-Century-Crofts, Inc., 1959.

Schilpp, P. A., *The Philosophy of John Dewey.* Evanston and Chicago: Northwestern University Press, 1939.

Taylor, Harold, *On Education and Freedom.* New York: Abelard-Schuman Limited, 1954.

Tenenbaum, S., *William Heard Kilpatrick.* New York: Harper & Row, Publishers, Inc., 1951.

Thomas, M. H., *A Bibliography of John Dewey, 1882–1939*. New York: Columbia University Press, 1939.

U. S. Bureau of Education, "Cardinal Principles of Secondary Education," *Bulletin* 35. Washington, D. C.: Government Printing Office, 1918.

White, Morton G., *The Origin of Dewey's Instrumentalism*. New York: Columbia University Press, 1943.

Wynne, John P., *Philosophies of Education*. Englewood Cliffs, N. J.: Prentice-Hall, Inc., 1947.

Chapter Seven

Experimentalism in Physical, Health, and Recreation Education

Bair, Donn E., "An Identification of Some Philosophical Beliefs Held by Influential Professional Leaders in American Physical Education." Ph.D. dissertation, University of Southern California, 1956. Published by Microcard Publications, The University of Oregon, Eugene, Oregon.

Brameld, Theodore, *Toward a Reconstructed Philosophy of Education*. New York: The Dryden Press, Inc., 1956.

Brightbill, Charles K., *Man and Leisure*. Englewood Cliffs, N. J.: Prentice-Hall, Inc., 1961.

Brubcher, John S., *Modern Philosophies of Education*, 3rd ed. New York: McGraw-Hill Book Company. Inc., 1962.

Butler, J. Donald, *Four Philosophies*, rev. ed. New York: Harper & Row, Publishers, Inc., 1957.

Cassidy, Rosalind, *New Directions in Physical Education for the Adolescent Girl in High School and College*. New York: A. S. Barnes & Co., 1938.

Clark, Margaret C., "A Program of Physical Education in a State Teachers College." Ph.D. dissertation, New York University, 1943.

Cobb, Louise Staples, "A Study of the Functions of Physical Education in Higher Education." Contributions to Education No. 876, Teachers College, Columbia University, 1943.

Cowell, C. C. and W. L. France, *Philosophies and Principles of Physical Education*. Englewood Cliffs, N. J.: Prentice-Hall, Inc., 1963.

Davis, Elwood C., *The Philosophical Process in Physical Education*. Philadelphia: Lea & Febiger, 1961.

————, ed., *Philosophies Fashion Physical Education*. Dubuque, Iowa: Wm. C. Brown Company, Publishers, 1963.

Dewey, John, *Democracy and Education*. New York: The Macmillan Company, 1916.

Downey, Robert J., "An Identification of the Philosophical Beliefs of Educators in the Field of Health Education." Ph.D. dissertation, University of Southern California, 1956.

Esslinger, Arthur A., "A Philosophical Study of Principles for Selecting Activities in Physical Education." Ph.D. dissertation, State University of Iowa, 1938.

Geiger, George R., "An Experimentalist Approach to Education," in *Modern Philosophies and Education, Fifty-fourth Yearbook* of the National Society for the Study of Education, Chairman J. S. Brubacher. Chicago: NSSE, 1955.

Hansen, Kenneth H., *Philosophy for American Education.* Englewood Cliffs, N. J.: Prentice-Hall, Inc., 1960.

Henry, N. B., ed., *Philosophies of Education, Forty-first Yearbook* of the National Society for the Study of Education. Chicago: University of Chicago Press, 1942, Part I.

————, *Modern Philosophies and Education, Fifty-fourth Yearbook* of the National Society for the Study of Education. Chicago: University of Chicago Press, 1955, Part I.

Hess, Ford A., "American Objectives of Physical Education from 1900–1957 Assessed in the Light of Certain Historical Events." Ph.D. dissertation, New York University, 1959. Published by Microcard Publications, The University of Oregon, Eugene, Oregon.

Hetherington, Clark, *School Program in Physical Education.* New York: Harcourt, Brace, & World, Inc., 1922.

Kaplan, Max, *Leisure in America.* New York: John Wiley & Sons, Inc., 1960.

Kilpatrick, W. H., *Education for a Changing Civilization.* New York: The Macmillan Company, 1926.

Kozman, H. C., ed., "Democratic Human Relations," in *First Yearbook* of American Association for Health, Physical Education, and Recreation. Washington, D. C.: AAHPER, 1951.

Larkin, Richard A., "The Influence of John Dewey on Physical Education." Master's thesis, Ohio State University, 1936.

Lynn, M. L., "Major Emphases in Physical Education." Ph.D. dissertation, The University of Pittsburgh, 1944.

McCloy, C. H., "Physical Education as Part of General Education," *Journal of Health and Physical Education,* XXXI (November 1928), 45.

————, *Philosophical Bases for Physical Education.* New York: Appleton-Century-Crofts, Inc., 1940.

Meyer, H. D. and C. K. Brightbill, *Community Recreation.* Englewood Cliffs, N. J.: Prentice-Hall, Inc., 1956.

Morland, Richard B., "A Philosophical Interpretation of the Educational Views Held by Leaders in American Physical Education." Ph.D. dissertation, New York University, 1958.

Neumeyer, Martin H. and Esther S. Neumeyer, *Leisure and Recreation,* 3rd ed. New York: The Ronald Press Company, 1958.

Sapora, Allen V. and Elmer D. Mitchell, *The Theory of Play and Recreation,* 3rd ed. New York: The Ronald Press Company, 1961.

Shepard, Natalie M., "Democracy in Physical Education: A Study of the Implications for Educating for Democracy Through Physical Education." Ed.D. dissertation, New York University, 1952.

Shivers, Jay S., "An Analysis of Theories of Recreation." Ph.D. dissertation, The University of Wisconsin, 1958.

Spears, Betty M., "Philosophical Bases for Physical Education Experiences Consistent with the Goals of General Education for College Women." Ph.D. dissertation, New York University, 1956.

Van Dalen, D. B., E. D. Mitchell, and B. L. Bennett, *A World History of Physical Education.* Englewood Cliffs, N. J.: Prentice-Hall, Inc., 1953.

Van Huss, W. D., "Orientation to Instructional Physical Education at Michigan State University," *Proceedings* of the College Physical Education Association, December 28–30, 1959, pp. 95–98.

Wegener, Frank C., "The Philosophical Beliefs of Leaders in American Education." Ph.D. dissertation, University of Southern California, 1946.

Williams. J. F., *The Principles of Physical Education,* 7th ed. Philadelphia: W. B. Saunders Co., 1959.

Williams, J. F. and W. L. Hughes, *Athletics in Education.* Philadelphia: W. B. Saunders Co., 1937.

Wilson, Charles C., *Health Education,* 4th ed. Washington, D. C.: National Education Association, 1948.

Wood, T. D. and Rosalind Cassidy, *The New Physical Education.* New York: The Macmillan Company, 1927.

Chapter Eight

Realism in Philosophy and Education

Adler, Mortimer J., "In Defense of the Philosophy of Education," in *Philosophies of Education.* Bloomington, Ill.: Public School Publishing Company, 1942.

Aquinas, St. Thomas, *Summa Theologica.* New York: Benziger Bros., Inc., 1947, Vols. I–III. Translated.

Aristotle, *The Works of Aristotle.* Oxford: The Clarendon Press, 1908–1931, Vols. 1–XI. Translated.

Breed, F. S., *Education and the New Realism.* New York: The Macmillan Company, 1939.

_____, "Education and the Realistic Outlook," in *Philosophies of Education.* Bloomington, Ill.: Public School Publishing Company, 1942.

Broudy, Harry S., *Building a Philosophy of Education,* 2nd ed. Englewood Cliffs, N. J.: Prentice-Hall, Inc., 1961.

Brubacher, John S., *Modern Philosophies of Education,* 3rd ed. New York: McGraw-Hill Book Company, Inc., 1962.

Butler, J. D., *Four Philosophies,* rev. ed. New York: Harper & Row, Publishers, Inc., 1957.

Cunningham, W. F., *Pivotal Problems in Education.* New York: The Macmillan Company, 1940.

de Houve, Franz, *Philosophy and Education.* New York: Benziger Bros., Inc., 1931.

Drake, Durant, ed., *Essays in Critical Realism.* New York: The Macmillan Company, 1920.

Feibleman, J. K., *The Revival of Realism.* Chapel Hill, N. C.: The University of North Carolina Press, 1946.

Holt, E. B., ed., *The New Realism*. New York: The Macmillan Company, 1912.

Justman, J. J., *Theories of Secondary Education*. New York: Bureau of Publications, Teachers College, Columbia University, 1940.

Kandel, Isaac L., *Conflicting Theories of Education*. New York: The Macmillan Company, 1939.

King, Beatrice, *Changing Man: The Education System of the U.S.S.R.* London: Victor Gollancz, Ltd., 1936.

————, *Russia Goes to School*. London: William Heinemann, Limited, 1948.

Lange, Frederick A., *History of Materialism*. Boston: James R. Osgood and Company, 1877, Vols. I–III.

McGucken, William J., *The Catholic Way in Education*. Milwaukee: Bruce Publishing Co., 1934.

————, "Intelligence and Character," *The National Catholic Educational Association Bulletin,* XXXVI (May 1940), 10–12.

————, "The Philosophy of Catholic Education," in *Philosophies of Education*. Bloomington, Ill.: Public School Publishing Company, 1942.

Maritain, Jacques, *Education at the Crossroads*. New Haven, Conn.: Yale University Press, 1943.

Montague, William P., "The Story of American Realism," *The Development of American Philosophy,* eds. Walter G. Muelder and Laurence Sears. Boston: Houghton Mifflin Company, 1940. Reprinted.

McLaughlin, Emmet, *American Culture and Catholic Schools*. New York: Lyle Stuart, Inc., 1959.

Pegis, Anton C., ed., *Basic Writings of Saint Thomas Aquinas*. New York: Random House, 1945, Vol. II.

Perry, Ralph B., *Present Philosophical Tendencies*. New York: George Braziller, Inc., 1955. Originally published in 1912.

Raby, Sister Joseph Mary, *A Critical Study of the New Education*. Washington, D. C.: The Catholic University of America Press, 1932.

Redden, J. D. and F. A. Ryan, *A Catholic Philosophy of Education*. Milwaukee: Bruce Publishing Co., 1942.

Reinhardt, K. F., *A Realistic Philosophy*. Milwaukee: Bruce Publishing Co., 1944.

Russell, Bertrand, *Education and the Good Life*. New York: Liveright Publishing Corp., 1926.

Santayana, George, *Realms of Being*. New York: Charles Scribner's Sons, 1927–1940, Vols. I–IV.

Sellars, R. W., *The Philosophy of Physical Realism*. New York: The Macmillan Company, 1932.

Somerville, John, *Soviet Philosophy*. New York: Philosophical Library, Inc., 1946.

Wegener, Frank C., *Problems and Principles of School and Society*. Dubuque, Iowa: Wm. C. Brown Company, Publishers, 1953.

Whitehead, Alfred North, *Science and the Modern World*. New York: New American Library of World Literature, Inc., 1948.

————, *The Aims of Education*. New York: The Macmillan Company, 1929.

Wild, John, *Plato's Modern Enemies and the Theory of Natural Law*. Chicago: University of Chicago Press, 1953.

————, "Education and Human Society: A Realistic View," in *Modern Phi-*

losophies and Education, ed. N. B. Henry. Chicago: University of Chicago Press, 1955.

_____, ed., *The Return to Reason*. Chicago: Henry Regnery Co., 1953.

Chapter Nine

Realism in Physical, Health, and Recreation Education

Adler, Mortimer J., "In Defense of the Philosophy of Education," in *Forty-first Yearbook* of the National Society for the Study of Education. Chicago: University of Chicago Press, 1942.

Bagley, William C., *Education, Crime, and Social Progress*. New York: The Macmillan Company, 1931.

Bair, Donn E., "An Identification of Some Philosophical Beliefs Held by Influential Professional Leaders in American Physical Education." Ph.D. dissertation, University of Southern California, 1956.

Brameld, Theodore, *Philosophies of Education in Cultural Perspective*. New York: The Dryden Press, Inc., 1955.

Broudy, Harry S., *Building a Philosophy of Education,* 2nd ed. Englewood Cliffs, N. J.: Prentice-Hall, Inc., 1961.

Brubacher, John S., *Modern Philosophies of Education,* 3rd ed. New York: McGraw-Hill Book Company, Inc., 1962.

Butler, J. Donald, *Four Philosophies,* rev. ed. New York: Harper & Row, Publishers, Inc., 1957.

Clark, Margaret C., "A Philosophical Interpretation of a Program of Physical Education in a State Teachers College," Ph.D. dissertation. School of Education, New York University, 1943.

Conant, James B., "Athletics: The Poison Ivy in Our School," *Look Magazine* (January 17, 1961).

Cowell, C. C. and W. L. France, *Philosophies and Principles of Physical Education*. Englewood Cliffs, N. J.: Prentice-Hall, Inc., 1963.

Davis, Elwood Craig, ed., *Philosophies Fashion Physical Education*. Dubuque, Iowa: Wm. C. Brown Company, Publishers, 1963.

Debinski, Benjamin, "Catholic Youth Work," in *Selected Papers Presented at the 42nd National Recreation Congress*. New York: National Recreation Association, 1961.

Educational Policies Commission, *The Central Purpose of American Education*. Washington, D. C.: National Education Association, 1961.

Finney, Ross L., *A Sociological Philosophy of Education*. New York: The Macmillan Company, 1928.

Holbrook, Leona, "The Philosophy of Realism." Paper presented at the Convention of the American Association for Health, Physical Education, and Recreation, March 19, 1961.

Kennedy, John F., "The Soft American," *Sports Illustrated* (December 26, 1960).

Mannes, Marya, "They're Cultural, But Are They Cultured?" *The New York Times Magazine* (July 9, 1961).

Maritain, Jacques, "Thomist Views on Education," in *Forty-first Yearbook* of the National Society for the Study of Education. Chicago: University of Chicago Press, 1942.

McCloy, Charles H., *Philosophical Bases for Physical Education.* New York: Appleton-Century-Crofts, Inc., 1940.

————, "A Return to Fundamentals," Proceeding of the College Physical Education Association, 1941.

————, "A Half Century of Physical Education," *The Physical Educator,* XVII, No. 3 (October 1960).

Morland, Richard B., "A Philosophical Interpretation of the Educational Views Held by Leaders in American Physical Education." Ph.D. dissertation, New York University, 1958.

Pope Pius XII, "Physical Culture and Youth," *Catholic Newsletter,* No. 288 (May 26, 1945).

————, "Sports and Gymnastics," *Catholic Mind,* No. 51 (September 1953), pp. 569–576.

————, "Christian Conduct Towards Athletics," *Catholic Mind,* No. 54 (July 1956), pp. 409–417.

Sanders, William J., in *The Public School and Spiritual Values, Seventh Yearbook* of the John Dewey Society, eds. J. S. Brubacher *et al.* New York: Harper & Row, Publishers, Inc., 1944.

Sapora, Allen V. and Elmer D. Mitchell, *The Theory of Play and Recreation,* 3rd ed. New York: The Ronald Press Company, 1961.

Wegener, Frank C., *The Organic Philosophy of Education.* Dubuque, Iowa: Wm. C. Brown Company, Publishers, 1957.

Whitehead, Alfred N., *The Aims of Education.* New York: The Macmillan Company, 1929.

Wild, John, "Education and Human Society: A Realistic View," in *Modern Philosophies and Education,* ed. N. B. Henry. Chicago: University of Chicago Press, 1955.

Note: During 1962, the author was privileged to serve as doctoral committee chairman for an outstanding young philosopher and historian of physical education—Harold J. VanderZwaag, now of DePaul University. His thesis involved a delineation of an essentialistic philosophy of physical education, a problem "based on the assumptions that (a) the systematic philosophy of essentialism can be identified, and that (b) a philosophy of physical education can and should be related to a systematic philosophy of education."

"The methodology of the study consists of three major steps: (1) Educational essentialism is identified in relationship to the problematic areas of general philosophical orientation, the educative process, the curriculum, educational administration, relationship between the school and community, and educational aims. Selected questions are considered under each problematic area in order to arrive at a basis for identifying essentialism. (2) The information provided by step one is used to draw implications concerning elements of essentialism in physical education. Similar problematic areas are considered. However, the category of general philosophical orientation is omitted from the second step. (3) Research data are presented which tend to support the implications for essentialism in physical education, as indicated in step two."

According to VanderZwaag, the most distinguishing elements of essentialism in physical education are as follows:

1. The physical educator is uniquely charged with responsibility for *education of the physical*. Education through the physical is an incidental part of the educative process.

2. Among the objectives of physical education, the *physical fitness* objective has top priority.

3. There is a definite *distinction between physical education and physical recreation* which should be reflected in a physical education program that is based on effort rather than interest.

4. *Drill* is a most meaningful concept in physical education. This is particularly reflected in the practice of physical skills and the use of physical conditioning exercises.

5. Variety in the physical education curriculum should be restricted to those activities which provide for *large-muscle* activity of a *strenuous* nature.

6. The concept of *discipline* connotes special responsibilities for the physical educator. In addition to sharing with all teachers the responsibility for enforcing the school's code of conduct, the physical educator is uniquely charged with the development and control of physical discipline and team discipline.

7. *Indoctrination* in physical education is justifiable when the indoctrination is in the form of *disciplined work*. In this context, indoctrination is used to inculcate the skills and attitudes which result from rigorous and vigorous physical activity.

8. The *social objectives* of physical education are *limited* to those of education generally. In other words, physical education is an equal part of what the essentialist calls "the educational arm of society." Physical education has no peculiar right to change the social pattern.

The bibliographical reference is as follows:

VanderZwaag, Harold John, "Delineation of an Essentialistic Philosophy of Physical Education." Ph.D. dissertation, The University of Michigan, 1962.

Chapter Ten

Idealism in Philosophy and Education

Adams, G. P. and W. P. Montague, *Contemporary American Philosophy*. New York: The Macmillan Company, 1930, Vol. II.

Barrett, Clifford, *Contemporary Idealism in America*. New York: The Macmillan Company, 1932.

Bogoslovsky, B. B., *The Ideal School*. New York: The Macmillan Company, 1936.

Bosanquet, Bernard, "Life and Philosophy," in *Contemporary British Philosophy,* ed. J. H. Muirhead. New York: The Macmillan Company, n.d., Series 2.

Brightman, E. S., *Nature and Values*. Nashville, Tenn.: Abingdon Press, 1945.

Brubacher, John S., *Modern Philosophies of Education,* 3rd ed. New York: McGraw-Hill Book Company, Inc., 1962.

Butler, J. Donald, *Four Philosophies,* rev. ed. New York: Harper & Row, Publishers, Inc., 1957.

Calkins, Mary Whiton, *The Persistent Problems of Philosophy,* 4th rev. ed. New York: The Macmillan Company, 1917.

Demiashkevitch, Michael, *An Introduction to the Philosophy of Education.* New York: American Book Company, 1935.

Educational Policies Commission, *Moral and Spiritual Values in the Public Schools.* Washington, D. C.: National Education Association, 1951.

Gentile, Giovanni, *The Reform of Education.* New York: Harcourt Brace & World, Inc., 1922. Authorized translation.

Greene, Theodore M., "A Liberal Christian Idealist Philosophy of Education," in *Fifty-fourth Yearbook* of the National Society for the Study of Education. Chicago: University of Chicago Press, 1955, Part I.

Hansen, Kenneth H., *Philosophy for American Education.* Englewood Cliffs, N. J.: Prentice-Hall, Inc., 1960.

Hocking, William E., *Human Nature and Its Remaking.* New Haven, Conn.: Yale University Press, 1918.

———, *The Meaning of God in Human Experience.* New Haven, Conn.: Yale University Press, 1928.

———, *The Self, Its Body and Freedom.* New Haven, Conn.: Yale University Press, 1928.

Hoernle, R. F. A., *Idealism as a Philosophy.* New York: Doubleday & Company, Inc., 1927.

Horne, Herman Harrell, *Idealism in Education.* New York: The Macmillan Company, 1910.

———, *Philosophy of Education,* rev. ed. New York: The Macmillan Company, 1927.

———, *This New Education.* Nashville, Tenn.: Abingdon Press, 1931.

———, "An Idealistic Philosophy of Education," in *Philosophies of Education.* Bloomington, Ill.: Public School Publishing Company, 1942.

Leighton, J. A., *Individuality and Education.* New York: Appleton-Century-Crofts, Inc., 1928.

Lodge, Rupert C., *Philosophy of Education,* rev. ed. New York: Harper & Row, Publishers, Inc., 1947.

Mayer, Frederick, *Philosophy of Education for Our Time.* New York: The Odyssey Press, Inc., 1958.

Royce, Josiah, *Lectures on Modern Idealism.* New Haven, Conn.: Yale University Press, 1919.

Schopenhauer, Arthur, "The World as Will and Idea," in *Masterworks of Philosophy.* New York: Doubleday & Company, Inc., 1946.

Ulich, Robert, *Conditions of Civilized Living.* New York: E. P. Dutton & Co., Inc., 1946.

Urban, W. M., *The Intelligible World.* New York: The Macmillan Company, 1929.

Chapter Eleven

Idealism in Physical, Health, and Recreation Education

Anderson, William G., *Methods of Teaching Gymnastics*. New York: Hinds and Noble, 1896.

A New Look at YMCA Physical Education. New York: Association Press, 1959.

Bair, Donn E., "An Identification of Some Philosophical Beliefs Held by Influential Professional Leaders in American Physical Education." Ph.D. dissertation, University of Southern California, 1956.

Bennett, Bruce L., "Religion and Physical Education," Paper presented at the Cincinnati Convention of the American Association for Health, Physical Education, and Recreation, April 10, 1962.

Boyd, Robert M., "The Southern Baptist Church Recreation Philosophy at Work." in *Selected Papers Presented at the 42nd National Recreation Congress*. New York: National Recreation Association, 1961.

Brightbill, Charles K., *Man and Leisure: A Philosophy of Recreation*. Englewood Cliffs, N. J.: Prentice-Hall, Inc., 1961.

Brubacher, John S., *Modern Philosophies of Education,* 3rd ed. New York: McGraw-Hill Book Company, Inc., 1962.

Brubacher, John S. *et al., The Public Schools and Spiritual Values*. New York: Harper & Row, Publishers, Inc., 1944.

Burke, Roger, "Idealism and Physical Education," in *The Philosophic Process in Physical Education,* ed. E. C. Davis. Philadelphia: Lea & Febiger, 1961.

Butler, J. Donald, *Four Philosophies*. New York: Harper & Row, Publishers, Inc., 1957.

Cahn, L. Joseph, "Contributions of Plato to Thought on Physical Education, Health, and Recreation." Unpublished Ed.D. dissertation, New York University, 1941.

Cowell, C. C. and W. L. France, *Philosophies and Principles of Physical Education*. Englewood Cliffs, N. J.: Prentice-Hall, Inc., 1963.

Clark, Margaret C., "A Philosophical Interpretation of a Program of Physical Education in a State Teachers College." Ph.D. dissertation, New York University, 1943.

Clements, Frances, Robert Tully, and Edward Crill, eds. *Recreation and the Local Church*. Elgin, Ill.: Bretheren Publishing House, 1956.

Davis, Elwood Craig, ed., *Philosophies Fashion Physical Education*. Dubuque, Iowa: Wm. C. Brown Company, Publishers, 1963.

Demarest, Gary, "Hero Worship Harnessed," *Journal of Health, Physical Education, and Recreation,* Vol. XXXI, No. 5 (May–June 1960), 30–31.

Downey, Robert J., "An Identification of the Philosophical Beliefs of Educators in the Field of Health Education." Unpublished Ph.D. dissertation, University of Southern California, 1956.

Educational Policies Commission, *Moral and Spiritual Values in the Public Schools*. Washington, D. C.: National Education Association, 1951.

Fellowship of Christian Athletes (The). n.d. Kansas City, Mo.: Fellowship of Christian Athletes, Inc. Pamphlet.

Hocking, William E., *Human Nature and Its Remaking*. New Haven, Conn.: Yale University Press, 1918.

Horne, Herman Harrell, *Philosophy of Education*, rev. ed. New York: The Macmillan Company, 1927.

_____, *This New Education*. Nashville, Tenn.: Abingdon Press, 1931.

_____, *The Democratic Philosophy of Education*. New York: The Macmillan Company, 1932.

_____, "An Idealistic Philosophy of Education," in *Forty-first Yearbook* of the National Society for the Study of Education. Chicago: University of Chicago Press, 1942, Part I.

Jaarsma, Cornelius, *Human Development, Learning & Teaching*. Grand Rapids, Mich.: Wm. Eerdmans Publishing Co., 1961.

Johnson, Elmer, "A History of Physical Education in the Young Men's Christian Association." Unpublished Ph.D. dissertation, University of Southern California, 1954.

Lee, Mabel and Miriam M. Wagner, *Fundamentals of Body Mechanics and Conditioning*. Philadelphia: W. B. Saunders Co., 1949.

Limbert, Paul M., "Physical Education as an Integral Part of YMCA Programme." Unpublished paper presented at the Fifth World YMCA Consultation on Health and Physical Education in Rome, September 12–14, 1960. Mimeographed.

Lozes, Jewell Helen, "The Philosophy of Certain Religious Denominations Relative to Physical Education." Master's thesis, Pennsylvania State University, 1955.

Matthias, E., *The Deeper Meaning of Physical Education,* trans. Carl Schrader. New York: A. S. Barnes & Co., 1929.

Morland, Richard B., "A Philosophical Interpretation of the Educational Views Held by Leaders in American Physical Education." Ph. D. dissertation, New York University, 1958.

Morris, Vance, "Striving for Perfection," *The Christian Athlete,* IV, No. 4 (December 1961), 10.

Moseley, Mary Louise, "A Study of the Philosophies of Camp Directors and of the Opinions of Campers as Related to the Spiritual Values Derived in the Field of Camping." Master's thesis, Woman's College, University of North Carolina, 1959.

Nash, Jay B., *Philosophy of Recreation and Leisure*. Dubuque, Iowa: Wm. C. Brown Company, Publishers, 1960. Published originally by the C. V. Mosby Company in 1953.

Neumeyer, Martin H. and Esther S. Neumeyer, *Leisure and Recreation,* 3rd ed. New York: The Ronald Press Company, 1958.

Resick, Matthew C., "Moral and Spiritual Values in Physical Education," *The Physical Educator,* Vol. XII, No. 1 (March 1955), 5.

Sapora, Allen V. and Elmer D. Mitchell, *The Theory of Play and Recreation,* 3rd ed. New York: The Ronald Press Company, 1961.

Shoemaker, Samuel M., *Fellowship of Christian Athletes* "Answer to America's Youth." Kansas City, Mo.: Fellowship of Christian Athletes, Inc., n.d. A sermon distributed in pamphlet form.

Steen, Barney, "Physical Education at Calvin College," *The Banner,* XCVI, No. 35 (September 1, 1961), 11 and 19.

Wilton, Wilton M., "A Comparative Analysis of Theories Related to Moral and Spiritual Values in Physical Education." Ed.D. thesis, University of California, Los Angeles, 1956.

"Physical Education, Sport, and Recreation," *World Communique,* January–February, 1961. (Published by the World Alliance of Young Men's Christian Associations, 37 Quai Wilson, Geneva, Switzerland).

Chapter Twelve

Systematic Philosophies and Some Persistent Problems

Adams, J., *The Evolution of Educational Theory.* London: Macmillan & Co., Ltd., 1915.

Ainsworth, Dorothy S., *The History of Physical Education in Colleges for Women.* New York: A. S. Barnes & Co., 1930.

Ashton, Dudley, "Contributions of Dance to Physical Education, Part I," *Journal of Health, Physical Education, and Recreation,* XXVI, No. 9 (December 1955).

————, "Contributions of Dance to Physical Education, Part II," *Journal of Health, Physical Education, and Recreation,* XXVII, No. 4 (April 1956).

Brightbill, C. K., *Man and Leisure: A Philosophy of Recreation.* Englewood Cliffs, N. J.: Prentice-Hall, Inc., 1961.

Brownell, C. L. and E. P. Hagman, *Physical Education-Foundations and Principles.* New York: McGraw-Hill Book Company, Inc., 1951.

Brubacher, J. S., *A History of the Problems of Education.* New York: McGraw-Hill Book Company, Inc., 1947.

Butts, R. F., *A Cultural History of Education.* New York: McGraw-Hill Book Company, Inc., 1947.

Bucher, C. A., *Foundations of Physical Education,* 3rd ed. St. Louis: The C. V. Mosby Company, 1960.

Carskadon, T. R. and G. Soule, *U.S.A. in New Dimensions.* New York: The Macmillan Company, 1957.

Cozens, F. W. and F. S. Stumpf, *Sports in American Life.* Chicago: University of Chicago Press, 1953.

Cubberley, E. P., *Readings in the History of Education.* Boston: Houghton Mifflin Company, 1920.

————, *State School Administration.* Boston: Houghton Mifflin Company, 1927.

————, *Readings in Public Education in the United States.* Boston: Houghton Mifflin Company, 1934.

Curti, M., *The Social Ideas of American Educators.* New York: Charles Scribner's Sons, 1935.

————, *The Growth of American Thought.* New York: Harper & Row, Publishers, Inc., 1943.

Davis, E. C., *The Philosophic Process in Physical Education*. Philadelphia: Lea & Febiger, 1961.

Dewey, J., *Democracy and Education*. New York: The Macmillan Company, 1916.

Dewhurst, F. F. and Associates, *America's Needs and Resources*. New York: The Twentieth Century Fund, Inc., 1947.

Diem, Carl, *Weltgeschichte des Sports und der Leibeserziehung*. Stuttgart, West Germany: J. G. Cotta'sche Buchhandlung, 1960.

Doell, C. E. and G. B. Fitzgerald, *A Brief History of Parks and Recreation in the United States*. Chicago: The Athletic Institute, 1954.

Douglass, P. F. *et al.*, eds. *Recreation in the Age of Automation*. Philadelphia: American Academy of Political and Social Science in *The Annals*, Vol. 313, September 1957.

Dulles, F. R., *America Learns to Play: A History of Popular Recreation, 1607–1940*. New York: Appleton-Century-Crofts, Inc., 1940.

Durant, Will, *The Life of Greece*. New York: Simon and Schuster, Inc., 1939.

Eby, F. and C. F. Arrowood, *The Development of Modern Education*. Englewood Cliffs, N. J.: Prentice-Hall, Inc., 1934.

————, *The History and Philosophy of Education*. Englewood Cliffs, N. J.: Prentice-Hall, Inc., 1940.

Ekirch, A. A., *The Idea of Progress in America*. New York: Columbia University Press, 1944.

Elsbree, W. S., *The American Teacher*. New York: American Book Company, 1930.

Educational Policies Commission, *Education for all American Youth*. Washington, D. C.: National Education Association, 1944.

Ellis, Havelock, *The Dance of Life*. New York: Modern Library, Inc., 1929.

Forsythe, C. E., *The Administration of High School Athletics*, 4th ed. Englewood Cliffs, N. J.: Prentice-Hall, Inc., 1962.

Freeman, K. J., *Schools of Hellas*. London: Macmillan & Co., Ltd., 1922.

Good, H. G., *A History of Western Education*. New York: The Macmillan Company, 1947.

Graves, F. P., *A History of Education Before the Middle Ages*. New York: The Macmillan Company, 1909.

————, *A History of Education During the Middle Ages*. New York: The Macmillan Company, 1910.

————, *A History of Education in Modern Times*. New York: The Macmillan Company, 1913.

Grutzner, Charles, *The Impact of Athletics on Education*. Washington, D. C.: Babe Ruth Sportsmanship Awards Committee, March 1951. Reprinted by permission of *The New York Times*.

Gwynn, J. M., *Curriculum Principles and Social Trends*. New York: The Macmillan Company, 1943.

Hartwell, E. M., *Physical Training*, U.S. Bureau of Education. Washington, D.C.: Government Printing Office, 1899.

H'Doubler, Margaret, *The Dance and Its Place in Education*. New York: Harcourt, Brace & World, Inc., 1925.

_____, *Dance, A Creative Art Experience.* New York: Appleton-Century-Crofts, Inc., 1940.

Huizinga, J., *Homo Ludens: A Study of the Play-Element in Culture.* Boston: The Beacon Press, 1950.

Kaplan, Max, *Leisure in America: A Social Inquiry.* New York: John Wiley & Sons, Inc., 1960.

Kozman, H. C., au. and ed., *Developing Democratic Human Relations, First Yearbook* of the American Association for Health, Physical Education, and Recreation. Washington, D. C.: AAHPER, 1951.

Larrabee, E., and R. Meyersohn, *Mass Leisure.* New York: Free Press of Glencoe, Inc., 1958.

Laurie, S., *History of Educational Opinion Since the Renaissance.* New York: David McKay Co., Inc., 1900.

Leonard, F. E., *Pioneers of Modern Physical Training,* 2nd ed. New York: Association Press, 1915.

Leonard, F. E. and G. B. Affleck, *The History of Physical Education,* 3rd ed. Philadelphia: Lea & Febiger, 1947.

Marique, P., *History of Christian Education.* New York: Fordham University Press, 1924–32, Vols. I–III.

Martin, John, *The Dance.* New York: Tudor Publishing Co., 1946.

McCloy, C. H., *Philosophical Bases for Physical Education.* New York: Appleton-Century-Crofts, Inc., 1940.

Meyer, A. E., *The Development of Education in the Twentieth Century.* Englewood Cliffs, N. J.: Prentice-Hall, Inc., 1939.

Monroe, J. P., *The Educational Ideal.* Boston: D. C. Heath & Company, 1906.

Monroe, P., *Cyclopedia of Education.* New York: The Macmillan Company, 1911–13.

_____, *Source Book of the History of Education.* New York: The Macmillan Company, 1921.

Mulhern, J., *A History of Education.* New York: The Ronald Press Company, 1946.

Nash, J. B., *Philosophy of Recreation and Leisure.* Dubuque, Iowa: Wm. C. Brown Company, Publishers, 1960. This book had been published originally by the C. V. Mosby Company, St. Louis, in 1953.

Neumeyer, M. H. and E. S. Neumeyer, *Leisure and Recreation,* 3rd ed. New York: The Ronald Press Company, 1958.

Oberteuffer, D., *Physical Education.* New York: Harper & Row, Publishers, Inc., 1951.

Page, Barbara, "The Philosophy of the Dance." *Research Quarterly,* IV, No. 2 (May 1933), 5–49.

Radir, Ruth A., *Modern Dance for the Youth of America.* New York: A. S. Barnes & Co., 1944.

Reisner, E. H., *Nationalism and Education Since 1789.* New York: The Macmillan Company, 1925.

_____, *Historical Foundations of Modern Education.* New York: The Macmillan Company, 1927.

Rice, E. A., J. L. Hutchinson, and Mabel Lee, *A Brief History of Physical Education,* 4th ed. New York: The Ronald Press Company, 1958.

Sachs, Curt, *World History of the Dance.* New York: W. W. Norton & Company, Inc., 1937.

Sapora, A. V. and E. D. Mitchell, *The Theory of Play and Recreation,* 3rd ed. New York: The Ronald Press Company, 1961.

Savage, H. J. *et al., American College Athletics.* New York: The Carnegie Foundation for the Advancement of Teaching, 1929.

Schwendener, N., *A History of Physical Education in the United States.* New York: A. S. Barnes & Co., 1942.

Scott, H. A., *Competitive Sports in Schools and Colleges.* New York: Harper & Row, Publishers, Inc., 1951.

Sharp, C., and O. P. Oppe, *An Historical Survey of Dancing in Europe.* New York: Minton, Balch & Co., 1924.

Snyder, R. A. and H. A. Scott, *Professional Preparation in Health, Physical Education, and Recreation.* New York: McGraw-Hill Book Company, Inc., 1954.

The New York Times, "Amateur Athletic Union vs. N.C.A.A.: Dispute Perils Sports Structure." January 21, 1962, pp. 1 and 5, Sports Section.

Ulich, R., *History of Educational Thought.* New York: American Book Company, 1945.

Van Dalen, D. B., E. D. Mitchell, and B. L. Bennett, *A World History of Physical Education.* Englewood Cliffs, N. J.: Prentice-Hall, Inc., 1953.

Vuillier, G., *History of Dancing.* New York: Appleton-Century-Crofts, Inc., 1897.

Weaver, R. B., *Amusements and Sports in American Life.* Chicago: University of Chicago Press, 1939.

Weir, L. H., *Europe at Play.* New York: A. S. Barnes & Co., 1937.

Weston, A., *The Making of American Physical Education.* New York: Appleton-Century-Crofts, Inc., 1962.

Wilds, E. H., *Foundations of Modern Education.* New York: Holt, Rinehart & Winston, Inc., 1942.

Williams, Jane E., *Ancient Art and Ritual.* London: Oxford University Press, 1943.

Williams, J. F., *The Principles of Physical Education,* 7th ed. Philadelphia: W. B. Saunders Co., 1959.

Woodward, W. H., *Vittorino Da Feltre and Other Humanist Educators.* London: Cambridge University Press, 1905.

Woody, T., *Life and Education in Early Societies.* New York: The Macmillan Company, 1949.

Zeigler, E. F., *A History of Professional Preparation for Physical Education in the United States, 1861–1948.* Eugene, Oregon: Microcard Publications, The University of Oregon, 1950.

Index

A

A priori, 12
  defined, 20, 317
A posteriori, defined, 20, 317
Absolute, defined, 317
Absolute idealism, 172
Absolutism, defined, 19, 317
Abstract, defined, 317
Adler, Mortimer, 127, 146
Administration, 261-63
  experimentalism in, 105-6, 262
  idealism in, 237-38, 262-63
  realists and, 159-60, 263
Aesthetics, 254
  defined, 23, 317
  experimentalists and, 77, 91-92
  idealists and, 183
  naturalists and, 40
  realists and, 119
Agassiz, Louis, 35
Agnosticism, defined, 20, 317
Aims, philosophical, 11
Aims and objectives, educational, 286
  the economy and, 257
  experimentalistic, 80-81, 99, 107-8
  idealistic, 188-92, 202-3, 238-39
  naturalistic, 49-51, 54-58, 64
  realistic, 123-28 137-55, 160-61
  See also Values
Allport, Vernon, and Lindzey, 310
Altruism, defined, 22, 317
American Association for Health, Physi-
    cal Education, and Recreation, 289
Analysis, defined, 317
Anaximander, 26
Anderson, William Gilbert, 204-5
Animism, defined, 317
Anthropomorphism, defined, 317
Aristotle, 24, 30, 75, 117, 126, 130
Art: philosophy contrasted with, 15
  realists and, 153-54
  See also Aesthetics

Artificial exercises, eliminating, 58
Asceticism, defined, 318
Associated learning, 103
Atheism, 115
  defined, 318
Athletics. *See* Sports
Atomism, defined, 318
Attitude development, 283-84
  experimentalists and, 99
  idealists and, 193
  testing, 310-16
Authoritarianism, defined, 20, 318
Average man's philosophy, 10
Averroës, 27
Axiology, 16, 17
  defined, 21-22, 318
  experimental, 21, 76-78
  idealistic, 182-86
  of naturalism, 22, 47-48
  realistic, 118-21
  See also Values
Axiom, defined, 318

B

Bacon, Francis, 24, 31, 46-47
Bacon, Roger, 27
Bair, Donn E., 147, 158, 159, 206, 207
Baptist Church, 226
Barnard, Henry, 35
Basketball, McCloy on, 92
Beauty: defined, 318
  See also Aesthetics
Behaviorism, 74
  defined, 318
Being, idealists and nature of, 171
Bennett, Bruce L., 219-20, 224, 226-27
Bergson, Henri, 25-26, 34
Berkeley, George, 33, 174
Bibliography, 324-45
Boas, George, 24

Body, 4, 81, 265-68
experimentalists and, 73-74, 266
idealists and, 202ff., 233-34, 267
naturalists and, 58-59, 61
realists and, 115, 267-68
See also Health education; Physical education; Physical fitness; Recreation education
Bosanquet, Bernard, 171
Bowne, Borden Parker, 35
Boyd, Robert M., 226
Brameld, Theodore, 98, 137, 146-47, 194, 237
Breed, Frederick S., 121-22, 124, 130
Brightbill, Charles K., 63-64, 95, 150, 230-31
Broudy, Harry S., 116, 120
on educational aims, 123, 125-26, 137
on educational method, 129-30, 155-56
on health education, 148, 267-68
on recreation, 152-53
on sports, 142-43
Brubacher, John S., 18, 49, 73, 80, 81, 122, 125, 127, 131, 139
on attitude development, 283-84
on idealism, 237
on novelty, 71
on recreation, 97
on tradition of freedom, 290
Burke, on idealism, 205
Burton, W. H., 78
Butler, J. Donald, 16-17, 46
compares philosophy and religion, 15-16
on idealists, 173, 182, 185, 194, 232-33, 234-36
on pattern of logic, 75-76
on realists, 114, 120, 127, 131

C

Cahn, L. Joseph, 203, 204, 217, 223, 232
Cairds, 34
Calkins, Mary Whiton, 176, 182-83
Camping, 230
Cardinal Principles of Education, 286
Carlyle, Thomas, 34, 35
Cartesian dualism. *See* Descartes, René
Categorical imperative, 318
Category, defined, 318
Catholic Church, 120
experimentalists and, 79-80
realism of, 122-23, 127-28, 131-32
and health education, 149, 267
and method, 155, 156, 157, 158
and physical education, 146-47
and recreation education, 154-55
and sport, 143-45

Causation, defined, 318
Cause and effect. *See* Determinism
Childs, J. L., 72, 83-84
Christianity, 8
idealism in, 31-32
and physical, health, and recreation education, 204, 209-10, 223-26, 236-37, 267
See also Catholic Church; Protestantism
Chronological narrative of philosophy, 24
Church: and state, separation of, 255
See also Catholic Church; Christianity; Protestantism; Religion
Church of the Brethren, 225
Church of Jesus Christ of Latter-Day Saints. *See* Mormons
Civilizations, Toynbee and, 6-9
Clark, Margaret C., 137, 147, 159, 232, 233-34
Clarke, H. H., 101
Clemens, Frances, 225
Clothing, 57
Coaches. *See* Sports; Teachers
Cobb, L. S., 87-88
Co-curricular activities, 259
Coleridge, Samuel Taylor, 34, 35
Comenius, John Amos, 32, 121
Comparative approach to history, 24
Comte, Auguste, 33, 46, 47
Conant, James B., 138-39, 143
Concept, defined, 318
Concomitant learning, 103
Consensus, possibility of, 283-90
Copernicus, 32
Cosmology: defined, 19-20, 318
history of, 24-29
idealistic, 171
realistic, 114-16
See also Metaphysics
"Course of development" approach, 23
Crill, Edward, 225
Creationism, defined, 19, 318
Critical idealism, 172
Critical naturalism, 46
See also Naturalism
Critical philosophy, 17
See also Epistemology; Logic
Critical realists, 35
Croce, Benedetto, 34
Culture: realists and, 153-54
See also Aesthetics
Curricula, 249
experimentalists and, 99-101
idealists and, 192, 195
realists and, 125-26, 129-30, 131, 158-59
See also Methodology
Cynicism, defined, 318

D

Dance, in physical education and recreation, 271-74
Danford, Howard G., 229
Darwin, Charles, 37, 38
Debates, 289, 295-300
Debinski, Benjamin, 154
Declarative sentences, 178-79
Deduction, 12, 20, 47, 177
  defined, 20, 318
Defects, physical exercise for, 288
Defects of formal education, 124-25
Definitions, 18-22, 317-23
Deism, defined, 19, 318
Demarest, Rev. Gary, 209
Democracy: experimentalists and, 78-79, 106
  idealists and, 195
  and nationalism, 255-56
  realists and, 121-22
Democritus, 26
Descartes, René, and Cartesian dualism, 24-25, 31, 36-37, 41, 170
Determinism, 115
  defined, 19, 318
Dewey, John, 36, 74-75, 77, 92, 95-97, 100
Dialectic, defined, 318
Dichotomy, defined, 318
Diet, 56
Dilettantism, defined, 318
Direct method, 131-32
Discipline: experimentalists and, 101
  idealists and, 194-95
Dogma, defined, 319
Dominant minority, 8-9
Double aspect theory, 319
Downey, Robert J., 94-95, 218, 235
Drill, 158, 287
Dualism: Cartesian. *See* Descartes, René
  defined, 19, 319
  epistemological, 116
Durant, Will, 13

E

Eastman, Charles A., 66
Eating, 56
Eclectic School, 84
Eclecticism, 292
  defined, 319
Economics, 256-58
Education, 249-90
  administration, 261-63
    See also Administration
  consensus about, 283-90
  economics and, 256-58

Education (*Cont.*)
  experimentalism in, 78-110
    aims, objectives of, 80-81
    process of, 81-84
  idealism in, 186-244
    aims, objectives of, 188-92
    process of, 192-96
  methodology, 258-61
    See also Methodology
  naturalism in, 48-66
    aims, objectives of, 49-51
    process of, 51-52
  philosophy contrasted with, 16
  politics and, 255-56
  professional preparation, 263-65
    See also Teachers
  realism in, 121-65
    aims, objectives of, 123-28
    process of, 129-32
  See also Health education; Physical education; Recreation education; specific philosophies
Educational Policies Commission, 148-49, 187, 212-14, 286
Effort vs. interest. *See* Interest
Egoism, defined, 22, 319
Elementary schools, Catholic, 127-28, 146, 156
Emergence theory, defined, 319
Emergent novelty, theory of, 71
Emerson, Ralph Waldo, 35
Empiricism, 20, 319
Environment, experimentalists and, 84, 100
Epicureanism, defined, 319
Epicurus, 26-27
Epiphenomenalism, defined, 319
Epistemology, 16-18, 249-50
  defined, 20, 319
  experimentalistic, 20, 69-70, 72-74
  idealistic, 173-82
  naturalistic, 46-47
  realistic, 116
Essentialism, 121, 122-23, 237, 257, 260
  defined, 319
  on educational spectrum, 251-52
  and professional preparation, 264-65
Eternity, defined, 319
Ethics, 229
  defined, 21-22, 319
  experimentalists and, 76-77, 80-81
  idealistic, 183
  realistic, 118-20
  See also Axiology; Morality; Religion
Evaluation: experimentalists and, 82, 90-91, 101

Evaluation: experimentalists and (*Cont.*)
    realists and, 158-59, 261
    See also Tests
Evans, Louis H., 209
Evil: defined, 319
    idealists and, 172-73
    naturalism and, 48
    See also Ethics
Evolutionism, defined, 19, 319
Examinations: sample, 301-4
    See also Evaluation
Exercise: eliminating artificial, 58
    See also Physical education; Recreation
        education
Existence theory, defined, 21
Existentialism, 29, 40-41
Experimental reasoning: defined, 319
    See also Problem-solving
Experimentalism, 38, 67-110
    aims, objectives, 80-81, 99, 107-8
    axiology of, 21, 76-78
    defined, 319
    in education, 78-110
        See also Administration; Method;
            etc.; Health education; Physical
            education; Recreation education
    epistemology of, 20, 72-74
    logic in, 74-76
    metaphysics of, 19-20, 70-72
    methodology of, 99-106, 108, 260
    strengths of, 109
    weaknesses of, 109-10
    See also Pragmatism
External proletariat, 8-9
Extracurricular activities, 259
    experimentalists and, 98
    idealists and, 191
    realists and, 142-43, 152-53

F

Fabricius, 32
Fallacy, defined, 319
Family: Spencer and, 50
    See also Home
Fatalism, defined, 319
Feeling, 12, 56-57
    See also Aesthetics
Feibleman, James, 114, 117
Fellowship of Christian Athletes, 209-10
Finney, Ross L., 145-46
Follen, Carl, 35
Friermood, Harold T., 208-9, 236
Free will, 71-72, 173
    defined, 19, 320
Freedom. *See* Free will; Individuals

G

Galileo Galilei, 32
Games: naturalism and, 61
    realists and, 152
    See also Recreation education; Sports
Gannett, Margaret Clark, 205-6, 218
Geiger, George R., 69, 80, 97, 137
Generalization, defined, 320
Gentile, Giovanni, 34
Gestalt, defined, 320
Girls: experimentalism and, 91
    naturalism and, 57-58
    See also Women
Glossary, 317-23
God, 19, 20
    defined, 320
    idealists and, 172, 186
    realists and, 115-16, 128
Good, defined, 320
Good, quoted on realism, 123
Government, 255-56
    experimentalists and, 79-80
    realists and, 122
    separation of church and state, 255
    Universal State, 7-8
Grades: experimentalists and, 91, 101
    realists and, 159, 261
Great-man approach to history, 23
Greece, ancient, 4, 5, 7, 8, 204, 205
    philosophy begins in, 11
Greene, Theodore M., 173-74, 188, 191,
        285, 291
    axiology of, 182, 183-84, 185
    and educational process, 192-93
Groos, Karl, 62-63
Growth-and-development approach, 195
Growth patterns of civilizations, 6

H

Hall, G. Stanley, 35, 63
Haller, Albrech von, 33
Hansen, Kenneth H., 130-31, 186, 188
Harris, William T., 35
Health education, 253-55, 265-68
    administration of. *See* Administration
    economics and, 256-58
    experimentalism in, 87ff., 93-95, 99-110,
        254, 266-67
    idealism in, 201ff., 217-20, 255, 267
    methodology of. *See* Methodology
    naturalism in, 54-62
    politics and, 255-56
    realism in, 136ff., 147-49, 155-60, 254-55,
        267-68
    values in, 253-55

Health services, 94, 285
Hebrew-Christian tradition, 31-32
Hedonism: defined, 22, 320
  in naturalism, 47-48
Hegel, Georg, 34, 35, 37, 41, 73
Heraclitus, 11, 30
Herbart, Johann F., 34
Hetherington, C., 92
History: of economics, 256-57
  of experimental epistemology, 72-73
  naturalists and, 52
  of philosophy, 11, 16, 24-42
  philosophy of, 3-9
  of play and recreation, 227-28
Hobbes, Thomas, 27, 46
Hocking, William E., 173, 183-85, 234
Hoernle, R. F. Alfred, 172
Holbrook, Leona, 147, 159
Home: experimentalists and, 79-80
  and health education, 148
  See also Family
Hook, on Murray, 28
Horne, Herman H., 187, 189-92, 193-94,
  202, 221
  on athletic contests, 233
  axiology of, 182 ,185-86
  on health education, 217-18, 267
  metaphysics of, 171, 174-75
  on recreation, 228-29
Howison, George H., 35
Hughes, W. L., 88-89
Humanism: defined, 320
  rational, 126-27, 130, 146, 154, 260
Humanities, 125-26
Hutton, James, 33
Huygens, Christian, 32
Hypothesis: defined, 320
  See also Problem-solving

I

Ideal, defined, 320
Idealism, 167-244
  aims, objectives of, 188-92, 202-31, 238-39
  axiology, 182-86
  defined, 320
  in education, 186-244
    See also Administration; Method;
    etc.; Health education; Physical
    education; Recreation education
  epistemology of, 173-82
  historical development of, 30-36, 38
  logic in, 177-78
  metaphysics of, 18-19, 20, 170-73

Idealism *(Cont.)*
  methodology of, 195-96, 231-38, 239-41,
    260
  strengths, 241-43
  weaknesses, 243-44
Ideas: defined, 320
  history of, 24
  relating of. *See* Logic
Illusion, defined, 320
Imitation, 194, 233
Immanent, defined, 320
Immortality, defined, 320
Imperative, defined, 320
Individualism, defined, 320
Individuals: experimentalists and, 78-80
  idealism and, 185-88ff., 203
  naturalists and, 48-49
  realists and, 121-23
  See also Ethics
Induction, 20, 177-78
  defined, 20, 320
  in naturalism, 46-47
Inference, defined, 320
Infinite, defined, 321
"Informal dialectic," 235
Inheritance theory of play, 63
Instinct theory, 63
Instrumentalism, 38, 69
  defined, 321
Interactionism, defined, 320
Interest: experimentalists and, 81, 91, 100
  idealists and, 194-95, 234
  realists and, 150-51, 157
    See also Catholic Church: realism of
Interest theory, defined, 21, 321
Internal proletariat, 8-9
Interscholastic sports: experimentalists
    and, 98-99
  idealism and, 210
  realists and, 142-43
  See also Sports
Intramural sports, 91, 99, 143
Introspection, defined, 321
Intuitionism, defined, 20, 321
Involvement. *See* Interest

J

Jaarsma, Cornelius, 210
Jackson, C. O., 141
James, William, 25, 73
Jews: and physical education, 226-27
  See also Hebrew-Christian tradition
Jones, R. W., 209, 237
Journal of Speculative Philosophy, 35
Jowett, Benjamin, 34

K

Kandel, Isaac L., 122
Kant, Immanuel, 22, 25, 33-34, 37, 46, 73, 172, 175, 183
Kennedy, Charles W., 212
Kennedy, John F., 139, 143, 149
Kepler, Johannes, 32
Kilpatrick, W. H., 99-100
Kierkegaard, Sören, 41
Knowledge, acquisition of. *See* Epistemology

L

Lamarck, Jean de, 33
Language philosophy, ordinary, 39, 40-41
Larkin, R. A., 89, 92-93, 99
Larrabee, on naturalism, 28
"Learning by doing," 84
Learning process. *See* Education; Methodology
Lee, Mabel, 216-17
Leibniz, Gottfried W., 32
Leisure, 274-78, 287
  experimentalists and, 97-98, 276
  history of, 227-28
  idealists and, 277
  naturalism and, 50-51
  realists and, 150, 151, 276-77
Leucippus, 26
Liberal education, 151, 191
Lieber, Francis, 35
Limbert, Paul, 208, 218-19, 236
Locke, John, 25, 32, 33, 73
Logic, 12, 17, 178-82
  defined, 20-21, 321
  experiment, 74-76
  idealistic, 177-78
  mathematical, 39
  of naturalism, 47
  realistic, 116-18
Logical atomism, 39-40
Logical positivism, 39, 40
Longfellow, Henry Wadsworth, 35
Longitudinal approach to history, 23
Lozes, Jewell Helen, 211, 224-25
Lucretius, 26

M

McCloy, C. H., 60-62, 64-65, 65-66, 92-93, 137, 158
McGucken, William, 128, 131
McLanen, Don, 209

Man: evolution of, 8
  nature of. *See* Cosmology; specific philosophies
  two views of, 249
Mann, Horace, 35
Mannes, Marya, 153-54
Marx, Karl, 34
Materialism, 38
  defined, 321
Materialistic realism, in Russia, 127
Mathematical logic, 39
Matthias, E., 211-12
Measurement. *See* Evaluation
Mechanism, defined, 321
Meliorism, defined, 22, 321
Metaphysics, 16, 17, 249
  defined, 18-20, 321
  of experimentalism, 19, 20, 170-72
  of idealism, 19, 20, 170-73
  of naturalism, 46
  of realism, 19, 114-16, 127
Methodist Church, and recreation, 224
Methodology, 258-61, 287
  experimental, 99-106, 108, 260
  idealistic, 195-96, 231-38, 239, 260
  naturalistic, 51, 58-60, 64-65
  in practice of philosophy, 12-13
  realistic, 155-60, 161-62, 260-61
Meyer, H. D., 95
Milesian school, 26
Mill, John Stuart, 118-19
Mind: experimentalists and, 73-74, 81, 83
  idealists and, 170, 174-75, 202-3, 222-23
  realists and, 115
Mitchell, Elmer D., 221-22
Monism: defined, 19, 321
  epistemological, 116
  idealists and, 172, 202-3
Moral imperative on education, 189
Moral (natural) law, 118, 119-20
  defined, 321
Morality: experimentalists and, 92-93
  idealists and, 211, 212, 213-15, 223, 255
  See also Axiology; Ethics; Values
Morland, Eichard B., 89-90, 100-1, 142, 157, 158, 216-17
Mormons, 219-20, 224, 267
Morris, Vance, 210
Moseley, Mary Louise, 230
Murray, Gilbert, 27
Mysticism, defined, 321

N

Nature, defined, 321
Nature study, 62, 63-64

Nagel, on nature's uniformities, 47
Naïve naturalism, 44-66
    aims, objectives of, 49-51, 54-58, 64
    axiology of, 47-48
    in education, 48-66
        See also Administration; Methodology;
            etc.; Health education; Physical
            education; Recreation education
    epistemology of, 46-47
    logic in, 47
    metaphysics of, 46
    methodology of, 51, 58-60, 64-65
    strengths, weaknesses of, 65-66
    See also Naturalism
Nash, Jay B., 229-30
National Education Association, 286
Nationalism, 255-56
Natural (moral) law, 118, 119-20
    defined, 321
Natural movement, the, 60
Natural sciences, in curriculum, 125, 126
Naturalism, 44-66
    aims, objectives of, 49-51, 54-58, 64
    axiology of, 22, 47-48
    defined, 321
    in education, 48-66
        See also Administration; Methodology;
            etc.; Health education; Physical
            education; Recreation education
    epistemology of, 46-47
    historical highlights of, 26-29, 38
    logic, 47
    metaphysics of, 46
    methodology of, 51, 58-60, 64-65
    strengths, weaknesses of, 65-66
Naturalistic realism, 125, 137, 267
    and methodology, 155-56, 158, 260
    and play and recreation, 154
Neorealists, 35
Neumeyer, Martin and Esther, 227-28
Newton, Isaac, 32
Nietzsche, Friedrich, 37-38, 41
Noumenon, defined, 321

O

Oberteuffer, Delbert, 215
Objectives, educational. *See* Aims and ob-
    jectives, educational
Ontology, defined, 19-20, 321
Optimism, defined, 21, 321
Ordinary language philosophy, 39, 40-41
Orientation, 1-42
    history of philosophy, 23-42
    to philosophy, 10-22
    philosophy of history, 2-9
Outdoor education, 62, 63-64, 230

P

Pantheism, 115, 116
    defined, 19, 321
Parallelism, defined, 322
Part-whole theory, defined, 21
Peaceful revolutions, 3-4
Peirce, Charles S., 34
Perennialism. *See* Catholic Church: real-
    ism of
Perfectionism, defined, 22, 322
Perry, Ralph Barton, 35, 118
Personality. *See* Individuals
Perspective, historical, 3
Pessimism, defined, 21, 322
Phenomenon, defined, 322
Philosophical analysis, 29, 38-39
    of university programs, 104-5
Philosophy, 2-42, 247-53
    aims of, 11-12
    and art, contrasted, 15
    branches of, 15-18
        See also Axiology; Epistemology;
            Logic; Metaphysics
    defined, 322
    and education, contrasted, 15-16
    of history, 3-9
        Toynbee's, 6-9
    history of, 11, 16, 23-42
    method involved in, 12-13
    modern, 36-42
    orientation to, 10-22
    personal, 247-48, 291-94
    and religion, contrasted, 15
    and science, contrasted, 13-15
    terms defined, 19-22
        See also Experimentalism; Idealism;
            Naturalism; Realism; etc.
Physical defects, exercise for, 288
Physical education, 253-55
    administration of. *See* Administration
    dance in, 271-74
    economics and, 256-58
    experimentalism in, 87-93, 99-110, 254,
        272-73
    idealism in, 201-17, 224-25, 225-26, 231-
        38, 255, 264, 273
    methodology of. *See* Methodology
    naturalism in, 54-62
    politics and, 255-56
    realism in, 136-47, 155-60, 254-55, 265,
        273-74
    values in, 253-55
    women and, 57-58, 91, 268-71, 279
    See also Sports

Physical fitness, 137-39, 265, 287-88
  See also Body; Health education; Physical education
Physics, 114, 115
Pius XII, 143-45, 149
Plato, 24, 30, 203-4, 217, 223, 232
Play: defined, 275
  experimentalists and, 95-97, 276
  idealists and, 221, 223, 277-78
  naturalists and, 58
  realists and, 149-50, 276-77
  See also Leisure; Recreation education; Sports
Pleasure. *See* Hedonism
Pluralism: defined, 19, 322
  idealists and, 172
Politics, 255-56
Polytheism, 115-16
  defined, 19, 322
Positivism: defined, 322
  logical, 39, 40
Pragmatism, 38
  defined, 322
  historical development of, 29-36
  logic in, 47
  See also Experimentalism
Preparation for life theory, 63
Pritchett, Henry S., 211
Problem-centered curriculum, 125-26
Problem-solving, 287
  experimentalists and, 74, 75, 76-77, 82-83, 99, 102-3
  realists and, 117, 125-26, 130
Progressions in philosophical study, 17-18
Progressivism, 71, 137, 141, 188, 189
  and classless society, 257
  in educational spectrum, 251-52
  and professional preparation, 264-65
  reconstructionists and, 98-99
  romantic naturalists, 49
  See also Experimentalism
Proposition, defined, 322
Protestantism, 186, 278
  See also specific denominations
Psychology, 73
Public health, 265-66
Pythagoras, 11

Q

Questions and answers, historical, 4-5

R

Raby, Sister Joseph Mary, 132
Rational humanism, 126-27, 130, 146, 154, 260

Rationalism, defined, 20, 322
Rauch, Frederick A., 35
Realism, 111-65
  aims, objectives of, 123-28, 137-55, 160-61
  axiology of, 118-21
  defined, 322
  in education, 121-65
    See also Administration; Methodology; etc.; Health education; Physical education; Recreation education
  epistemology of, 116
  historical development of, 29-36
  logic in, 116-18
  metaphysics of, 18-19, 114-16, 127
  methodology of, 155-60, 161-62, 260-61
  and politics, 256
  strengths of, 162-64
  weaknesses of, 164-65
Reality, questions about. *See* Metaphysics
Recapitulation theory of play, 63
Reconstructionism, 98, 260
Recreation: defined, 275
  See also Leisure; Play; Recreation education; Sports
Recreation education, 253-55
  administration of. *See* Administration
  dance in, 271-74
  economics and, 256-58
  experimentalism in, 87ff., 95-110, 276
  idealism in, 201 ff., 220-38, 277-78
  methodology of. *See* Methodology
  naturalism in, 54-64
  politics and, 255-56
  realism in, 136ff., 149-60, 276-77
  values in, 253-55
  women and, 268-71
  See also Women
Redden, John D., 122, 131, 132
Reflective thought, 13
Relativism, defined, 20, 322
Relaxation: Whitehead on, 151-52
  See also Leisure; Play
Religion, 212
  experimentalism and, 77
  and the future, 9
  and the greatest good, 22
  history and, 5
  idealistic, 183-85, 189
  in naturalism, 48
  realistic, 119-20
  in Universal State, 7-8
  See also Christianity; specific groups
Research, 51-52, 288-89
  historical, 5-6
Resick, M. C., 213-14
Revelation, 127-28
  defined, 20, 322

Revolutions, peaceful, 3-4
Rickey, Branch, 209
Rights, education and the availability of, 157
Roman Catholic Church. *See* Catholic Church
Romantic naturalism, 49
Rome, ancient, 4, 5, 7, 8
    Universal State, 7
Rousseau, Jean Jacques, 27-28
Royce, Josiah, 35
Ruggedness, need for, 55-56, 57-58
    See also Body
Russell, Bertrand, 39
Russia, 127
Ryan, Francis A., 122, 131, 132

S

Safety, 285
St. Louis Philosophical Society, 35
Sanders, William J., 154
Santayana, George, 35, 120
Sapora, Allen V., 221-22
Sargent, Dudley Allen, 204-5
Schneider, view of nature of, 46
Scholasticism, defined, 322
School. *See* Education
Schopenhauer, Arthur, 37, 183
Science, 12
    contrast of philosophy with, 13-15
    in curriculum, 125, 126
    realists and, 117
    role of, 250-51
    separation of philosophy from, 11
Secondary schools, Catholic, 127-28, 146, 147
Self-expression theory of play, 221-22
Self-instruction, 52
Self-preservation. *See* Naturalism
Sellars, Roy Wood, 35, 119
Sensations: importance of, 56-57
    See also Feeling
Sentences, declarative, 178-79
    Shoemaker, Samuel, 210
Silver, Rabbi D. J., 227
Skepticism, defined, 20
Social intelligence, 90, 92
Social issues, involvement in, 286-87
Social sciences, 125, 126
Society: classless, 257-58
    experimentalists and, 77-80
    idealism and, 185-88
    naturalism and, 48-49
    realists and, 120-23
    and women, 270
    See also Ethics; Government

Socrates, 204
Sophists, 30
Soul, 243
    defined, 322
    idealists and, 171, 222-23
Spectatoritis, 98
Spectrum, educational, 251-53
Speculation, 11, 12
    defined, 323
    See also Axiology; Metaphysics
Spencer, Herbert, 28, 37, 46, 47, 49-50ff., 62, 63
Spengler, Oswald, 6
Spinoza, Baruch, 25, 32
Spiritual monism, 172
Spiritual pantheism, 115, 116
Spiritual pluralism, 172
Spiritual values, 211, 212, 213-15
    in outdoor education, 230
    See also Idealism
Spiritualism, defined, 323
Sports, 278-80, 288
    experimentalists and, 91-93, 98-99, 279
    idealism and, 209-10, 213-14, 234, 279-80
    naturalists and, 61
    realism and, 142-44, 152-53, 279
    for women, 270-71
    See also Women
    See also Physical education; Recreation education; specific sports
State. *See* Government
Steen, Barney, 211, 219
Steinhaus, Arthur H., 208, 236
Stoicism, defined, 323
Study of Values, 310
Subject matter, realists and, 125-26, 129-30
Subman, 8
Summum bonum, 22, 323
Supernaturalism. *See* Catholic Church; realism of

T

Teacher Education Beliefs Indicator for Health Education, 94-95, 218
Teachers, 263-65
    experimentalists and, 94-95, 102-3
    idealism and, 193-94, 233, 234, 238, 264
    naturalists and, 51
    realists and, 158, 264
Technical learning, 103
Teleology, defined, 19, 323
"Tendency of the time" approach, 24
Term papers, sample, 304-10
Tests: recommended, 301-4
    See also Evaluation
Thales, 26

Theism, defined, 19, 323
Themes of action, Toynbee's, 6-7
Thomas Aquinas, St., 31, 118, 126
Time of Troubles, Toynbee's, 7, 8
Total fitness, 88-89
  See also Body
Toynbee, Arnold J., 6-9
Transcendentalism, defined, 323
Transfer of training, 156-57, 243
Tully, Robert, 225

U

Ulrich, Celeste, 101
Unification of field, experimentalists and, 88-89, 93-94, 95
Unified philosophy, achieving of, 248-49
Unity of mind and body, 81, 202-3
  See also Body; Mind
Unity of universe: idealists and, 172
  realists and, 115
Universal State, 7-8
Universe. *See* Cosmology
University programs, 103-5
Urban, William M., 171
Utilitarianism, defined, 22, 323
Utopia, defined, 323

V

Values, 190-91, 211, 212, 213-15, 253-55
  recreation and, 222-23
  systems of. *See* Axiology
  See also Aims and objectives, educational

Verifiability principle, 40
Vesalius, Andreas, 33
Vienna Circle, 40
Virtue, defined, 323
Vivas, Eliseo, 48
Vocational education, 191

W

War, and health, 265
Wegener, Frank C., 138, 292
Western civilization, 7, 8-9
Whitehead, Alfred North, 39, 114, 123-24, 138, 150-52
Wild, John, 114, 116, 118, 119, 121, 124, 125, 157
Will: defined, 323
  See also Free Will
Williams, Jesse Feiring, 60, 64, 65, 88-89, 98, 102
Wilton, Wilton M., 214, 225-26
Windelband, Wilhelm, 16
Wittgenstein, Ludwig, 40-41
Women, 57-58, 91, 268-71, 279
Woody, Thomas, 4, 15-16
Work: experimentalists and, 96-97, 276
  realists and, 150, 276
World. *See* Cosmology
World War II, 206
Wrestling, 102-3

Y

YMCA, 140, 204, 207-9, 219